RETRIEVING NICAEA

RETRIEVING NICAEA

The Development and Meaning
of Trinitarian Doctrine

Khaled Anatolios

Foreword by Brian E. Daley

Baker Academic
a division of Baker Publishing Group
Grand Rapids, Michigan

Published by Baker Academic
a division of Baker Publishing Group
P.O. Box 6287, Grand Rapids, MI 49516-6287
www.bakeracademic.com

Printed in the United States of America

Library of Congress Cataloging-in-Publication Data

Anatolios, Khaled, 1962–
    Retrieving Nicaea : the development and meaning of Trinitarian doctrine / Khaled Anatolios ; foreword by Brian E. Daley.
        p.   cm.
    Includes bibliographical references (p.   ) and indexes.
    ISBN 978-0-8010-3132-8 (cloth)
    1. Trinity—History of doctrines—Early church, ca. 30–600. 2. Dogma, Development of. 3. Council of Nicaea (1st : 325) 4. Council of Constantinople (1st : 381) I. Title.
BT109.A52 2011
231′.0440901—dc22   2011012337

11   12   13   14   15   16   17   7   6   5   4   3   2   1

For Meredith

At your baptism in the Jordan, O Christ, the worship of the Trinity was revealed. For the Father's voice bore witness to you, calling you his beloved Son, and the Spirit in the form of a dove confirmed the truth of these words. O Christ, our God, you have revealed yourself and enlightened the world. Glory to You!

Troparion for the Feast of Theophany, Byzantine Divine Liturgy

Contents

Foreword

S ince at least the late 1960s, Christian theology in virtually all of our churches
has shown once again a vital interest in reflecting on the trinitarian mystery
of God. Theological themes have their fashions, of course, with periodical ups and
downs in their popularity. Like other aspects of recognized church doctrine, the
conception of God as Trinity seemed, to many traditional Christians in the late
nineteenth and early twentieth centuries, to be formulated already with a clarity
that left it beyond discussion. To liberals and modernists, on the other hand, it often
seemed quaintly irrelevant: an inherited, incurably paradoxical way of thinking about
the divine Mystery that defied both rational explanation and practical applicability.
Many of us have probably heard sermons on Trinity Sunday, for instance, or on other
occasions where a reference to God's threefold simplicity seems called for, that begin
with words like those a friend of mine once was shocked to hear on a bright Sunday
morning following a gathering of patristic scholars: "Today we celebrate our belief
that God is one in nature, subsisting eternally in the three Persons of Father, Son,
and Holy Spirit. We don't know how to explain this, or even to say exactly what it
means—so let us, instead, try to love one another!" God's trinitarian being has come
to seem, for many modern Christians, far removed from what faith is really about.

Yet the Trinity is so deeply written into the language and liturgical use of the
church that Christians can hardly escape it altogether. Drawing on Jesus's commission
in Matthew 28:19, Christian communities, as far back as we know, have normally
baptized new members "in the name of the Father, and the Son, and the Holy Spirit"
as an immersion into the divine power that underlies both Jesus's commands and
his promise always to be present with his disciples. Since the beginning of Christian
records, liturgical forms of blessing and doxologies at the conclusion of homilies have
invoked God's favor and praised God's glory with this characteristic, yet intractably
puzzling, formulation. For some contemporary Christians, trinitarian formulations
seem inappropriate because they do not feature the "inclusive language" we want
to use for God; for others, they are simply unintelligible. Do we really need them?

So speculative Christian thinkers have begun again to look for a vocabulary and a conceptuality that might serve as a contemporary vehicle for unpacking and applying the trinitarian mystery that our tradition presents as the heart of faith. Hegelians have drawn on that philosopher's highly structured form of historical idealism to seek out its implications for how we conceive of God and suggest that somehow absolute spiritual being must always be understood as threefold. Other thinkers—especially from the Reformed tradition—have followed Jürgen Moltmann in the attempt to develop a "social model" of the Trinity. "Process" theologians have argued for a divine Trinity whose being actually develops to fullness in inseparable involvement with the development of creation. The Orthodox John Zizioulas and the Catholic Catherine Mowry LaCugna have drawn on the Continental tradition of personalist philosophy to suggest a way of approaching trinitarian doctrine that begins with the relational, interpersonal character of conscious being itself. In his famous reflection on trinitarian doctrine that first appeared in the German collection *Mysterium Salutis*, Karl Rahner has tellingly reminded modern theologians that our way of thinking about what God is, in God's eternal being, is for Christian faith identical with the way God has revealed himself in sacred history—enunciating there his oft-quoted principle that the "immanent Trinity" *is* the "economic Trinity," and vice versa.[1] And Hans Urs von Balthasar, in his reflection on the liturgy of the Holy Week Triduum in that same collection, has suggested that the death and burial of Jesus, as Son of God, really introduces abandonment and death as well as vindication and new life into the eternal inner relationships that form God's own being.[2] All of these approaches—and numerous others—to conceiving of the Trinity in new ways, ways related to the main themes of modern church life and modern philosophy, have drawn new criticisms. But they also testify at least to the growing consciousness among Christian thinkers that we cannot talk responsibly about God, as Christians, without somehow shaping our speech in explicitly trinitarian terms.

Theoretical models of the Trinity, however, whether ancient or modern, always seem doomed to failure if they are taken to be models for rational explanation—for actually making sense of how we can confess the Father, the Son, and the Holy Spirit, whom Christians invoke in liturgy and prayer, to be at the same time both radically one and simple and irreducibly three. The reason, of course, is that our thought and speech about God as Trinity is not, in any sense, a theory or hypothesis intended to explain how God has touched us in history. So trinitarian language always resists further explanation; it simply confesses, proclaims. And the reason is that the Trinity is not a theory so much as a summary of biblical faith, the briefest and most lapidary of Christian creeds.

As Christians, believers commit themselves to the faith of Israel, as Jesus and his disciples did: they take as utterly fundamental the ancient Hebrew profession of

1. Karl Rahner, "Der Dreifaltige Gott als Transzendenter Urgrund der Heilsgeschichte," in *Mysterium Salutis: Grundriss heilsgeschichtlicher Dogmatik*, ed. Johannes Feiner and Magnus Löhrer (Einsiedeln: Benzinger, 1965), 2:328 (ET: Karl Rahner, *The Trinity*, trans. Joseph Donceel [New York: Crossroad, 1967], 21).

2. Hans Urs von Balthasar, "Der Zugang zur Wirklichkeit Gottes," in *Mysterium Salutis*, 2:15–43.

faith in a single God (Deut. 6:4) and the engagement to "have no other gods besides" him (Exod. 20:3). With Jesus, they dare to call this transcendent, ultimate divine mystery, whom no one can define or imagine, by the name "Father"; they seek to live in utter obedience to his will (see Luke 22:42) and commit their lives into his hands (see Luke 23:46). In the risen Jesus, proclaimed by the witness of his disciples to the world, they recognize one who makes God personally present and visible today, who brings to fulfillment, in unexpected ways, the full prophetic promise of Israel's history. They dare to say with the disciples, "Jesus is Lord," recognizing him not simply as an eschatological prophet or even simply as Israel's promised Messiah but as one who is literally the Son of God, God's Word made flesh, "God with us." And in the very process of making this confession, they recognize that God is present and active among them in yet another way, mysteriously enabling them to grasp more fully the identity of Jesus and to walk with him on his way to the Father. "No one can say 'Jesus is Lord,'" Paul reminds the Corinthians, "except by the Holy Spirit" (1 Cor. 12:3).

The events of Easter and Pentecost, in other words, are for New Testament Christianity the beginning of a new depth of human awareness of God's transcendent, ineffable reality and nearness, working in history to save us from self-destruction. More important, this astonishing revelation is the reason Christians affirm that these three distinct ways our forebears have had of conceiving God's working are—taken together—a revelation of *what God is*. God *is* the invisible presence in the burning bush and on the top of Sinai, the one who guided Israel throughout its history, whom Jesus spoke to as his Father; God *is* the rabbi from Nazareth who proclaimed the kingdom, who was crucified and then raised from the dead, whom the disciples recognized as "Lord"; God *is* the sudden, irresistibly powerful Holy Spirit of Pentecost and of the continuing life of the church, the interior "advocate" sent by Jesus from the Father (John 15:26) to bear witness to him and to guide his followers "into all truth" (John 16:13). For Christians, all three of these figures and voices in the history of revelation remain distinct—related intimately to one another, working along with one another, but not simply the same as one another—yet all, taken together, *are* what Christians mean by "God." And salvation for the Christian is nothing less than to be caught up into this manifold divine mystery, this unified yet textured and endlessly reciprocal life of God. It is to be moved by the Spirit to call Jesus "Lord," to be Jesus's disciple, to be made part of Jesus's ecclesial body, and so to walk with him on his way to the Father in obedience and in hope. It is to be identified by the Spirit, through trinitarian baptism, with Jesus Christ; to become "sons and daughters in the Son," children of the Father with Jesus; and so to be embraced within the life of God.

In the first five centuries of Christian history, theologians came only haltingly, only gradually, to a recognition of the contours of this staggering mystery of salvation and to the words and expressions that would enable them to put that recognition into human language. From the late second century on, many spoke of the three names of the baptismal formula as a "Triad," a *trias*; step by step, with the help of the best conceptions available to them from philosophy and literature for thinking about the world and human existence, they built up patterns of thought and language that would let them speak faithfully of this divine Triad within the boundaries of biblical faith. In classical patristic usage, most of the "-ologies" by which Christians today analyze the facets of faith were still unknown; "Christology," "eschatology," "soteriology," "Mariology," and so on, as subdivisions of the wider project of theology, are all creations of post-Reformation scholasticism, Protestant and Catholic. The overarching term for speaking about what God has done in history to reveal and to save was *oikonomia*: God's "household management" within creation, God's plan to share and rebuild the life that began with the act of creation itself and reached its culmination in the incarnation of his Son. To speak of God as God has shown himself to be—to try, on the basis of what humans have seen of his *oikonomia*, to reach beyond history into his own inconceivable life—was alone *theologia*: talking and thinking about *God*!

By the last quarter of the fourth century, halting Christian attempts to do *theologia* in the biblical and liturgical tradition had led, by unpredictable twists and turns, to what later generations generally think of as "the doctrine of the Holy Trinity": the formulated idea that the God of Jewish and Christian revelation *is* Father and Son and Holy Spirit, as one reality or substance, operating outward in creation always as a unity, yet always internally differentiated by the relationships of origin that Father and Son and Holy Spirit have with one another—the ways each one *is*, with the others, the single mystery of God. By the conventions of the late fourth century, first formulated in Greek by the "Cappadocian Fathers," these three constituent members of what God is came to be referred to as *hypostases* ("concrete individuals") or, more misleadingly for us moderns, as *prosōpa* ("persons"). As St. Augustine would remark in his monumental treatise *On the Trinity*, when we speak of the distinguishing relationships we have come to recognize between Father, Son, and Holy Spirit, and are asked to say in what sense they are three, we speak of "three *hypostases*" or "three individuals" or "three persons" simply for lack of a better term:

> For the sake, then, of speaking of things that cannot be uttered, that we may be able in some way to utter what we can in no way express fully, our Greek friends have spoken of one essence, three substances (= *hypostases*), but the Latins of one essence or substance, three persons—because, as we have already said, essence usually means nothing else than substance in our language. . . . And provided that what is said is understood only in a mystery, such a way of speaking is sufficient, in order that there might be something to say when we are asked what those three are, which the true faith pronounces to be three.[3]

But the relationship of these three remains mysterious as well as crucially important for salvation; their unity remains as central to their divine identity as their distinction. So St. Gregory of Nazianzus, rejecting the notion that each of the three "persons" has responsibility for a different aspect of salvation or a different region of creation, insists,

> This is not what we are saying; "For this is not the division of Jacob" (Jer. 10:16), as my theologian puts it. But each of them is one with what is united to it, no less than it

3. *Trin.* 7.4.7; see also 5.8.10 and 6.8.9.

is with itself, by identity of substance and power. This is the structure of [God's] unity, as far as what we have understood of it allows us to say.[4]

God's identity is ultimate self-identity, like that of a conscious subject, even while it remains a dynamic, self-giving, internally related identity of three agents who, each and all together, realize God's being, God's subjectivity, and God's unified action in eternally distinct ways. Each of these agents *is* the unique God!

These passages, like so many others in the classical tradition of Christian speech about the mystery of God, seem to bend the structures of linguistic coherence, to push the limits of normal meaning to the breaking point. What they reveal is that statements about God as one substance and three *hypostases* are, first of all, boundary statements: statements that mark out, in the name of the community of Christian faith and worship, the limits of what represents biblical and ecclesial faith from what lies outside it. As boundary statements, they are also rules of religious grammar: formal principles for the use of language within the ongoing tradition of the church's belief. They are summaries of all that Christian faith proclaims about God, about God's work in Jesus and God's continuing work through the Spirit in the church, about human salvation and transformation by sharing in their mutual gift of life. Yet even so— perhaps for the very reason that they are not attempts at giving a satisfying explanation of God—their content and meaning remain inexhaustibly rich and provocative, irretrievably beyond what any of us can understand or explain. They are simply the halting beginnings of developed Christian *theologia*.

What my dear friend and colleague Khaled Anatolios offers us in this book, *Retrieving Nicaea*, is nothing less than a retelling of how and in what terms the Christian community of the first five centuries learned to speak in this challenging yet normative way, and why their speech is important for us as believers. It is not simply another attempt to reconstruct the tangled early history of trinitarian dogma or an essay in late antique social or intellectual history. It is rather, in my view at least, a work of profound theology: a brilliant summary of the conflicts and debates that originally led the church to articulate just what God is for a Christian, as substance and person, and of the beginnings of some accepted answers to the questions that troubled many believers in the controversies surrounding the Council of Nicaea (325). Every later generation of Christian theologians, in one way or another, has had to carry on the process of forming answers to the questions raised then concerning God's being. The process, by the very terms of the discussion, never reaches a fully satisfying conclusion. Yet, as Prof. Anatolios reminds us, we are blessed by the fact that these first theologians, these first writers to "talk about God" in what we call trinitarian terms, were also great theologians: great thinkers, great writers, individuals of great devotion and great faith. As we attempt to carry on their work today, joining intelligently and generously in their debates is probably the best place for any of us to begin. We can learn from them, perhaps better than from many more recent thinkers, both the

4. *Or.* 31.16.

terms of the discussion and the spirit of devout and eloquent brilliance that such a discussion inevitably requires of us if we are to carry it on well. This book, in fact, does just that, and does it supremely well; it brings us—with clarity and insight—face to face with the origins of trinitarian doctrine as a theological conversation on which our salvation, in one way or another, ultimately depends. The subject, after all, as Gregory of Nazianzus reminds us, is nothing less than God.[5]

Brian E. Daley, SJ
Catherine F. Huisking Professor of Theology
University of Notre Dame
Holy Thursday, 2011

---

5. *Or.* 27.3.

Preface

The composition of this book has been animated by a double conviction: that the development of trinitarian doctrine is the key to its meaning, and that the contents of this meaning constitute the entirety of Christian faith. It represents the trinitarian debates of the fourth century as a crucial and irreversible stage in the church's appropriation of the gospel of Jesus Christ that simultaneously identified the God whom Christians worship with Jesus's relationship to his Father in the Spirit and interpreted the entirety of Christian life and faith as bearing the imprint of this identification. The full exposition and substantiation of this double claim would require many more volumes dealing with ancient personages not treated in this book as well as modern themes and questions. An original schema that included substantive treatments of the likes of Basil of Caesarea, Gregory of Nazianzus, Hilary of Poitiers, and Ephrem the Syrian had to be abandoned in favor of a narrower but more intensely focused approach that attempts to highlight the comprehensive range of trinitarian faith as virtually coextensive with the entire breadth of Christian faith in the theologies of Athanasius and Gregory of Nyssa while highlighting the epistemology of trinitarian faith in Augustine. The concluding chapter, outlining in very broad strokes "the systematic scope of Nicene trinitarian doctrine," can also easily be extrapolated into a much more extensive treatment in explicit dialogue with modern theology. While this project can thus be materially broadened in both the directions of ancient and modern theology, its present form amounts to a concession to the limits of space and time that nevertheless attempts to lay a sufficient foundation for the demonstration of its double claim. Rather than purporting to be an exhaustive *Dogmengeschichte*, it is a hopeful, if not quixotic, effort to engage both historical and systematic theologians in a conversation about the enduring value of the historical development of trinitarian doctrine for its systematic exposition.

I have adapted parts of two earlier published pieces for this manuscript. Chapter 1 involves a reworking of material from my chapter "Discourse on the Trinity" in *Constantine to 600*, vol. 2, *The Cambridge History of Christianity*, ed. W. Löhr and

F. Norris (Cambridge: Cambridge University Press, 2007), 431–59; chapter 2 incorporates material from my "The Immediately Triune God: A Patristic Response to Schleiermacher," *Pro Ecclesia* 10 (Spring 2001): 159–78.

I am thankful to a number of colleagues for reading parts or all of this manuscript and offering helpful comments and suggestions, including Gary Anderson, John Baldovin, John Behr, John Cavadini, Boyd Taylor Coolman, Brian Daley, Kevin Hart, George Hunsinger, Robert Imbelli, Richard Lennan, Bruce Marshall, John Milbank, John R. Sachs, Kelley McCarthy Spoerl, and Markus Vinzent. It has been a special pleasure to work with James Ernest, senior editor at Baker Academic. Since I was already admiringly familiar with James's own significant scholarship on Athanasius, I started out with high expectations. But what I did not expect was a throwback to the famed, perhaps legendary days when milk and bread were delivered to one's front door and editors took meticulous interest in every matter of style and substance. James's profound and extensive erudition, keen intelligence, attention to every detail, and unfailingly good humor have made the collaboration of preparing this manuscript for publication a truly memorable pleasure.

Finally, and above all, I want to express my deepest gratitude to my wife, Meredith, whose companionship has lightened the burdens and greatly multiplied the rewards of my every labor since I have been gifted with her presence. The crowning joy of completing this work is to dedicate it to her.

Abbreviations

General

ET	English translation	LXX	Septuagint

Modern Editions

CCSL	Corpus christianorum, series latina
CSCO	Corpus scriptorum christianorum orientalium
CSEL	Corpus scriptorum ecclesiasticorum latinorum
GCS	Griechischen Christlichen Schriftsteller
GNO	*Gregorii Nysseni Opera*. Leiden: Brill, 1960–.
LCL	Loeb Classical Library
NPNF[2]	*Nicene and Post-Nicene Fathers*, Second Series
OECT	Oxford Early Christian Texts
PG	Patrologia graeca
PL	Patrologia latina
SC	Sources chrétiennes
TDNT	Kittel, Gerhard, ed. *Theological Dictionary of the New Testament*. Translated by Geoffrey Bromiley. 10 vols. Grand Rapids: Eerdmans, 1964.
Urk.	Opitz, H., ed. *Urkunden zur Geschichte des Arianischen Streites*. Berlin: de Gruyter, 1934.

Greek and Latin Sources

Alexander of Alexandria

Ep. Alex.	*Letter to Alexander of Byzantium*

Ambrose

Spir.	*On the Holy Spirit*

Apollinaris of Laodicea

Fr.	Fragments

Aristotle

Cat.	*Categories*

Asterius

Fr.	Fragments

Athanasius

C. Ar.	*Orations against the Arians*
C. gent.	*Against the Greeks*
Decr.	*On the Council of Nicaea*

Ep. Aeg. Lib.	Letter to the Bishops of Egypt and Libya
Ep. Afr.	Letter to the Bishops of Africa
Ep. Fest.	Festal Letters
Ep. Serap.	Letters to Serapion on the Holy Spirit
Inc.	On the Incarnation
Syn.	On the Councils of Ariminum and Seleucia
Tom. Antioch.	Tome to the Antiochenes
Vit. Ant.	Life of Anthony

Augustine

Civ.	City of God
Doctr. chr.	De doctrina christiana
Serm.	Sermons
Trin.	De Trinitate

Basil of Caesarea

C. Eun.	Against Eunomius
Ep.	Epistles
Spir.	On the Holy Spirit
Vita	Vitae philosophorum

Eunomius of Cyzicus

| Apol. | Apology |

Eusebius of Caesarea

Com. Isa.	Commentary on Isaiah
Dem. ev.	Demonstration of the Gospel
Eccl. theol.	Ecclesiastical Theology
Hist. eccl.	Ecclesiastical History
Laud. Const.	In Praise of Constantine
Marc.	Against Marcellus
Prep. ev.	Preparation for the Gospel
Theoph.	Theophany
Vit. Const.	Life of Constantine

Gregory of Nazianzus

| Ep. | Epistles |
| Or. | Orations |

Gregory of Nyssa

C. Eun.	Against Eunomius
Cat. Or.	Catechetical Oration
Comm. Cant.	Commentary on the Song of Songs
De virg.	On Virginity
Ep.	Epistles
Eus.	To Eustathius
Spir.	Against the Macedonians on the Holy Spirit

| Vit. Mos. | Life of Moses |

Hilary of Poitiers

| Coll. Ant. | Collectanea Antiariana Parisina |
| De syn. | On the Synods |

Irenaeus

| Haer. | Against the Hereies |

Jerome

| Ep. | Epistles |

Justin Martyr

| 1 Apol. | First Apology |
| Dial. | Dialogue with Trypho |

Marcellus of Ancyra

| Fr. | Fragments |

Methodius of Olympus

| De lib. arb. | On Free Will |

Origen

| Comm. Jo. | Commentary on Job |
| Princ. | On First Principles |

Philostorgius

| Hist. eccl. | Ecclesiastical History |

Plato

Crat.	Cratylus
Phaedr.	Phaedrus
Rep.	Republic
Tim.	Timaeus

Plotinus

| Enn. | Enneads |

Seneca

| Ep. | Epistles |

Socrates

| Hist. eccl. | Ecclesiastical History |

Sozomen

| Hist. eccl. | Ecclesiastical History |

Tertullian

| Prax. | Against Praxeas |

Introduction

Development as Meaning in Trinitarian Doctrine

In this book I aim to exhibit the intelligibility of trinitarian doctrine by interpreting the writings of key Christian thinkers of the fourth and early fifth centuries. My premise is that if we wish to understand trinitarian doctrine, we must observe how it came to be formulated in the councils of Nicaea (325) and Constantinople (381) and how such formulations were interpreted in the immediate aftermath of these councils. The approach taken here rejects as simplistic any sharp distinction between "historical theology" (as "what it meant then") and "systematic theology" (as "what it means now"). Rather, it traces the logic whereby trinitarian doctrine developed in order to find resources for contemporary appropriation of this doctrine. We cannot ignore the historical development and gain direct access to the objective referents of the normative statements of trinitarian doctrine; we must creatively re-perform the acts of understanding and interpretation that led to those statements. In other words, in order to grasp trinitarian doctrine creatively in our own setting, we must "retrieve Nicaea."

In this perspective, "Nicaea" refers not to the historical event of 325 in and of itself but rather to that event as appropriated and interpreted by those who over the succeeding decades claimed to be—and later were generally accepted as being—in continuity with its declaration of the consubstantiality of the Father and the Son. They understood that declaration to entail both unity of being and real distinction between Father, Son, and Spirit. This book contends that their interpretations were not based on arcane speculations about unity and diversity in God, or about the nature of substance and persons, but rather expressed coherent construals of the entirety of Christian existence. Many voices today lament the isolation and abstractness of trinitarian theology and ask how it connects with lived Christian faith; we can address those concerns fruitfully by retrieving the doctrine in the course of its development.

1

Because of the particular challenges that trinitarian faith has always posed to understanding, as well as the various shortcomings of modern strategies for apprehending the meaning of trinitarian doctrine, we should see the creative "indwelling of the tradition"[1] whereby this doctrine was constructed as an indispensable maneuver in appropriating trinitarian faith. Indeed, the peculiar difficulties of understanding trinitarian doctrine are not distinctly modern discoveries. The North African bishop Augustine already presented the unique character of these difficulties clearly in the fifth century.[2] In every other doctrine, says Augustine, we can at least understand the objective referents of the individual terms of the proposition recommended to faith, even if we have no direct access to the whole reality to which the entire proposition refers. For example, Christian faith proposes that Jesus the Christ rose from the dead. A potential believer must accept or reject this faith proposition without direct empirical access to the event of Jesus's rising from the dead. But at least in this case we apprehend the objective referents of the proposition enough to know what we are being asked to believe. We have experience of people both living and dying, and we can ascertain that we are being asked to believe that after Jesus died, he continues to live. But this is not the case with the proposition that God is triune, which seems to predicate of God a three-in-oneness of which God is apparently the only instance. What then do we believe when we believe that God is Trinity? And what meaning can such faith have for us, both cognitively and existentially?

A more modern perspective on the question of the intelligibility of trinitarian doctrine comes from the Enlightenment philosopher Immanuel Kant. Kant concluded that because what trinitarian doctrine predicates of God is not accessible to human experience, it is simply not intelligible; therefore it is meaningless in its reference to God.[3] More recently, Karl Rahner has given classic expression to another modern challenge to the meaningfulness of trinitarian doctrine, this time posed from within Christian faith. Rahner proposes that the Western postscholastic development of the doctrine has located its meaning in a realm that is abstracted from Christian "piety" and theology and thus has no existential meaning for most Christians.[4] Since Rahner's clarion call for an existentially accessible meaning for trinitarian doctrine, there has been much talk of a "renewal" of trinitarian theology.[5] But given Rahner's original pastoral motivation, one can still legitimately ask whether this putative renaissance has really borne fruit in the experience of ordinary Christians.[6] Are our churches today

---

1. The phrase is originally from Polanyi, as developed in his *Personal Knowledge* and *Knowing and Being*.
2. *Trin.* 8.4.6–8.
3. *Religion within the Limits of Reason Alone*, book 4, "General Observation."
4. See his seminal article, "The Method and Structure of the Treatise 'On the Triune God,'" in *Trinity*, 9–48.
5. For an account and critique of the modern claim for a renewal in trinitarian theology, see Marshall, "Trinity," esp. 190–200.
6. When I invoke the category of "experience," I do not intend to denote an area of human existence that is separate from thought, conceptuality, doctrine, etc., but rather the entirety of human existence to the extent that it is consciously interpreted by the human subject and becomes the object of what Newman called "real assent." See Newman, *An Essay in Aid of a Grammar of Assent*, esp. 49–92.

any more imbued with a trinitarian consciousness than the functionally unitarian Christianity lamented by Rahner?

Three Trajectories in Modern Trinitarian Doctrine

Among modern approaches to retrieving the meaning of trinitarian doctrine, we can identify three major trajectories. The first trajectory, for which Friedrich Schleiermacher is a seminal figure, concedes Kant's objection that trinitarian doctrine says nothing intelligible about God's intrinsic being. The meaning of trinitarian doctrine resides rather in what it says about our relation to God, namely, "the being of God in Christ and in the Church."[7] "Son" and "Spirit" in this schema refer to how the presumably singular divine essence interacts with the world, not to eternal differentiations within the divine essence itself. And yet Schleiermacher recognizes that trinitarian doctrine does apparently intend to predicate something of the divine being. Consequently—and problematically—he separates the meaning of the doctrine from the doctrine itself: "Hence, it is important to make the point that the main pivots (*Hauptangelpunkte*) of the ecclesiastical doctrine—the being of God in Christ and in the Christian Church—are independent of the doctrine of the Trinity."[8] Several recent theologians, including Piet Schoonenberg, Catherine LaCugna, and Roger Haight, have adopted Schleiermacher's approach.[9] The inner contradiction that plagues this approach is most dramatically presented by LaCugna's work, which attempts the baffling balancing act of insisting both on the urgent meaning of trinitarian doctrine for Christian existence as revelatory of God's "being as communion" and yet cautioning that trinitarian doctrine does not really mean that God *is* Trinity.[10] I will not here

7. Schleiermacher, *Christian Faith*, 741.

8. Ibid.; *Der Christliche Glaube*, 2:461. Recently, Francis Schüssler Fiorenza has endeavored to defend Schleiermacher from the charge that he marginalized trinitarian doctrine, contending instead that its position at the end of *The Christian Faith* is intended to indicate the status of the doctrine as the "capstone" of Christian confession. See his "Schleiermacher's Understanding of God as Triune," 171–88. However, Fiorenza's defense of Schleiermacher is not relevant to our present concern, which is not with Schleiermacher's subjective intentionality in his evaluation of the status of trinitarian doctrine but rather with his construal of the actual contents of the doctrine. Inasmuch as he refuses to concede that it refers to eternal distinctions in the divine being, his construal of that doctrine is effectively marginal with respect to the mainstream Christian tradition, regardless of his estimation of the relative rank of the doctrine in relation to other aspects of the Christian confession.

9. See thesis 25 in Schoonenberg, "Trinity—the Consummated Covenant," 114; LaCugna, *God for Us*, esp. 209–41; Haight, *Jesus: Symbol of God*, 480–83; and Haight, "The Point of Trinitarian Theology," 191–204.

10. LaCugna approvingly summarizes Zizioulas thus: "Human persons exist in the first place because God subsists as triune love" (*God for Us*, 266). However, she explicitly rejects the notion of "intradivine relations" in God and of "Trinity" as a predication of God's intrinsic being: "And, as the history of the doctrine of the Trinity shows, as soon as we begin to argue on the basis of such intradivine distinctions, we leave the economy behind. As soon as we leave the economy behind, the doctrine of the Trinity has no bearing on life or faith" (ibid., 227); "The doctrine of the Trinity is not ultimately a teaching about 'God' but a teaching about *God's life with us and our life with each other*" (ibid., 228; original italics).

attempt a detailed refutation of this approach. Suffice it to say that it objectively deconstructs not only the plain sense of trinitarian affirmations—whatever that doctrine purports to say about God, it clearly intends to say something about God in God's very being—but indeed the intelligibility of Christian revelation as a whole. After all, this revelation has been traditionally understood as divine self-disclosure and self-communication. The latter point was already made in the nineteenth century by the German Lutheran theologian Isaak Dorner: "The economic Trinity . . . leads back to immanent distinctions in God himself, all the more so because in the world of revelation we have to do not merely with a teaching of truths, but with the true *being* of God in the world, with God's actions, indeed with his self-communication."[11]

A second trajectory exactly reverses Schleiermacher's disjunction of God's being from God's relation to the world: trinitarian doctrine, this view insists, asserts that the form of God's salvific self-communication to the world coincides with the form of divine being. While Rahner is by no means the originator, even in modern times, of this notion,[12] his oft-quoted *Grundaxiom* has become its most celebrated expression: "The 'economic' Trinity is the 'immanent' Trinity and the 'immanent' Trinity is the 'economic' Trinity."[13] As Dorner insisted in the quotation cited above, some version of this approach—positing an essential continuity between the form of God's self-presentation to the world and God's own being—is necessary not only for a correct interpretation of trinitarian doctrine but, indeed, for an authentic notion of divine revelation. The Christian account of divine revelation and of divine "faithfulness" posits a correspondence between who God is and how God presents himself to the world. But at least two difficulties attend Rahner's particular presentation of this position. The first has been pointed out by Yves Congar and others: Rahner's axiom seems to strictly conflate God's eternal trinitarian being with the economic features acquired by the Trinity in God's work of salvation.[14] One can hold that the eternal Trinity is the subject of the economy of salvation without holding that the features of "the economic Trinity" are exactly those of the eternal Trinity. In fact, the development of Nicene orthodoxy hinges on the insistence that, at least in one crucial respect, the "form" or appearance of the economic Trinity does *not* correspond to that of the eternal immanent Trinity. A strict and unqualified conflation of the economic Trinity with the immanent Trinity would entail that the subordination of the incarnate Son to the Father reflects the same order of subordination in the immanent Trinity. But a large part of the logic of Nicene theology consists precisely in overcoming this inference.

Of course, Rahner's own understanding of his axiom did not entail a wholesale transposition of all the features of the "economic Trinity" onto the "immanent Trinity." The central thrust of his application of this axiom was the insistence that the two modes of God's self-communication—in concrete history and as the horizon of

---

11. As cited in Marshall, "Trinity," 195 (my italics).
12. As noted in ibid.
13. Rahner, *Trinity*, 22.
14. See Congar, *I Believe in the Holy Spirit*, 3:11–18.

the self-transcendence of human subjectivity—correspond to the eternal modes of divine self-communication and differentiation in the eternal generation of the Son and the procession of the Spirit:

> In line with this idea, we might point out here that the incomprehensible, primordial, and forever mysterious unity of transcendence through history and of history into transcendence holds its ultimate depths and most profound roots in the Trinity, in which the Father is the incomprehensible origin and the original unity, the "Word" his utterance into history, and the "Spirit" the opening up of history into the immediacy of its fatherly origin and end. And precisely this Trinity of salvation history, as it reveals itself to us by deeds, is the "immanent" Trinity.[15]

This quotation clearly brings out the second difficulty in Rahner's implementation of his own trinitarian *Grundaxiom*, and that is its abstraction from the concrete particularities of the scriptural narrative. Rahner complains about the "isolation" of trinitarian doctrine "from other dogmatic treatises telling us something about ourselves conducive to our real salvation."[16] However, his own approach does not so much delve into the continuities and discontinuities between the biblical narrative of creation and salvation and the Trinity as the subject of this narrative; rather, he comprehensively enfolds the dialectic of history and spirit/transcendence into divine life and being. Thus, in actual practice, his identification of the immanent Trinity with the economic Trinity pays little attention to the narrative particularities of the economy. All this is not to deny that his trinitarian theology is substantially biblical in its deepest thrust. My point is that his axiom needs to be more thoroughly integrated with particular details of the scriptural narrative.

Other theologians committed to Rahner's fundamental principle have more explicitly applied this project to the particular details of the biblical narrative and in so doing have reached controversial conclusions. Thus Karl Barth and, more recently, Robert Jenson have sought to reassert the ontological identity between the eternal Word and the incarnate Word, to the point of affirming that the eternal Word is in some sense eternally incarnate, or at least *incarnandus*.[17] Raising such questions simply underscores the point that an approach to trinitarian theology that probes continuities between the narrative of the economy and the very being of God will always encounter difficulties that reverberate to the core of the mystery of Christian revelation. These difficulties cannot be resolved by a mere formal statement of the identity of the immanent and economic Trinity. Moreover, Rahner's axiom and the complexities of its implementation should make us ask how such complexities were dealt with in the historical construction of the doctrine itself. What light does this

15. Rahner, *Trinity*, 47.
16. Ibid., 15.
17. See Jenson, *Triune Identity*, 138–45, and his discussion of Barth therein. For a defense of Barth on this point, with the clarification that for Barth, the Son is always *incarnandus* by grace and not by nature, see Hunsinger, "Election and the Trinity," esp. 182–83 (thesis 5).

history shed on our contemporary efforts to identify continuities and discontinuities between trinitarian being and the trinitarian economy?

A third trajectory in the effort to locate the meaning of trinitarian doctrine is probably the dominant one in the modern Western Christian tradition: the search for an appropriate creaturely analogy. Historically, in the West, the regnant version of this approach is the so-called "psychological analogy," presumed to be originated by Augustine, further developed by Aquinas, and elaborated in a contemporary idiom by Bernard Lonergan.[18] In this version we glimpse a certain semblance of the divine trinitarian being, however remotely and imperfectly, when we attend to the processions of intellect and will from the human mind. More recently, however, theologians have critiqued the psychological analogy as modalist in its trinitarian doctrine and individualistic, in a proto-Cartesian manner, in its anthropological implications.[19] Instead, the version of the analogical strategy that is currently most favored is the "social analogy," which in certain versions presumes to retrieve another trinitarian image from Augustine that is further developed by Richard of St. Victor. Augustine spoke of the Trinity in terms of lover, beloved, and the love between them;[20] Richard of St. Victor spoke of lover, beloved, and co-beloved.[21] In some quarters, the central question of the meaning of trinitarian doctrine seems to be the choice between the psychological and the social analogies. This centralization of the role of analogies in mediating the meaning of trinitarian doctrine tends to spill over from systematic theology to historical studies, where the trinitarian theologies of figures foundational to the tradition are often interpreted principally in terms of their preferred analogies. Moreover, the search for the meaning of trinitarian doctrine through analogies is probably the default position of most practicing Christians, at least in the Western churches. To the extent that they are stirred to seek this meaning, and to the extent that pastors are moved to supply it, recourse is typically made principally to analogies. I recall a sermon on Trinity Sunday in which the preacher suggested the analogy of a father, a mother, and their baby sleeping in the same bed, the bed corresponding to the one essence!

The use of analogies has been pervasive in the history of Christian reflection on the divine Trinity. But, going beyond skirmishes over which analogy is most adequate, one has to question the whole approach in which analogies become the primary location of trinitarian meaning. When the meaning of trinitarian doctrine is located principally in some particular creaturely analogue, it becomes separable from other aspects of the Christian mystery. Instead of trinitarian meaning being embedded in the whole nexus of Christian faith, it tends to be reduced to the features of the analogue itself. One can after all espouse "relationality" or wonder at the mind's differentiated unity

18. A contemporary defender of this approach asserts, "For over one thousand years the psychological analogy for the Trinity was the high point of Trinitarian theological reflection" (Ormerod, "Psychological Analogy," 281).

19. See, for example, the critique of Gunton in *Promise of Trinitarian Theology*, esp. 42–48.

20. *Trin.* 8.10.14.

21. Richard of St. Victor, *De Trin.* 3:11–19.

in the acts of knowing and willing without actually confessing and worshiping the Triune God as Father, Son, and Spirit. In that case, one could capture the meaning of trinitarian doctrine without ever subscribing to Christian faith. At the very least, the doctrine of the Trinity is then in danger of becoming simply another item in the list of Christian beliefs. Thus a Christian would be someone who believes that God created the world from nothing, that Jesus arose from the dead, and that God is in some way like a shamrock leaf (or human consciousness, or human relationships). Surely Rahner is right: the meaning of trinitarian doctrine must have a more intrinsic connection to the structure and texture of the whole of Christian life and faith.

Locating the Intelligibility of Trinitarian Doctrine

The difficulties of discerning the meaning of trinitarian faith, or the realization that the content of the objective propositions articulating this doctrine is so elusive, should lead us to ask, what intelligibility attended their original formulation? To return to Kant's contention that these propositions are simply nonsensical, we can and must nevertheless ask, what sense did these propositions have for the people who articulated them? They at least seem to have thought they understood what they agreed and disagreed about! Augustine already clearly discerned the central and crucial difficulty in extracting meaning from trinitarian doctrine: the objective reference of the statements of trinitarian faith is not directly available to human perception and is thus ultimately incomprehensible. We cannot directly perceive with the mind's eye what we are saying about God when we say that God is Trinity. But this aporia should lead us back to the intentionalities that generated these statements. If we cannot comprehensively ascertain what predicating Trinity of God objectively entails with reference to God's own being, can we not nevertheless ask what Athanasius, Gregory of Nyssa, and Augustine meant when they affirmed such incomprehensible things? By reappropriating their acts of meaning and judgment, maybe we will also learn to affirm the things they said and to mean them approximately as they meant them.

Some may worry that the approach propounded here will follow the Schleiermacher trajectory and deny the objective reference of trinitarian doctrine to divine being. But that is far from the case. The difference between the Schleiermacherian approach and the one recommended here hinges on the crucial distinction between reference and full comprehension. I do not deny that trinitarian doctrine refers to God's being. But I do insist, along with the mainstream of Christian tradition, that trinitarian doctrine says things about God that are not fully comprehensible. My point is that the meaning of trinitarian doctrine should not be sought primarily in the objective reference of a narrow set of "trinitarian" propositional formulae (since this objective referent is also asserted to transcend full comprehension by human intelligence) but rather in the exigencies that led to their articulation. If we ask what these exigencies are, the answer proposed in this book is that these exigencies involved the entirety of Christian faith and life and thus provide a demonstration of the systematic scope of trinitarian doctrine. Trinitarian doctrine emerged not from some isolated insight into the being of God, such that its meaning might be grasped from a retrieval of that singular insight, or from some creaturely analogue that somehow approximates that insight. Rather, orthodox trinitarian doctrine emerged as a kind of meta-doctrine that involved a global interpretation of Christian life and faith and indeed evoked a global interpretation of reality. Its historical development thus presents a dramatic demonstration of Karl Rahner's characterization of trinitarian doctrine as the summary of Christian faith. To appropriate the meaning of trinitarian doctrine today, one must learn from the systematic thrust of its development how the entirety of Christian faith and life means the Trinity. Put differently, the suggestion is that we may *perform* the meaning of trinitarian doctrine by learning to refer to the trinitarian being of God through the entirety of Christian existence. The point is not to shift from objective reference to subjective intention but rather to retrieve the intentions of the theologians who had a formative role in the doctrine's expression, precisely in order to thereby learn how to correctly refer to God's trinitarian being. That retrieval leads us to identify the "sentences" that signify the divine Trinity as constituting the whole of Christian existence and not merely some subset of "trinitarian" propositions.

For some, the above proposal will evoke resonances of George Lindbeck's "cultural-linguistic mode" in his now classic, *The Nature of Doctrine*. In that work, Lindbeck notoriously dismisses not only "experiential-expressive" models of doctrine, in which doctrines are conceived as symbolizations of interior states, but also those of "traditional orthodoxies" in which doctrines are understood as conveying cognitive information in a direct correspondence between doctrinal propositions and the objective realities to which they refer. Lindbeck's own "cultural-linguistic" model understands doctrines as "idioms for the construction of reality and the living of life . . . [and] as communally authoritative rules of discourse, attitude, and action."[22] Setting aside for the moment the controverted question of whether this cultural-linguistic model completely annuls the truth-telling function of doctrine, I would like to propose that at least a variation of it helps us to grasp the real import of fourth-century trinitarian doctrine.[23] I would contend that the development of fourth-century trinitarian orthodoxy did indeed involve claims to objectively refer to the positive reality of the Triune God—yet not in the manner of a direct cognitive correspondence between propositions and their referents but rather by way of prescribing "authoritative rules of discourse, attitude, and action" that ensure the success of the act of referring to the Triune God. If this is true, then it is not fourth-century trinitarian orthodoxy that corresponds to Lindbeck's characterization of "traditional orthodoxies," but rather modern reductionist readings of this tradition.

Throughout this book, I will try to substantiate that position by demonstrating that the historical development of trinitarian doctrine took place through a syntax

22. Lindbeck, *Nature of Doctrine*, 18.
23. For a defense of Lindbeck against the charge that he is "soft on truth," see Marshall, "*The Nature of Doctrine* after 25 Years," in *Nature of Doctrine*, 25th anniv. ed., xvii.

that enfolded the entirety of Christian existence. Consequently, the retrieval of this systematic dimension of the historical development is an indispensable element for any subsequent "systematic" treatment of trinitarian doctrine, or indeed of Christian theology in general.

I further propose two fundamental principles that underlay the historical development of trinitarian doctrine, whose retrieval is indispensable for a contemporary appropriation of this doctrine. First, the construction of a particular set of interpretations of the primacy of Christ—as applied to the entire Christian narrative but especially as informing the notion of divine transcendence—was central to the development of trinitarian doctrine. The previous statement is in fact strongly ironic, since it is a celebrated motif in contemporary trinitarian theology that the greatest deficiency of "classical" trinitarian theology and Christology is that it begins with a non-christological "Hellenistic" conception of divine transcendence and that this deficiency is now being redressed by efforts to rethink divine transcendence from the perspective of the person and work of Jesus Christ.[24] In fact, I argue that a christological reconception of divine transcendence was foundational for the deep structure of the developing trinitarian grammar of what came to be associated with "Nicene" faith. Conversely, a contemporary appropriation of Nicene trinitarian doctrine amounts to an understanding and assenting to a particular account of the primacy of Christ and of the re-envisioning of divine transcendence and indeed of all of Christian faith and experience from that vantage point.

A second crucial element in the development of trinitarian doctrine was the clarification of a theological epistemology. According to the terms of this epistemology, trinitarian doctrine does not allow us to encompass the being of God within the confines of human knowing, but it does regulate our being and knowing so as to enable us to successfully relate ourselves to God, who is really Trinity. Moreover, this regulation of our being and knowing constitutes a global interpretation and performance of the whole of Christian existence. Although we cannot encompass God's trinitarian being within our human knowledge, we can know and glorify God as Trinity and be consciously and thankfully incorporated into trinitarian life. Thus appropriating the meaning of trinitarian doctrine involves learning to think, live, and pray so as to refer to God's being as Trinity while at the same time learning to disavow a comprehensive epistemic hold on the God to whom we thus refer ourselves. Consequently, the full disclosure of the meaning of our trinitarian affirmations (which, to repeat, constitute the whole of Christian existence) remains an eschatological hope rather than a present possession, though Christian faith involves an authentic foretaste of the substance of this hope.

A helpful modern metaphor for the kind of knowledge that trinitarian doctrine offers, and that the development of this doctrine demonstrates, is Jean-Luc Marion's

---

24. For some examples of this motif, see Pannenberg, *Systematic Theology*, 2:290; Moltmann, *Crucified God*, 87; Barth, *Church Dogmatics* IV/1, 179–85.

notion of the "saturated phenomenon."[25] A saturated phenomenon involves an excess of presencing that so overtakes and overwhelms the knower that she cannot objectify the source of this saturation and enclose it within her cognitive grasp. Similarly, the meaning of trinitarian doctrine, or the apprehension of the trinitarian being of God, cannot be epistemically enclosed or objectified. Rather, we appropriate the meaning of trinitarian doctrine by learning to identify and interpret the various aspects of Christian existence precisely as saturated by the God who is Trinity; conversely, we learn to identify the God who is Trinity through the saturated phenomenon that is Christian existence as a whole and in all its aspects. The historical development of trinitarian doctrine offers foundational insights into this reciprocal process.

How does the project of retrieving trinitarian doctrine as proposed here relate to the three modern approaches described above?

1. The first approach, which denies that trinitarian doctrine can in any way function as a description of divine being, is fundamentally incompatible with the Nicene development of trinitarian doctrine, as Schleiermacher himself was well aware.[26] The present proposal insists that trinitarian doctrine does successfully refer to divine being while conceding that the propositions of trinitarian doctrine do not encompass the divine being.

2. With regard to the second approach, which asserts the identity of the "immanent" Trinity and the "economic" Trinity, the retrieval here proposed accepts that the trinitarian economy yields real knowledge of God's being but does not simplistically conflate the trinitarian being of God with all the features of the trinitarian economy. The Nicene development of trinitarian doctrine involves a global interpretation of Christian life and faith that asserts a series of interlocking continuities and discontinuities between the trinitarian being of God and the trinitarian economy. Only by appropriating the strategies whereby these continuities and discontinuities constitute a coherent interpretation of Christian life and faith can we learn the meaning of trinitarian doctrine.

3. With respect to the search for trinitarian analogies, the Nicene development of trinitarian doctrine does allow for the use of various analogies, psychological, social, and otherwise—meteorological, in one instance![27] But it never makes an isolated analogy, or even a network of analogies, the main locus of trinitarian meaning. That locus is always, at least implicitly, the entire field of Christian existence.

How This Book Proceeds

It should be evident by now that the project of interpreting the development of trinitarian doctrine according to the terms outlined above is far removed from standard analyses that recount the history of this development as different versions of unity and

---

25. See Marion, *In Excess*.
26. Schleiermacher, *Christian Faith*, 172.3.
27. Cf. Gregory of Nyssa's analogy of the rainbow in *Ep.* 38 (= Ps. Basil).

diversity, or equality and inequality, between the "persons," or by way of word studies of "nature" and "person." There is ineluctably a hermeneutical circle between the kind of meaning that trinitarian doctrine is presumed to have and a given expositor's reconstruction of the development of this meaning. Standard textbook accounts of the development of trinitarian doctrine are beholden to typical preconceptions of the meaning of trinitarian doctrine, some of which we have just discussed. The meaning of trinitarian doctrine is presupposed to be contained in a set of isolated propositions containing such key terms as *ousia* and *hypostasis*, or to be manifest in the choice of certain analogies, or determined by an isolated key principle such as "Christ must be God in order to save us." Accordingly, the story of the development of trinitarian doctrine and the main voices within that narrative are treated principally in terms of their use of these key terms, their use or lack of use of certain analogies, and similar considerations.[28] But the inadequacy of that approach is manifest in its obvious *post factum* character. It does not bring to light the motivating intelligibility that pushed certain persons to these formulations, analogies, and judgments about the relation of the divine "persons" but simply narrates earlier traces of the final formulations of the doctrine. The result is not a creative reconstruction of a process of discovery that can be reenacted in acts of understanding and judgment but a lexical archaeological expedition.

I hope the approach propounded here gains a certain measure of hermeneutical transparency by explicitly announcing the hermeneutical circle that governs it. In reading the relevant texts, I have come to the conclusion that the development of Nicene trinitarian doctrine involved most decisively not so much the creation of a certain vocabulary, or the use of certain analogies, or indeed any one thing, but rather comprehensive interpretations of many aspects of Christian faith and life. Thus its proponents insisted that what was at stake was the interpretation of Christian life as a whole. Consequently, my interpretation of the development of Nicene trinitarian theology privileges precisely this systematic thrust. Of course every perspective has its limitations, and I am glad to concede this fact from the outset. Both material and formal limitations necessarily attend the particular perspective deployed here.

Materially, this book does not aspire to anything like the breadth of a comprehensive *Dogmengeschichte* of the development of trinitarian doctrine. Moreover, it does not attempt to offer a detailed historical account of the various alliances and ecclesial-political networks that informed the fourth-century controversies, though it

28. In *Nicaea and Its Legacy*, Ayres makes some significant overtures toward transcending this approach with sporadic appeals to a "Nicene culture," and to that extent his approach is complementary to mine. I have registered my own conviction that this more comprehensive approach needs to be more consistently implemented in his treatment of fourth-century theology in Ayres, Behr, and Anatolios, "*Nicaea and Its Legacy*: A Discussion," 141–75. John Behr's work could also be interpreted as reading the development of trinitarian doctrine as an extended interpretation of the "primacy of Christ" (though he does not use this phrase) and to that extent is also complementary to one of the structural trajectories of the approach presented here. See his *Way to Nicaea* and *Nicene Faith*. For a more systematic exposition of what I have referred to as the principle of the primacy of Christ, see his *Mystery of Christ*.

does interact with contemporary scholarship that deals with such issues. Furthermore, the particular focus on the systematic thrust of developing trinitarian theologies in the fourth century has severely restricted the number of theologians treated in depth. If one seeks the meaning of trinitarian doctrine especially in the use of the language of natures and persons, or in the use of analogies, then a broad analysis of the use of such language or various analogies is needed. But since I am trying to show how the development of trinitarian theology entailed a global interpretation of Christian faith and life as a whole, it seemed more pertinent to focus on a very few major figures and to show how their trinitarian doctrine involved such global interpretations.

Further limitations then come into play. Once the parameters of the notion of "trinitarian theology" are so enlarged as to be effectively coincident with the whole of theology, an exposition of a major figure's trinitarian theology becomes a much larger undertaking. Some creative selection therefore becomes necessary in presenting these figures. Thus for Athanasius and Gregory of Nyssa, my focus is broader; I portray these figures as representatives of the systematic thrust of Nicene trinitarian theology in relation to other aspects of Christian faith. The chapter on Augustine has the narrower goal of elucidating the epistemology of trinitarian faith in his classic work *On the Trinity* (*De Trinitate*). My focus throughout is on elements I consider relevant to the project of a contemporary appropriation of the meaning of trinitarian doctrine. To say this is to admit to the ineluctable "fusion of horizons" that attends every act of interpretation. It is also once again to destabilize the division of the tasks of historical and systematic theology. The present work purports to be a creative systematic retrieval of systematizing elements within the historical development of trinitarian doctrine.

Formally, perhaps the most crucial limitation of the present work is precisely that it is not a history. It does not attempt to offer any detailed sociocultural context for the fourth-century doctrinal debates. For example, I make no effort to familiarize the reader with the economic and social conditions of Athanasius's Egypt, though I try to contextualize his theological judgments in relation to contemporaries with whom he was in conversation. Questions about Athanasius's personal motivations (Did he champion Nicene theology in order to consolidate his own hold on episcopal power? To what extent did he authorize violence against his opponents?) are not entertained. Someone offering a history of the fourth century or of Athanasius himself would need to treat all such questions. The present study seeks only to illumine some of the interconnections that Athanasius and others drew between trinitarian commitments and other aspects of Christian faith. It treats Athanasius as essentially a systematic theologian in his own right, someone who claims to offer a certain vision of the coherence of Christian faith.

The claim underlying this approach is that such an account of Athanasius's theology, focusing on how it organizes the internal data of Christian faith (Scripture, liturgical rites, etc.), is intelligible in its own right. I do not deny the validity of investigating other elements of historical context, but I do reject an *a priori* presupposition that doctrinal controversies are not intelligible in the terms in which they actually present themselves, namely, as debates over how the various givens of Christian experience can be organized into a coherent whole. It would be interesting to explore further how various strategies for constructing the coherence of Christian experience interacted with the wider culture. But the aim of this study is simply to present certain versions of Nicene coherences. Moreover, it presents them with the further claim that they are still intelligible and indeed are perennially relevant to attempts to construe the meaning of trinitarian doctrine as embedded in Christian faith as a whole. This book does not set out to elucidate the conditions that make possible this continuity of intelligibility across historical distance. Such an elucidation, which properly belongs to the field of fundamental theology, would aim to explain how historicity and sociocultural variation interact with the structures and interactive presencing of human consciousness and the external world in such a way that a twenty-first-century Christian may recognize fourth-century theology as both intelligible and attractive.[29] The present book presupposes that such can be the case, and that presupposition will be validated if a sufficient number of readers are able to understand it and find in it constructive resources for their reasoned appropriation of Christian faith.

Of the chapters that follow, the first will quickly sketch the history of trinitarian debate between the Council of Nicaea in 325 and the Council of Constantinople in 381, assess current schemes for categorizing the positions of the various parties to that debate, and propose what I believe to be a more helpful way of categorizing two main trajectories. The second chapter will present a theoretical model of doctrinal development in general and apply it to certain figures representing both trajectories. As I have already signaled above, succeeding chapters will treat three major figures who, in distinct and overlapping ways, represent Nicene trinitarian theology as an integral interpretation of Christian faith: Athanasius of Alexandria, Gregory of Nyssa, and Augustine of Hippo. The conclusion will make explicit the constructive and systematic underpinnings of this historical enquiry by proposing a number of theses that I take to be key components of "Nicene" trinitarian theology.

---

29. For an exemplary account of just such a fundamental theology, see now Guarino, *Foundations of Systematic Theology.* By "fundamental theology" I mean that branch of theological discourse that explicitly considers the presuppositions and methods that enable theological enquiry, reflecting on such topics as revelation, faith and reason, and the uses of Scripture and tradition. Among notable modern treatments, see O'Collins, *Fundamental Theology,* and Fries, *Fundamental Theology.*

1

Fourth-Century Trinitarian Theology

History and Interpretation

This chapter will first narrate, in fairly broad strokes, the fourth-century doctrinal debates, then discuss how to best categorize the conflict of doctrinal positions in these debates so as to render them theologically intelligible. The narration of events between the Council of Nicaea in 325 and the Council of Constantinople in 381 will be presented with a minimum of interpretation; its aim is simply to acquaint the reader with the main figures and events. The second section will propose that a useful strategy for interpreting the debates of this period is to distinguish between theologies that see the unity of the Trinity as a unity of being and theologies that see this unity as a unity of will.

Before Nicaea[1]

The church of the fourth century inherited a tradition of trinitarian discourse that was pervasively embedded in its worship and proclamation, even if it was lacking in conceptual definition. The early Christians were monotheists who gave unqualified adherence to the *Shema* of Deuteronomy: "Hear, O Israel, the LORD is our God, the LORD alone" (Deut. 6:4). Yet they expressed belief in Jesus Christ as Savior in terms that referred to Jesus as the Son, Word, and Wisdom of God and as the one who

---

1. The following section is adapted from my "Discourse on the Trinity," in *Constantine to 600*, vol. 2, *The Cambridge History of Christianity*, ed. W. Löhr and F. Norris (Cambridge: Cambridge University Press, 2007), 431–59. Copyright © Cambridge University Press, 2007. Used with permission.

grants his disciples the grace of adoption through the bestowal of God's Spirit (cf. Gal. 4:4–7). The first centuries of Christian theological reflection assimilated confessions of both the oneness of God and the triadic form of Christian discipleship with varying degrees of concern for conceptual clarity and logical synthesis.

The first major debate concerned with conceptualizing the Christian experience of God as Trinity and bringing into coherence the emphases on divine unity and triadic distinction occurs in the third century. Tertullian (fl. 200), Hippolytus (ca. 170–ca. 236), and Novatian (mid-third century) all oppose doctrines that insist on the radical singularity of God and that reduce the distinctions between Father, Son, and Spirit to modes of appearance or activity. Tertullian insists that the unity of God must be interpreted through the trinitarian "economy" and attempts terminological differentiations that make it possible to speak of God in terms of a monotheistic trinitarianism: Father, Son, and Spirit are one in "substance," "condition," and "power" (*substantia, status, potestas*) while three in "degree," "form," and "aspect" (*gradus, forma, species*).[2] After the work of Tertullian, Hippolytus, and Novatian, the conceptions of God as a radically singular being and of Son and Spirit as merely modes of divine operation came to be associated with a certain Sabellius and with Paul of Samosata, third-century figures whose writings are no longer extant and who are therefore known to us only through the reports of their opponents. Nevertheless, their impact was such that it became *de rigueur* for the articulation of a Christian doctrine of God to reject a "Sabellian" or "Samosatene" interpretation of divine unity.

This lesson was well learned by Origen, arguably the greatest and most influential theologian of the third century, whose teaching cast a large shadow on the trinitarian controversies of the fourth century.[3] With Origen, there is a pronounced emphasis on Father, Son, and Spirit as distinct subsistences (*hypostaseis*) and on the eternal generation of the Son from the Father. Origen spoke of varying degrees of transcendence among the three *hypostaseis*, though he strictly differentiated the divine Trinity from creation.[4] More fatefully, he conjectured that God's eternal sovereignty, mediated by the preexistent Word and Wisdom, implied the existence from eternity of the creation over which he is sovereign.[5] This line of reasoning seemed to indicate an intrinsic link between the eternal generation of the Word from the Father and the everlasting existence of the creation. As Origen's speculation about the everlasting existence of creation came under severe critique, most notably in the later part of the third century by Methodius of Olympus, the doctrine of creation from nothing was brought to the foreground of theological reflection.[6] This critique led to a further question: if only the one God was unoriginated (*agen[n]ētos/agenētos*), did the derivation of the Son from

2. *Prax.* 2.

3. On the influence of Origen as setting the stage for the fourth-century controversies, see Williams, *Arius*, 131–57; Ayres, *Nicaea*, 20–30; Simonetti, *La crisi ariana nel IV secolo*, 55–60.

4. Cf. *Princ.* 1.1.8; 1.2.10. See Anatolios, "Theology and Economy in Origen and Athanasius," 165–71.

5. *Princ.* 1.2.10.

6. On the significance of Methodius, see especially Patterson, "Methodius, Origen, and the Arian Dispute"; Williams, *Arius*, 167–71; Behr, *Nicene Faith*, 1:38–48; Barnes, *Dynamis*, 184–89.

the Father also involve a kind of "creation from nothing"?[7] Thus, when Constantine's reign began in the early fourth century, Christian discourse used a trinitarian grammar, but it was not clear how best to conceive the relations and respective status of Father, Son, and Spirit vis-à-vis the created realm.

The Early Stages of Controversy

The trinitarian controversies of the fourth century constitute what is arguably the most crucially formative period in the development of the Christian doctrine of God. The fifth-century historian Socrates gives a plausible rendering of the outbreak of the debate. He tells us that an Egyptian presbyter, Arius, took issue with the preaching of Alexander, the bishop of Alexandria, on the mystery of "the unity of the holy Trinity."[8] Alexander's doctrine prominently stressed Origen's idea of the eternal generation of the Son from the Father. In contrast, the doctrine of Arius combined Origen's emphasis on the real distinctions within the Trinity with an unflagging insistence on the utter singularity of the one unoriginated and Unbegotten God. Thus, while we can speak of a divine Trinity, only the first entity (*hypostasis*) is truly and fully God. The unity of this Trinity, composed of unequal *hypostaseis*, is a unity of will rather than of substance. This doctrine does not deny the Son's divinity but presumes the framework of a graded hierarchy of transcendence in which it is possible to speak of variation in degree within the divine realm.[9] The fluidity of this model of divinity allowed Arius to balance scriptural attributions of divine honor to the Son with a strict interpretation of biblical monotheism. Given the demarcation between the unoriginate God and the creation from nothing by divine will, the Son must be placed in the latter category. His generation from the Father is thus the first and highest instance of creaturehood. Following Origen's insistence that all creatures are changeable by nature and equipped with the freedom of moral self-determination, Arius contended that the Son also is changeable by nature. Yet because of his foreseen merits, the Son was granted an unparalleled share of divine glory. Thus his divine status is a consequence of grace rather than nature.

The controversy between Arius and Alexander was exacerbated by factionalism within the Egyptian church dating back to the Diocletianic persecution as well as by different styles of theological discourse within the Egyptian Christian tradition. Both the political unification under Constantine and the centrality to Christian teaching of the issues under discussion ensured that the controversy would quickly cross Egyptian boundaries and spread throughout the Roman Empire. After Constantine defeated his Eastern rival, Licinius, and became sole emperor in 324, he quickly addressed the threat to unity created by this ecclesial debate. A church council was

---

7. On the lack of distinction between *gen[n]ētos/genētos* and their corresponding privatives in the fourth-century debates, see Hanson, *Search*, 203–6.

8. *Hist. eccl.* 1.5.

9. Ayres is right to stress the importance of recognizing "the . . . flexibility with which the term 'God' could be employed in these debates" (*Nicaea*, 14).

held in Nicaea in 325, attended by both Arius and Alexander as well as other bishops and theologians predominantly from the Eastern part of the empire. This council rejected Arius's slogan, "there was once when the Son was not," asserting that the Son's generation from the Father was of a different order than that of creation: "God of God, Light of Light, true God of true God, begotten not made." It used the term *homoousios* ("of the same substance") to designate the relation between the Son and the Father, less as a positive attempt to describe divine being than as an apophatic pronouncement ruling out any suggestion that the Son was created from nothing. The creed of Nicaea ran as follows:

> We believe in one God, Father Almighty, Maker of all things visible and invisible. And in one Lord Jesus Christ, the Son of God, begotten from the Father, only-begotten, that is, from the substance of the Father, God from God, light from light, true God from true God, begotten not made, consubstantial (*homoousion*) with the Father, through whom all things came into being, those on heaven and on earth; who for us humans and for our salvation came down and was incarnate and became human, suffered and rose again on the third day, ascended into the heavens, and is coming to judge the living and the dead.
>
> And in the Holy Spirit.
>
> But as for those who say, "there was once when he was not," and "before being begotten he was not," and that "he came into being from non-being," or who declare that the Son of God is of another *hypostasis* or *ousia*, or alterable or changeable, these the Catholic and Apostolic Church anathematizes.[10]

The Christian imagination has tended to portray the Nicene council as ushering in the victory of Athanasian "orthodoxy" over "the Arian heresy" with the inspired confession of the *homoousios*. However, the reception of Nicaea was a far more convoluted process than such a rendering suggests. In point of fact, the Council of Nicaea resulted in more confusion than resolution, at least in the short term, and neither Arius nor Athanasius was a primary figure in the immediate aftermath of the council.[11] Arius's slogan "there was once when the Son was not" embarrassed even those who were uncomfortable with the teaching of Nicaea. The task of articulating an alternative theology to that propounded by Nicaea passed to the leadership of Eusebius of Nicomedia, Eusebius of Caesarea, and Asterius. Eusebius of Nicomedia was an early supporter of Arius but shunned references to the Son's origination from nothing. His own theology emphasized the divine title "unbegotten" (*age[n]nētos*) as applicable only to one. Eusebius is wary of any language of communication of substance as suggesting "two unbegottens" or a materialistic fragmentation of the divine substance. The Son, who is produced by the

---

10. Critical edition in Dossetti, *Il simbolo di Nicea e di Costantinopoli*, 226–41.

11. The decline of Arius's public standing after the Council of Nicaea does not preclude the theory, put forward by Parvis, that the decades immediately following Nicaea (325–345) were theologically dominated by pro-Arius and pro-Alexander factions, conceived as "two ongoing, though continually modified alliances"; see Parvis, *Marcellus of Ancyra*, 38. Support for Arius's basic assertion of the non-coexistence of Father and Son was not usually coupled with an allegiance to his person as the acknowledged leader of an organized party or "school."

Father's will, differs from the Father in substance and power but is united to him through a "likeness of disposition."[12] Eusebius of Caesarea, the illustrious church historian and theological disciple of Origen, also disowned Arius's doctrine of the Son's origination from nothing, but he likewise rejected Origen's teaching on the eternal generation of the Son.[13] Eusebius of Caesarea had reluctantly agreed to the Nicene *homoousios*, but his own doctrine, often articulated in terms of the Son's being the "image of the Father's substance," is centrally concerned with maintaining the clear priority of the Father over the Son. Asterius's doctrine is also distinguishable from that of Arius in several important respects. Not only does he avoid speaking of the Son's origination from nothing, but he also identifies the Son as "the unchanging image of the substance and will and glory and power" of the Father.[14] This is a decisive modification of Arius's stress on the incomparability of the Father. Moreover, Arius's doctrine that God was not always Father is replaced with the notion that fatherhood can be eternally predicated of God as a generative capacity that precedes the generation of the Son.[15] Yet, Asterius did share fundamental common ground with Arius in his affirmation that the Son is not integral to the divine essence but a creature, produced by the Father's will.[16]

In the decades following Nicaea, we witness the rise of two important figures who were largely responsible for the designation of non-Nicene theology as "Arian," Marcellus and Athanasius. Marcellus, bishop of Ancyra, was present at the Council of Nicaea and interpreted its teaching in a distinctly monistic direction. God is a single being, one *prosōpon*, of whom no plurality can be predicated. Marcellus's theology of divine oneness dealt with the plethora of scriptural titles applied to Jesus by insisting that they all apply only after the incarnation, with the exception of the title *Logos*. The *Logos* is not distinct from God, just as a human word is not distinct from its speaker.[17] It is enunciated in the act of creation and is only differentiated from God in the incarnation. This differentiation will cease once the redemptive work of Christ is accomplished and the Son becomes subject to the Father (cf. 1 Cor. 15:24).[18] Marcellus propounded his theology by way of a denunciation of Asterius's doctrine of the Son as a subordinate *hypostasis* produced by the Father's will. His own theology and his attempts to present this teaching as the true interpretation of Nicaea made Nicene doctrine at least as problematic, in the eyes of many, as the teaching of Arius. Branded as a "new Sabellius" by the authoritative figure Eusebius of Caesarea, Marcellus was deposed by a synod in Constantinople in 336. While exiled in Rome, he joined forces with his fellow exile Athanasius in a polemical campaign against those whom they called "Arians."

Athanasius had been present at the Council of Nicaea as a young deacon accompanying his bishop, Alexander. He succeeded Alexander as bishop of Alexandria in

12. *Letter to Paulinus* 3.
13. *Eccl. theol.* 2.12.
14. Fr. 10 (Vinzent).
15. Fr. 14 (Vinzent).
16. Fr. 16 (Vinzent).
17. Fr. 87 (Vinzent).
18. Fr. 87 (Vinzent).

328, embarking on a forty-six-year reign over the Church of Egypt, punctuated by seventeen years of exile. The first of these exiles began in 335, when Athanasius's opponents, who included both Melitians and supporters of Arius, charged that he had used violence and bribery to achieve episcopal election while below the canonical age. While deposing Athanasius, the Council of Tyre declared Arius's doctrine orthodox. Although Athanasius later interpreted the judgment against him as motivated by "Arian" sympathies, we do not have any explicit public refutation of "Arianism" from Athanasius until the early 340s, some fifteen years after the Council of Nicaea, when he pens his *Orations against the Arians*.

Together, Marcellus and Athanasius were at the center of doctrinal tensions in the 340s, in the course of which contrasting doctrinal pronouncements issued from councils in Eastern and Western parts of the empire. After the death of Constantine in 337, the government of the empire was divided among his three sons, Constantinus and Constans in the West and Constantius in the East. The differences between East and West at that time are well illustrated by two councils from this period, the Council of Antioch in 341 and the Council of Serdica in 343. The former followed failed negotiations between Pope Julius and the Eastern bishops to convoke a synod in Rome. Meeting separately, the bishops of Antioch indignantly denied being followers of Arius. But their main theological opponent was Marcellus, whose doctrine they countered by insisting that Father, Son, and Spirit are three *hypostaseis*. They shunned the language of unity of substance, employing the biblical term "image" to designate the relation between Father and Son (cf. Col. 1:15). The unity of the Trinity was expressed in volitional rather than ontological terms: "one in concord" (*symphōnia*). The Council of Serdica, convoked by the Western emperor Constans, was also originally intended to bring together East and West. But the Western insistence that Athanasius and Marcellus be in attendance proved unacceptable to the Eastern bishops, and the two sides met separately.[19] At Serdica, the Western bishops defended Athanasius and Marcellus, the latter having persuaded the council attendees that "Arians" had misrepresented his views. The profession of faith promulgated by this council is designed primarily to rule out any form of subordinationism as "Arian." Any attenuation of the Son's divinity is proscribed, and the unity of Father, Son, and Spirit is expressed as "one *hypostasis*."

Crisis and Resolution

The 350s saw the emergence of several more starkly defined theological positions that were to have the cumulative effect of bringing the debate to clearer resolution.

19. The designations of "Western" and "Eastern" here refer to the geographical location of the respective councils. As Ayres has pointed out, the provenance of the attendees at these councils did not always strictly correspond to these designations (*Nicaea*, 123). At the same time, the notion of an East/West theological divide in the fourth-century debates was sometimes articulated during these very debates. See Hilary of Poitiers, *On the Synods*. See also Anatolios, "Dynamics of Reception."

Acacius of Caesarea (who succeeded the illustrious Eusebius as bishop) and Eudoxius of Antioch were at the vanguard of a movement whose doctrine seemed Arius-like in its subordinationism, even though its proponents rejected the label "Arian" and the doctrine that the Son was created "from nothing." This type of theology, having its roots in the teaching of Eusebius of Caesarea rather than Arius himself, clearly insisted that the Son was a creature and a product of the Father's will. With arguments that were often based on scriptural accounts of the human limitations of the incarnate Word, it did not shy from reiterating the incomparable superiority of the Father to the Son and clarified, further, that the Spirit in turn was inferior to the Son. Its preferred designation for the relation of the Son to the Father was *homoios*—the Son was "like" the Father—though this likeness was understood very much in a subordinationist vein. This "homoian" theology found expression in a series of councils in the 350s, in both East and West, under the patronage of the emperor Constantius. It reached a climax at the Council of Sirmium in 357, which combined an outright rejection of the Nicene *homoousios* with an undisguised subordinationism: "And nobody is unaware that this is Catholic doctrine, that there are two Persons of the Father and the Son, and that the Father is greater, and the Son is subjected in common with all the things which the Father subjected to him."[20]

Heterousians and Homoiousians

An even starker subordinationism is found in the theology propounded by Aetius and Eunomius, variously referred to as "heterousian," "anomoian," or "neo-Arian." This theology differed in key ways from the theology of Arius, most notably in replacing Arius's doctrine that the Son does not know the Father with the teaching that the knowledge of God's substance is available to all rational creatures and is manifest in the divine names. Most centrally, for both Aetius and Eunomius, the primary name of the divine nature is *age[n]nētos*, unoriginate and unbegotten. Therefore, the Son, as begotten, is of a different nature than the true God. The unbegotten nature of God precludes any communication of being either in the act of an (intra-divine) generation or an incarnation. Unlike the homoians, Aetius and especially Eunomius were not shy of applying *ousia* language to God in order to declare unflinchingly the incomparable difference in ontological status between Father and Son.

The emergence of radical expressions of anti-Nicene subordinationism in the 350s prompted significant reactions. The successor of Marcellus, Basil of Ancyra, still wary of the Sabellian overtones of the Nicene *homoousios*, nevertheless insisted that the relation of the Son to the Father must be articulated as "like according to essence" (*homoios kat' ousian*) in order to preclude attributing creaturehood to the Son. This position came to be identified with the term *homoiousios* ("like in essence"), though Basil of Ancyra did not use it. Athanasius goes further, emerging in the 350s as a leading promoter of Nicaea. In his *On the Nicene Council* (*De decretis*), Athanasius

---

20. Second Creed of Sirmium of 357; in Hanson, *Search*, 345.

defended Nicaea against those who disapproved of its terminology as non-scriptural. He explained that the Nicene bishops were forced to resort to the term *homoousios* in order to safeguard the intent of scriptural language. This intent is manifest in the scriptural titles of the Son—such as Word, Wisdom, Radiance—which represent him as correlative to the Father's being. The Nicene *homoousios* was the only way to rule out interpretations of scriptural language that imputed creaturehood to the Son. Even the terminology of likeness of essence, which in the theology of Basil of Ancyra lacked subordinationist overtones, was inadequate as leaving the way open to a homoian interpretation.[21]

As the decade wore on, developments in ecclesial politics under the influence of the Eastern emperor Constantius served to undermine the position of the homoiousians and further polarize pro-Nicene and anti-Nicene forces. In 359, Constantius convoked twin councils, the Western contingent of which met at Ariminum (Rimini) in Italy and the Eastern at Seleucia, near Antioch. The councils were presented with a creed (known as the "Dated Creed" of 22 May, 359), which attempted a compromise between a homoian theology that rejected language of community of substance between Father and Son and the homoiousian theology of Basil of Ancyra. But the Western synod simply reasserted its fidelity to Nicaea, while the Eastern attendees, divided between homoians and followers of Basil of Ancyra, failed to reach a consensus. Constantius then forced both synods to sign a version of the Dated Creed that settled matters in a homoian direction, describing the Son as "like" the Father and omitting the original qualification of "in all respects." In 360, the homoian Acacius presided over another council in Constantinople, at which Basil of Ancyra and his followers were deposed.

As anti-Nicene positions became more explicit in the 350s, the supporters of Nicaea rallied to negotiate a consensus among those who believed in the full divinity of the Son and the Spirit. Such a consensus required a clearer articulation of a non-modalist interpretation of the Nicene *homoousios* as well as a *rapprochement* among those who wished to confess the complete divinity of both Son and Spirit but advocated different terminologies: *homoousios* as opposed to *homoios kat' ousian* ("like in substance") and "one *hypostasis*" as opposed to "three *hypostaseis*." We find significant traces of such theological diplomacy in the writings of Athanasius from that period. Though a leading advocate of the Nicene confession of the unity of Father and Son, he clarifies that God is a Trinity "not only in name and linguistic expression but Trinity in reality and truth. Just as the Father is the 'One who is' (Exod. 3:14), so likewise is his Word the 'One who is, God over all' (Rom. 9:5). Nor is the Holy Spirit nonexistent but truly exists and subsists."[22] He also concedes that those who follow the "likeness of essence" terminology of Basil of Ancyra are substantially in accord with his own (Nicene) teaching,[23] though he continues to prefer *homoousios*. We find similar conciliatory moves in Hilary of Poitier's *On the Trinity*, written in the early

21. *Syn.* 53.
22. *Ep. Serap.* 1.28; Anatolios, *Athanasius*, 227.
23. *Syn.* 41.

years of the 360s. Hilary was careful to interpret *homoousios* in a way that clarified the real distinction between Father and Son, thus avoiding the specter of modalism, and was even more explicit than Athanasius in allowing the legitimacy of *homoiousios*.[24]

A significant development in the movement toward a pro-Nicene consensus was a council headed by Athanasius at Alexandria in 362. This council met to address a schism between followers of two pro-Nicene bishops at Antioch: Paulinus, who confessed the one *hypostasis*, and Melitius, who confessed three *hypostaseis*. This council decided to allow both usages, as long as both the unity and the distinction were safeguarded and neither an "Arian" subordinationism nor a "Sabellian" modalism was intended. The Alexandrian council thus based its terminological tolerance on an admission from each side of the validity of the other's emphasis: on the one side, unity of the substance; on the other, the irreducible reality of the three divine subsistents. However, the lack of terminological consensus continued to undermine the commitment to tolerance, which was further tested by attempts to integrate *hypostasis* language with the language of *prosōpon* or, in Latin, *persona*.

The Differentiation of Ousia and Hypostasis

Indications of the tense history that followed upon the seeming resolution of the Alexandrian council are found in the epistles of Basil of Caesarea and Jerome.[25] Basil had originally exhibited some discomfort with the Nicene *homoousios* as vulnerable to modalistic interpretations. His acceptance of this term was conditioned by his construction of an accompanying set of terminology to designate the threeness of God: Father, Son, and Spirit are each a distinct *hypostasis*, with a unique manner of subsistence (*tropos hyparxeōs*). Basil, a supporter of Melitius, pressed the followers of Paulinus to adopt the language of three *hypostaseis* in order to safeguard Nicene theology from a Sabellian interpretation. The "Paulinians" were not insensible to that concern but considered it sufficiently addressed by acknowledging that each of the Trinity is a distinct person, or *prosōpon*. But Basil deemed this stratagem inadequate, since the term *prosōpon* could mean simply "role" or "manifestation," and thus even a Sabellian could subscribe to such a confession: "It is not enough to count differences in the Persons (*prosōpa*). It is necessary also to confess that each Person (*prosōpon*) exists in a true *hypostasis*. The mirage of persons (*prosōpa*) without *hypostaseis* is not denied even by Sabellius, who said that the same God, though he is one subject, is transformed according to the need of each occasion and is thus spoken of now as Father, now as Son, and now as Holy Spirit."[26]

Meanwhile, Jerome became embroiled in the controversy, expressing his shocked disapproval of the language of three *hypostaseis* to Pope Damasus and articulating the tri-unity as "one substance, three persons" (*una substantia, tres personae*).[27] Jerome's

---

24. *Syn.* 71.
25. On the following, see Halleux, "'Hypostase' et 'Personne,'" 313–69, 625–70.
26. *Ep.* 210.5.36–41.
27. See Jerome, *Ep.* 15.4.

discomfort with the three-*hypostaseis* language of Basil and Meletius is readily explicable since the Greek term *hypostasis* can be literally transcribed into Latin as *substantia*. It was under such pressures that Basil came to insist on a distinction between the signification of the terms *ousia* and *hypostasis*. As Jerome had protested, such a distinction was rather novel inasmuch as the two terms were regularly employed as synonyms. Nevertheless, the construction of such a distinction became invaluable inasmuch as the affirmation of being that underlies both terms ensured that both the unity and the distinction within the Trinity were confessed as having equally radical ontological status. At the same time, the two terms were distinguished by Basil as having the same relation as that of the common to the particular.[28] Thus, *ousia* signified the unity of being, while *hypostasis* referred to the particular mode of being that is irreducibly distinct in each of the three. In this way, the Nicene *homoousios* came to be supplemented by an equal emphasis on the distinctions within the Triune God.

The Holy Spirit in the Trinity

Another important development beginning in the late 350s, which led to a clearer definition of a pro-Nicene trinitarianism, was the foregrounding of the question of the status of the Holy Spirit. In the aftermath of the dispute between Arius and Alexander on the relation between Father and Son, the Council of Nicaea adverted to the Holy Spirit in what might seem like a mere afterthought: "And we believe in the Holy Spirit." Arius himself largely bypassed the subject of the Spirit, though he would have certainly considered the Spirit to be a creature. In subordinating the Son to the Father, the homoians as well as Eunomius also maintained that the Spirit in turn was subordinate to the Son and not an object of worship. But the subordinationism of the Spirit was not always conceived in tandem with that of the Son. In some circles, in the late 350s and 360s, it was combined with an acknowledgment of the equality of the Son to the Father. This was the case with two movements that have been called *tropici* and Macedonians. The former was a group of Egyptian Christians who based their subordination of the Spirit to the Father and Son chiefly on scriptural grounds, most notably Amos 4:13 ("I, who establish thunder and create spirit"), Zechariah 1:9 ("These things says the angel that speaks within me"), and 1 Timothy 5:21 ("I adjure you in the sight of God and Christ Jesus and the elect angels"). Their opponents presumably branded them *tropici* as a pejorative allusion to their use of scriptural figures or "tropes" in their argumentation. On the basis of the aforementioned biblical texts, the *tropici* concluded that the Spirit was created as an angel, the chief of God's "ministering spirits" (cf. Heb. 1:14). Their reasoning was also based on the premise that the equality of the Son to the Father is constituted by the relation of generation; since the Spirit lacks such a relation to the Father, it is external to the divine nature. This point was given a rhetorical cast by saying that if the Spirit were integral to the divine nature, it would have to be another Son, as a brother of the

---

28. Basil, *Ep.* 214.4.

Son, or even a son of the Son, and thus grandson of the Father.[29] The "Macedonians" were named after Macedonius, the bishop of Constantinople, though his connection with this doctrine is tenuous, the most prominent exponent of this view being rather Eustathius of Sebaste. The Macedonians also believed in the full divinity of the Son, under the rubric of "likeness of essence," but withheld both worship and confession of divinity from the Spirit, using scriptural and logical arguments that were largely similar to those of the *tropici*.[30]

The development of these subordinationist views of the Spirit was countered chiefly by Athanasius and Basil of Caesarea. In his *Letters to Serapion on the Holy Spirit*, written between 358 and 361, Athanasius dismissed as specious the exegetical arguments of those who denied the divinity of the Holy Spirit: the biblical reference to the created spirit in Amos pertains not to the divine Spirit but to the spirit of creatures. Since the Scriptures attribute to the Spirit the creative and sanctifying work of God, the Spirit must be God. Moreover, this work is brought to consummation in the individual Christian through the sacramental event of baptism, in which the Spirit is an agent. If the Spirit were not God, baptism would not be an initiation into divine life. Athanasius analyzed the patterns of scriptural language to come to the conclusion that "the Spirit has the same relation of nature and order with respect to the Son as the Son has with respect to the Father."[31] As to the precise distinction between the Son's generation and the Spirit's, he maintains an apophatic silence.

In his treatise *On the Holy Spirit*, written in 374–375, Basil follows Athanasius's line of reasoning that the scriptural account of the names and activities of the Spirit indicates his divinity, and he also dwells on the Spirit's agency in Christian baptism. He deals with Aetius's argument that the differences in liturgical prepositions ("from the Father, through the Son, in the Spirit") indicate differences of essence by showing that each of these prepositions is variously applied in the Scriptures to all three. Ultimately, however, Basil refrains from directly calling the Spirit "God" or *homoousios*, choosing to make the point in the more experiential language of worship: the Spirit possesses "equal honor" (*isotimia*) with the Father and the Son.[32] Many of the arguments of Athanasius and Basil are reproduced in the writings of Western defenders of Nicene doctrine, though already the Greek apophaticism regarding the procession of the Spirit is attenuated in the West by references to the double procession of the Spirit from Father and Son.[33]

In the writings of Athanasius and Basil we see the clear confession of the full divinity of the Holy Spirit becoming another significant ingredient in the formation of a pro-Nicene consensus that was now spreading in both East and West. But the polarization between East and West continued on the political front. Constantius, who had lent forceful support to the homoian position, died in 361. He was succeeded briefly by

29. Athanasius, *Ep. Serap.* 1.15. See Hanson, *Search*, 748–52; Simonetti, *La crisi*, 362–67.
30. On Macedonian theology, see Hanson, *Search*, 760–72; Simonetti, *La crisi*, 480–85.
31. *Ep. Serap.* 1.21.
32. *Spir.* 6.13.
33. Cf. Epiphanius, *Panarion* 62.4.1; Ambrose, *Spir.* 1.11.120.

his cousin Julian, who had renounced Christianity and sought to purge the empire of Christian influences, and by Jovian, who showed signs of favoring pro-Nicenes during his brief reign. In 364, imperial authority was again divided, now between Valens in the East (364–378) and Valentinian in the West (364–375). Valens was an active promoter of the homoian cause, while Valentinian followed a non-interventionist policy that was nevertheless sympathetic to the Nicene position. Upon his death in 375, Valentinian was succeeded by his son Gratian, who adopted a policy of general tolerance. The more fateful succession followed upon the death of Valens, who died at the hands of the Goths in the battle of Adrianople in 378. He was succeeded in 379 by Theodosius, who quickly showed himself to be a strong supporter of the emerging pro-Nicene consensus. He issued an edict in 380 (*Cunctos populos*) that announced the single divinity of Father, Son, and Spirit to be the official doctrine of the empire and another in January 381 (*Nullis haereticis*) that expressly forbade anti-Nicene factions to congregate in churches. The stage was thus set for a pro-Nicene council, which was called to meet in Constantinople, in 381.

The Council of Constantinople

The Council of Constantinople—often called the First Council of Constantinople (although it was not the first council ever held at that city), and traditionally reckoned as the "second ecumenical council"—was attended by approximately one-hundred-fifty Eastern bishops. The large majority of these were already sympathetic to pro-Nicene theology, with the exception of about thirty "Macedonian" bishops. Negotiations with the Macedonian party were attempted but proved to be unfruitful, and they walked out of the council proceedings. The first canon of the Constantinopolitan council reconfirmed the Council of Nicaea and anathematized all those who rejected the full and equal divinity of either Son or Spirit, making reference to "Eunomians" and "Arians," as well as "semi-Arians," that is, those who accepted the full divinity of the Son but did not accord the same status to the Spirit. It equally rejected the modalist doctrine of Marcellus and his Western disciple Photinus, as well as the teaching of Apollinaris, which was consistent with Nicene theology in its trinitarian doctrine but asserted that the incarnate Word did not assume a fully human soul. At the Council of Chalcedon of 451, a creed said to be the confession of faith of the Council of Constantinople was read out by the archdeacon of that city. The acts of Chalcedon thus present us with the first record of a Constantinopolitan Creed, which runs as follows:

> We believe in one God, Father Almighty, maker of heaven and earth and of all things visible and invisible; and in one Lord Jesus Christ the Son of God, the Only-begotten, begotten by the Father before all ages, Light from Light, true God from true God, begotten not made, consubstantial (*homoousion*) with the Father, through whom all things came into being, who for us human beings and for our salvation came down from the heavens and was incarnate by the Holy Spirit and the Virgin Mary and became human, and was crucified for us under Pontius Pilate and suffered and was buried and

rose again on the third day in accordance with the Scriptures and ascended into the heavens and is seated at the right hand of the Father and is coming again with glory to judge the living and the dead, of whose kingship there will be no end; and in the Holy Spirit, the Lord and Life-giver, who proceeds from the Father, who is co-worshiped and co-glorified with the Father and the Son, who has spoken through the prophets; and in one holy, catholic and apostolic Church. We confess one baptism for the forgiveness of sins; we wait for the resurrection of the dead and the life of the age to come. Amen.[34]

The lack of any clear reference prior to Chalcedon of a creed produced by the Council of Constantinople has led some modern scholars to question whether this creed was in fact promulgated on that occasion. But the consensus of modern scholarship is that the witness of the Chalcedonian council was correct; the lack of reference to a "Constantinopolitan Creed" prior to Chalcedon reflects the council's own understanding that its confession of faith was not a new creed but rather a restatement of Nicene faith.[35] It is also likely that the Council of Constantinople drew on an earlier Western creed that was a pro-Nicene restatement of the Old Roman creed, supplemented by an enlargement of the confession of the divinity of the Holy Spirit.[36] The Constantinopolitan redaction of the earlier Western creed amounts to a highly condensed summary of both the content and form of Basil of Caesarea's approach to the subject. It declares the Spirit's divinity not by applying ontological terminology but by ascribing divine titles and activities—"the Lord, the Life-Giver"—and by affirming the equality of the Spirit to Father and Son as an object of honor and worship. Apart from the development of the confession of the Spirit, there are various discrepancies between the creeds of Nicaea and Constantinople, which tend to give credence to the theory of a mediating creedal formula redacted by Constantinople. Among these discrepancies, we can note two of some significance: first, the omission of the Nicene anathema against those who speak of the Son as another "*hypostasis*" from the Father, reflecting the terminological *rapprochement* achieved by the Council of Alexandria of 362; and, second, the addition of the statement that Christ's kingship will not end. The latter addition was inserted as a rebuttal of what was considered to be the doctrine of Marcellus, namely, that the expansion of the divine activity from monad to triad would eschatologically retract into the monad, and thus the kingdom of Christ will be re-enfolded into the kingdom of the Father.

Categories and Interpretation

Subsequent tradition has viewed the Council of Constantinople as a validation of Nicaea, a view shared by the attendees of Constantinople themselves. From this

---

34. Critical edition in Dossetti, *Il simbolo di Nicea e di Costantinopoli*, 244–50.

35. For a full treatment, see Kelly, *Early Christian Creeds*, 296–331.

36. This is the thesis of Abramowski, "Was hat das Nicaeno-Constantinopolitanum (C) mit dem Konzil von Konstantinopel 381 zu tun?" 481–513.

perspective, the intervening debates and conflicts between the two councils have been read as conflicts over Nicaea. Arius is regarded as the prime culprit of Nicaea, and therefore all opposition to the Nicene formula was interpreted as "Arian," an interpretive strategy originally devised by Athanasius and Marcellus. Athanasius himself has been hailed as the first defender and spokesperson for Nicene theology. Hence the interpretive schema that categorizes all the tortuous controversy between Nicaea and Constantinople as a struggle between "Arians," on the one side, and Nicene theology, defended most prominently by Athanasius and the Cappadocians, on the other. This narrative schema, though much maligned of late for its oversimplification, is not entirely lacking in either historical foundation or theological justification. There are certain fundamental doctrinal continuities between Arius and others who were uncomfortable with the outcome of Nicaea, despite significant discontinuities. And although Athanasius probably was not a significant figure at Nicaea and maintained a discreet silence about that council for over a decade, he did emerge in the 350s as one of its leading defenders. Certainly the Cappadocians saw themselves as aligned with Athanasius rather than Arius.[37] Moreover, we have seen that Constantinople did see itself as a confirmation of Nicaea, thus enclosing the intervening debates within a single trajectory in which the central question was seen to be that of the validity of "Nicene" doctrine. A theological reading of the historical development of trinitarian doctrine needs to account for the intelligibility of this perspective rather than dismiss it altogether.

At the same time, modern scholarship has raised important questions about the validity of this interpretive schema as a straightforward description of the fourth-century conflicts. The notion of two fairly homogenous parties, one following Arius, the other led by Athanasius and loyal to Nicaea, runs afoul of the complex actual history. As a significant example of this complexity, we have noted that a personal allegiance to Arius was not at all a persevering feature of anti-Nicene theology.

Recent Categorizations

Understandably, modern scholarship has endeavored to replace the traditional schema with new categorizations. Before joining this effort, we need to acknowledge the perspectival and interpretive nature of any such endeavor. The main obstacle to an objective naming of conflicting parties is that the parties themselves shunned any self-naming other than reasserting their own claim to represent the apostolic and or-thodox faith of the Catholic Church while depicting their opponents as "heretics." All naming, therefore, must to some degree be imposed by the historical interpreter from without. A narration that foregrounds differences between theological positions will necessarily privilege certain doctrinal emphases of certain parties at a certain period of the conflict in order to derive categories that will then be superimposed over the whole controversy, and all this from the theological perspective of the interpreter.

37. E.g., Gregory of Nazianzus, *Or.* 21; Basil, *Ep.* 69.

This is demonstrably the case in two recent significant proposals for categorizing the issues in the fourth-century trinitarian debates. Joseph Lienhard has suggested that the earlier stages of the controversy, from the Arius-Alexander confrontation to 361, may best be described as a collision between "miahypostatic" and "dyohypostatic" theologies.[38] The former trajectory affirmed Christianity's fundamental monotheism by speaking of Father and Son as a single *hypostasis*, dismantled the Hellenistic chain of being, and interpreted salvation as ontological deification. The latter trajectory affirmed the biblical trinitarian identification of God by speaking of Father and Son as two *hypostaseis* but at the cost of a subordinationism that retained the Hellenistic graded chain of being, and interpreted salvation in terms of moralism, as taking "place in the order of will."[39] The Cappadocian "resolution" involved a synthesis of key elements from both trajectories and a rejection of the limitations of both. While there is much to recommend this strategy for mapping the earlier stages of the controversy, it is not without its limitations. One criticism leveled against it is that it overemphasizes the centrality of *hypostasis* language as "the decisive factor in the controversies."[40] If we are attempting a theological reading of the controversy as a whole, a more serious limitation is that the Cappadocian/Constantinopolitan resolution looks more like a "third element" than a development (much less a mere reiteration) of an earlier "Nicene" position. From a historical point of view, this approach seems to contradict the self-understanding of the Cappadocians and Constantinople itself that they were validating Nicaea and were fundamentally in continuity with the Alexander-Athanasius trajectory. Indeed, on the merely literal level of *hypostasis* language, the fact that the Cappadocians would have to be designated as dyohypostatic would seem to suggest more continuity with the Arius-Asterius-Eunomius trajectory. The fact that the doctrine of Nicaea was explicitly miahypostatic while that of Constantinople was implicitly dyohypostatic raises serious theological issues about the development of doctrine. Placing so much weight on *hypostasis* language merely exacerbates these difficulties.

Another recent approach, proposed by Michel Barnes and Lewis Ayres, has been to identify two large "trends" in the fourth-century debates, one emphasizing sameness between Father and Son, the other emphasizing diversity.[41] But, as Ayres himself immediately acknowledges, most (or rather, all) fourth-century accounts do both.[42] The difference then is reduced to, in Ayres's own terms: "preference of emphasis."[43] But that fairly vague criterion is difficult to apply in a way that respects the integrity of a given position in its own self-understanding. Asterius, for example, considerably

38. Lienhard, "Arian Controversy," 415–36.

39. Ibid., 424.

40. Ayres, *Nicaea*, 41n1. It should be noted, however, that while Lienhard designates the two trajectories through their use of *hypostasis* terminology, his analysis broadens into other considerations, as indicated above, such as the God-world relation and the character of human salvation.

41. Barnes, "Fourth Century as Trinitarian Canon," 47–67; Ayres, *Nicaea*, 41.

42. "Most theologians combine these tendencies, but almost all use one set as primary, as governing how the other should be understood" (*Nicaea*, 41).

43. "Some prefer language that emphasizes the *sameness* of Father and Son, while others emphasize *diversity* between the two" (*Nicaea*, 41; original italics).

modified Arius's account of the unlikeness between Father and Son—to the extent of designating the Son as "the exact image of the substance, will, glory and power of the Father."[44] Did Asterius prefer to emphasize the difference between Father and Son over the sameness? Yes, compared to Alexander; no, compared to Arius. It seems that, after all, the criterion of sameness/difference is only serviceable to the extent that one is secretly referring to the "right answer" of just how simultaneously same and different Father and Son should be and assigning grades by reference to that right answer. If all significant theological positions in the fourth-century debates included accounts of both sameness and difference with respect to the relation between Father and Son, we need a heuristic strategy for mapping these debates that corresponds more directly to the variations between these accounts of sameness-difference rather than the general criterion of "preference of emphasis." It hardly needs to be said that both Barnes and Ayres provide valuable interpretations of these accounts, but these interpretations supersede and go well beyond the categorization strategy centered on the criterion of preference of emphasis with respect to sameness and difference in the Father-Son relation.

Ultimately, these hermeneutical caveats do not entirely discredit the particular categorizations cited above, much less disallow all categorization; rather, they highlight the need for hermeneutical transparency and modesty. Since all schemas for narrating these debates are inevitably perspectival and interpretive, the essential requirement is to acknowledge one's own interpretive perspective. The interpretive perspective attempted here seeks a broad view of the doctrinal conflicts stretching from Nicaea to Constantinople. The aim is to make sense of the traditional understanding that each group—those who came to approve of Nicaea and those who disapproved—had its commonalities while also providing a way to talk about the tensions, differences, and developments within each group. A narrative that will make sense of the contours of these debates must be able to shed some light on the intelligibility of later construals that condensed their complexities into the two main lines of pro-Nicene and anti-Nicene. Is there any sense at all to the notion that, from a later perspective, Arius, Asterius, and Eunomius belong together, despite all their differences, and that Alexander, Athanasius, and the Cappadocians also manifest continuities that are more significant than discontinuities? This is a question of theological interpretation and not simply of "objective" history, but such categorizations cannot be simply constructed out of thin air without historical foundations. We must strive to understand the different theological positions on their own terms.

Unity of Being and Unity of Will

My proposal is to distinguish between theologies that spoke of the unity of the Trinity as a unity of being and those that spoke of a unity of will. This schema has three main hermeneutical virtues.

---

44. Fr. 10 (Vinzent).

First, it eschews the polemical ploy, practiced by all parties in these controversies, of depicting their opponents in terms of sheer otherness in favor of a framework that sees their differences as arising within common ground. This move does not claim moral virtue (as if it were simply more peaceable and tolerant to see things that way) but interpretive virtue: it makes better sense of what transpired in these debates. The fundamental starting point for all parties was the church's confession of faith in Father, Son, and Holy Spirit. This was the starting point no less for Arius than for Athanasius or Marcellus. Even theologies that were later deemed subordinationist or modalist were nevertheless, on their own terms, trinitarian. Again, all parties allowed for both sameness and difference within the Trinity. The essential distinction, from within the common ground of confession of the Trinity as differentiated unity, was whether the divine Trinity was united according to a unity of being, or by unity of will. To say this is not to prejudge the question of just how that unity was conceived; it does not presume, for example, that numerical oneness or equality is a necessary feature of that unity so conceived.

Second, the categorization of the different positions in these terms is in keeping with the way the theologians involved in these debates expressed themselves. Every significant figure in these debates had a position with reference to this distinction, and that position was central to his doctrine of God.

Third, identifying two main trajectories of fourth-century theology along these lines helps us to see a certain coherence within the debates between Nicaea and Constantinople. Thus, Alexander, Athanasius, and the Cappadocians, despite undeniable differences and developments, all designated the relation between Father and Son in terms of unity of being. Arius, Asterius, Eusebius, and Eunomius, again despite all their divergences, insisted that the relations between Father and Son pertained to will, not to being. But identifying these lines of continuity within the two trajectories need not blind us to the tensions and developments within each trajectory, but rather helps us to make better sense of these developments. There is undeniably a development of a theology of the triune being of God from Alexander to the Cappadocians and Augustine, as there is a development of the theology of the divine will from Arius to Eunomius.

In the end, the construction of schemas that categorize individuals for the sake of plotting a coherent narrative has to be seen for what it is: a provisional hermeneutical device. Its validity is proportionate to the particular issues that it can illuminate. The historian or interpreter is responsible for choosing these issues and is thereby involved in a constructive and systematic, and not merely archaeological, task. For the sake of theological elucidation, these categorizations, which are inevitably abstract, since their very function is to generalize, should not supplant the more concrete task of interpreting individual theological systems in the native context of their own integrity. The rest of this book will be occupied with that task.

2

Development of Trinitarian Doctrine

A Model and Its Application

In John Henry Newman's classic *Essay on the Development of Christian Doctrine* and elsewhere, the question of the development of doctrine has been largely restricted to asserting or evaluating claims to continuity in the face of apparent change. Development of doctrine therefore tends to be treated more or less exclusively within fundamental rather than positive dogmatic theology, as pertaining to questions of the infallibility and continuity of the church's faith. According to the perspective proposed here, however, development of doctrine is to be conceived as the dynamic and complex process of cumulative interpretation that constitutes the meaning of a doctrine. The issue then is not simply how apparent changes can be enfolded within continuity, though that is not an insignificant question, but, more radically, the intelligibility of a given doctrine from within the process of its development.[1] While it is beyond the scope of our present discussion to provide a detailed theory of doctrinal development in explicit dialogue with Newman and more recent theologians, a rudimentary sketch of such a theory can be offered as a heuristic device for understanding the tumultuous debates of the fourth century as a formative episode in Christian consciousness. The developmental model proposed here derives its basic framework from the French Catholic

---

1. This model has certain affinities with the "reception" model developed by Rush, who states that "a reception-model traces the dynamics of the history of doctrines in a way that provides hermeneutical principles for their interpretation" ("Reception Hermeneutics," 127). For a more extended treatment, see further his *Reception of Doctrine*.

philosopher Gabriel Marcel (1889–1973).[2] A central motif of Marcel's philosophy is a distinction between what he calls "primary reflection" and "secondary reflection." Eschewing any facile dualism between reflection and experience,[3] Marcel speaks of the exigency of reflection as occasioned by a kind of "break" in the flow of experience. Such a break may be as trivial as losing my watch and pausing to wonder what I did with it or as morally grave as facing the fact that one has lied to a friend.[4] In either case, one's experience "bump[s] into some sort of obstacle."[5] According to Marcel, the act of reflection, which is called forth by a break in the flow of experience, has the character of a "readjustment" or retrieval; I re-collect my movements to discern where I could have left my watch, or I try to retrieve an acceptable notion of myself in the face of my immoral act. The resulting adjustment in my self-understanding may go well beyond the triggering circumstances: I may recognize a general tendency to carelessness or absent-mindedness; or, I may recall an occasion when I harshly judged a friend for a similar act. The result, says Marcel, is that "I am now able to communicate at a broader level with myself, since I have, as it were, introduced the self that committed the dubious act to the self that did not hesitate to set itself up as the harsh judge of such acts in others. Such self-appropriation then can lead to fuller intersubjective communication: 'I am now able to enter into far more intimate communication with my friend.'"[6]

Within this evocation of reflection as intending a reintegration of experience, Marcel introduces his distinction between primary and secondary reflection. He summarizes the distinction thus: "Roughly, we can say that where primary reflection tends to dissolve the unity of experience which is first put before it, the function of secondary reflection is essentially recuperative; it reconquers that unity."[7] Primary reflection dissolves the unity of experience by seeing the object as abstracted from my relationship with it. Marcel's crucial example for this mode of objectification is my seeing my body as "*a* body," as if it were a "something" detachable from "myself." But secondary reflection reasserts and reappropriates the concrete link between myself and the object of my experience. Here I recognize the mysterious reality of this body as "*my* body"—"myself"; I recognize myself as embodied.[8]

In applying this model to religious experience, we can begin with the distinction between primary and secondary reflection. Primary reflection, as the normal

---

2. The following section is adapted from a portion of my earlier essay, "The Immediately Triune God: A Patristic Response to Schleiermacher," *Pro Ecclesia* 10 (Spring 2001): 159–78. Used with permission.

3. "If I take experience as merely a sort of passive recording of impressions, I shall never manage to understand how the reflective process could be integrated with experience. On the other hand, the more we grasp the notion of experience in its proper complexity, in its active and I would even dare to say in its dialectical aspects, the better we shall understand how experience cannot fail to transform itself into reflection, and we shall even have the right to say that the more richly it is experience, the more, also, it is reflection" (Marcel, *Reflection and Mystery*, 83).

4. Ibid., 78–79.

5. Ibid., 79.

6. Ibid., 80.

7. Ibid., 83.

8. Ibid., 92–102.

and default surface level of experience, tends to acquiesce in the objectification and fragmentation of experience. I simply acknowledge and register different experiences as objects of my intentional consciousness. Primary reflection represents a doctrinal faith such as Christianity as a series of items to which I assent, each one of these items having its own discrete objectivity within the unexamined flow of my experience: I believe that God created the world, that God is good, that there will be a resurrection of the dead, and so on. Breaks will arise in this flow of experience because the ever-newness and strangeness of God will always challenge our closed, narrowly constructed coherences, and also because the comprehensive scope of Christian faith, as a global interpretation of reality, will always confront competing interpretations. Positively engaged, such breaks should occasion a reunification of experience on the level of secondary reflection. They can bring about a deeper integration of transcendent truths that are never finally enclosed within human grasp but continually beckon into unfathomable depths. Seen in this light, continuity is not merely static adherence to a set of propositions but also a dramatic and sometimes tumultuous process of continually retrieving the truth of the saving relationship with God in Christ—a truth in which this person or community is involved, but which remains beyond their grasp. From this perspective, the inherently systematic character of doctrinal development also becomes readily apparent, inasmuch as the process, at its deepest level, entails reconstructing coherence in the face of the threat of incoherence.

The phenomenology of the transition from primary reflection to secondary reflection can be a very helpful model for properly locating trinitarian doctrine in relation to Christian faith as a whole. Within the dialectic of primary and secondary reflection, the development of trinitarian doctrine cannot be simply another item of primary reflection, as if people decided at some point to add to the list of Christian beliefs the odd notion that God is both three and one. Rather, it represents a secondary reflection that was motivated by the necessity of reconceiving the entirety of Christian faith in light of certain breaks in the flow of Christian experience. The very formulation of trinitarian doctrine has nevertheless objectified it, making it simply another item in the list of Christian beliefs. Thus instead of appropriating trinitarian doctrine as a unification of Christian experience, we are stuck on asking how to conceptualize the objective referent to which that item of faith refers. What we need is a reinvolvement in the secondary reflection that brought about the formulation of trinitarian doctrine. We need to reexperience the disruptive breaks that led to the development of trinitarian doctrine as secondary reflection in order to "make strange," and thus rediscover, the holistic meaning of trinitarian doctrine.[9] Therein lies the particular and indispensable virtue of engagement with the process of the development of the doctrine.

9. The phrase has been popularized by John Milbank; see his *Word Made Strange.* On the manifestation of the alterity of a text as enabling the reception of its classic force, as argued by Hans Robert Jauss, see Rush, "Reception Hermeneutics," esp. 127–31.

Common Experience at the Threshold of Nicaea

In applying this model particularly to the trinitarian debates of the fourth century, we need to answer two preliminary questions: (1) What were the common elements of the "flow of experience" at the threshold of Nicaea? (2) What elements were agitating this flow of experience and creating "breaks" that required reintegration? Answering these questions will position us to see how various theologians' efforts to reintegrate Christian experience in light of these agitations gave rise to the doctrinal debates surrounding the Nicene council. We can answer the first question by citing six significant elements of faith shared by all parties to the trinitarian controversies. Three of these elements pertain to what later came to be called fundamental theology, and three to positive or dogmatic theology.

Elements of a Common Fundamental Theology

1. There was general agreement on the contents of the scriptural canon, its normativity as the prime source of divine revelation, and the attribution of its ultimate authorship to the Holy Spirit. Thus all parties in the trinitarian conflicts constructed their arguments in scriptural terms, without any disagreements on canonicity.

2. There was also general agreement that apostolic tradition is a normative interpreter of scriptural revelation and that the office of bishop is concretely linked to this tradition. Thus all parties claimed continuity with apostolic tradition and sought validation of their positions by groups of bishops—hence the many councils in the course of these debates.

3. There was a shared sense both of the primacy of faith and of the necessity of applying reason to faith. Later interpretations tend to depict one side of these debates as faith-based and the other as rationalistic and philosophical—a rhetorical ploy that was used by the antagonists themselves—but in fact each side presented itself as offering a reasonable interpretation of faith and as employing a faithful mode of reasoning.

Elements of a Common Doctrinal Confession

COMMON AFFIRMATIONS

All parties to the trinitarian controversies affirmed this fairly substantial list of fundamental principles and beliefs:

1. All parties and individuals accepted the Trinity as the object of Christian faith and worship. There were different understandings of the relations between the three, or their relative ontological standing, but references to Father, Son, and Spirit were inscribed into the grammar of Christian faith through liturgical formulae, creeds, and, of course, the rite of baptism, so that all took for granted that Christian faith and worship was oriented to Father, Son, and Spirit.

2. Everyone agreed that God created the world from nothing. We must say more about this belief presently, but for now we can simply note that general consensus

had emerged that the world was created from nothing rather than from preexistent matter and that the world was not coexistent with God.

3. Finally, but most importantly, everyone affirmed the lordship or primacy of Christ. Despite some differences, theologians broadly agreed on what was involved in affirming Christ's lordship. We can count seven elements of a common christological confession.

a. All parties confessed Jesus Christ in the context of worship.[10] The question was precisely how to interpret such worship. Each party claimed that its own doctrinal position was consistent with the confession of Christ as Lord and that its opponents' doctrine was not.

b. The lordship of Christ was verbalized through the exalted titles scripturally applied to him, such as God, Lord, Word (*Logos*), Wisdom, Power, Light, Life. These scriptural conceptualizations of Christ's primacy were variously styled as *epinoiai* (by Origen, Arius, and Gregory of Nyssa) or *paradeigmata* (by Athanasius).[11] Regardless of how they were designated, any serious participant in the fourth-century debates was compelled to explain how these titles applied to Christ.

c. There was general consensus on the preexistence of Christ. Recent scholars tend to fit earlier debates into a "high Christology"/"low Christology" framework, but no significant participant in these debates espoused such a low Christology as to deny that the divine *Logos* preexisted the world.

d. There was broad agreement that the preexistent Christ was the Creator of the world and in some sense the paradigm of creation, or at least contained the paradigms of creation. The scriptural basis for this general belief was found in texts that spoke of creation as by and through the Word, and of the world as "in Christ" (cf. John 1:1; Col. 1:16). More generally, this belief was predicated on a biblical Wisdom Christology. A crucial text in this respect was Proverbs 8:22: "He created me as the beginning of his ways, for his works." For some, the interpretation of this text involved identifying Christ both as created and also as Creator of the rest of creation.

e. All believed that Jesus was both human and divine and that this combination of humanity and divinity was salvific. There may have been different understandings of what "human" and "divine" mean, but all significant participants in the fourth-century debates agreed that Jesus's being human at least ruled out gnostic docetism; his humanity was not mere appearance. On the other hand, everyone could agree that Jesus was not "a mere man" (*psilanthrōpos*), as Paul of Samosata was alleged to have asserted. Everyone had to find a way to call the preexistent Christ "God."

f. All parties to these debates presumed that Jesus Christ was the Savior of the world. Later scholars have tended to designate a given position as motivated by soteriological concerns over against, say, cosmological concerns, but in fact no theological position was simply without soteriological concerns.

10. In considering the experience of worship as the primary element of christological confession, I am indebted to the work of Larry W. Hurtado, who presents the experience of worshiping Jesus as constitutive of the scriptural witness; see his *Lord Jesus Christ*.

11. See Orbe, *La Epinoia*.

g. Finally, Jesus's work of salvation was universally conceived within a trinitarian grammar; the Spirit is somehow involved in the work of salvation, and the salvation worked by Jesus gives greater access to the Father.

Common Negative Boundaries

Moreover, there was also a set of commonly acknowledged negative boundaries within which the discussion was framed. These help explain sensitivities that were formative of both affirmations and critiques of opponents' views. We can note at least four such "heresies" that everyone tried to avoid in their own teaching and to impute to their opponents. Whether or not one's opponents explicitly and intentionally held to the specified heresy in its original form, one welcomed any excuse for pinning these labels on them.

1. The first of these was Manichaeism, the notion that the universe was governed by two opposing forces, of good and evil. No party to the trinitarian debates actually held that belief, but accusing one's opponents of Manichaeism served to emphasize one's own affirmation of one original principle and sole ruler of the universe. The characterization of God as "unbegotten" or "unoriginated" (*agen[n]ētos*) also served this assertion. The doctrine of the eternal coexistence of Father and Son seemed to posit two unoriginated beings and was thus vulnerable to the charge of Manichaeism.

2. Another marker was gnostic emanationism, the doctrine of a kind of natural overflow from one divine being to another within the *plērōma* of the divine realm. The Nicene notion of the Father's begetting of the Son by nature was again vulnerable to this charge. Those who disagreed with the doctrine of an eternal begetting of the Son that was continuous with the divine nature as such asserted the primacy of divine will as the antidote to emanationism. This problematic involved questions of how to apply the categories of divine nature and will in the relations between Father, Son, and Spirit.

3. Whatever Paul of Samosata had actually taught, the name of "the Samosatene" was associated with the notion that Jesus was *psilanthrōpos* ("mere man") and that his divinity came about when God "adopted" his humanity. Everyone shunned association with such a doctrine.

4. Finally, the equally shadowy figure of Sabellius was invoked to critique any doctrine that undermined the real differentiation between Father, Son, and Spirit, as if they were ultimately the same thing.

The Break in Pre-Nicene Experience

Taken together, the positive and negative markers outlined above constituted a large portion of the common flow of Christian experience. We can say that these items inhabited the primary reflection of Christians in that period. What then were the agitating factors that created a break in this flow of experience, necessitating the recuperative efforts of a doctrinal secondary reflection? We can list at least three major sources of destabilization that evoked a recasting and reinterpretation of the unity of Christian reflection.

1. First among these was an emerging clarity on the radical difference between God and the world. The careful articulation of this radical difference has since that time become a fundamental fixture in Christian theology. A modern theologian continues to speak of this "Christian distinction" as the lynchpin of Christian theology.[12] But at that time, the framing of this distinction was still relatively new. Aristotle had taught that the whole universe was "unbegotten," and had always existed.[13] Plato had spoken of a creation of the world by the Demiurge, but this "creation" was the imposition of design and order on preexistent matter—an interpretation that was taken over by some Christian apologists.[14] Even with the widespread acceptance of the notion of creation from nothing, Origen proposed that God, as eternally Almighty, was always Lord and Master over a creation that always existed, even if it did always exist from nothing![15] In the third century, a bishop from Asia Minor, Methodius of Olympus, criticized what he deemed to be Origen's "Hellenizing" doctrine and insisted on a punctiliar eruption of creation from nothing into existence. God alone was unbegotten, sole existent, uniquely prior to everything that came to be through him.[16] The term "unbegotten" (*agen[n]ētos*) was to carry much of the weight of this newfound clarity on the radical difference between God and the world. This development constituted an agitation or break within the flow of Christian experience inasmuch as it needed to be creatively integrated with another fundamental principle of Christian experience, the primacy of Jesus as Lord. According to everyone's understanding of Scripture, even the preexistent Christ was begotten, caused by the Father. Moreover, although Creator, he was also closely associated with creation, as its paradigm, "the beginning of God's works" (Prov. 8:22; cf. Col. 1:17). In a fairly standard interpretation of the latter scriptural phrase, Origen explains that "in this very subsistence of wisdom there was implicit every capacity and form of the creation that was to be."[17] How then to reconcile the primacy of Christ, closely bound with his double relation to both God and creation, with this newly maximized sense of divine primacy—the radical difference between God and world and God's absolute priority and freedom from any kind of posteriority (or being caused)? In the tensions evoked by these questions, a reexamination and reintegration of the elements of Christian experience was being called forth. The question of the relation between Father and Son was closely bound to questions about the nature of divine transcendence and the relation between God and creation.

2. A second source of agitation was recent controversy and confusion as to the existence and soteriological significance of Jesus's human soul.[18] For Origen, Jesus's

---

12. See Sokolowski, *God of Faith and Reason*. David Burrell sees this distinction as foundational to all three Abrahamic religions; see his *Freedom and Creation*.

13. Aristotle, *De caelo* 1.3.270b.

14. Plato, *Timaeus* 28; cf. Justin Martyr, *1 Apol.* 10.

15. *Princ.* 1.2.10; pref.4.

16. *De lib. arb.* 5–6, 22.

17. *Princ.* 1.2.2 (ET: Butterworth, *On First Principles*, 16).

18. For an excellent analysis of this issue, see Behr's discussion of Paul of Samosata in *Way to Nicaea*, 213–20.

human soul mediated between the divine *Logos* and the human flesh of Jesus. In Origen's theological system, Jesus's human soul also functioned to mediate between divine grace and human freedom. Origen's framework included the hypothesis of souls that preexisted the material embodiment of the present world. Only one of these souls clung faithfully to the divine *Logos* and thus deserved to become the human soul of Jesus, divinized by its union with the *Logos*.[19] The alleged teaching of Paul of Samosata brought further suspicion on any emphasis on Christ's human soul. As we have noted, the latter was reputed to have taught that Jesus was an integral human being, with both a human body and human soul, who was merely "adopted" by divine grace. Midway through the fourth century, the question of Jesus's human soul became an explicit point of debate, especially between Apollinaris and the Cappadocians. But at the threshold of Nicaea, the question of Christ's human soul already evoked the larger and more general question of the location of christological mediation between God and world. If not in the human soul, at what point in Christ's divine-human being should we locate the *pro nobis*, the "for us"? At the threshold of Nicaea, this question was motivating a secondary reflection on the mutual relations of different aspects of Christian faith: Christology, trinitarian theology, divine grace, and human freedom.

3. A third source of agitation toward secondary reflection was a drive to systematization, motivated by forces both internal and external to the church. In the late antique period, various philosophical schools produced systematic manuals articulating their distinct worldviews and programs for attaining wisdom and happiness.[20] We can find traces of this approach among the apologists, especially Justin Martyr. But once again Origen is the pivotal figure. In *On First Principles*, Origen attempts a presentation of Christian faith as a unified body of knowledge, a science (*epistēmē*) in the Aristotelian sense.[21] The construction of such a Christian science, which has divinely revealed Scripture as the source and goal of its reflection, involves probing the consistency between the constitutive parts of revealed Christian faith in order to attain a vision of the whole:

> Everyone therefore who is desirous of constructing out of the foregoing [rule of faith] a connected body of doctrine must use points like these as elementary and foundational principles, in accordance with the commandment which says, "Enlighten yourselves with the light of knowledge" (Hos. 10:12 LXX). Thus by clear and cogent arguments he will discover the truth about each particular point and so will produce, as we have said, a single body of doctrine, with the aid of such illustrations and declarations as he shall find in the holy Scriptures and of such conclusions as he shall determine to follow logically from them when rightly understood.[22]

19. *Princ.* 2.6.4–7.
20. See Hadot, *Philosophy as a Way of Life*, 60–61.
21. See Daley, "Origen's *De Principiis*," 3–21.
22. *Princ.* 1; pref. 10 (ET: Butterworth, *On First Principles*, 10).

As he both indulged in tantalizing speculation and insisted on organic consistency, Origen modeled a creative striving for synthesis and coherence in Christian thinking. His example made it more difficult to simply ignore internal tensions in the Christian worldview. The changing social location of the legitimized church in the Constantinian era gave further impetus toward this systematization. Now that it was fully incorporated into the political life of the empire, the church needed to strive for a unified and consistent expression of its faith, both for identifying itself to the world and for furthering the unity of the empire.[23] In the ensuing controversies, the church would not always have the leisure to contemplate issues at its own pace. Often it would be driven toward consistency in the expression of its faith by political powers aiming to minimize the social unrest that doctrinal disagreement could engender.

Thus, at the eve of Nicaea, we find a church that is driven by internal and external pressures to articulate its beliefs in a coherent manner. The flow of its experience was being agitated by new developments in its ongoing reflection on the implications of the message of Jesus Christ as Lord. Aside from external pressures, we can locate the central point of this agitation in the newly developing break between its allegiance to the primacy of Christ and its newfound clarity on what constitutes divine primacy as such. The latter conception identifies an essential feature of divine primacy in terms of being uncaused, absolutely and unqualifiedly prior—in a word, "unbegotten" or "unoriginated," *agen[n]ētos*. But the primacy of Jesus, as Savior, as God "for us," has always been conceived in terms of his identification with creation, obviously in his humanity but also to some extent even in his divinity. Moreover, Scripture frames the primacy of Christ in terms of his derivative relation to the Father: the Son sent by the Father to do the Father's will. How can the primacy of Jesus, as Mediator between the world and the Father, be harmonized with the conception of divine primacy as absolute, unbegotten priority? Around this central break in the flow of Christian experience, other aspects became patient of different interpretations according to one's fundamental orientation with regard to that central question: how to read the christological narrative presented by Scripture, how to interpret Christian worship, how the world is related to God, and so on.

Trinitarian Theologians of Unity of Will

Among the various strategies devised by different theologians to execute the reintegration of Christian experience, we can identify two main trajectories. Some affirmed the primacy of Christ by associating him with the *being* of the Father, thereby christologically reconstructing the category of absolute transcendence. Others affirmed the primacy of Christ by associating him with the *will* of the Unbegotten, thereby reasserting the recently clarified insistence on the sovereign freedom of the biblical

23. Lyman, "Hellenism and Heresy."

God and his distinction from all that is caused. The remainder of this chapter treats some notable figures from both trajectories.

Arius

Arius, who was born in Libya, was a respected ascetic and presbyter at the church of the Baucalis in Alexandria at the time of the outbreak of his controversy with the bishop of Alexandria, Alexander. An indication of both his reputation as a teacher and of an initially positive relation with Alexander is given by the fourth-century historian Sozomen, who reports that Alexander "honored him as a highly skilled dialectician, for he was reputed to be not lacking in these arts."[24] Such a portrait would seem to support Rowan Williams's characterization of Arius as identifying himself with the Alexandrian "school" tradition of which Origen was the most illustrious representative.[25] Arius and Alexander could not reconcile their differences over how to conceive the relation between the Father and the Son, however, and Arius was excommunicated from the Egyptian church sometime in the early 320s. Both Arius and Alexander appealed to surrounding bishops for support, and in response to the expanding controversy, the emperor Constantine convened the Council of Nicaea in 325. There Arius's doctrine was condemned and Arius was exiled, as were some of his key supporters. However, appeals on his behalf by prominent bishops, such as Eusebius of Nicomedia and the erudite and respected Eusebius of Caesarea, led Constantine to ask Alexander to accept Arius back into communion. Both Alexander and his successor, Athanasius, rebuffed this request. At the Council of Tyre, in 335, Athanasius himself was deposed and Arius reinstated. The latter decision was reaffirmed by another council in Constantinople in 336. Before Arius could return to Alexandria, however, he suddenly died, reportedly in a public bathroom, a circumstance interpreted by his opponents as dramatic divine judgment.[26]

Arius in the Flow of Christian Experience

As Maurice Wiles has noted, subsequent Christian tradition has depicted Arius as the archetypal heretic, the paradigmatic "other" against which orthodoxy defines itself.[27] But, of course, if Arius's relation to Christian tradition was merely one of sheer otherness, the refutation of his teaching would not have become so constitutive a feature of Christian doctrine. Neither could we make sense of the fact, reported by Athanasius himself, that many Christians could readily interpret the teaching of Arius and his supporters as a plausible and acceptable version of Christian faith.[28] The framework that we have adopted allows us to make sense of that fact by locating Arius first of all within the common flow of Christian experience of that time. Moreover,

---

24. Sozomen, *Hist. eccl.* 1.15.3.
25. *Arius*, 84–86.
26. Athanasius, *Ep. Aeg. Lib.* 19; Epiphanius, *Pan.* 69.10.3.
27. Wiles, *Archetypal Heresy*; cf. Williams, *Arius*, 2–25.
28. *C. Ar.* 1.1.

Arius himself did not create the break in Christian experience that was dramatized by the debates in which he was involved. Arius simply responded to this crisis by his own interpretive reintegration of the various elements of Christian faith—a reintegration meant to restore the common flow of Christian experience. The otherness of Arius with respect to subsequent orthodoxy is therefore best understood not as the invasion by an alien force of the pristine untroubled integrity of Christian experience but rather as one response to a conflict of interpretation within a common horizon of Christian experience. This perspective enables us to make sense of the fact that the refutation of Arius eventually became integral to the reinterpretation of Christian experience that constitutes the development of orthodox trinitarian doctrine.

In placing Arius within the common flow of Christian experience, we have to first of all reject the temptation to construe him primarily as a rationalist who succumbed to the lure of Platonic reason. There are philosophical elements in his interpretation of Christian faith, but his argumentation seems to have been, for the most part, overtly scriptural. Arius used scriptural predications in his description of God, "the God of the law and prophets and the New Covenant,"[29] and his depiction of the primacy of Christ was also formulated in terms of the scriptural titles of christological exaltation (*epinoiai*): Word, Wisdom, Power, and so on.[30] Moreover, Alexander reports that Arius and his supporters made extensive use of scriptural texts to support their doctrine of the ontological inferiority of the Son, particularly texts that pertain to his suffering humanity: "Recalling all the words about the salvific suffering, humiliation, self-emptying, poverty, and other attributes that the Savior took on for our sake, they pile these up to impugn the supreme deity that was his from the start."[31]

Arius also endeavored to identify himself within apostolic tradition. Rowan Williams raises the intriguing possibility that underlying the initial conflict between Arius and Alexander was a lingering tension in the Egyptian church between episcopal authority and the model of the charismatic teacher, exemplified by Origen.[32] Nevertheless, we find Arius striving to find support for his teaching by alliances with bishops. Indeed, he goes so far as to impute his own teaching to Alexander himself—clearly a rhetorical maneuver, but it acknowledges the principle of episcopal validation of apostolic tradition: "Our faith, which we have learned from our forefathers and which we have also learned from you, holy father, is this . . ."[33] When agreement with Alexander proved unworkable, he sought episcopal support elsewhere.

Finally, in order to properly secure Arius's position within the common flow of Christian experience, we have to resist the anachronistic characterization of him as an antitrinitarian theologian. That characterization simply misses the complexity of the situation. In his confession of faith to Alexander, Arius makes what seems to be a simple statement that is nevertheless fraught with hidden complexities. He writes

29. Arius, *Letter to Alexander*, Urk. 6.2.
30. *Thalia*, in Athanasius, *Syn.* 15.
31. Alexander, *Letter to Alexander of Byzantium*; Theodoret 1.4, Urk. 14.
32. *Arius*, 84–86.
33. Arius, *Letter to Alexander*, Urk. 6.

simply, "So there are three *hypostaseis*."[34] This statement turns out to be surprisingly revelatory of Arius's complex position as both standing within the common flow of Christian experience and yet caught by a certain turbulence that threatens the stability of this standing. What makes this statement so intriguing is that in this same confession of faith, Arius has been insisting with monotonous repetition that the God whose supreme attribute is oneness is other than and prior to the Son and has failed even to mention the Holy Spirit. The stark affirmation "there are three *hypostaseis*" does not say *where* they are! In "God"? Clearly not, for we are told that the *one God* is "the monad" and that the three *hypostaseis* are dissimilar in essence and glory. Indeed, in this epistle, the Son is nowhere called "God." But if not "in God," what or where then are these three *hypostaseis*? In reality in general? Surely not, for there are very many *hypostaseis* in reality as a whole. We have to ask, then, what subset of reality is Arius partitioning off by that apparently simple statement, "So there are three *hypostaseis*"? We have to say that it is the set of beings that form the object (or objects) of Christian confession. So we find Arius occupying a tense position in which he is involved in the common flow of Christian experience but is also making certain clarifications that trouble that flow. On the one hand, Arius finds himself involved in the trinitarian grammar of Christian faith, in which the three *hypostaseis* seemingly form a certain unity at least as a single prediction of Christian faith, and yet, on the other hand, he also makes radically monotheistic qualifications that destabilize the unity of that predication.

THE PRIMACY OF CHRIST AND THE PRIMACY OF GOD

We have already identified the central break in the flow of Christian experience that led to the Nicene reinterpretation of Christian faith as the tension involved in reintegrating confession of Christ's primacy with a heightened redefinition of the absolute primacy of God over creation. Arius's theology is best understood as an attempt to achieve that reintegration by depicting the relation of the Father and the Son in terms of the divine will, as the exemplary manifestation of the primacy of the one God as Creator over the creation, which came to be from nothing and to which he is related by his sovereign will. The absolute primacy of the one God is designated by the titles of "unbegotten/uncaused" (*agen[n]ētos*) and "sole" (*monas*). "God" is that being who is characterized by an absolute and unqualified priority, without any shadow of posteriority, and such a being by definition is absolutely unique. The positing of a second who is equal to such a being is clearly self-contradictory, as that would assert the notion of "two" in which neither is "second"— in Arius's terms, "two Unbegottens."[35] Such an assertion smacks of Manichaean dualism. In his emphasis on the absolute and unqualified priority of the one Unbegotten, Arius could rely on scriptural testimony as well as on the third-century development of a clarified doctrine of creation from nothing. Methodius of Olympus had asserted this notion of a

34. Arius, *Letter to Alexander*, Urk. 6.13.7.
35. Arius, *Letter to Alexander*, Urk. 6.13.12.

punctiliar origination of creation from nothing in reaction to Origen's alleged belief that it was necessary for God's eternal almightiness that there be always a creation over which God presides as Lord.[36] There is a general consensus now that Arius was dependent on Methodius's critique of Origen and developed it into the more radical assertion that even the only-begotten Son has a punctiliar origin that is posterior to the existence of the Unbegotten monad.[37] It may also be that Arius found philosophical resources for asserting the absolute sovereignty and priority of the biblical God in emerging Neoplatonism, which tended to elevate the first principle beyond any secondary and intermediate "divine" beings.[38] Such a first principle is characterized by its inaccessibility to participation by lesser beings. Yet Arius's God is still to be distinguished radically from a Platonic first principle inasmuch as Arius's God is related to his creation, in true biblical fashion, through his sovereign and deliberate will.

When it comes to integrating such a radicalized conception of divinity as absolute priority (God as unbegotten/unoriginated) with confession of the primacy of Christ, Arius is prepared to admit that Christ's primacy does not meet this strict standard. The Alexandrian tradition to which Arius belonged featured a Wisdom Christology in which even the preexistent divinity of Christ was associated with creation, as containing its paradigms.[39] Thus even the divinity of Christ was somehow implicated with creation. Moreover, Christian faith is directed not abstractly to the preexistent Christ, but simply to Jesus Christ, a man who lived among other human beings, suffered, died, and was exalted in his resurrection. As a hermeneutically purifying mental exercise, one might weigh one's indoctrinated shock at Arius's assertion that the Son is a creature against the uncontroversial assertion that *Jesus Christ* is a creature. For Arius, the creaturehood of Jesus Christ, which is indubitable at the most obvious and empirical level, must extend also to his preexistent "divinity." This line of thinking underlies the exegetical strategy reported by Alexander in which the human limitations and suffering of Christ become evidence of his attenuated divinity. Of course, even on the level of the preexistent divinity, Christ was "second" as "begotten" of the Father and therefore not "first" and "unbegotten." Between the preexistent Christ and the unique Unbegotten must lie the radical chasm between what is uniquely first and everything else: the nothingness that can only be overcome by the sovereign will of the unique Unbegotten. The Son, therefore, is a creature who originated from

36. On Methodius's doctrine of creation, see Williams, *Arius*, 168–71; Patterson, "Methodius, Origen, and the Arian Dispute"; and Patterson, *Methodius of Olympus*.

37. Cf. Stead, "Platonism of Arius," 30; Williams, *Arius*, 168–71; Patterson, "Methodius, Origen, and the Arian Dispute." Ayres mentions Methodius's critique of Origen as part of the background that shaped fourth-century theology in general (*Nicaea*, 29–30); Behr, *Nicene Faith*, 1:149.

38. This thesis is extensively argued by Williams in *Arius*, esp. 215–32. Christopher Stead offers a detailed refutation of Williams's contention of direct Neoplatonic influence in "Was Arius a Neoplatonist?" In his 2001 revision of *Arius*, Williams concedes that he overstated the case of direct literary influence but still maintains that philosophical developments that tended to accentuate the higher transcendence of the first principle may have created a climate in which "affirming the substantial difference of the Logos from the Father was an intellectual necessity for theology" (265).

39. Cf. Origen, *Princ.* 1.2.2.

nothing through the sovereign and gracious will of the Unbegotten: "He was not before he was begotten and created and appointed and established; for he was not unbegotten."[40] The relation between the eternal God and the created Son thus in no way implicates the *substance* of the one God but is strictly consequent upon the *will* of the one God: He "came into being by the Father's will. By God's will the Son is what he is and as great as he is."[41]

In the relatively scarce extant material that we can attribute to Arius, he employs language of substance, relation, and participation to construct affirmations and negations about the relation of Father and Son. But the intelligibility of his thought is to be found not so much in any technical definitions of these terms but rather in his attempts to render a biblically coherent account of the relation of absolute divine primacy to the primacy of Christ. Manlio Simonetti outlines five exegetical routes by which Arius and his early supporters interpreted the scriptural data on the relation between Father and Son. These were based on (1) passages that referred to divine oneness (e.g., Deut. 6:4); (2) passages that identify the Father as the source of the powers and dignities of the Son (e.g., Luke 10:22); (3) passages that employ the language of "making" and "creating" with reference to the Son, the paradigmatic example being the reference to Wisdom, understood to be the preexistent Christ, in Proverbs 8:22: "He created me as the beginning of his ways for his works"; (4) attributions of passibility and change to the human Jesus, understood as indications of an inferior divinity; and (5) passages where language of "generation" and other exalted christological titles are applied to other creatures (e.g., Isa. 1:2).[42]

The complexity of Arius's hermeneutical strategy is seen in his intriguing doctrine, according to Athanasius's reporting of Arius's *Thalia*, that there are two Words and Wisdoms in God. While we cannot be sure that Athanasius's wording is entirely accurate, the doctrine can probably be safely attributed to Arius inasmuch as it is strictly consistent with his theological project as a whole. Theologians of this period can speak conceptually of divine "being" or "substance," but their language for naming and imaging God comes primarily from Scripture. As we noted earlier, by Arius's time there was a well-established tradition of naming the primacy of Christ by reciting the litany of exalted titles that Scripture applies both to the divine presence and power and to Christ, such as Word, Wisdom, and Power. This scriptural linguistic pattern was the basis for a biblical articulation of the correlativity of Father and Son, and it was used very pointedly in this manner by Origen: God is always wise and almighty through his Wisdom and Power.[43] In his efforts to draw a clear boundary between the absolute primacy of the one God and the primacy of Christ, and to render all this in scriptural terms, Arius was doubly constrained. He could not deny outright the

---

40. Arius, *Letter to Eusebius of Nicomedia*, Urk. 1.5.

41. *Thalia*, in Athanasius, *Syn.* 15. An allusion to the Son's coming into being through the Father's will can be found in all three of Arius's extant writings; cf. *Letter to Eusebius of Nicomedia*, Urk. 1.3.1; *Letter to Alexander*, Urk. 6.12.9–10.

42. Simonetti, *La crisi*, 52–53.

43. *Princ.* 1.2.10.

attribution of these exalted titles to Christ, nor could he deny their strictly theological overtones as biblical descriptions of divine presence and power. Moreover, his opponents were quick to expose how Arius's doctrine seemed to violate these scriptural patterns: if the Son was not before he was created, then inasmuch as the Son is biblically designated as Word, Wisdom, Power, Truth, and so on, we must also say that God was once irrational (*alogos*) and without wisdom, power, and truth.[44] In this framework, Arius's doctrine of two Words and two Wisdoms becomes intelligible. In effect, this doctrine regulates the interpretation of the linguistic overlap by positing that in their strictly theological sense these terms apply to the one God, while in a more attenuated sense they apply to the Son's creaturely participation in the "grace" by which the one God wills the Son to share in his glory. Thus "Wisdom came into existence through Wisdom, by the will of the one who is wise. And so it is conceived in countless manifestations (*epinoiai*): spirit, power, and wisdom, God's glory, truth, image, Word."[45] In this way, the doctrine of the one God who brings the Son into being by his sovereign will governs the interpretation of the christological titles of Christ.

THE ROLE OF SOTERIOLOGY

Among the titles and characterizations of Christ in the Scriptures, perhaps the most crucial for Christian experience is that of Christ as "Savior." An important moment in the modern interpretation of the Nicene-"Arian" controversy was the publication of Gregg and Groh's *Early Arianism: A View of Salvation*.[46] Gregg and Groh argued that the central focus of Arius's theology is not so much a cosmology or a maximal insistence on divine transcendence but a view of salvation in which Christ is conceived as an exemplar showing how a creature may attain salvation through the exercise of free will. Over against Athanasius's emphasis on the difference between Christ and humanity, Arius and the early Arians focused on the solidarity of Christ as "one of us" in his creaturehood. This "early Arian" or "voluntarist" view of salvation, as a reward for virtue freely chosen, is contrasted with the "essentialist" view of Athanasius, in which salvation is conceived as graced participation in divine life.[47] The greatest contribution of Gregg and Groh is simply to recommend looking at Arius's theology from a soteriological perspective over against the traditional inclination to think of Athanasian-Nicene theology as soteriological and Arius's theology as cosmological. But their particular rendering of that soteriology is plagued with problems: it downplays Arius's explicit emphasis on divine transcendence, and it ignores Arius's insistence that Christ is in fact not like other creatures, even apart from the likelihood that he also taught that Christ did not have a human soul.[48] Indeed, in this important respect, Gregg and Groh seem to have fallen into the trap of seeing Arius principally

---

44. *Henos sōmatos*, Urk. 4b.13.
45. *Thalia* (ET: Williams, *Arius*, 103).
46. Gregg and Groh, *Early Arianism*.
47. Ibid., esp. 161–91.
48. In his *Letter to Alexander*, Arius calls the Son "the perfect creation of God but not as one among the creatures, begotten but not as one among begotten beings" (Urk. 6.12.11–12).

through his opponents' eyes, accepting at face value the charge, leveled frequently by Athanasius, that he rendered Christ into a mere creature like all other creatures. But if we are to locate Arius properly within the common flow of Christian experience, we must take seriously his obvious and explicit efforts to give a substantial account of the unique primacy of Christ and his incomparability with other creatures.

Perhaps the key problem in Gregg and Groh's rendering of Arius's soteriology is that they seem beholden to a Western, post-Augustinian conception of what soteriology is. In the latter framework, the key questions of soteriology are about will, freedom, grace, and the interaction of human and divine agency in the moral life. Such a preconception of soteriology does not succeed in integrating other arguably more prominent themes in Arius's theology, most especially the ever-present emphasis on the unqualified unique transcendence of the one God. But if we put aside such a preconception of what we mean by "soteriology," we find a most surprising witness for the radicality of the soteriological perspective in Arius's theology: Athanasius himself. On the most basic and general level, soteriological discourse is about Christ's benefits "for us," and Athanasius charged that Arius's theology located the "for us" at the very origin of Christ's preexistent divinity.[49] In light of modern characterizations of the controversy, it is ironic indeed that Athanasius should complain that Arius's theology is too soteriological. Nevertheless, Athanasius's critique can help us to trace the soteriological perspective in Arius to its very roots. Along the way, we will have to shed anachronistic preconceptions in which soteriology, cosmology, and accounts of divine transcendence occupy discrete realms of discourse.

We have already seen how Arius fully subscribed to a newly clarified insistence on the absolute and unqualified priority of the one God over against creation. In Arius's theology, any being that is in any sense posterior to the Unbegotten can only be considered as coming into being as the effect of the sovereign will of the one who is unqualifiedly prior. The bringing about of this effect is called creation; the effect itself must be called a creature; and, from the perspective of the creature, what precedes this effect is nothing. Given all of the above, we must say that the Son, as begotten and caused by the one God, is a creature who came to be from nothing. But Arius staked his claim to a coherent interpretation of Christian faith not by devaluing the Son as a creature like all other creatures, despite his opponents' caricatures, but by proposing a positive and carefully constructed reinterpretation of the primacy of Christ. This reinterpretation was centered on the dialectical mediation of the Word between God and the world. We can dismiss this conception of the Word's mediation as "cosmological" and as having affinities with Hellenistic "mediatorial" schemes, but we must contend with the fact that this perspective also tries to integrate a biblical soteriological perspective by designating the Word's very being as "for us"—as Athanasius himself concedes. A kinship with Greek mediatorial schemes should not cause us to lose sight of the scriptural soteriological framework in which this scheme is reconstituted. In Arius's conception, the Word comes to be as the first and preeminent creature who is

49. *C. Ar.* 2.30; cf. *Henos sōmatos*, Urk. 4b.9.

the primordial and unsurpassable representation and sign of the ineffable glory of the one God. In his preexistent divinity, the Word accomplishes this mediation through his work of creating all other creatures, and this work of mediation is continued into his visible and empirically accessible humanity.

The positive aspect of Arius's emphasis on the Son as mediating access to the ineffable and unique Unbegotten is admittedly in some tension with his assertions in the *Thalia* that the Son does not fully know the Father or even himself:

> God is inexpressible to the Son,
> For he is what he is for himself, and that is unutterable,
> So that the Son does not have the understanding that would enable him to
>   give voice to any words expressing comprehension.
> For him it is impossible to search out the mysteries of the Father, who exists in
>   himself;
> For the Son does not know his own substance,
> Since, being a son, he came into actual subsistence by a father's will.
> What scheme of thought, then, could admit the idea that he who has his
>   being from the Father
> Should know by comprehension the one who begot him?[50]

This christological apophaticism is magnified when we contrast it with the later Eunomian claim that the divine essence is knowable. The real character of Arius's doctrine, however, lies not in a complete epistemological dissociation between the Son and the Father but rather in a dialectical movement between the Son's incomplete knowledge of the Father and his rendering epistemic access to the Father. As to the assertion that the Son cannot attain to a comprehensive knowledge of the Father, some have suggested that Arius was influenced both by Origen's speculations and by developments in emerging Neoplatonism, which posited the One as beyond the subject-object duality of intellection.[51] In both cases, there is a more or less explicit contrast between what is radically and absolutely simple and what attains to simplicity through multiplicity. The second hierarchical principle, of unity-in-multiplicity, cannot attain a complete and simple grasp of the first principle in its native simplicity.

---

50. Arius, *Thalia* (ET: Williams, *Arius*, 103).

51. Kannengiesser suggests a direct link to Plotinus, *Enn.* 5.3.7, and rejects the notion that Origen advocated the kind of epistemological breach between Father and Son that is found in Arius; see Kannengiesser, *Holy Scripture and Hellenistic Hermeneutics*, 32–40; Williams is sympathetic to the thesis of Neoplatonic influence but notes ambiguities and tensions in Origen that might have been radicalized by Arius, such as Origen's seemingly inconclusive discussion of the question of whether the Father is glorified in himself in some way beyond the Son's glorification of the Father (*Arius*, 199–214). See Origen, *Comm. Jo.* 32.28–29. Stead rejects the theory of Plotinian influence and considers Arius's doctrine as a response to Alexander's doctrine of the ineffability of the Son's being, developing that notion by emphasizing the transcendent ineffability of the Father even with respect to the Son ("Was Arius a Neoplatonist?" 46–47). Löhr also notes the link with Origen's discussion and further notes overlapping resonances between Arius's stress on the unknowability of the Father and the Valentinian *Tripartite Tractate*. See Löhr, "Arius Reconsidered: Part Two," 125–27.

Alongside such philosophical considerations, Arius seems to be again pressing the basic point of the difference between Creator and creature. A creature by definition cannot encompass the being of its Creator; the passivity of the creature in respect to the givenness of its own being renders it also unable to actively search out a comprehensive view of its own essence. So Arius appears here once again to be following through on his project of properly relativizing the primacy of Christ in relation to the unique and Unbegotten God.

But Arius simultaneously gives a positive account of the primacy of Christ by inserting into the apophatic framework sketched above a characterization of the Son's role as granting humanity positive access to the ineffable God. The Word's being *refers us* to the Unbegotten God:

> We call him unbegotten on account of the one who by nature is begotten;
> We sing his praises as without beginning because of the one who has a
> beginning.
> We worship him as eternal because of him who was born in the order of time.
> The one without beginning established the Son as the beginning of all
> creatures.[52]

Rowan Williams sees a parallel between Arius's *Thalia* and "the (Plotinian) paradox that the first principle is known for what it is through its opposite."[53] One could say that in Arius's theological-christological epistemology, the Son is the supreme negative theology in person. But as in most negative theologies, the "greater unlikeness" is also complemented by some likeness that refers us to its supereminent source. Even when the relation seems to be one of pure contrast, as in "unbegotten/begotten" and "without beginning/having beginning," the overall context leads us to see that the contrast is specified and informed by the particular manifest glory of the Word, who is

> God's glory, truth, image, Word.
> You should understand that he is thought of too as radiance and as light
> The Higher One is able to beget an equal to the Son,
> But not one more renowned, higher or greater than he.[54]

If we cannot see all of this as soteriology, that is, I have suggested, because of a particularly modern, post-Augustinian, and Western narrowing of that concept. In Arius's own milieu of fourth-century Alexandrian Christianity, the breakdown and christological retrieval of true knowledge of God is an eminently soteriological motif. This much again we can glean from Athanasius himself, inasmuch as this motif figures as an explicitly soteriological theme in *On the Incarnation*.[55] Whether we construct a

---

52. Arius, *Thalia* (ET: Williams, *Arius*, 101–2).
53. Arius, *Thalia* (ET: Williams, *Arius*, 223).
54. Arius, *Thalia* (ET: Williams, *Arius*, 103).
55. See, e.g., *Inc.* 11–16.

genealogy of Arius's logic by positing an uncritical adoption of a Platonic mediatorial cosmology or, following Athanasius, by decrying his locating the "for us" too radically at the origin of the very divinity of the Word, what is most unhelpful is to sunder the unity of divine transcendence, christological mediation, and soteriology in Arius's scheme. For Arius, the Son and Word comes to be as the first and preeminent created manifestation and mediator of the glory of the Unbegotten; precisely inasmuch as his being is bound up with this work of mediation, he is "for us" through and through. Moreover, this work of mediation-salvation is fulfilled when the incarnate Word enables his disciples to give due worship to the ineffable Unbegotten God: "We worship him as eternal because of him who was born in the order of time." Precisely as the "perfect creature," the Son is the exemplary worshiper of the one God, the one whose unique and unsurpassable access to the glories of the one God enables him to recognize the ineffable transcendence of the Unbegotten and to communicate this knowledge of the ineffability of the Unbegotten to those who worship with him and through him. Rowan Williams suggests that the *Thalia* is alluding to the practice of a primitive Alexandrian liturgy in which the Son and the Spirit are depicted as leading the angelic praises before the divine throne. Whether or not parts of the *Thalia* were intended as "a gloss" on liturgical texts, Williams's conclusion seems to fit in with the theology of the *Thalia* as a whole:

> In this, as in other respects, Arius appears as someone pressing the apparent logic of existing practice toward a potentially unwelcome conclusion: if a *worshiper* of God, then not God in any defensible sense, though the term may be used, by a kind of scripturally licensed courtesy, as an address to the Son. . . . If a being who reveals to us the utter incomprehensibility of the Father, then a being who shares with us the epistemic distance between God and all other subjects, since he can only reveal this incomprehensibility by pointing beyond himself to the mystery of his origins.[56]

As for Arius's ascribing to the Word/Son free will and the attainment of divinity as a merited reward for his virtues, that too should not be read in terms of a modern schema of Christ's solidarity with other human beings as "just like us." Rather, it belongs in an Origenian framework that simply applies to Christ's divinity one of the necessary features of a created rational being. Origen insisted both that the Son is "unchangeable and unalterable" and that all rational beings possess a free will that can incline toward either good or evil: "There is none among rational creatures who is not capable of both good and evil except the nature of God."[57] Thus, in an Alexandrian-Origenian framework, to assert that the Son does not belong to the very nature of the unique Unbegotten God necessitates imputing to the Son a will that is free and, in principle, changeable. With characteristic consistency, Arius seems to have been willing to take that step. But he greatly mitigates the resulting dilution of Christ's primacy by insisting that the divinity gained by the Word's exercise of free will was preveniently

56. "Angels Unawares," 361.
57. *Princ.* 1.8.3.

and originally supplied by God in anticipation of future merits, a doctrine redolent of Origen's teaching on Christ's human soul.[58] From the origin of his existence the Son and Word was "divine," in a sense secondary to the Unbegotten but unique in relation to all other creatures. Whether or not such a schema of a prevenient grace that both anticipates and yet is somehow proleptically consequent upon future merit is coherent or intelligible, the paradox inherent in it bespeaks Arius's true concern: to affirm consistently the consequences of the Son's creaturehood while keeping the primacy of Christ unique in relation to all other creatures. One connotation that does not seem intended at all is that the divinity of the Son is something that he has in common with humanity.

THE CONSISTENCY OF ARIUS

While the location of the center or heart of a given theological system is perhaps in the end a matter of interpretive perspective, we can at least maintain that the internal consistency of Arius's doctrine comes into view once we see that his project is fundamentally concerned with integrating a strict definition of divine transcendence with a relativized but, in his view, scripturally adequate conception of the primacy of Christ. The highest level of divine transcendence is defined in terms of absolute simplicity and unqualified priority: the one God is therefore unbegotten/uncaused/*monas*. Therefore, God is not always Father; the Son did not always exist; the three *hypostaseis* are unlike each other in substance. In relation to this one God, the Son/Word/Wisdom, as secondary and caused, is a creature whose existence has a beginning as the effect of the will of the one God. But the Son is also "God," albeit in a secondary sense, as the created and necessarily incomplete representation and mediation of divine glory. Like all created beings, the Son is alterable by nature. But the primacy of Christ consists in his being granted an original and unsurpassable share in divine glory, which is not a participation in divine substance but in the freely bestowed grace of God's benefits. The Word is therefore not like the other creatures but is the exemplary and uniquely "perfect creature." This exemplarity is coincident with his mediation of the transcendent glory of the Unbegotten, which begins with his work of creation and comes to fruition in his enabling his disciples to become true worshipers, in his company, of the ineffable One Unbegotten. In terms of our overarching framework of trinitarian theologies of will over against trinitarian theologies of substance, we should note that Arius does not go so far as to say that Father, Son, and Spirit simply share the same will. In speaking of a trajectory that conceives of the Trinity in terms of unity of will, we are not necessarily speaking in all instances of *identity* of will. What we find in Arius is rather the assertion that the ultimate ground of Christ's primacy is his origination as the perfect creature who alone is directly effected by the one God's sovereign will. The affirmation of a "unity of will" is more explicitly deveolped by Arius's early supporter, Asterius.

58. See Lorenz, *Arius judaizans*, 211–24.

Asterius

Asterius was born in Cappadocia and, like Arius, was reputed to be a student of Lucian of Antioch. Before the eruption of the controversy between Arius and Alexander, Asterius was a "sophist," a teacher of rhetoric and philosophy. Because he sacrificed to the pagan gods during the Diocletianic persecution, he was disqualified from holding church office. Nevertheless, his theological talents were widely recognized, and he became a prominent participant at the important Council of Antioch of 341. Asterius was one of the early supporters of Arius and, prior to the Nicene council, penned a short defense of Arius, the *Syntagmation*, of which we have fragments quoted by some of his contemporaries. According to Athanasius, Asterius propagated his defense of Arius through a preaching and lecturing tour that took him through "Syria and elsewhere."[59] The only other extant writing of Asterius, of which we again possess only fragments, is a defense of a letter penned by another supporter of Arius, Eusebius of Nicomedia, and addressed to Paulinus of Tyre.[60] This letter was the basis for the condemnation and deposition of Eusebius at the Council of Nicaea. Asterius's defense of Eusebius integrates what he considers to be the main point of the latter's doctrine, that "the generation of the Son is to be attributed to the will of the Father,"[61] with the description of the Son as God from God, "the unchanging image of the essence and will and glory and power" of God.[62] The latter depiction of the Son resurfaces in the "Dedication Creed" of the Council of Antioch of 341, at which Asterius himself was present (though he died shortly thereafter) and whose creed was the most prominent alternative to the creed of Nicaea in the 340s.[63] Thus Asterius affirms the foundations of Arius's doctrine regarding the essence of the Son as the product of the Father's will, which is external to the Father's essence, but he also modifies this doctrine by emphasizing the nearness of Father and Son. This combination is typical of Asterius's theological project.

ASTERIUS AS CONTINUATOR OF ARIUS

In systematicians' standard summaries of the controversies surrounding the Council of Nicaea, the figure of Asterius does not loom large. But in fact Asterius is at least as much the object of Athanasius's polemic as Arius. He has yet to be sufficiently

---

59. *Syn.* 18.

60. Apart from these fragments, there is a set of *Homilies on the Psalms* attributed to Asterius, but their authenticity is questionable, as has been argued extensively by Kinzig in *In Search of Asterius*.

61. Fr. 5 (Vinzent).

62. Fr. 10 (Vinzent).

63. We have no conclusive evidence to determine if it was Asterius himself who was responsible for inserting this phrasing into the "Dedication Creed" or if the source of this phrasing is an earlier creed by Lucian of Antioch. The latter version is based on the report of the church historian Sozomen (*Hist. eccl.* 3.5). Lienhard accepts this version: "Asterius is quoting a creed, and not vice-versa; he could hardly have reworked his letter into a conciliar creed" (*Contra Marcellum*, 97n137). Hanson, referring to some comments by Philostorgius in which he criticizes Asterius for a similar phrasing, concludes that Asterius "had some influence on the composition" of the Dedication Creed (*Search*, 289).

appreciated as a crucial mediating figure between the theologies of Arius and Athana-sius.[64] Although he was an energetic supporter of Arius and was faithful to important basic elements of Arius's theology, Asterius also adjusted Arius's theology in ways that implicitly concede some of its weaknesses. In seeking to overcome these weaknesses, Asterius in fact enlarged the common ground between a developing theological tra-dition that shared some of its basic insights with Arius and the opposing trajectory, which was developing Alexander's theological commitments. The creation of this larger common ground enabled Athanasius to capitalize on Asterius's concessions and, by conflating Arius's theology with that of Asterius, to attempt a refutation of Arian-Asterian theology from within its own framework. A sketch of these dynam-ics will shed light on the accumulating insights that were emerging as constitutive aspects of trinitarian doctrine.

We can identify three main features of Asterius's continuity with the theology of Arius.[65] First, with regard to the doctrine of God, Asterius continued Arius's con-ception of absolute divine primacy as defined by the characteristics of eternity and priority in the order of causality, that is, God is unbegotten/uncaused. "Unbegotten" becomes an even more crucial identifying marker of absolute divinity for Asterius than it was for Arius, supplanting Arius's primary stress on the absolute divinity as singular, *monas*.[66] As "only-begotten," the Son's essence is created and made and is other than and posterior to the essence of the Father.[67] As with Arius, the relation between Father and Son is depicted predominantly in terms of the will of the Unbe-gotten. The Son has no participation in the divine essence but is entirely the product of the divine will.[68] Any similarity between Father and Son is the effect of the Father's will and does not amount to a participation in the essence of the Father; rather, the active power of the Father is reproduced in the Son. Whether or not we can speak of direct influence, there does seem to be a certain affinity here with the emerging "Neoplatonism" of Plotinus and Porphyry, whereby the notion of "participation" is undergoing a reinterpretation in which "the lower reality is constituted or formed in this or that respect by the active life of the higher, but *does not reproduce the 'essence' of the higher.*"[69] Therefore, Asterius interprets the Johannine dominical saying "I and the Father are one" as referring to "their exact correspondence (*symphōnia*) in all thoughts and works."[70] It is with reference to this framework of unity of will and activity that

64. The best modern treatment of Asterius's theology is Vinzent, *Asterius*, esp. 38–71; see also Hanson, *Search*, 32–41; Lienhard, *Contra Marcellum*, 89–101; Kopecek, *History of Neo-Arianism*, 28–56. On Athanasius's preoccupation with Asterius in the *Orations against the Arians*, see Kannengiesser, *Athanase d'Alexandrie*, esp. 151–81.

65. For comparisons between Asterius and Arius, see especially Kopecek, *Neo-Arianism*, 1:29–34; Vinzent, *Asterius*, 63–71.

66. See Vinzent, *Asterius*, 64–65.

67. Fr. 34, 35 (Vinzent).

68. Cf. Fr. 16, 18–20 (Vinzent).

69. Williams, *Arius*, 220.

70. Fr. 39 (cf. Vinzent, *Asterius*, 102); cf. Fr. 40 (Vinzent).

we should understand Asterius's notion of the Son as "exact Image" of the Father.[71] In this way, Asterius is able to incorporate the biblical designation of the Son as Image, which Arius generally downplayed, without compromising Arius's insistence on the nonparticipation of the Son in the substance of the Father.

Second, Asterius continues Arius's characterization of the primacy of Christ in terms of the Word's being the uniquely exemplary and unsurpassable creature.[72] As with Arius, the primacy of the preexistent Christ is at all points bound up with his mediatorial role. One aspect of this mediatorial role is that the Son represents an attenuation of the supreme transcendence of the Unbegotten. Apart from this attenuation, creation could "not withstand the immediate hand of God."[73] Thus only the Son is created by the Father alone; all other beings are created by the Father through the Son as "a subordinate assistant" (*hypēretēs*) to the Unbegotten.[74] A correlative aspect to the Son's mitigation of supreme transcendence is that he exemplifies all creaturely participation in the beneficent activity of the Unbegotten to the highest degree. In this respect, the primacy of the Son can be summed up by saying that he is "the first" in relation to the rest of creation: "He illuminates and shines upon all those that are in the intelligible cosmos."[75] As with Arius, this conception of the Son as Mediator locates the soteriological *pro nobis* not primarily in the incarnation event but at the very origin of the being of the Son: "He is Reason (*Logos*) for the sake of rational beings (*logika*), Wisdom for the sake of those who are made wise, and Power for the sake of those who are empowered."[76]

A third area of continuity between Arius and Asterius is the program of a scriptural exegesis in support of the clear distinction between the absolute primacy of the Unbegotten and the exemplary creaturehood of the Son. Among Asterius's fragments, we can discern two main strategies in service of this program. First, as we have already noted, Asterius interprets scriptural language of the unity of Father and Son (as in John 10:30, "the Father and I are one") as denoting oneness of will and activity rather than of substance. As with Arius, Asterius considers that ascribing the genesis of the Son to the will of the Father is the only way to avoid gnostic emanationism and the attribution of *pathos* to God.[77] Second, with regard to the exalted titles of Christ, such as *Logos*, Power, and Image, Asterius endeavors to show that Scripture applies such titles also to creatures. Therefore, in light of scriptural linguistic usage, these titles denote the exemplary creaturehood of the Son and not his sharing in the being

71. "The original which the image images without alteration is nevertheless not the being of the original but its creative power [*dessen schaffende Kraft*]. The hypostatic difference in being between the original and the image does not amount to any difference in power. The being of the original must be absent in its image, while a non-essential association in power [*nichtwesenhafter Zusammenhang in der Kraft*], that is, a dynamic association between original and image, remains" (Vinzent, *Asterius*, 46; my translation).

72. Fr. 10, 23, 35 (Vinzent).

73. Fr. 26 (Vinzent).

74. Fr. 34 (Vinzent, *Asterius*, 100).

75. Fr. 23 (Vinzent, *Asterius*, 94).

76. Fr. 71 (Vinzent, *Asterius*, 132).

77. Fr. 5 (Vinzent).

of the Unbegotten. Inasmuch as some of those titles, in particular Word (*Logos*), Wisdom (*Sophia*), and Power were scripturally aligned with divine presence and activity, Asterius also followed the strategy of distinguishing instances that referred to properties of the divine being of the Unbegotten from instances that referred to the Son's exemplary creaturely participation in the dynamic effects of these properties—and to other creatures' participation in these properties through the Son's mediation.[78] Thus Asterius, like Arius, configured the scriptural linguistic field that identifies Jesus Christ by distinguishing between the Unbegotten, on the one side, and the Only-begotten and other begotten creatures, on the other side.

ASTERIUS AS REVISER OF ARIUS

But within this essential continuity of perspective with Arius's theology, Asterius also initiated significant developments both with regard to the conception of what constitutes absolute divine primacy and with regard to an account of the primacy of Christ. As to the former, we have already noted that Asterius downplayed Arius's repetitive insistence on the title *monas*, preferring to designate absolute divinity by the attributes of eternity and unbegottenness. More significantly, Asterius attenuated Arius's radical apophaticism and his stress on the sheer otherness separating God from creation. As a significant example, while Arius seems to have shrouded the title "Unbegotten" with mystically undefinable content, Asterius had a much more transparent definition that links God and creation within the category of being while preserving the distinction between the Unbegotten and creation; the Unbegotten is "that which has not been made but always is."[79] As a further qualification of Arius's radical apophaticism, Asterius distinguishes between exclusive and nonexclusive properties of the Unbegotten.[80] Exclusive properties include unbegottenness and eternity; these are not shareable. Nonexclusive properties, such as divine wisdom, can be shared with creatures. Creation's sharing of these nonexclusive properties must again be understood in light of Asterius's more explicit distinction between the essence of the Unbegotten and his efficacious power. The Unbegotten is related to every other being, beginning with the only-begotten, only by will and not by essence.[81]

Asterius's most fateful adjustment along those lines is his retrieval of the title "Father" as an eternal identification of God. A consideration of this retrieval highlights not only Asterius's strategic role in the dynamics of the fourth-century trinitarian debates but also the systematic questions that became pressing as theologians tried to integrate their conceptual commitments with the whole *nexus* of shared Christian faith. From the singularity of the Unbegotten God, Arius had drawn the strict

78. Fr. 64, 59 (Vinzent).

79. Fr. 2 (Vinzent, *Asterius*, 82); on this point, see further Kopecek, *Neo-Arianism*, 1:29–30; Vinzent, *Asterius*, 66.

80. See Vinzent, *Asterius*, 41–44.

81. Fr. 14–16 (Vinzent). Vinzent comments: "For Asterius, it is the creative power [*schöpferische Kraft*] and not the being itself, which for him is exclusive, that can enter into relation and thus has the capacity to be non-exclusive" (Vinzent, *Asterius*, 43; my translation).

consequence that this God was not always Father, since the designation "Father" necessitates the coexistence of the Son. Asterius also applied the language of eternity and unbegottenness only to the one eternally Unbegotten God, and he was also equally committed to the proposition that the Son was a creature and posterior to the eternally Unbegotten God. And yet Asterius was clearly uncomfortable with the conclusion that God is not always Father—a conclusion that seemed jarringly discordant with the linguistic texture of Christian experience. Fourth-century Christians did not need historical-critical biblical scholarship to perceive the "Abba-consciousness" of Jesus. Then as now, a straightforward reading of the Gospels suffices to disclose that one of the primary benefits of being a disciple of Jesus is to be related to God as Father, an experience that is re-inscribed into Christian consciousness with every repetition of the Lord's Prayer. So Asterius wanted to retrieve the title "Father" as a properly radical identification of God without accepting the eternal coexistence of Father and Son. His resolution was to explain that the Unbegotten God is indeed eternally Father—not, however, because he eternally begets a Son who coexists with him, but rather because he possesses an eternal generative potency that is actuated when he wills to create the Son as the first of creatures.[82]

As we shall see, this elegant resolution of Asterius's dilemma came at a price: in conceding fatherhood as an eternal attribute of God, he left Athanasius a more promising terrain on which to do battle for the eternity of the Son than that afforded by Arius's theology.

A similar dynamic is at play with regard to the conception of the primacy of Christ. Asterius is in fundamental continuity with Arius in conceiving of that primacy as a primacy of creaturehood; Christ is the first and exemplary creature, the one who mediates between lesser creatures and the Unbegotten, the latter being otherwise inaccessible in his unmitigated transcendence. But as with his conception of what constitutes absolute divine primacy, Arius was unflinching in drawing out the strict consequences of his belief in the Son's creaturehood. If the Son is a creature, then he cannot possess comprehensive knowledge of the one God, nor indeed of himself, though he can in some way refer us to the unfathomable one who resides in a glory not fully accessible even to him. Once again, the tensions between Arius's bold pronouncements and the surface level of Christian experience cause Asterius to adjust Arius's theology. Athanasius was able to deploy a host of Johannine and other texts to reassert that an intractable feature of Christian discipleship is the assurance that Christ grants us knowledge of the Father because he himself knows the Father and is indeed the Image of the Father: the one who sees Jesus has seen the Father (John 14:9). Arius's cryptic and esoterically oracular effort to give an account of the epistemic role of the Son in relating Christian disciples to the One, as expressed in the *Thalia* through the portrait of Christ as a negative theology in person, was clearly inadequate to Asterius, as it must have been to many. Indeed, we are told by the historian Philostorgius

82. Fr. 14 (Vinzent).

that "the disciples of Lucian" disagreed with Arius on precisely this point.[83] For his part, Asterius departs decisively from Arius's language and conception in this matter. Arius had been quite uncomfortable with designating the Son as Image, preferring to designate the Son's positive role of epistemic mediation by a dialectical stress on the contrast between Son and Father. But Asterius, as we have noted, describes the Son not simply as Image but as "unchanging Image of the essence and will and power and glory" of the Father.[84] Here again we see Asterius's efforts to attune Arius's doctrine to the common discourse of Christian experience, simultaneously creating common ground with opponents of Arius and giving them openings for attack. Athanasius consistently used Image language to designate the Son, even though such language was favored also by those, like Asterius, who rejected equality of being between Father and Son. But it was typical of Athanasius to exploit common ground with his opponents, especially common ground with scriptural foundations, in order to expose what he considered to be inconsistencies between this common ground and his opponents' overall systems. In this case, he was tireless in posing the dilemma: How can the Son be "exact Image" of the Father if their very being is dissimilar? How can a creature be the "exact Image" of the Creator?

With regard to absolute divine primacy and the primacy of Christ, the relation between Arius and Asterius seems to confirm the characterization of Arius as a theological "expert" in the Origenian tradition—someone who sees himself as dispensing profound Christian wisdom to the spiritually mature even at the cost of making bold adjustments to the common discourse of Christian experience. Arius was willing to make provocative statements such as "the Son came into being from nonexistence," "God was not always Father," and "the Son does not fully know himself or the Father," in order to safeguard what he considered to be the deep structure of genuine piety, which included a proper appreciation of the superiority of the one God and Creator over the preexistent Christ, who is the supremely glorified creature and exemplary glorifier of the one God. While essentially faithful to that fundamental insight, Asterius displays a much different theological temper. He seems to consistently be preoccupied with adjusting Arius's theology so as to accommodate the ordinary patterns of Christian discourse without retracting a basic commitment to the ontological superiority of the Unbegotten over the Son. The development of this theological trajectory from Arius to Asterius and its interaction with the trajectory espousing trinitarian unity of being demonstrates that none of these theologians was simply creating a theology on his own. They were all interacting within a common narrative, a common set of Christian experiences; they deployed different features of this common narrative and experience in order to construct various "coherences" of Christian life. At the center of these various coherences was the question of how to integrate a fitting conception of absolute divine primacy with the lordship of Christ. Notwithstanding all their

---

83. *Hist. eccl.* 2.3; Williams conjectures that Arius wrote his *Thalia* partially to deal with "Lucianist" objections (*Arius*, 162–67).

84. Fr. 10 (Vinzent, *Asterius*, 86)

differences, Arius and Asterius agreed that the integration must finally be attributed to the sovereign will of the one Unbegotten. Both the existence and the lordship of Christ, going back to his preexistence as Word, Son, and Wisdom, is the effect of the will of the one Unbegotten and cannot be insinuated into the essence of the Unbegotten.

Eusebius of Caesarea

Eusebius of Caesarea (ca. 260–ca. 339), heir to Origen's Palestinian library and chosen orator for Constantine's tricennial celebration, was the most erudite bishop of his time and a prominent figure in both ecclesiastical and imperial circles. He wrote biblical commentaries, apologetic works, theological polemics, and the first large-scale history of the church. Through his teacher, Pamphilus, Eusebius became an admirer of Origen and collaborated with Pamphilus in *A Defense of Origen*. Eusebius was an early supporter of Arius, though he also departs from Arius's doctrine at key points and is generally closer to the theology of Asterius. At the Council of Nicaea, Eusebius reluctantly agreed to the *homoousios*, though he was suspicious of its modalist connotations. This suspicion seemed to be vindicated by the interpretation of Nicaea presented by Marcellus, who was Eusebius's primary polemical target. Eusebius also attended the Council of Tyre in 335, which reinstated Arius and deposed Athanasius and Marcellus.

THE FATHER-SON RELATIONSHIP

Eusebius integrates the themes of absolute divine primacy and the primacy of Christ within an elaborate schema centered on the sovereignty of the divine will. He defines absolute divine primacy clearly in his *Demonstration of the Gospel*: "Now common to all [people] is the doctrine of God, the first and eternal, alone, unbegotten and supreme cause of the universe, lord of lords and king of kings."[85] Here we see something of Eusebius's intellectual temper and his apologetic concern. For him, the fact that the doctrine is commonly held establishes its rational appeal; hence, "in regard to the first cause of all things let this be our admitted form of agreement."[86] Absolute divine primacy means primarily eternity and unqualified priority in the order of causality (first, unbegotten, supreme cause). For Eusebius, as for Arius and Asterius, the term *agen[n]ētos* is especially indicative of absolute primacy; the Son—who though preexistent is caused or begotten (*gen[n]ētos*)—is therefore excluded from this level of primacy. Clear links have been documented between this conception of absolute divine primacy and Middle Platonism, particularly Numenius's first principle, characterized as simple, indivisible, the good-in-itself that so transcends creation that he cannot properly be called Creator.[87] Indeed, Eusebius himself was keen to establish and

---

85. *Dem. ev.* 4.1.

86. *Prep. ev.* 11.14. On Eusebius's apologetic motivations, see Lyman, *Christology and Cosmology*, 108.

87. On the Middle Platonic background of Eusebius's theology, one can still profitably read Ricken's triptych of articles: Ricken, "Die Logoslehre des Eusebios von Caesarea und der Mittelplatonismus"; "Nikaia als Krisis des altchristlichen Platonismus"; and "Zur Rezeption der platonischen Ontologie

celebrate these links as evidence for the luminous universality of Christian truth. But it would be a mistake simply to dismiss Eusebius's conception of absolute divine primacy as "Platonic." What starkly differentiates his conception from Numenius and other Platonic schemes is the emphasis on divine willing.[88] It is true that, like Numenius, Eusebius tends to speak of the creative (demiurgic) function particularly in relation to the Word. However, the Word/Son himself is generated by the sovereign will of the Father: "The Son is the image of the Father by intention and deliberate choice (*kata gnōmēn kai proairesin*). For God willed (*boulētheis*) to beget a Son."[89] In this way, the chain of willing, which in Eusebius coincides with the hierarchical chain of being, begins with the highest principle, the Father himself. Other Middle Platonic schemes do not relate the supreme cause actively to everything else through the initiative of his sovereign will. At the same time, Eusebius's theology of the sovereignty of divine will should not be reduced to arbitrary voluntarism. Rather, the sovereignty and absolute efficacy of the divine willing always has the character of manifesting the goodness of the divine nature: "The fact that he wills it is the sole cause whereby all existent things come into being and continue in being. It comes of his will and he wills it because he is good by nature. For nothing else is essential by nature to a good person except to will what is good. And what he wills, he can effect."[90] Thus Eusebius's conception of absolute divine primacy encompasses a double emphasis on God as supreme and first cause and on the goodness of the divine nature as informing and motivating the intentional exercise of that causality.

Within this framework, Eusebius's conception of the primacy of Christ can be best summed up in his description of the preexistent Son as the begotten principle (*archē*) that is "first born and fellow worker of the Father's will and image of him (*pros auton apeikonismenēn*)."[91] Throughout his career, Eusebius is consistent in both affirming the Son's primacy in relation to the rest of creation and yet subordinating that relative primacy to the absolute primacy of the Unbegotten/Uncaused Father.[92] It was principally in order to defend what Eusebius considered to be this foundational tenet of Christian monotheism that the prelate originally found ground for common cause with Arius.

Yet there are some interesting lines of development in his work. In his letter to Alexander defending Arius, Eusebius cites as one of the accusations leveled against Arius and his supporters that they asserted that "the One who is begot the one who

---

bei Eusebios von Kaisareia, Areios, und Athanasios." More recently, Holger Strutwolf has interpreted Eusebius as creatively synthesizing elements from both Numenius and Plotinus (*Die Trinitätstheologie und Christologie des Euseb von Caesarea*).

88. As noted by Lyman: "Eusebius thus combines the strongest contemporary definitions of transcendence and voluntarism to assert God's absolute creative power" (*Christology and Cosmology*, 96).

89. *Dem. ev.* 4.3.

90. *Dem. ev.* 4.1.

91. *Prep. ev.* 7.15. In *Eccl. theol.* 2.7, Jesus's saying, "I have come . . . not to do my own will, but the will of him who sent me" (John 6:38), is applied to the preexistent Christ.

92. For traces of this subordination persisting in his latest work, see *Eccl. theol.* 1.20; 2.7.

was not"; Eusebius's rejoinder is: "I am amazed that anyone can say otherwise."[93] Such amazement would be consistent with his earlier assertion in the *Demonstration of the Gospel* (probably written before the outbreak of the controversy) that the Father "precedes the Son and has preceded him in existence, inasmuch as He alone is unbegotten."[94] Yet, by his last work, the *Ecclesiastical Theology* (written shortly before his death in 339), Eusebius can speak easily of the "coexistence always and at all times" of the Father and Son[95] and has become emphatic that it is incorrect to say that the Son is from nothing; at this point, talk of the "preexistence" of the Father has dropped out. There is, however, an underlying consistency beneath what is perhaps only a development of emphasis. In *Ecclesiastical Theology*, Eusebius is attacking the doctrine of Marcellus, which he interprets to be saying that the Word is the active rationality of the Father, something like an accident within the divine substance rather than a subsistence.[96] In this context, affirming the "coexistence" of the Son with the Father is meant to indicate primarily the *real existence* and hypostatic subsistence of the Son alongside the Father; thus the recurring refrain descriptive of the Son in this work: "living and subsisting."[97] Talk of the "preexistence" of the Father, in the ambience of anti-Marcellan polemic, would be too redolent of Marcellus's own conception, in which the Son is originally an "inner word" within the Father that is extrapolated and achieves subsistence only with a view to the divine act of creation.[98] But even in this late work, Eusebius is careful to steer clear of designating the coexistence of Father and Son as *eternal*. In opposing the doctrine of Marcellus of Ancyra, it still seems self-evident to him that eternity cannot be predicated of the Son. To make the Son co-eternal with the Father is to make him co-unbegotten and thus to posit two gods; he rebukes Marcellus for speaking of the Son as "eternal" (*aïdios*), which Eusebius himself qualifies, "that is, unbegotten."[99]

But Eusebius's consistent insistence on the secondary status of the Son and his repudiation of Origen's doctrine of eternal generation are qualified by one puzzling earlier text, from the *Demonstration*, that seems to concede eternal generation:

> The scope of the theology we are considering far transcends all illustrations and is not concerned with anything physical, but imagines with the acutest thought a begotten Son, not at one time non-existent and existent at another afterwards, but existent before endless ages (*pro chronōn aiōniōn*) and pre-existent and always with the Father as his Son and yet not unbegotten but begotten from the unbegotten Father, being the only-begotten, the Word, and God of God, who teaches that he was not cast forth from the being of the Father by separation or scission or division but unspeakably and, as far as

93. *Letter of Eusbeius of Caesarea to Alexander of Alexandria*, Urk. 7; 15.2–3.
94. *Dem. ev.* 4.3; cf. *Dem. ev.* 5.1.
95. E.g., *Eccl. theol.* 2.14.14–15: "*synōn kai symparōn autō aei kai pantote*"; cf. *Eccl. theol.* 3.3.56; 3.4.6.
96. *Eccl. theol.* 2.14.
97. *Eccl. theol.* 1.16; 1.20; 2.6; 2.14; 2.16; 2.17; 2.24; 3.1; 3.3.
98. See below, 197.
99. "*Aidion, tout' estin agenēton*" (*Eccl. theol.* 2.3.3; 2.12.2; cf. *Letter to Euphration*, Urk. 3.4–6).

we are concerned, unthinkably brought into being from all time, or rather before all times, by the Father's transcendent and inconceivable will and power.[100]

If we wish to make Eusebius's theology entirely consistent, we are compelled to ask how exactly the relation between Father and Son is to be conceived if eternal generation, generation in time, and origination from nothing are all, at various points, excluded. First, with regard to Eusebius's method and style as a doctrinal theologian, it has to be said that he is generally less concerned with conceptual coherence than with appropriate boundaries. In this case, one boundary is the absolute divine primacy of the Unbegotten, which excludes the eternal generation of the Son. Another is the primacy of Christ, which excludes the Son's creation from nothing. Eusebius is clear on the necessity of these two negations, less clear on how the space between is coherent. More positively, Eusebius insists on a certain apophaticism with regard to the generation of the Son that is demarcated by contrasting it with the relation between God and creation. As Simonetti notes, whereas Arius tends to interpret "generation" language through the lens of creation language (wherein "creation" means "from nothing"), Eusebius considers the meaning of "generation" language as applied to the Son to be ultimately ineffable but distinct from "creation" language.[101] Indeed, this apophaticism tends to become starker in the latter stages of Eusebius's career. In the *Ecclesiastical Theology*, he glosses John 3:36 ("whoever believes in the Son has eternal life") by pointing out that the Lord does not promise eternal life to those who know how he is begotten!

Second, with regard to the passage quoted above where Eusebius explicitly denies that "the Son was at one time non-existent and existent at another time afterwards," Rowan Williams's assessment seems correct: "This passage is indeed puzzling; but what it might mean is simply that there is no point *within the history of the universe* at which the Son does not exist alongside the Father."[102] Eusebius's formulation seems carefully designed to make the Son prior to all *time* and it is consistent with contemporaneous philosophical discourse on the notion of timeless derivation.[103] It is also consistent, in some measure, with the language of Arius, who despite asserting that the Son "did not exist prior to his begetting" nevertheless is similarly able to speak of the Son's generating the Father "before endless ages" (*pro chronōn aiōniōn*) and who also similarly identifies eternality with unbegottenness.[104]

Third, a rather cryptic passage where Eusebius denies that any creature came to be from nothing might give some indication of how he can deny the eternity of the Son and yet insist that he did not come to be from nothing. The context of this denial shows that its point is not really to negate that creatures came from nothing, much

---

100. *Dem. ev.* 4.3 (ET: Ferrar, *Proof*, 168, altered).
101. Cf. *Eccl. theol.* 1.9.10; see Simonetti, *La crisi*, 62–63.
102. Williams, *Arius*, 172 (original italics).
103. See Williams, *Arius*, 181–88; Meijering, "ΗΝ ΠΟΤΕ ΟΤΕ ΟΥΚ ΗΝ Ο ΥΙΟΣ."
104. "The Statement of Faith of Arius and His Colleagues to Alexander of Alexandria," Urk. 6; Athanasius, *Syn.* 16.

less to affirm that they came to be from the divine essence, but rather to insist that the proper terms for construing the relation between God and everything else are not "divine substance" and "nothing" but rather "divine power" and "will":

> And the fact that he wills it is the sole cause of the coming into being and continuing in being of all that exists. . . . What he wills, he has the power to effect. Therefore, having both the will and the power, he has ordained for himself, without hindrance or obstacle, everything beautiful and useful both in the visible and invisible world, making his own will and power as it were a kind of material ground of the genesis and constitution of the universe. So it is no longer appropriate to say that anything that exists must have come from non-being, for what comes from non-being would not be anything. For how could non-being cause something else to be? Everything that has ever existed or now exists derives its being from the One, the only existent and pre-existent Being, who said, "I am the one who is." As the only and everlasting being, he is himself the cause of existence to all those to whom he has granted being from himself by his will and power and gives to all things, richly and ungrudgingly from himself, their being as well as their powers and forms.[105]

Thus, in the last analysis, when Eusebius denies both that the Son's generation took place in time and that it was co-eternal with the existence of the Unbegotten, what he gains is not clarity with respect to the question of the status of the Son's generation in relation to time and eternity. Rather, he clarifies that the Son's generation is not posterior to any temporal "once," neither is it inseparably and mutually related to the Father's being but rather is a product of his "will and power."

Positively, Eusebius's account of the primacy of the preexistent Christ is governed by the scriptural designation of the Son as Image. This motif has a double meaning for Eusebius. The Son is called only-begotten God and Image "because of his primary likeness and also for the reason that he was appointed by the Father as his good minister . . . in order that the universe might be guided by him."[106] The first meaning is brought out by Eusebius's treatment of an aligned biblical motif that designates the relation between Father and Son as radiance emanating from light. This motif derives from the biblical characterization of God as light and of Christ as the "radiance" and expression of God's subsistence (*hypostasis*; Heb. 1:3). We shall see that, for Athanasius, this motif will become a privileged way of talking about the mutuality of being between Father and Son. A light without radiance is not merely a deficient light, but not a light at all; it belongs to the very nature of light to be radiant, and its luminous emanation is thus integral to its very being. By contrast, Eusebius's treatment of this element explicitly repudiates the element of necessary and inseparable coexistence as inapplicable in the case of the divine nature, substituting for it his characteristic emphasis on the sovereignty of the Father's will. Eusebius exploits the scriptural ambivalence between the more ontological description of Christ as image

---

105. *Dem. ev.* 4.1 (ET: Ferrar, *Proof*, 164, altered).
106. *Dem. ev.* 4.2; cf. *Eccl. theol.* 1.8.1.

of God's subsistence (*hypostasis*) in Hebrews and the description of Wisdom as mirror of divine activity (*energeia*) in Wisdom 7:26. Clearly the latter characterization takes precedence for Eusebius. The passage in which Eusebius discusses the relation between Father and Son as light and radiance runs as follows:

> And as the Father is one, it follows that there must be one Son and not many sons, and that there can be only one perfect God begotten of God and not several. . . . Even so, light being of one essence, we are absolutely obliged to regard the perfect thing that is begotten of light to be one also. For what other thing would it be possible to conceive of as begotten of light except only the ray which proceeds from it and fills and enlightens all things? . . . And analogously to this there can be nothing like the Supreme Father who is unspeakable light nor a true copy of him except only the one whom we are able to call the Son. For he is the radiance of the eternal light and the unblurred mirror of the activity of God, and the image of his goodness (Wis 7:26). Thus it was said, "Who being the radiance of his glory and the express image of his person (*hypostasis*)."
>
> But there is the exception that in the realm of sense, the radiance is inseparable from the light, while the Son exists in himself in his own essence apart from the Father. And the ray has its range of activity only from the light, whereas the Son is something different from a channel of energy, having his being in himself. Moreover, the ray is coexistent with light and somehow mutually related to it (for there could be no light without a ray); they exist together and simultaneously. But the Father precedes the Son and has preceded him in existence, inasmuch as he alone is unbegotten. The One, perfect in himself and first in order as Father and the cause of the Son's existence, receives nothing towards the completeness of his existence from the Son; the other, as Son begotten of him that caused his being, came second to him, whose Son he is, receiving from the Father both his being and the character of his being. Yet again, the ray does not shine forth from the light by its deliberate choice (*kata proairesin*), but because of something which is an inseparable accident of its essence. But the Son is the image of the Father by intention and deliberate choice (*kata gnōmēn kai proairesin*). For God willed (*boulētheis*) to beget a Son and established a second light, made to be in all things like himself.[107]

This important passage signals some of the distinctive emphases of Eusebius's theology. Like Asterius, and unlike both Arius and the general pattern of Middle Platonism, Eusebius does not contrast the Son to the Father as the refraction of primal unity into multiplicity.[108] Rather, the Son images the Father's oneness in a way that is nevertheless still external to that oneness and in no way qualifies it. The image of light and radiance is thus used not so much to designate the essential oneness *between* Father and Son but rather that they are each "one," while the relation between them is consistently described by reference to the categories of will, intention, and deliberate choice (*boulē, gnōmē, proairesis*). At the same time, Eusebius always stresses the derived character of the Son's existence. Scriptural passages that refer to the "receiving" of Christ are applied globally to the being of the preexistent Son. The biblical

---

107. *Dem. ev.* 4.3 (ET: Ferrar, *Proof*, 166–67, altered).
108. As noted by Lyman, *Christology and Cosmology*, 111.

motif of the "receiving" of Christ links together the two aspects of the Son as Image. The Son receives his likeness to the Father, coincident with his very being, in order to mediate the Father's sovereign will, and thus "he is appointed by the Father as his good minister."[109] As with Arius and Asterius, the *pro nobis* is thereby located at the very origin of the Son's being and characterizes his being wholly and not merely in the incarnation. In a manner especially close to Asterius, the mediatorial being and function of the Son consist in the mitigation of the Unbegotten's transcendence.[110] In this way, the very being of the Son is an expression of the Father's goodness and the benevolence of his intentions toward creation.

Roots and Implications of Eusebian Trinitarianism

Once again, we should note that this mediatorial scheme, traditionally dismissed as "cosmological," is in fact also radically soteriological, a way of conceiving the Son as radically "God for us." Because the Father is "all good," he does not wish creation to be deprived of "the greatest good" of communion with him. However, communion with "the Father's unbegotten and incomprehensible essence" can only be accessed through "the mediated supply" provided by the "secondary being" of the Son. As the first and highest creature, he possesses "the most certain and intimate association with the Father and equally with him rejoiced in that which is unspeakable," but it is precisely his inferiority to the Father that enables him to "descend with all gentleness and conform himself in such ways as were possible to those who were far distant from his own height and because of their weakness crave amelioration and aid from a secondary being."[111] The primacy of the Son thus foundationally consists in his mitigated imaging of the transcendent Unbegotten. This descent begins with the Son's mediating the will of the Father in the act of creation and achieves its climax in the act of the Son's incarnation and his human salvific work. The fact that Eusebius locates the mediating function of the Son in his divine being can perhaps shed some light on his denial of a human soul of Christ.[112] In an Origenian framework, the human soul mediates between the *Logos* and the flesh. But in Eusebius, the mediation of divine transcendence is located in the very being of the *Logos*. In the incarnation, the "mediated supply" of the divinity of the *Logos* becomes manifest in human flesh; to further mediate this already "mediated supply" would threaten to make Jesus Christ into a "mere man."[113]

Although Eusebius acknowledges the salvific value of Christ's death as "a sacrifice for sins," his main soteriological theme is the incarnate Son's role as teacher, providing "true teaching of the knowledge of the Father and of holiness."[114] Indeed,

109. *Dem. ev.* 4.2; cf. *Eccl. theol.* 1.20.
110. See *Eccl. theol.* 1.13; 2.17; cf. Asterius, Fr. 26 (Vinzent).
111. *Dem. ev.* 4.6 (ET: Ferrar, *Proof of the Gospel*, 173–74, altered).
112. Though Hanson considers Eusebius "ambiguous" on this issue (*Search*, 54), the presence of a human soul in Christ is clearly rejected in *Eccl. theol.* 1.20.
113. *Eccl. theol.* 1.20.
114. *Dem. ev.* 4.10.

even the death of Christ itself is presented as a teaching about his lordship over sin and death.[115] Eusebius makes use of all the traditional soteriological motifs, including deification, but they are all conditioned by the overarching framework of benevolent rule and enlightened obedience, in which Jesus Christ is the teacher and exemplar of both divine rule and human obedience. As Rebecca Lyman rightly points out, this emphasis is not "an external or merely moral instruction, but rather constitutes access to transforming power to heal both body and soul."[116] The key to Eusebius's soteriology, which is consistent with his voluntarist metaphysics, is that it is consistently framed within the interactivity of divine and human willing. Such interactivity does not preclude ontological transformation but causes it. As salvific teacher, Christ manifests and enacts the benevolent will of the Father as an appeal to the human will; positively answering that appeal is what gives humanity access to the transformative divine power. Moreover, an integral appreciation of the theme of Christ as teacher in Eusebius would have to take account of the fact that the exemplarity of Christ is not only moral but also doxological. The preexistent Christ is minister to the Father, not only as a subordinate assistant, but also as worshiper of the Father's glory; the earthly ministry of Jesus Christ is an expression of his divine worship of his "God and Father."[117]

The concrete christocentrism of Eusebius's theology is evident in a personal creedal confession, which he presents in his major anti-Marcellan work, *Ecclesiastical Theology*. Here Eusebius says that there are three objects of Christian confession: Jesus Christ, "from the seed of David and the holy Virgin"; the preexistent Son who dwells in him; and "God his Father."[118] Given the specific polemical context, it is perhaps not fair to judge this statement as if it were meant to be a comprehensive account of the faith and to evaluate its omissions accordingly. Nevertheless, it is indicative of two features shared widely by the theology of the time. First, it uncovers how the framework of theological debate was centrally determined by the question of the identity of the concrete person, Jesus Christ. Even though that question involved a host of related issues—such as how to construe the relation between the divinity of the Father and that of the Son, and how creation as a whole is related to God—these questions are only relevant and intelligible in light of the central question of the identity of Jesus Christ. Second, at this stage of theological discussion, prior to the 360s, the conversation did not yet include a focused discussion on the identity of the Holy Spirit. Up to that point, there is a gap between the explicit thematic formulation of theological questions relating to the identity of Jesus Christ, which often leaves the Spirit out of account, and the grammar of Christian experience, which invokes Father, Son, and Holy Spirit as "the Trinity." Eusebius testifies to the latter aspect when he speaks comfortably of "the holy and blessed Trinity of Father and Son and Holy Spirit"[119]

115. *Dem. ev.* 4.12.
116. *Christology and Cosmology*, 122.
117. *Prep. ev.* 7.16; *Hist. eccl.* 10.4.68–70; *Eccl. theol.* 2.7.
118. *Eccl. theol.* 1.6.
119. *Prep. ev.* 11.20; 13.13; *Eccl. theol.* 1.6.1–2; *Marc.* 1.1.10.

and when he differentiates the Spirit from the angels: "But none of them can be equaled to the Spirit who is the Paraclete. Therefore, only this Spirit is numbered in the holy and thrice-blessed Trinity."[120] On the level of theological conceptualization, however, Eusebius's relative neglect of the Holy Spirit is such that Hanson can say that "it is only by courtesy that Eusebius can be described as having a doctrine of the Trinity."[121] Eusebius conceives of the Spirit as the next level down in the chain of being and willing that descends from the Father and the Son. While he is ambiguous on the neuralgic question of the creaturehood of the Son, he is clear that the Spirit is a creature, the first to come into existence through the agency of the Son.[122] The Spirit is a self-subsistent being who indwells those who are sanctified and bestows on them the gifts of holiness.[123] In one passage, Eusebius says that the Spirit is neither God nor Son.[124] However, such a statement is more difficult to interpret than at first appears. This is so not only because the notion of divinity is still fairly elastic at this point, such that many could speak of the Son as divine but not "true God," but also because Eusebius in particular is preoccupied with scriptural titles. Eusebius's presentation of the Spirit follows a scriptural literalism: the Spirit is not scripturally identified as either God or Son. If "all things came to be through the Son," then the Spirit is the first of the creatures who came into existence through the Son; the Spirit sanctifies the faithful and is one of the "holy Trinity."

EUSEBIUS'S LEGACY: AMBIGUITY AND POLITICAL THEOLOGY

With a view toward tracing the emergent systematic logic of trinitarian doctrine through the century, we can note two other significant aspects of Eusebius's theology. First, with regard to his theological style, we have already noted Eusebius's high tolerance for ambiguity and lack of concern with logical contradiction. This aspect of Eusebius's theological character is in stark contrast to the great Alexandrian whom he admired, Origen. Origen's theology was driven by the exigency of coherence. His much-noted speculative impulse was not typically the fruit merely of ecstatic mystical insight but rather of the necessity for a spiritual interpretation that saw beyond the fragmentariness of the letter of Scripture toward a vision of the interconnected whole. A paradigmatic example is one we have already mentioned: if God is both eternal and almighty, then there must be always a creation over which he is almighty; if the Son is God's Power, then the Father is always almighty over creation through the Son.[125] Eusebius exhibits a far different theological temper. As remarked earlier, Eusebius is less concerned with internal coherence than with staking the appropriate boundaries of an "ecclesiastical theology" in a manner that does not violate a literal reading of Scripture. The contrast I am drawing attention to is not between allegorical

---

120. *Eccl. theol.* 3.5.21.
121. Hanson, *Search*, 56.
122. *Eccl. theol.* 3.6.3.
123. *Eccl. theol.* 3.6.5.
124. *Eccl. theol.* 3.6.3.
125. *Princ.* 1.2.9–10.

and literal readings of Scripture—Eusebius has no trouble with allegory *per se*—but between a theological style that is driven by the impulse to coherence and one that is motivated primarily by setting limits without too much concern for the interconnection between these limits (as seen in his failure, discussed above, to clarify how the Son can be both not eternal and not "from nothing").[126]

In the subsequent course of the fourth-century development of trinitarian doctrine, the impulse to reach consensus on such questions by way of studied ambiguity would reassert itself repeatedly. The climax of this trajectory was the prohibition of the language of being at the Council of Sirmium of 357. Such a prohibition was essentially anti-systematic and, in a certain sense, anti-theological; it attempted to legislate a return to the free play of scriptural language without the imposition of the hermeneutical control of doctrine. Of course, as often happens in such cases, there was a doctrinal agenda behind this legislation of ambiguity. Nevertheless, in rejecting all such efforts to reassert a scripturally sanctioned ambiguity, the Council of Constantinople set trinitarian doctrine within a certain construal of the relation between faith and reason. Trinitarian doctrine indeed transcended the reach of reason but could not neglect logical coherence.

A second significant feature of Eusebius's theology of divine will is his derivation of a political theology from his theological metaphysics. We should not leap to the conclusion that a trinitarian theology based on ontological subordinationism, with Father and Son relating within a hierarchy of will and obedience, will necessarily lead to a monarchical political theology. But in Eusebius this is exactly what happens.[127] Eusebius's account of the relation between Father and Son extends seamlessly into a comprehensive vision of reality in which the chain of being coincides at every level with a chain of willing, of command and obedience. The metaphysical, cosmic, and worldly spheres can all be encompassed by the conception of good government. Good government begins with the sovereign willing of the Unbegotten, which manifests the goodness of his nature. The primordial act of this willing occurs when the Father brings forth the Son and "cast[s] in him of the seeds of the constitution and government of the universe."[128] As the Son is vice-regent of the Unbegotten Father, so is the emperor the vice-regent of the Word. Reality is pervasively a monarchy, ordered by a chain of benevolent command and freely embraced obedience. The rupture of this order by sin has been repaired by the incarnate Word, and the emperor presides over the continuance of this redeemed order. Earthly government now once again images the orderly hierarchical stream of divine government:

126. This characterization of the contrast between Eusebius and Origen has affinities with Lienhard's comparison of Eusebius's ecclesial and practical style to Origen's more speculative and mystical approach (*Contra Marcellum*, 128).

127. In this regard, the classic account of the connection between trinitarian and political theology, Erik Peterson's *Der Monotheismus als politisches Problem*, is still worth reading. In more recent theology, the issue has been taken up especially by Jürgen Moltmann; see, for example, his *Trinity and the Kingdom*, 192–200.

128. *Dem. ev.* 4.5.

And so the Almighty Sovereign himself grants an increase of both years and children to our most pious emperor, and renders his sway over the nations of the world still fresh and flourishing, as if it were even now springing up in its earliest vigor. . . . Invested as he is with a semblance of heavenly sovereignty, he directs his gaze above and structures his earthly government according to the pattern of that divine original, feeling strength in its conformity to the monarchy of God. And this conformity is granted by the universal Sovereign to humanity alone among all the creatures of this earth, for he who alone is the author of sovereign power decrees that all should be subject to the rule of one. Certainly, monarchy far transcends every other constitution and form of government, for that democratic equality of power, which is its opposite, is rather more aptly described as anarchy and disorder. Hence, there is one God, and not two or three or more; for to assert a plurality of gods is plainly to deny the being of God at all. There is one Sovereign and his Word and royal law are one, a law not expressed in syllables and words . . . but the living and subsisting Word, who himself is God and who administers his Father's kingdom on behalf of all who are after him and subject to his power. His attendants are the heavenly hosts; the myriads of God's angelic ministers; the super-terrestrial armies of unnumbered multitude; and those unseen spirits within heaven itself whose agency is employed in regulating the order of this world. Ruler and chief of all these is the royal Word, acting as Regent of the Supreme Sovereign. . . . And the Father, having constituted him the living Word and Law and Wisdom, the fullness of all blessing, has presented this best and greatest gift to all who are the subjects of his sovereignty. . . . For he only is wise who is the only God; he only is essentially good; his only is mighty power, the Parent of Justice, the Father of reason and wisdom, the fountain of light and life, the dispenser of truth and virtue, in a word, the author of empire itself and of all dominion and power.[129]

Eunomius of Cyzicus

Eunomius was born in rural Cappadocia and studied rhetoric and philosophy in Antioch, Constantinople, and Alexandria. He was a student and secretary of Aetius, whose *Syntagmation* presents in terse syllogisms the two main principles of Eunomius's theology: that the title *agen[n]ētos* directly describes the divine essence and that, consequently, the different title which describes the Son, begotten (*gen[n]ētos*), indicates a different essence. Aetius and Eunomius are often identified, with reference to the doctrine of "difference in essence," as "heterousians." (Textbooks often refer to them also as "neo-Arians" or "anomoians," for reasons that will become clear below.) Although they shared substantially the same beliefs, the difference in style between Aetius's *Syntagmation* and the extant writings of Eunomius help explain why the latter's version of their common beliefs proved more popular, and why heterousian doctrine is more typically described as "Eunomian" rather than "Aetian." Aetius's short treatise is a collection of highly compressed statements of logical conundrums raised by assertions that the Father and the Son are the same or similar in essence. The accusation leveled against the heterousians that they were mere logic-choppers or

---

129. *Coet. sanct.* 3.3–8 (ET: NPNF² 1:584–85, altered).

rationalist "technologues" sticks much easier to the theological style of Aetius than it does to Eunomius. While also concerned with logical consistency and advancing many of the same kinds of arguments as Aetius, Eunomius was able to articulate his doctrine in a more traditional expository and creedal framework that drew upon scriptural references. Though exiled by Constantius in 358, along with Aetius, Eunomius was vindicated by the Council of Constantinople of 360. Many participants at this council were hostile to language affirming the sameness or likeness of essence between the Father and the Son. Their preferred description of the Son, as "like according to the Scriptures," relied on scriptural exegesis that indicated the ontological inferiority of the Son to the Father, even while finding ways to understand the biblical motif that the Son was nevertheless "like" (*homoios*) the Father. Eunomius, originally under suspicion for asserting that the Son was "unlike" the Father, explained in the apology that he penned at the eve of this council that he affirmed the Son's likeness to the Father "according to the Scriptures" but that this likeness should not be understood as a likeness of essence. It seems that Eunomius, though vindicated at the Council of Constantinople of 360, continued to be plagued by accusations of heresy by some of his own clergy and eventually left Cyzicus and returned to Cappadocia.[130] Aetius and Eunomius attempted to solidify their ecclesial position by appointing their own bishops in various parts of the Eastern empire, but the accession of the emperor Theodosius proved to be fatal to their movement. Theodosius banished Eunomius and prohibited the "heterousians" from public assembly for worship. Eunomius himself was condemned at the Council of Constantinople of 381, and it was further legislated that "heterousians," who practiced a single-immersion baptism, must be re-baptized if they wished to be admitted into the orthodox church. Eunomius died around 396.[131]

Like or Unlike the Father?

As we have seen, Aetius and Eunomius quickly achieved a notoriety fueled by allegations that they described the Son as "unlike" (*anomoios*) the Father. In response to these charges, they protested that they did not designate the Son as wholly unlike the Father but only unlike with respect to essence. Their qualification of the language of likeness is distinctive within the trajectory of trinitarian theologies of will. It is often pointed out that Eunomius differs markedly from Arius on the question of knowledge of God because Arius spoke of the one God as ineffable while Eunomius held that the term "Unbegotten" conveys true knowledge of the divine essence. As we shall see, even on this point, there is perhaps less substantial difference than at first appears. But with regard to what kind of likeness obtains between Father and Son, Aetius and Eunomius are better seen as a return to the theology of Arius himself.[132] Athanasius reports Arius as saying, in the *Thalia*, that the Son is "entirely different

---

130. *Hist. eccl.* 4.26.5–6; see Hanson, *Search*, 613–14.

131. For a very insightful intellectual biography of Eunomius, see further Vaggione, *Eunomius of Cyzicus*.

132. See Kopecek, *Neo-Arianism*, 1:3.

from and unlike (*anomoios*) the Father's substance."[133] Even if this phrase is not an exact quotation, it is entirely consistent with Arius's pattern of contrasting Father and Son throughout the *Thalia* and his reluctance to speak of the Son as Image of the Father. As we have seen in Asterius and in Eusebius of Caesarea, both these features of Arius's theology were deemphasized by subsequent accounts within the trajectory of trinitarian theologies of will. Both Asterius and Eusebius could comfortably designate the Son as Image of the Father, even as Image of the Father's essence. For Eusebius, the title "Image" was the primary characterization of the Son.

Eusebius's theology became foundational to the homoian doctrinal stream described in chapter 1. Homoians continued to defer to the scriptural patterns of Christian discourse (i.e., the designation of the Son as Image of the Father) by using the language of "likeness" to designate the Son's relation to the Father. But, even if they sometimes connected this likeness with "substance" language, as Eusebius himself, it was clear that these theologians did not envision any sharing of substance between Father and Son, and they tended to accent much more prominently the notion that the likeness between Father and Son referred to the realm of will and activity rather than essence. But, of course, those theologians who saw the unity of Father and Son as integral to divine being itself also made prominent use of the language of likeness. Inasmuch as this scriptural motif constituted common ground between the two trajectories, it tended to favor the maximal ascription of likeness endorsed by those who referred that likeness to the realm of being itself. This fact was polemically exploited in an argument that we see frequently in Athanasius and others: how can the Son be truly like the Father if he is not really, in reality and being, like the Father? It was typical of Aetius's and Eunomius's theological temperament to seek to overcome such ambiguity and to assert clearly the respective ways in which the Son was both like and unlike the Father. In doing so, they were recognizing that the kind of qualification to Arius's theology represented by Asterius and Eusebius was destabilizing the key fundamental principle of the ontological difference between Father and Son.

Logic and Piety

The term that Eunomius himself tended to use in his insistence on such clarity of distinctions is "exactitude" (*akribeia*). His opponents were ruthless in their exploitation of this self-designation, depicting him as a "technologue" who was vulgarizing the divine mystery by petty and arrogant reasoning. They opposed Eunomius's self-styled *akribeia* with an appeal to *eusebeia*, which can be translated as "piety" or "devotion."[134] In fact, Eunomius *was* an acute dialectician, probably better versed in contemporary philosophical discussions than his Cappadocian opponents and not shy of posing logical

133. *C. Ar.* 1.6.
134. Maurice Wiles challenges this caricature in his "Eunomius: Hair-Splitting Dialectician or Defender of the Accessibility of Salvation?" As elaborated above, my own assessment of Eunomius's approach would replace the "or" in that title with "and."

conundrums in the style of his teacher, Aetius.[135] Moreover, a certain claim to rational precision and dialectical prowess seems to have permeated the Aetian-Eunomian movement as a whole. The evidence of this ethos ranges from the ridiculous to the sublime. In the work of the Eunomian historian Philostorgius, we find stories of how Aetius's and Eunomius's prowess in debate caused the physical death of their opponents—a Manichaean died after debating with Aetius, and Basil of Caesarea apparently died of a heart attack after reading Eunomius's *Apology*.[136] On the sublime side, we find in the *Apostolic Constitutions*, which shows traces of emanating from Eunomian circles, repeated liturgical invocations for divine "knowledge."[137] In the latter vein, Eunomius's *akribeia* is a striving for precise and careful reasoning within a matrix of faith governed by creed and canon. Such care in reasoning is not hubris but a proper appropriation of the objectively revealed structure of Christian piety. Inasmuch as this structure is trinitarian in its grammar, theological *akribeia* is first and foremost a matter of making the appropriate trinitarian distinctions: "Let us turn to that very profession of faith by which those who wish to do so may acquire an easy and convenient knowledge of our opinion. . . . After first setting out as a kind of rule (*kanōn*) and standard of knowledge that pious (*eusebē*) and governing tradition which has come down from the fathers, they should agree to use that as the exact criterion (*akribei kritēriō*) by which to judge what is said."[138] Eunomius then cites a trinitarian profession of faith in the Father, "from whom are all things," and the Son, "through whom are all things," and the Spirit, "in whom . . . is given every grace."[139] The different prepositions are clearly meant to preview the exposition of the essential dissimilarity between Father, Son, and Spirit. For our immediate purposes, however, the fundamental point is that far from announcing the autonomy of reason, *akribeia* designates the accurate construal of revealed Christian faith as received "from the fathers." It is concerned with how "the honor due to God" should be appropriately rendered in view of the differentiations between Father, Son, and Holy Spirit. Ultimately, then, the motivation is doxological.

The Trinity according to Eunomius

Eunomius's *Apology* is structured according to this pattern of trinitarian *akribeia*, setting out the appropriate way to render proper honor to the Unbegotten God, to Jesus as Lord, and to the Holy Spirit. The exactitude of piety requires giving due honor in the first place to the Unbegotten God. Such honor is oriented precisely to

135. On Eunomius's knowledge of contemporary Neoplatonic debate as considerably greater than that of the Cappadocians, see Mortley, *From Word to Silence*, esp. 135, 137.

136. *Hist. eccl.* 3.15; 8.12.

137. Kopecek, "Neo-Arian Religion." Kopecek notes that "the Neo-Arians tended to downplay affective worship in favor of self-consciously intellectual worship, a worship of intellectual assent to God's revelation of his essence and of his activity in the world. . . . One of the most important intended results of the eucharistic mystery is knowledge" (172–73).

138. *Apol.* 5. I have slightly altered the translation of Vaggione, *Eunomius*, 37, 39, e.g., translating *gnōmona* as "standard of knowledge" rather than "norm" in order to maintain the resonance of the "*gnōsis*" root.

139. *Apol.* 5.

being-unbegotten as the determining characteristic of supreme divinity. Eunomius seems to be well acquainted with strands of contemporary Neoplatonic theology, which distinguished between grammatically negative descriptions of the highest principle and privations.[140] A privation is the lack of a prior positive reality, whereas naming the highest principle by negative language does not signify the privation of a prior positive reality but rather positively signifies a reality that is itself absolutely prior and hence utterly incomparable.[141] Eunomius's theology of divine naming further draws upon an ongoing philosophical debate, extending back to Plato's *Cratylus*, as to whether names are given by nature or constructed by human convention. Eunomius firmly insists that the divine name *agen[n]ētos* ("Unbegotten") is given by God directly, inscribed in human nature and indicated by revelation, and enables direct perception of the absolute priority and self-existence of the true God: "According to both innate knowledge and the teaching of the fathers, we have confessed one God who does not come into being by another nor by himself."[142] The absoluteness of unbegottenness, for Eunomius, thus strictly precludes any notion of derivation; positing such derivation within the divine essence violates both reason and the honor due to God. Radical ontological derivation, by which a being exists through the agency of another, is the definition of creaturehood. The positive reality that is prior to all such derivation is signified by the title "Unbegotten," so identifying the divine essence as unbegotten is the first and highest way to honor God:

> When we say "Unbegotten," then we do not imagine that we ought to honor God only in name, in conformity with human invention; rather, in conformity with reality, we ought to repay him the debt which above all others is most due God: the acknowledgment that he is what he is. . . . He is not such, however, by way of privation; for if privatives are privatives with respect to the inherent properties of something, then they are secondary to these positive properties. But birth has never been an inherent property of God! He was not first begotten and then deprived of that quality so as to become unbegotten! Indeed, to say that God has been deprived of anything at all is impious in the extreme as being destructive of the true notion of God and his perfection. . . . So, then . . . the "Unbegotten" is based neither on invention nor on privation and is not applied to a part of him only (for he is without parts), and does not exist within him as something separate (for he is simple and uncompounded), and is not something different alongside him (for he is one and only he is unbegotten), then the Unbegotten must be unbegotten essence.[143]

I have suggested at various points that the significance of the title "Unbegotten" was bound up with the project of sustaining the Christian distinction between God

140. See Mortley, *From Word to Silence*, 2:137.

141. Eunomius "exploits the Aristotelian/Neoplatonist logic of privation in order to emphasize that privation implies the ontological priority of the state of which the privation is being predicated" (ibid., 2:139).

142. *Apol.* 7.

143. *Apol.* 8 (Vaggione, 41, 43).

and the world over against the Greek philosophical tendency to make them coordinate. Never one to let his reasoning remain implicit, Eunomius formulates this logic explicitly. To insist on unbegottenness as the essential descriptor of the highest God is to assert God's absolute priority with respect to the processes of causality. If this priority is not strictly maintained, and if the products of God's causal activity are conceived as implicating the divine essence itself, then the created world can also be conceived as implicating the divine essence. That, says Eunomius, would take us right back to the Greeks, "the pagans":

> If we purify our notions of these matters with exactitude (*akribōs*), we will understand that God's mode of activity is not human but effortless and divine. We must not think that the [divine] activity is some kind of motion or division of his essence. This is in fact what those who have been led astray by pagan sophistries do have to suppose because they have united the activity to the essence and therefore present the world as coterminous with God.[144]

As this quotation makes clear, Eunomius's insistence on the positive incomparability of the Unbegotten with respect to creation also entails a radical differentiation between divine being and divine willing.[145] The being of the Unbegotten is absolutely prior and impervious to any process of causality, whereas divine willing is an activity in the order of causality and the term of such activity is always external and posterior to the divine essence. Moreover, Eunomius insists that divine willing, even considered from the perspective of divine agency, can never be eternal. If the divine agency were eternal, so would be the term of the activity of that agency. The logical end of such a chain of reasoning, as we have seen, would make the world coordinate with God (back to Origen!). It is crucial to see that, for Eunomius, the Unbegotten is not so much first cause or prime mover as utterly and self-sufficiently beyond all processes of causality, even with respect to the active agency of causality. God-acting-as-cause is, as it were, a secondary, temporary, and separable realm from God-as-Unbegotten; the latter is a description of the divine essence, while the former in no way implicates the essence. Michel Barnes has shown that Eunomius adjusts a prevalent contemporary account of the sequence of causality in order to emphasize this disjunction between essence and activity. The standard pattern posits an essence as having an essential capacity (*dynamis*) for a corresponding activity (*energeia*) that causes an effect, or product (*ergon*). But Eunomius usually, if not always, erases from this sequence the stage of essential capacity (*dynamis*), which links essence and activity.[146] For Eunomius, the activity is simply external to the essence and coterminous not with the essence but with its product.

All this bears directly on the Father-Son relation. The Son, as only-begotten of the Father, is clearly caused by another, the Father. Inasmuch as causality is a form of

144. *Apol.* 22 (ET: Vaggione, *Eunomius*, 63, altered).
145. See Barnes, *Dynamis*, 188–91.
146. Ibid., 190–91, 215–18.

activity, Eunomius considers that seeing the begetting of the Son as somehow internal to the divine essence amounts to conflating divine essence with divine action—a
conflation that would dissolve the absoluteness of divine priority so as ultimately
to make the world coordinate with God. Thus the first principle of pious *akribeia*,
by which the honor of the Unbegotten can be safeguarded, is to maintain a strict
separation between the perfection and eternity of divine being and the contingent
economy of divine willing:

> We . . . do not consider it unhazardous to have to unite the action to the essence. We
> recognize that the divine essence is without beginning, simple, and endless, but we also
> recognize that its action is neither without beginning nor without ending. . . . There is
> no need, therefore, to accept the half-baked opinions of outsiders and unite the action
> to the essence. On the contrary, we must believe that the action which is the truest and
> the most befitting God is his will and that this will is sufficient to bring into existence
> and to redeem all things, as indeed the prophetic voice bears witness: "Whatever he
> willed to do, he did."[147]

The second stage of Eunomius's elucidation of trinitarian *akribeia* in the *Apology*
gives an account of the primacy of Christ. Not surprisingly, Eunomius is constrained
to emphasize that confessing the primacy of Christ must not subvert the preeminence
of the Unbegotten, which is the primary object of religious piety (*eusebeia*). Thus an
accurate assessment of the primacy of Christ must first concede the unlikeness of essence between the preexistent Christ and the Unbegotten. Such a concession is not a
denigration of Christ, who himself acknowledged, "The Father who sent me is greater
than I" (cf. John 14:28).[148] As we have seen, the fundamental feature of this unlikeness
is that the essence of the Unbegotten is not itself implicated in any activity, whereas
the essence of the Son is the product of divine activity, "begotten before all things by
the will of its God and Father."[149] Indeed, the term "Father" designates neither the
eternal essence of the Unbegotten nor an eternal capacity (*dynamis*) for action, much
less an eternal action. It only names the agency of the begetting of the Son, which
is external and posterior to the divine essence. As we have noted, in insisting on the
essential unlikeness between Father and Son, Eunomius is reverting to the language
of Arius and reacting against intervening accommodations of the superiority of the
Unbegotten to the patterns within Christian discourse that emphasized Christ's likeness to the Father. But by rejecting these developments, Eunomius also retrieves the
problem of explaining the scriptural language of likeness between Father and Son.
He does this by once again employing the fundamental distinction between divine
essence and activity. As begotten, the Son is simply unlike in essence to the Unbegotten God. However, he is like the Father inasmuch as he reflects the will and power of
the divine agency designated by the term "Father": "Accordingly, if this argument has

147. *Apol.* 23 (Vaggione, 65).
148. *Apol.* 10.
149. *Apol.* 12 (Vaggione, 49).

demonstrated that God's will is an action and that this action is not essence, but that the Only-begotten exists by virtue of the will of the Father, then of necessity it is not with respect to the essence but with respect to the action (which is what the will is) that the Son preserves his similarity to the Father."[150] This principle is then applied to the christological title "Image": "The word 'image,' then, refers the similarity back not to the essence of God but to action unbegottenly stored up in his foreknowledge prior to the existence of the first-born and of the things created 'in him.'"[151]

Having qualified his positive account of the primacy of Christ by locating it within the secondary level of divine activity, as distinguished from the level of the divine essence, Eunomius nevertheless insists on the priority of the preexistent Christ in relation to the rest of creation. As the "image and seal of the [Unbegotten's] power and action," the Son mediates the efficacious power of the divine will to the rest of creation, beginning with the activity of creation itself: "Since he alone was begotten and created by the power (*dynamei*) of the Unbegotten, he became the perfect minister of the whole creative activity and purpose of the Father."[152] The Son performs his creative and salvific work always in the subordinate mode of obedience to the Father: "Obedient with regard to the ordering and creation of all existing things, obedient with regard to all governance . . . obedient in his words, mediator in doctrine, mediator in law. . . . He became obedient unto the cross and unto death."[153] Though Eunomius's scant extant texts focus predominantly on metaphysical relations rather than explicitly soteriological themes, it seems consistent with his thought to see obedience as the crucial soteriological category.[154] As is typical of this trajectory of the account of Christ's primacy, the "for us" does not take place merely within the event of the incarnation but is inscribed into the very being of the Son. Jesus Christ is Savior because his very being, both "before" and "after" the incarnation, is an obedient manifestation of the creative and healing power of the Unbegotten. If we can take the *Apostolic Constitutions* as a witness to Eunomian liturgical life, we find that Christ's role as obedient servant also has a doxological dimension, as we saw with Arius: "Christ's role is that of the prototypical worshiper of God."[155]

Eunomius completes his trinitarian account of Christian faith in the *Apology* with his confession of the Holy Spirit, the third stage of trinitarian *akribeia*. As the Son is created by the Father, the Spirit is created by the Son. He is third in dignity, order, and nature. There is perhaps an Origenian influence in the statement that the Spirit is

---

150. *Apol.* 24 (Vaggione, 65).

151. *Apol.* 24 (Vaggione, 65).

152. *Apol.* 15 (Vaggione, 53). This passage represents an exception to Eunomius's general pattern of dropping out the category of *dynamis* from his account of the divine causal sequence; cf. also *Apol.* 24, where Eunomius speaks of the Father's *dynamis* as stored up in the Son.

153. *Confession of Faith* (Vaggione, 155).

154. On the centrality of this theme in Eunomius as well as Western "homoians," see Meslin, *Les Ariens*, 311–13.

155. Kopecek, "Neo-Arian Religion," 169.

not involved in the work of creation but is active in the work of sanctification, "filled with the power of sanctification and instruction."[156]

The Place of Eunomius in the Ongoing Debate

We can note three significant features of Eunomius's location within the trajectory of trinitarian theologies of will. First, Eunomius provided a radical and provocative resolution to a longstanding tension within that trajectory between an emphasis on the incomparability of the Unbegotten and the scriptural characterization of the Son as Image of the Father. We have seen that Asterius and Eusebius both mitigated Arius's contrast between Father and Son and found ways to use Image and likeness language in relating Father and Son. Eunomius sets clear limits to such qualifications by insisting on the difference in essence between the Unbegotten and the Only-begotten and explaining that all likeness must be relegated to the level of divine activity, not the level of being. This move represents a significant retrieval of Arius's original theology.

The second major contribution of Eunomius to further fourth-century trinitarian debate is that he shifted the discussion into an epistemological key. Eunomius's whole theology centers on the knowledge of God: what we know about God and how words about God signify. Here also, Eunomius's affinity with Arius is closer than has been generally acknowledged. Much has been made of the contrast between Arius's stress on the incomprehensibility of the One and Eunomius's insistence that we have reliable knowledge of the divine essence as unbegotten. But, as Raoul Mortley has shown, Eunomius's theology is better understood as a Christianized Neoplatonic apophaticism than as the mystery-exploding rationalism caricatured by his opponents, ancient and contemporary.[157] Admittedly, Eunomius's articulation of the principle that the word *agen*[*n*]*ētos* describes the divine essence is not found in Arius's theology. But it is a development that is meant to safeguard precisely the ineffability and incomparability of the Unbegotten. We find no indication in Eunomius that the word *agen*[*n*]*ētos* provides mystical knowledge of God. Rather, his foundational epistemological principle simply insists that the positive fact of God's absolute incomparability and priority is given to human rationality and witnessed to in divine revelation. This word indeed describes the divine essence, but only to the extent of presenting it as categorically not passive with respect to causality. As with Arius, it is precisely knowledge of God's otherness, not analogical knowledge, that draws positive connections between knowledge of God and knowledge of the world. At any rate, Eunomius clearly ensured that epistemological questions would be at the forefront of trinitarian discussion.

The third significant contribution of Eunomius's theological approach is his clear and precisely rendered distinction between the realms of divine being and divine willing. Here again, we see consistency with Arius, for whom the One is utterly self-contained and ineffable in his being but positively related to creation, beginning with the Son, through his will. Eunomius's contribution consists in his clear and precise

156. *Apol.* 25 (Vaggione, 69).
157. Mortley, *From Word to Silence*, esp. 2:157–59.

affirmation of the priority of divine being and the sovereign contingency of divine willing. Eunomius interprets the conception of the eternal coexistence of the Father and the only-begotten Son as inserting activity, and so a kind of mutability or motion and thus passibility, into the divine essence. With regard to defining divine primacy as such, the question evoked by Eunomius is whether divine perfection can accommodate activity and movement *within* divine being. Eunomius's provocation on this issue will call forth from some of his theological opponents a clear affirmation that trinitarian theology does indeed involve the characterization of God as motion. So Gregory of Nazianzus can describe the unity of the divine essence as an "identity of motion," and we shall see that there is also a kineticism that pervades the theological vision of Gregory of Nyssa.[158] Moreover, Eunomius grounds the distinction between God and world in the distinction between divine being and divine willing. He thus raises the question of how the divine activity of the Son's generation is to be distinguished from the divine activity of creating the world.

With Eusebius and Eunomius, the interpretation of the church's trinitarian confession of faith principally by relating Father, Son, and Spirit through the category of divine will achieves climactic expression. Throughout, this trajectory has reintegrated a fitting conception of the primacy of Christ with a radical conception of divine primacy by making absolute priority in the order of causality the essential marker of unqualified divinity. The attribute "unbegotten" becomes the crucial description of the divine essence—implicitly in Arius, explicitly in Eunomius. Whatever philosophical resources they used to articulate this conception, its proponents believed it was founded on biblical conceptions of the absolute sovereignty of the living God and the radical difference between God and world. They were able to incorporate the equally central biblical conception of God's positive relation to the world by invoking the scriptural motif of God's will. They typically portrayed the primacy of Christ by depicting the being of the preexistent Christ as the first and greatest product of the divine will and as the mediator of divine power and activity to the rest of creation. This role is coextensive with the Son's being as such and extends within a continuum that runs from the Word's agency in creation to the consummation of Christ's salvific work. With Eusebius, this vision receives unprecedented breadth of expression in his account of the chain of being as a chain of willing, extending from the Unbegotten through the Only-begotten to the emperor and the rest of creation, encompassing all reality within the good government of the Unbegotten. Eunomius renders the chain of divine being-willing with greater theological precision by demarcating radically between being and willing. He sees the fullness of divine being as coterminous with the designation of "Unbegotten." All references to God that designate activity of any kind, including the act of generating the Son, are ascribed to the divine will, which is external to divine being. Within the framework of this radical rupture between divine being and divine willing, the unity of Father, Son, and Spirit as an ineradicable pattern of Christian discourse is rendered in terms of the mediation of the sovereign

---

158. Gregory of Nazianzus, *Or.* 29.2; on Gregory of Nyssa, see below, esp. 238–39.

divine will: from the Unbegotten to the Only-begotten in the work of creation and salvation, and from the Only-begotten to the Holy Spirit in the work of sanctification.

Trinitarian Theologians of Unity of Being

Whatever ambiguities may attach to the signification of the Nicene *homoousios*, its clear intent of describing the relation of Father and Son in the language of being aligned it unmistakably with theologies of the "unity of being" rather than "unity of will." Our overarching project of reconstructing the systematic scope of "Nicene" trinitarian doctrine will thus involve broad interpretations of three major theologians who exemplify this trajectory: Athanasius, Gregory of Nyssa, and Augustine. For the moment, however, we will linger over three lesser figures in that tradition, who were nevertheless crucial in delineating the nexus of issues surrounding the Council of Nicaea and its reception: Alexander of Alexandria, Marcellus of Ancyra, and Apollinaris of Laodicea.

Alexander of Alexandria

Alexander was bishop of Alexandria from 312 to 328. The beginning of his episcopacy was already complicated by the divisions in the Egyptian church emanating from the Melitian schism. These complications intensified greatly with the outbreak of the controversy with Arius. As we stated earlier, it seems more likely that Arius was reacting to Alexander's Origenistic emphasis on the eternal correlativity of Father and Son than that Arius spontaneously started producing slogans asserting the ontological inferiority of the Son. Rowan Williams suggests that the conflict between Arius and Alexander be contextualized in light of ambivalence at Alexandria in that era about the role of the bishop. Traditionally venerated with the title "Papa," the bishop of Alexandria was accorded primacy throughout the Egyptian church, and yet his authority within Alexandria was qualified by a strong notion of a presbyterial communion "with the bishop as president of a college of near-equals."[159] That situation can help explain both Arius's self-presentation as a theological expert correcting the incautious theological extravagances of his bishop and Alexander's sovereign frustration at Arius's subversion of his own authority: "They . . . refused to remain any longer in submission to the Church."[160]

At the same time, it is clear that for Alexander the issue is not merely ecclesiastical politics but a crucial cornerstone of Christian faith. He summoned a council of Alexandrian clergy that presented Arius with a confession of the faith they deemed as orthodox. Upon rejecting this confession, Arius and his supporters were excommunicated by Alexander and began their campaign of soliciting support from bishops outside Egypt. Vindicated by Nicaea's anathematization of Arius's teaching, Alexander

159. Williams, *Arius*, 42.
160. *Ep. Alex.*, Urk. 14.3 [*Hē philarchos*].

subsequently rejected any overtures to readmit Arius to communion in Alexandria, a policy faithfully continued by his successor, Athanasius. Practically all the extant material from the pen of Alexander issues from his epistolary campaign to defend his excommunication of Arius and alert fellow bishops of the theological dangers of Arius's doctrine.[161] The central principles of Alexander's refutation of Arius became foundational for Athanasius's theological and polemical program against the "Arians." Moreover, significant continuities run from Alexander's theology all the way to the fruition of the unity-of-being trajectory in the Cappadocians.

CREATOR AND CREATION

If the most radical distinction in the unity-of-will theologies is between divine being and divine will, the most radical distinction in unity-of-being theologies is that between Creator and creation. It is true that the will theologians also demarcate strictly between Creator and creature, but their demarcation is rendered ambivalent by the crucial qualification that the Son is both creature and Creator. Theologians of will thus finally invoke the primary distinction between the divine being of the Unbegotten and what exists as the effect of the divine will as constituting the most basic differentiation. Eusebius and Eunomius actually come to interpret origination from nothing as origination from the divine will. Moreover, we have seen that Eunomius interprets even the divine appellations "Father" and "Creator" within the more radical being-will framework, as naming the activities of divine willing, which are secondary to the essence of the Unbegotten. In the trajectory of trinitarian theologies of unity of being, it is Alexander who initiates the central argument that the Creator-creature distinction constitutes mutually exclusive categories that allow for no middle term; the notion of a created Creator is simply nonsensical. The immediate payoff of this line of reasoning is the conclusion that if the Son is Creator, as the Scriptures attest and Arius acknowledges, then he can in no way share in the properties of creatures.

Part of the logic of this position lies in the literal sense of scriptural language that the Son is Creator of *all* (cf. John 1:3): if the Son himself is created, then all things are not created by him, or he created himself, or else he is not among all things.[162] But in addition, this position radicalizes the Platonic opposition of being-becoming by integrating it into the Christian framework of an absolute and mutually exclusive distinction between Creator and creature. The category of "Creator" becomes strictly equivalent to that of "being" (*to on*); to create means not merely to impose form upon formless matter but also to be in full and immediate possession of being, and thus

---

161. Here I will confine myself to Alexander's undisputed and most substantive epistle, sent to his namesake, Alexander of Byzantium (*Ep. Alex.*, NPNF[2] 3:35–41, Urk. 14). Another letter, *Letter to All Bishops* (*Henos sōmatos*), might well have been drafted by his then secretary, Athanasius (see Stead, "Athanasius's Earliest Written Work"; Ernest, *Bible in Athanasius of Alexandria*, 105–7, esp. 106n4). Athanasius's *First Letter to Virgins* also presents an extended quotation from Alexander; see Brakke, *Athanasius and the Politics of Asceticism*, 286–88.

162. *Ep. Alex.*, Urk. 14.17; 14.23.

to own the capacity of granting being to the nonexistent. This capacity to give being is only possible for one who owns being and is not part of the realm of becoming:

> If all things were made by him (cf. John 1:3), how is it that he who thus granted existence to all could at any period have no existence himself? The Word, the creating power, can in no way be defined as of the same nature (*physis*) as the things created if indeed he was in the beginning and all things were made by him and were called by him out of nonbeing into being. That which is (*to on*) must be opposite and entirely separate from the things which came into being from non-being. This shows that there is no separation between the Father and the Son . . . all things having been granted an origin of existence by the Father through the Son.[163]

THE SON AND THE UNBEGOTTEN

If one essential element of Alexander's response to Arius is to assert the Son's status as Creator in order to deny categorically that he is a creature, the complementary task, prescribed both by the biblical narrative and Arius's interpretation of it, is to clarify the distinction and relation between the Son and the Unbegotten. To begin with, Alexander certainly affirms the distinction and rejects the charge that he makes the Son out to be another Unbegotten.[164] The title "Unbegotten" designates "the proper honor" of the Father and the reality of his being "without cause," while the Son's existence, as "begotten," is derived from the Father.[165] Consequently, we find inchoate patterns in Alexander for distinguishing the individual existences of Father and Son. Indeed, if we invoke Lienhard's categorization of miahypostatic versus dyohypostatic traditions, there is probably more ground for placing Alexander in the dyohypostatic tradition. He never refers to Father and Son as one *hypostasis*, and he characteristically associates *hypostasis* language regarding the Son with the Son's particular existence as distinguished from that of the Father: "John . . . declares his particular *hypostasis* (*tēn idiotropon hypostasin*) in the following words, 'In the beginning was the Word . . .'";[166] "The Father alone is Unbegotten, but the ineffable *hypostasis* of the Only-begotten is beyond the keenest conception of the minds of the evangelists and even of angels."[167]

---

163. *Ep. Alex.*, Urk. 14.17–19.
164. *Ep. Alex.*, Urk. 14.19.
165. *Ep. Alex.*, Urk. 14.52.
166. *Ep. Alex.*, Urk. 14.16.
167. *Ep. Alex.*, Urk. 14.19. Ayres downplays Alexander's use of *hypostasis* language: "Alexander also uses the term *hypostasis*, but in the majority of his uses—even when he talks of the Son's *hypostasis*—the term seems to mean 'existence' or 'nature.' We never find him using *hypostasis* as a technical term for the individual existence of one of the divine persons, and he never speaks of there being two or three *hypostaseis*" (*Nicaea*, 45). As the above quotations show, Alexander did use the language of *hypostasis* to designate the particularity of the Son in his distinction from the Father. Moreover, there is one instance where Alexander could be speaking of two *hypostaseis*: "'I and the Father are one.' When the Lord says this, he is not calling himself 'Father' nor is he supposing that the natures which are two in *hypostasis* are one" (*oude tas tē hypostasei dyo physeis mian einai saphēnizōn*) (Urk. 14.38). However, this instance is not conclusive both because whatever affirmation is being made about the Father and Son is enfolded within a negation (the Lord is *not* supposing this) and because it is grammatically possible, although more strained,

In affirming the distinction between Father and Son, Alexander refers to the title "Only-begotten" as indicating the "middle" (*mesiteuousa*) status of the Son's existence, between the "Unbegotten" Father and creation. Manlio Simonetti takes this reference as grounds for attributing an "attenuated subordination" to Alexander's theology.[168] But this is to interpret "middle" in too quantitative a sense, as if it places the Son ontologically halfway between the Unbegotten and creation, as in Platonic mediatorial schemes. One must resist the impulse to invoke Plato just because "middle" language is used. In this context, the category "middle" has not so much an ontological-quantitative or spatial designation as a logical signification. Alexander is simply rejecting the false dilemma that says if the Son is not unbegotten he must be created; the notion of "middle" here designates a logical space for invoking a category that is distinct from both "unbegotten" and "created": "These uninstructed people charge that one of these alternatives must hold: either he must be believed to come from non-being or there are two unbegotten beings. In their ignorance and lack of theological expertise, they do not realize how vast must be the distance between the uncreated Father and creatures . . . and that the only-begotten nature of the one who is the Word of God by whom the Father created the universe out of non-being, standing as it were in the middle between the two, was begotten of the self-existent Father."[169]

Yet, within his account of the distinction between Father and Son, Alexander finds various ways to designate their unity of being. The first of these responds to Arius's radical apophaticism of the one Unbegotten through a christological restructuring of the category of divine incomprehensibility. Perhaps every theology must ultimately invoke the ineffability of the divine mystery. But theologies, as well as the experiences they inculcate, are crucially determined by where the mystery is located. For Arius, the ultimate mystery is the supremely ineffable reality of the one Unbegotten, and this way of specifying the location of ultimate divine mystery remains a consistent tenet of the trajectory of trinitarian unity of will. Alexander, however, clearly and persistently attempts to present the mystery of the Unbegotten as mutually coordinate with the mystery of the Only-begotten, such that they are really two aspects of the same mystery. This christological restructuring of the notion of divine mystery tends to be inserted into affirmations of the very distinction between Father and Son, as in the previously quoted statement: "The Father alone is Unbegotten, but the ineffable *hypostasis* of the only-Begotten is beyond the keenest conception";[170] "How can anyone presume to enquire into the *hypostasis* of the Word of God?"[171]

---

to translate it as Ayres does: "that the two *physeis* in the *hypostasis* are one." But it militates against the latter translation that we cannot find another instance where Alexander uses *hypostasis* to designate the single being of Father and Son. For these reasons I agree with Hanson, who in turn agrees with Simonetti, that "Alexander . . . uses *hypostasis* to express the individual reality of the Son, and can use it elsewhere to describe that of the Father. A doctrine of three *hypostaseis* would not of itself have been regarded by him as scandalous" (Hanson, *Search*, 143). See also Simonetti, *La crisi*, 60.

168. Simonetti, *La crisi*, 58.
169. *Ep. Alex.*, Urk. 14.44–45 (ET: NPNF[2] 3:39, altered).
170. *Ep. Alex.*, Urk. 14.19.
171. *Ep. Alex.*, Urk. 14.20.

The equality of Father and Son is in this way rendered apophatic by affirming that Father and Son are *equally incomprehensible*. A scriptural touchstone for insisting on the radical incomprehensibility of the Son is found in Isaiah 53:8: "Who can declare his generation?" There is no graded hierarchy between the supreme mystery of the Unbegotten and the lower mystery of the only-begotten; the two mysteries coexist within the Father-Son relationship itself:

> And, therefore, our Savior in his kindness to those men who were the pillars of the whole world, desiring to relieve them of the burden of striving after this knowledge, told them that it was beyond their natural comprehension, and that the Father alone could discern this most divine mystery. "No man," he said, "knows the Son except the Father and no one knows the Father except the Son" (Matt. 11:27). I think it was in reference to this subject that the Father said, "My secret is for me and mine" (Isa. 24:16 Vulgate).[172]

Knowledge of God is thus in the first place a transaction between the Father and the Son, and the mystery of God is identified with that relationship itself rather than exclusively with the Unbegotten. Positive access to the knowledge of God is coincidental with access to the mutuality of that relation, which in turn is predicated upon a correct confession of the true nature of that mutuality.

Another of Alexander's strategies for speaking of the essential relatedness of Father and Son, derived from Origen, is making the Father-Son relationship constitutive of the idea of divine perfection.[173] Again, we can say that all Christian theologies will necessarily attribute perfection to God, but they invoke different elements of the biblical narrative to give content to the notion of divine perfection. We have seen that Eunomius makes explicit a foundational premise of the unity-of-will trajectory by simply equating the summit of divine perfection with unbegottenness, while before him Eusebius had spoken of the divine goodness as manifest in the character of divine willing. For Alexander, however, divine perfection is coincident with the ontological relation of Father and Son: "And the Son being always present with him, the Father is always perfect, lacking in no good thing."[174] This conception of divine perfection as constituted by the Father-Son relation relies on biblical passages correlating divine glory with Christ. As a prime example, the Letter to the Hebrews identifies Christ as the "radiance" of divine light (cf. Heb. 1:3), which Alexander associates in turn with the designation of Christ as Image of the Father. The perfection of the Son's reflection of the Father's *hypostasis* means that he is "immutable and unchangeable, all-sufficient and perfect, like the Father, lacking only his 'unbegotten.' He is the exact and precisely similar image of his Father. For it is clear that the image fully contains everything by which the greater likeness exists, as the Lord taught us when he said, 'My Father is greater than I.'"[175] As Alexander understands it, the superiority of the

172. *Ep. Alex.*, 14.21.
173. Origen, *Princ.* 1.2.9.
174. *Ep. Alex.*, Urk. 14.26.
175. *Ep. Alex.*, Urk. 14.47.

Father to the Son resides not in his possessing a higher or more sublime condition of being but simply in the fact that he is the original possessor of the being that he shares fully and perfectly with the Son, without there being any gap (*diastēma*), ontological or temporal, between the Father's original possession of perfect being and the Son's reflected possession of it. Alexander also uses the patterns of scriptural correlation linking the identity of Christ with that of the Father in a negative, polemical mode to deny that divine perfection is prior to and separable from the Father's relation to the Son. Such a separation is inserted into the biblical patterns of correlation to yield such discomfiting statements as: there was once when God was without wisdom, power, brightness, and so on.[176] We shall see that Alexander's most illustrious disciple, Athanasius, exploits this rhetorical-exegetical strategy relentlessly.

Worship, Salvation, and Father-Son Unity

According to Alexander, the ultimacy of Christ, as strictly integral to divine perfection, is substantiated and demonstrated by the public worship of the church. The content of worship directed to Christ is specified by the trinitarian confession, which affirms that the Son is both co-eternal with the Father and perfectly images the Father's divinity, while maintaining the Father's priority as the Unbegotten source of the Son: "We must render him worship *only* piously and religiously, attributing to him the 'was' (John 1:1) and the 'always' and the 'before all ages,' not rejecting his divinity but attributing to him a perfect likeness in all things to his Father, while at the same time we glorify the Father's unique property (*idiōma*) as Unbegotten, as the Savior himself says, 'The Father is greater than I' (John 14:28)."[177] I have italicized "only" in the above quotation as it seems to indicate that Alexander is deliberately articulating an interpretation of the content of Christian worship that is meant to contradict Arius's alternative version in which Christ leads his disciples in adoration of the Unbegotten. The church itself is defined as the community that confesses the unqualified divinity of Christ, and it is on the basis of just this conception of the church that Alexander feels justified in excommunicating Arius and his supporters: "We unanimously expelled them from the Church which worships the divinity of Christ."[178]

Alexander's soteriology is linked to his teaching on the unity by nature of the Father and the Son in two significant ways. First, he defines the content of Christian salvation precisely as being enfolded into the Father-Son relation. Through the incarnation, Jesus Christ's divine "sonship by nature" opens up to offer the possibility for us to enjoy a "sonship by grace." The acknowledgment by creatures of this salvific integration by grace into Christ's natural sonship determines the content of Christian worship:

Therefore, our Lord, being the Son of the Father by nature (*physei*), is worshiped by all. As for those who have put off the spirit of bondage and by brave deeds and progress in

---

176. *Ep. Alex.*, Urk. 14.27.
177. *Ep. Alex.*, Urk. 14.52 (ET: NPNF² 3:40, altered; my italics).
178. *Ep. Alex.*, Urk. 14.6.

virtue have received the spirit of adoption through the kindness of the one who is Son of God by nature, they become sons by adoption.[179]

Inasmuch as the language of filiation is scriptural, the supporters of Arius also interpreted it in their own way, a fact reported by Alexander himself. But their interpretation of it served simply to underscore that the category of "sonship" could apply to creatures and was not therefore necessarily a prerogative of absolute divinity. In this case, the notion of humanity's being "adopted" by God has no reference to the divine nature as such. For Alexander, however, salvation as adoption bears a real relationship to the Father-Son relation that constitutes the perfection of divine being.

Second, Alexander invokes the Origenian concept that salvation depends on being strictly assimilated to divine immutability.[180] Arius, himself following Origen's emphasis that all creatures are by definition mutable, had to conclude that the Son also, as a creature, possessed a nature susceptible to alteration. We have seen that he attempted to mitigate the shock of that conception by explaining that the Son's alterable nature was rendered *de facto* inalterable by a prevenient divine grace, an explanation that also echoes Origen's account of Christ's human soul.[181] Alexander rejects this account on the basis of a soteriological schema whereby human "sonship by grace" is ontologically anchored in the natural immutability of the "sonship by nature" enjoyed by the Son. From this perspective, Alexander reads the history of divine salvific intervention as God's offer of adoption to humanity, an offer that falters because humans fail to receive it. In this context, Alexander invokes the divine complaint in Isaiah 1:2: "I have nourished and brought up children and they have rebelled against me." This divine complaint was addressed definitively only when humanity was adopted by grace into the natural sonship of the divinity of Christ. Human salvation, characterized as adoption into divine life, can only be secured if it is founded on the ontological and divinely immutable filiation of the Son.[182]

Alexander's trinitarian confession thus concedes Arius's central assertion that unbegottenness is unique to the Father but also insists that divine perfection is not limited or fully defined by that attribute alone but rather encompasses the coordinate mysteries of the Father's unbegottenness and the Son's only-begotteness as the perfect Image and radiance of the Father. In the course of synthesizing these emphases, Alexander provides a clear, albeit preliminary, account of unity and distinction, an account that involves discernible efforts to create linguistic categories for both unity and distinction. Acknowledging the distinctness of the attributions of "unbegotten" and "only-begotten," Alexander invokes language to articulate that distinction, such as the statement that "unbegotten" is the proper honor (*oikeion axiōma*) of the Father and that the Father alone has the property (*idiōma*) of unbegottenness.[183] At the

179. *Ep. Alex.*, Urk. 14.3.
180. Origen, *Princ.* 1.5.5; 1.8.3.
181. Origen, *Princ.* 2.6.4. This correspondence is noted by Lorenz, *Arius judaizans*, esp. 211–24.
182. *Ep. Alex.*, Urk. 14.34.
183. *Ep. Alex.*, Urk. 14.52.

same time, the Son's being belongs (*idios*) inalienably and inseparably to the Father.[184] But the heart of Alexander's account of the unity of Father and Son is not so much a vocabulary but a conception of how the coordinate distinct "honors" of the modes of being of Father and Son together constitute divine perfection, the orientation and content of human worship, and the content of salvation. Alexander thus deals with the crisis of a more intense and clarified sense of the primacy of divine transcendence not by relativizing the primacy of Christ, as did Arius, but by christologically restructuring divine primacy such that the ineffable mystery of the Son's being only-begotten is strictly correlative to the Father's "proper honor" of being unbegotten. The Son's perfect imaging of the Father grounds both human worship and salvation, whereby humanity is incorporated by grace into the natural filiation of the Son to the Father. As is typical of this stage of the debate, Alexander includes a reference to the Holy Spirit in his confession but without significant elaboration: "We confess, as the sacred Scriptures teach us, one Holy Spirit who moved the holy ones of the Old Testament and the divine teachers of . . . the New."[185]

Marcellus of Ancyra

Marcellus was born around 280. We first hear of him as the bishop of Ancyra, in Galatia, as an attendee of a synod in 314. He also attended the Council of Nicaea and was an enthusiastic supporter of the Nicene *homoousios*, though he interpreted it in his own distinctive and controversial manner, attributing all real differentiation between Father and Son to divine economic activity rather than divine being. After Nicaea, he wrote a refutation of Asterius, which was in turn answered by Eusebius of Caesarea in two writings, *Against Marcellus* and *Ecclesiastical Theology*. Eusebius's writings drew attention to Marcellus's seemingly modalist interpretation of Nicaea, resulting in condemnations by Eastern synods in 336 (Constantinople), 341 (Antioch), and 343 (Serdica). Marcellus fared better in the West. After presenting Pope Julius with a confession of faith that adhered closely to the Roman creed, he was vindicated by a Roman synod in 340 and spent his exile in Rome with the deposed Athanasius. The Alexandrian bishop, while recognizing the value of Marcellus's polemic against Asterius and the "Arians," was eventually led to break off communion with Marcellus in the mid-340s but held back from explicit condemnation of Marcellus's doctrine.[186] Between the 340s and the Council of Constantinople (381), Marcellus's position became increasingly identified as the opposite and equally erroneous extreme on the far side of Arius, while an emerging consensus identified itself by negating these two extremes. The Council of Constantinople reiterated the condemnation of Marcellus, and its creed rejected what was considered to be a

---

184. On the significance of *idios* language in the Alexandrian tradition, see Louth, "Use of the Term *IDIOS*."

185. *Ep. Alex.*, Urk. 14.53.

186. For a balanced account of Marcellus's complex relationship with Athanasius, see Lienhard, "Did Athanasius Reject Marcellus?"

feature of Marcellus's doctrine in affirming that Christ's kingship will have no end. Marcellus died in the early 370s.

MARCELLUS'S DISTINCTIVE SYNTHESIS

With respect to the unity-of-being and unity-of-will trajectories in trinitarian theology, Marcellus's position is ambivalent. Superficially, his fervent support of the Nicene *homoousios* and equally fervent polemic against Asterius seem to place him squarely in the first trajectory, but the deeper structure of his thought shows significant affinities with the second. As we analyze the systematic scope of the development of trinitarian doctrine, Marcellus's distinctive synthesis of Christian doctrine throws considerable light on how conceptions of God as Trinity are intertwined with questions of God's relationship to the world and the relationship of humanity and divinity in the person of Jesus Christ. These questions come to the fore when we analyze how Marcellus configures his accounts of the doctrine of God and the primacy of Christ. His doctrine of God places the strongest possible emphasis on the singularity of God, a feature that he shares with his opponent, Asterius. Divine being can only be described as one *dynamis*, *prosōpon*, and *hypostasis*. (Marcellus preferred the first two terms to *ousia-hypostasis* language.[187]) However, the singularity of divine being becomes functionally complex through God's relation to creation. Thus the act of creation begins with the Word's emanation from the divine being. In Marcellus's account, the primacy of Christ is affirmed by insisting that his divinity, the Word, has its radical origin within the divine being as such and cannot ultimately be differentiated from the divine being. Any differentiation it has from the divine being is provisional and temporary; in the beginning and in the end, the Word is simply within God and in no way another alongside the one God.

We can best approach Marcellus's understanding of God-Word unity and differentiation by noting his arguments against Asterius's preference for the title "Image" and for his own preferred title, "Word." He rejects the title "Image" because it implies a real distinction of being between the image and its archetype: "The image is not image of itself but of something else."[188] Marcellus chastises Asterius for holding that "God is as distinct from his Word as a man is distinct from his image."[189] For his part, Marcellus considers "Word" the only title that is strictly applicable to the divinity of Christ. He conceives of the generation of the Word primarily by analogy with human speaking. The central significance of this analogy, for Marcellus, is that the word achieves real differentiation from the speaker only in the act of speaking. Thus, for Marcellus, we can say that before the act of generation, there was "silence" because the Word was in God.[190] With respect to God's immanent being, there is no real differentiation between God and the Word; they are one *prosōpon* and one

187. On Marcellus's theological vocabulary, see Lienhard, *Contra Marcellum*, 51–56; Parvis, *Marcellus*, 65.
188. Fr. 114 (Vinzent).
189. Fr. 51 (Vinzent).
190. Fr. 76 (Vinzent).

power. Differentiation occurs only as the divine power (*dynamis*), which is coextensive with divine being, broadens out in its external activity (*energeia*).[191] This schema is used to gloss John 1:1: "In the beginning was the Word" means that the Word was originally "in the Father by power" (*dynamei en tō patri*); "And the Word was with God" means that the Word was extrapolated so as to be "with the Father by activity" (*energeia pros ton theon*).[192]

This framework is given another scriptural rendering when Marcellus deals with a *locus classicus* for discerning the trinitarian God in the act of creation, Genesis 1:26: "Let us make man in our image and likeness." The plural reference has been typically considered to be a revelation of trinitarian being; the same text had been used by Justin Martyr to indicate that Father and Son are "two" and "numerically distinct."[193] Marcellus denies that it means the Father and the Son are two. Interpreting the first person plural as referring to God and his Word, he rejects the notion that the plurality in question consists of a dialogical exchange between distinct speakers. Rather, in an interpretation much ridiculed by Eusebius of Caesarea, there is only one speaker, who is summoning his reason, just as the builder of a statue, "aware that his reason (*logos*) is working with him, by which he thinks and is accustomed to doing everything . . . encourages *himself as he would another*, saying, 'Come, let us make a statue' . . . for the whole creation came into being by the Word."[194] Of course, Marcellus's point is that the reason of the artist is in fact not "another" with respect to the artist; the plurality is merely a linguistic device that dramatizes what is essentially a monologue and not a dialogue. In sum, there is no dialogue in God's immanent being. Another contrast with Justin Martyr underscores the same point. One way that Justin traces indications of trinitarian being in the Old Testament is by discerning the different "voices" or personas (*prosōpa*) of the Father and the Son.[195] But Marcellus is emphatic that the God who speaks throughout the Scriptures is a single, undifferentiated subject; the Word is not to be conceived as a co-speaker with the Father but rather as an instrument of the Father's speech. It is therefore inappropriate to ask which of the Trinity is the speaker when God speaks in the Scriptures; there is only one who speaks, and that is the Father who speaks through his Word: "What is said by the Father is expressed (*sēmainetai*) through the Word."[196]

As the above account implies, Marcellus's view of the primacy of Christ is founded on his identification of Christ's divinity with his status as the internal Word of the Father who is ultimately not to be differentiated from the Father as in any way "another." But, while one pole of Marcellus's theology was a firm insistence on the singularity of divine being *in se*, the other was established on an equally strong affirmation of the real difference between the divinity and humanity of Jesus Christ. Marcellus thus

191. Fr. 48 (Vinzent).
192. Fr. 70 (Vinzent).
193. *Dial.* 62.
194. Fr. 98 (Vinzent, my italics); see the criticisms of Eusebius, *Eccl. theol.* 1.7.
195. See Slusser, "Exegetical Roots of Trinitarian Theolgy."
196. Fr. 87 (Vinzent, *Markell*, 74).

exemplifies the second of two patterns by which accounts of trinitarian unity and distinction are typically correlated with accounts of the person of Christ, as identified by Brian Daley: "A theology that emphasizes the threeness of the persons of God . . . tends to stress the oneness of person in Christ the Savior. . . . On the other hand, a theology with a weak conception of the distinctions of persons in God—a theology with a more 'modalist' way of conceiving God's being—tends to stress the twoness of natures or substances in Christ."[197] Indeed, Marcellus does not flatly deny the unity of Christ's "natures." He comfortably uses the language of unity (*henōsis*),[198] joining (*synaptō*),[199] and assumption (*analēpsis*)[200] to link Christ's humanity with his divinity. Nevertheless, to the extent that Marcellus insists on the lack of difference between the divinity of Christ and the one God, he is compelled to the exact same extent to attribute to the humanity all differentiation between Jesus Christ and the one God of humanity. The more the humanity of Jesus is differentiated from his divinity, the easier it is to integrate that divinity without qualification into the being of the one God. For example, the title "Image," which implies a differentiation between Father and Word that Marcellus finds inadmissible, can be suitably applied to the humanity of Jesus. Jesus Christ is Image of the Father through the visibility of his humanity; and indeed, in his humanity, he is also Image of the divine Word: "For it is not possible for anyone to know either the Word or the Father of the Word apart from this image."[201] By emphasizing the singular integrity of the Father, who possesses *Logos*, while relegating all differentiation to the relation between Christ's humanity and divinity, Marcellus is thus able to attach maximal significance to the tensions between humanity and divinity in the scriptural narrative. He mocks Asterius's efforts to interpret the unity of Father and Son as a unity of will and "agreement" because it underrepresents not only the fullness of Christ's divinity but also the real difference of will and lack of agreement that attaches to his humanity (as evidenced, for example, by the agony of Gethsemane).[202]

THE FATE OF CHRIST'S HUMANITY

The underlying tension in Marcellus's account of the relation between humanity and divinity comes to the fore in his awkward handling of the question of what happens to the humanity of Christ after the consummation of his saving work, another feature of Marcellus's theology that was excoriated by Eusebius.[203] This was not a widely controverted question to which Marcellus was constrained to offer a response. Rather, it arises inevitably out of the presuppositions and tensions of his own theological vision in a way that provides a paradigmatic illustration of the nexus of key doctrinal issues in "trinitarian" theology. In interpreting this logic, we can begin with our *leitmotif*:

197. Daley, "One Thing and Another," 21.
198. Fr. 7, 28 (Vinzent).
199. Fr. 4 (Vinzent).
200. Fr. 33 (Vinzent).
201. Fr. 55 (Vinzent).
202. Fr. 74 (Vinzent).
203. *Eccl. theol.* 3.8.

the central issue motivating the development of fourth-century trinitarian thought was the reintegration of the principle of divine primacy with that of the primacy of Christ. The complexity and even idiosyncrasy of Marcellus's position is manifest in the fact that, despite his vehement opposition to Arius's supporter Asterius, he accepted Arius's primary presupposition, the identification of absolute divine primacy with singularity.[204] Marcellus, like Arius, accepts *monas* as the primary attribute of God.[205] The singularity of God is not merely a philosophical postulate but a scriptural commandment that governs right worship; in this context, Marcellus invokes the divine injunction, "You will worship the Lord your God and him alone shall you serve" (cf. Deut. 6:13; Matt. 4:10; Luke 4:8).[206] But unlike Arius and Asterius, Marcellus was unwilling to maintain the uniqueness of the absolute God by positing "a second God, separated from the Father in *hypostasis* and power (*dynamis*)."[207] Instead of making Christ a second God, Marcellus simply enfolds his divinity strictly within the unqualified singularity of the one God.

What threatens this synthesis is the apparent difference between divinity and humanity in the scriptural accounts of Jesus's life (notably the agony in Gethsemane). Marcellus's key "trinitarian" problem, then, was how to reconcile a commitment to unqualified divine singularity with the distance between God and Jesus Christ *in Jesus's human life*. Marcellus is determined to locate that distancing entirely outside of divine being and wholly in the sphere of divine activity *ad extra*. It belongs to the working out of the divine economy, not to theology proper. Hence a radical disjunction between theology and economy: theology is exclusively governed by the principle of radical simplicity; only the economy allows for interactivity between God and what is other than God. All this can be held together up until the incarnation, when the Word's union with humanity occasions a differentiation between the Word and the Father. If there is no room for differentiation within the divine being, then the Word must ultimately let go of the humanity in order to be reintegrated into the divine simplicity. This is the logic that apparently constrained Marcellus to say that the kingship of Christ will come to an end.[208] That statement appears to denigrate the primacy of Christ, but Marcellus says his real intention is to safeguard the eternal kingship of the Word. Once the Word is retracted back into the Father, the "partial kingship" exercised through the humanity will come to an end, which is also a fulfillment (*telos*). But what becomes of Christ's humanity? When Marcellus directly asks what happens to the flesh of Christ after the fulfillment of his "partial kingship," his disarming answer is that he does not know—Scripture does not tell us. But clearly there is no place for it in the Word's retraction into the Father after Christ subjects all things to himself in order to then subject himself to the God and Father (1 Cor. 15:28), "so that the Word might thus be in God, just as He was before the existence

204. Cf. Parvis, *Marcellus*, 66.
205. Fr. 92 (Vinzent).
206. Fr. 91 (Vinzent).
207. Fr. 91 (Vinzent, *Markell*, 80).
208. Fr. 101, 102 (Vinzent).

of the world, for before that there was nothing but God alone."[209] For his own purposes, Marcellus has thus consistently safeguarded the primacy of Christ by refusing any ultimate and lasting differentiation between the Word and the one God. But, as Eusebius of Caesarea witheringly pointed out, the soteriological consequences of this approach are highly dubious. If the possibility is entertained that the humanity of Jesus will in the end be "left behind, devoid of the Word," then what will become of our humanity, whose glorification is bound up with that of Jesus? And if the ultimate glorification of Jesus entails the re-absorption of the Word, without hypostatic remainder, into the singular divinity of the one God, then will our glorification also require our annihilation as subsistent beings—other than, and in relation to, God?[210]

THE FUTURE OF MARCELLAN THEOLOGY

Marcellus's theology eventually became a negative marker, identified with a modalist Sabellianism, against which other theologies touted their orthodoxy. The "Sabellianism" of Marcellus was marked off as one heretical extreme, as equidistant from the correct faith as the subordinationism of Arius.[211] Some modern scholars have tried to modify that judgment and to recommend Marcellus as someone who was prolonging an earlier tradition of economic trinitarianism, perhaps somewhat past its time.[212] But the issue here is not so much to pass judgment on Marcellus's orthodoxy as to see how the complexities and aporias of his theological reasoning illuminate systematic connections that are intrinsic to the developing meaning of trinitarian doctrine. In this case, the most significant connections are between the doctrine of God, the relation between God and creation, and Christology. And the central issue can be stated thus: Marcellus's doctrine of God depicts divine being as a monologue—God is singular, *monas*; in his own being, he is silent; in relation to creation, he utters his Word (*Logos*). On the other hand, the biblically depicted account of God's relation to creation is clearly a dialogue, since creation is other than God. As we have seen, the fact of this radical difference was a pervasive emphasis throughout the fourth-century debates. Jesus Christ, as the human incarnation of the Word, encompasses that dialogue in his own being. But since, for Marcellus, dialogue is not internal to God, neither can Jesus Christ, as a dialogical being in his divinity-humanity, be wholly reintegrated into divine life. Rather, in the end as in the beginning, God's life will again be simply a monologue. The dialogue of the union of humanity and divinity in Jesus Christ must once again be resolved into the monologue of divine life. Marcellus's doctrine of God simply lacks sufficient differentiation to ground and encompass the human-divine differentiation within Christ's being. The moral of the story: the deep structure of trinitarian faith involves grounding the God-world difference in an intra-divine

---

209. Fr. 109 (Vinzent).

210. *Eccl. theol.* 3.15.

211. Basil, *Ep.* 69; cf. *Tom. Antioch.* 5–6; see Barnes, "Fourth Century as Trinitarian Canon."

212. See Parvis's portrait of Marcellus as following in the Irenaean tradition, in *Marcellus*, 31–37. A balanced summary account of Marcellus's theology on its own terms is found in Lienhard, *Contra Marcellum*, 51–68.

difference—not merely as a postulate of abstract metaphysical calculation but as the indispensable basis of the christological narrative and its soteriological import.

Just as Marcellus's theology raises complex issues about the systematic meaning of trinitarian doctrine, it also complicates attempts to neatly compartmentalize the major protagonists in the fourth-century doctrinal debates. While he has been associated with Athanasius and aligned with the miahypostatic tradition, it is arguable that, from the point of view of his doctrine of God, he has just as much in common with Arius. Like Arius, Marcellus defined the divine essence by its singularity. Moreover, Marcellus aligns himself more with the unity-of-will trajectory in his tendency to see the relation between God and creation as utterly without ground in God's own being and completely derivative of God's *ad extra* activity. When we turn to Athanasius, we shall see that the latter's theological perspective is quite incompatible with Marcellus's. However, where Marcellus does agree with Athanasius and the trajectory of Nicene-Constantinopolitan theology is in his insistence on the absolute primacy of Christ in his divinity. This was apparently enough to earn him the forbearance, if not the endorsement, of Athanasius.

Apollinaris of Laodicea

Apollinaris was born around 315, the son of a priest also named Apollinaris. Both father and son were excommunicated for listening to a hymn in honor of Dionysius by the pagan sophist Epiphanius. Later the son was again excommunicated by the local bishop, George of Laodicea, for welcoming Athanasius into his home when the latter was on his way back to Alexandria from exile. These incidents reveal both Apollinaris's independent spirit and his staunch support of Athanasius and Nicaea. By the time of the Alexandrian Council of 362, Apollinaris had been consecrated as bishop of Laodicea and was represented by a party of monks at that council. Apollinaris's troubles began in the mid-370s when an Antiochian presbyter, Vitalis, became enamored of Apollinaris's theology and subsequently came under suspicion. The central issue was Apollinaris's conviction that in the incarnation, the *Logos* took the place of the human soul, or mind (*nous*), of Christ. After personally presenting this teaching to Pope Damasus, who initially affirmed Apollinaris's orthodoxy but soon afterward expressed hesitation on the subject, Vitalis returned to Antioch. Rather than serve under either of two rival pro-Nicene bishops divided over theological terminology, Melitius and Paulinus, Vitalis was consecrated by Apollinaris as yet another bishop of the same see (along with a fourth, the anti-Nicene Euzoius). Official censure of Apollinaris began in the late 370s, with a Roman synod headed by Damasus, and was reiterated by an Antiochian council in 379 as well as the Council of Constantinople. All three of the Cappadocians took up pens against the doctrine of Apollinaris. In the course of this anti-Apollinarian polemic, Gregory of Nazianzus framed his famous soteriological maxim, "What is not assumed is not healed."[213] Apollinaris died in 392.

213. *Ep.* 101.

For our purposes, the significance of Apollinaris, like that of Marcellus, resides in the disclosure of important links between trinitarian and christological doctrines that become manifest in his theological project. If Marcellus exemplifies the pattern in which the ultimate singularity of God is correlated with an emphasis on the difference between humanity and divinity in Christ, Apollinaris represents the opposite paradigm. He combines an emphasis on the three distinct subsistences—or *prosōpa*, in his preferred terminology—with a strongly unitive Christology that denies ascribing duality to Christ with the same vigor that Marcellus rejected any qualification of divine ontology as other than singular.[214] In Marcellus's scheme, there is ultimately no intra-divine difference that can enfold the difference between humanity and divinity in Christ; the latter difference can stand precisely because it does not need to be integrated into the unqualified divine singularity. With Apollinaris, however, the difference between Father and Son is a genuine ontological distinction that is enfolded by the divine consubstantiality. In this schema, the humanity of Christ can be integrated into the Son's relation to the Father but, it seems, only by being harmonized with the divinity to a degree that compromises its own integrity.

TRINITY AND THE CHRISTOLOGICAL *PRO NOBIS*

Yet another key to exploring these trinitarian-christological connections is the relationship of Christ's *pro nobis* to different trinitarian options. The scriptural narrative presents Jesus the Christ as Savior, the one who embodies and enacts God's saving purposes "for us." The question is precisely where to locate the "for us" in the divine-human constitution of Jesus Christ. We have seen that those who attributed a subordinate status to the divinity of Christ tended to locate the "for us" at the very origin of Christ's divine being. The Son was generated to be the mediator of God's gracious purposes in the work of creation and salvation. In this model, the "for us" extends in a continuum from the very origin of Christ's divinity into his human incarnation, death, and resurrection. Jesus's human work for us corresponds to his attenuated and more immanent divinity. We have seen this model explicitly in Arius, Asterius, and Eusebius, and this is the model that underlies the anti-Nicene attachment to the much-controverted Proverbs 8:22, "He created me as the beginning of his ways *for the sake of his works* (*eis erga autou*)." The "creation" of the Son is for the sake of the "works" of the rest of creation. On the other hand, those who ascribed an absolute and unqualified divinity to the Son did not locate the *pro nobis* at the origin of Christ's divine being but rather at the point of his taking on human flesh. In this model, the Son's existence is a function not of the mediation of God's purposes for creation but of the inherent perfection of divine being; in the incarnation the Son takes on a new form of existence wholly for the sake of creation. The rudiments of this model are present in Origen and Alexander, and it is of fundamental importance

214. On the pervasive use of *prosōpon* language in Apollinaris, see Lienhard, "Two Friends of Athanasius," 64. As Lienhard points out: "Apollinaris clearly preferred to call the Word a *prosōpon*, but he understood that term as equivalent to, or meaning, *hypostasis*" (65).

to theologians who endorse Nicene doctrine, as we shall presently see in the cases of Athanasius and Gregory of Nyssa.

Each of these models had its own vulnerabilities, requiring distinct theological remedies. The main weakness of the model that locates the "for us" at the origin of the divinity of Christ is that it tended to subvert the notion of Christ's lordship, since, even in his divinity, Christ was conceived as merely a means to the end of human flourishing. We shall see that Athanasius made much of the preceding objection. In turn, the main weakness of the model that identified the "for us" with the incarnation is that it replaced the continuity of christological being in the former model with an element of disruption. Whereas the former model had the appearance of a more unitive Christology, the latter tended to appear divisive, a teaching of "two Christs."[215] The two models represented distinct options for relating the humanity and divinity of Christ, not merely in theoretical metaphysical terms but also as distinct interpretations of the christological narrative. Was the humanity of Christ simply a soteriological extension of an attenuated divinity, such that the divinity and humanity belong together within a continuum of Christ's *being* "for us"? Or was it a radical reversal of the most differentiated modes of being, wherein the fully transcendent Creator became a suffering creature "for us and our salvation"?

Approaching the issue in terms of christological continuity and disruption enables us to make better sense of the fourth-century trinitarian debates than do modern frameworks of emphasizing the humanity versus emphasizing the divinity, or Christology "from above" and Christology "from below." For a modern reader, it is striking and puzzling, for example, that Arius's Christ represents both an inferior divinity and a superhuman humanity insofar as he does not possess a human soul. Whereas this seems contradictory if one is trying to determine whether his intention is really to emphasize the divinity or the humanity, it is utterly consistent with a commitment to christological continuity. The commitment to such continuity tended to exert pressure on *both* the divinity and the humanity to make them structurally reconcilable; the divinity is attenuated with a view to the humanity, and the humanity is elevated with a view to the divinity. On the other hand, a commitment to a christological narrative of disruption involves a typical recourse to a rhetoric of paradox that includes an unflinching emphasis on the discontinuity between Christ's divine being and his human lowliness.

Apollinaris's distinct location within this developing problematic can be highlighted by elucidating its interaction with Marcellus's account. As Kelley McCarthy Spoerl has shown, it was in large part an interpretation of Marcellus's Christology as resolvable into "two Christs" that motivated Apollinaris's extremely unitive Christology.[216] With regard to the location of the christological *pro nobis*, Marcellus, typically, is hard to categorize. On the one hand, the generation of the Word, which inaugu-

---

215. See the insightful analysis of this point by Vaggione, *Eunomius of Cyzicus*, 109.

216. "Apollinarian Christology and the Anti-Marcellan Tradition." A fuller presentation of her thesis and a very helpful reading of Apollinaris's major work, *Kata meros pistis*, is found in Spoerl, "A Study of the *Kata Meros Pistis*." More recently, Spoerl has argued that Apollinaris is also influenced by Eusebius

rates the Word's differentiation from the Father, is a working of the divine activity (*energeia*) for us. But this outward generation of the Word, for Marcellus, is not the origin of Christ's divine being but a secondary stage that belongs to the outworking of divine activity *ad extra*. In his immanent being, internal to the Father, the Word exists in the silence of the perfection of divine singularity. The absolute divinity of the preexistent Christ is thus integral to the divine being and is not merely functional, "for us." Therefore, Marcellus dealt with Proverbs 8:22 by locating the "creation for the sake of the works" at the point of the incarnation and not in the absolute origin of the divinity of the preexistent Christ.[217] Notwithstanding his ambiguity about the status of the Word's outward generation, Marcellus thus belongs ultimately within the model in which the *pro nobis* is located not at the very origin of Christ's divinity but rather in his human economy. Consequently, Marcellus's Christology followed the model of disruption and reversal rather than continuity. We have seen that, despite the employment of the language of unity, Marcellus gave maximal scope to the differences between humanity and divinity in Christ, indeed to the point where the divinity seems to simply abandon the humanity in order to recover its integrity within divine singularity. Just as Marcellus's account of the relation of the Father and the Son seemed to substantiate fears that Nicene doctrine was modalist, his account of the loose and tense unity between Christ's humanity and divinity seemed to confirm the suspicion that the disruptive element in Nicene Christology amounted to the positing of "two Christs."

OVERCOMING THE CHRISTOLOGY OF DISRUPTION

Apollinaris was a strong supporter of Nicene doctrine whose attitude to Marcellus, another supporter of Nicaea, could be expressed by the adage, "With friends like that, who needs enemies?" In pointed contrast to Marcellus's modalist-leaning interpretation of *homoousios*, Apollinaris insisted that Father, Son, and Spirit are three distinct *prosōpa*.[218] Because he was committed to the absolute and unqualified divinity of Christ, Apollinaris had to locate the *pro nobis* not at the origin of the divinity itself but in the human economy. Consequently, he was committed in some measure to a Christology of disruption rather than continuity, a Christology that had to deal with the extremes of a fully transcendent divinity and an enfleshed humanity and with Christ's being both *pro se* and *pro nobis*. But Apollinaris recoiled from the "two Christs" entailed by the divisive Christology of Marcellus and others, like Eustathius of Antioch, who spoke explicitly of Jesus's human soul. Again, the issue was not some abstract metaphysical speculation but the integrity and intelligibility of the experience of Christian worship and the message of salvation. For Apollinaris, a divisive Christology threatened to deconstruct the doxological core of Christian life by positing two sets of worship. Such an error not only fragments

---

of Caesarea's polemic against Eustathius of Antioch's doctrine of a human soul of Christ ("Apollinarius and the First Nicene Generation").

217. Cf. Fr. 35 (Vinzent).

218. *Kata meros pistis* 13–15.

the act of worshiping but also renders unintelligible Christ's own self-understanding as the recipient of such worship:

> If the same one is a complete human being and God as well, and the pious spirit does not worship a human being but worships God, it will be found both worshiping and not worshiping the same one—which is impossible. Moreover, humanity itself does not judge itself to be an object of worship . . . but God knows himself to be an object of worship. Yet it is inconceivable that the same one should both know himself to be an object of worship and not know it. Therefore, it is inconceivable that the same one should be both God and a whole human being. Rather, he exists in the singleness of a commingled incarnate divine nature, with the result that worshipers bend their attention to God inseparable from his flesh and not to one who is not worshiped and another who is.[219]

The oneness of Christ's person, for Apollinaris, is thus experientially appropriated through the unity and integrity of the act of worship: "We confess that the Son of God became Son of Man, not merely in name but in truth, having taken flesh from the Virgin Mary, and that the same one is Son of God and the same Son of Man, and that there is one *prosōpon* and one is the worship of the Word along with the flesh he assumed."[220] Having safeguarded the distinctions within the Trinity such that the act of worship is really directed to three who are united in consubstantiality, the dividing of Jesus Christ into two threatens to make the Trinity experienced in Christian worship a foursome: "We do not say that we worship four *prosōpa*: God, and the Son of God, and a human being, and the Holy Spirit."[221]

A divisive Christology also breaks down the integrity and efficacy of Christian salvation. Only divinity can be the agent of salvation, and only divine immutability can safeguard the inherent instability of mutable humanity. The humanity of Christ can be a medium for the divine salvific agency, but it cannot be a co-agent of acts of salvation. For all these reasons, Apollinaris's decisive step, designed to mitigate the element of disruption in a Christology that acknowledged both a fully transcendent divinity and Christ's sharing in the human condition, was to assert that the *Logos* replaced the human spirit, or mind (*nous*), in Christ. In this model, there is still a *kenōsis* of the *Logos* in assuming human flesh, but there is no enduring tension or dichotomy between the human and the divine. The divinity simply rules the humanity; the unity of divinity and humanity is resolved in the salvific monarchy of the *Logos* over the subservient flesh. In Apollinaris's reckoning, Christ's humanity was still genuine, inasmuch as a human being was constituted of flesh ruled by spirit (*nous*), and so was Christ, even if his human flesh was ruled by the divine *Logos*.[222]

219. Fr. 9 (Lietzmann) (ET: Norris, *Christological Controversy*, 107–8, altered).
220. *Kata meros pistis* 28.
221. *Kata meros pistis* 31.
222. See Norris, *Christological Controversy*, 22.

The legacy of Apollinaris and his significance in the systematic reconstruction of emerging trinitarian doctrine resides in his exposing the structural problematic of the trinitarian position that attributed absolute status to the Son's divinity and thus located the *pro nobis* in the humanity. As we saw, this model was necessarily bound up with a Christology of disruption and reversal. Apollinaris's radical attempts to resolve this disruption and to hold in tandem both the irreducible difference between the divine and human status of the Son and a unitive account of Jesus Christ was roundly rejected by other supporters of Nicaea. This rejection was based on an insistence that the scriptural christological narrative and its soteriological vision required that Christ's humanity be truly integral. Overcoming the element of disruption and reversal intrinsic to Nicene Christology cannot involve a truncation of Christ's humanity. But Apollinaris's provocation made it clear that a Nicene account of the coordinate divinity of the Word and the Father, which necessarily involves a maximal contrast between Christ's absolute divinity and his humanity, must find a different way to conceive of the unitive principle within this maximal difference. This task then became constitutive of subsequent efforts to articulate accounts of the unity of being of Father, Son, and Holy Spirit.

This chapter has attempted to provide a broad and schematic reading of a range of issues involved in the doctrinal debates of the fourth century. In order to provide a rudimentary framework for understanding these debates as a process of development that is constitutive of the meaning of trinitarian doctrine, I have proposed a model of development based on Gabriel Marcel's distinction between primary and secondary reflection. Elements of trinitarian faith were embedded in the primary reflection of the early church that constituted the flow of Christian experience. A constellation of agitating factors contributed to the exigency of a secondary reflection oriented to retrieving the unity of Christian experience in the face of challenges to that unity from within and without: for example, the pressure to present a coherent account of its faith in its newly legitimized social location and the need to reconcile a clarified appreciation of the transcendence of God as without cause or origin with a coherent account of the primacy of Christ, who is scripturally designated as originated both in his divine and human status.

I suggested that the latter issue was the galvanizing center around which revolved two distinct strategies for recovering the unity of Christian experience, both of which were attempts to preserve what their proponents believed to be distinctly Christian truths. One trajectory staked its foundation on the biblical witness of God's sovereign freedom benevolently manifested in his relation to the world. This trajectory considered it of primary importance to insist on God's priority as uncaused (*agen[n]ētos*) relative to everything that is caused by his sovereign and beneficent will. In this trajectory, the primacy of Christ was conceived in terms of his being an instrument and mediator of God's benevolent will toward creation and simultaneously a model of humanity's obedience to God's benevolent purpose. This approach dealt with the trinitarian grammar of Christian faith by conceiving Son and Spirit as being uniquely associated with the benevolent will of the uncaused God, the first products and primary mediators of that good will. A distinct trajectory, which parsed trinitarian grammar in terms of unity of being, was foundationally based on the christological reconfiguration of divine transcendence. While the relation between God and creation is still conceived in terms of a radical ontological otherness, the relation between Christ, in his divinity, and the God he addressed as Father (and, ultimately, the Spirit) was considered to be constitutive of the perfection of divine being. As early as Alexander, and persisting throughout the diverse configurations of doctrinal issues treated by theologians within this trajectory, there is a consistent emphasis that the relation between God and Jesus Christ in his divinity, rather than God's priority as uncaused, provides the core content of divine transcendence.

One benefit of the model of development sketched above is that it explains that both trajectories involved global interpretations of Christian faith. Questions of worship, the character of salvation, the nature of Christ's salvific mediation, and the God-world relation, among others, were demonstrated to be implicated in the basic trinitarian options of unity of being and unity of will. At the same time, the taxonomy of these two trajectories is appropriately used to make intelligible the interactivity between all the significant players, rather than to box them into hermetically sealed compartments. Asterius corrected Arius's denial of the title "Father" to the one God by ascribing a generative capacity to the Unbegotten and thereby provided Athanasius with further ground for arguing that generativity was constitutive of the divine essence as such. Apollinaris apparently took to heart criticisms of those who saw Nicene Christology as positing "two Christs" and tried to redress it in a manner that highlighted the need for a christological model that could synthesize the Nicene patterns of a Christology of disruption with a balancing emphasis on Christ's unity of person, a process that links together the trinitarian debates of the fourth century to the christological debates of the fifth.

The model of development proposed here and the identification of these two broad trajectories could be applied to a much more detailed account of the fourth-century debates than the present enquiry allows. For the sake of retrieving Nicene doctrine in its systematic scope, we now proceed to an account of how this scope is configured in the trinitarian theologies of three significant interpreters, Athanasius of Alexandria, Gregory of Nyssa, and Augustine of Hippo. Athanasius and Gregory of Nyssa are two figures who belong in the first trajectory but integrate some of the concerns of the other, ultimately conceding that will is an applicable category not only with respect to the relation between God and creation, but even within the divine being. In both cases, we will also note, among other themes, their christological reinterpretation of divine transcendence, which I proposed as a foundational principle in the development of Nicene trinitarian theology. Augustine will be considered in a further chapter as someone who expounds a straightforward account of trinitarian unity of being that is largely untroubled by questions of willing within the Trinity. In Augustine's case, we will be concerned rather with his construction of a christocentric trinitarian epistemology, which I suggested is a second foundational principle in the development of Nicene theology.

3

Athanasius

The Crucified Lord and Trinitarian Deification

Athanasius was born in Egypt around 295. A tenth-century Arabic chronicle of Coptic Patriarchs reports that he was born to pagan parents and that his widowed mother converted to Christianity at his instigation when he was a teenager.[1] It also reports that he was taken into the household of Bishop Alexander at an early age and tutored in Scripture and theology. The reliability of all the details of this hagiographical account is uncertain, but we do know that the young Athanasius, barely thirty years old at most, was present at the Council of Nicaea as Alexander's secretary. With the death of Alexander three years after Nicaea, in 328, Athanasius became bishop of Alexandria. He inherited a church embroiled in the doctrinal disagreements between Alexander and Arius and still suffering from the disturbances of the Melitian schism. Melitius was an Egyptian bishop who a couple of decades earlier had drawn the ire of the then bishop of Alexandria, Peter, by consecrating bishops outside his jurisdiction while Peter was imprisoned during the Diocletianic persecution. The tension between the two bishops apparently also came to involve disagreements over the handling of those who had lapsed during the persecution, with Peter adopting a lenient approach, which Melitius criticized.[2] At the beginning of Athanasius's episcopacy, the Melitians had set up rival bishops throughout Egypt. Although the Council of Nicaea had attempted to reintegrate Melitians with the greater church of Egypt, the

---

1. Severus ibn al-Mukaffa, *History of the Patriarchs* 4.1, 407.
2. For a full and nuanced account of the issues involved in this controversy, see Williams, "Arius and the Melitian Schism"; *Arius*, 32–47.

Melitians were angered by Athanasius's appointment as bishop and charged that he was underage and had used illicit means to gain the episcopal office. The Melitians and the supporters of Arius were allied in their opposition to Athanasius and initiated other charges against Athanasius, accusing him of heavy-handed and violent behavior.[3] Athanasius's popularity among his own people grew with his tenure as bishop and was further consolidated by his integration of the growing monastic community of Egypt with his own episcopal authority and doctrinal stance.[4] However, outside of Egypt, disapproval of his resolute opposition to Arius and his supporters, together with the ill repute garnered by his opponents' accusations, resulted in his legendary series of exiles, constituting seventeen of his forty-six years as bishop of Alexandria. He died in 373.[5]

In retracing the systematic range of Athanasius's trinitarian theology, we shall focus on five themes: (1) his account of the divinity of the Crucified as the Christian story of salvation; (2) his construction of a trinitarian hermeneutics; (3) his analysis of the dialectic of Scripture and doctrine in speaking about God; (4) his theology of the Holy Spirit; and (5) his vision of Christian life as participation in the Triune God.

The Divinity of the Crucified and the Christian Story of Salvation

The second half of Athanasius's double treatise *Against the Greeks–On the Incarnation* has long been regarded as a Christian classic. One important feature of a classic text is that it can construct and project a world from within its own internal dynamics. And indeed, many have been able to derive a great deal from *On the Incarnation* without placing it in its historical setting—which to some extent is fortunate, because we cannot be certain of the precise historical circumstances of its writing.[6] The crucial question is whether it was composed before or after the outbreak of the controversy between Arius and Alexander. Up until fairly recently, it was widely held that Athanasius wrote this work prior to the eruption of this debate. The main rationale for this position is that Athanasius makes no explicit mention of this debate in the work. But it has been pointed out that Athanasius does not explicitly mention Arius in any extant text composed before 335, fully seven years after his accession to the episcopal throne.[7] But Athanasius, though often prolix in his literary style, is also a man of strategic silences. Given the emperor Constantine's impatience with the emerging doctrinal debate and his own embattled position among other Eastern bishops, it seems that Athanasius considered it most prudent at this stage to defend what he considered to be

3. For an account of these charges, a review of modern scholarship, and a defense of Athanasius, see Arnold, *Early Episcopal Career of Athanasius*.

4. See especially Brakke, *Athanasius and the Politics of Asceticism*.

5. For fuller treatments of Athanasius's life and turbulent ecclesial career, see especially Anatolios, *Athanasius*, 1–39; Martin, *Athanase d'Alexandrie*; Tetz, "Zur Biographie des Athanasius"; Tetz, *Athanasiana*.

6. On questions of the dating, see Anatolios, *Athanasius*, 26–30; Ernest, *Bible in Athanasius*, 44–50, 423–24.

7. See Kannengiesser, "La date de l'apologie d'Athanase."

orthodox Christian doctrine without explicitly mentioning Arius and his supporters. The modern scholarly consensus places the composition of this text after the outbreak of doctrinal disagreements between Alexander and Arius. I have argued elsewhere from the treatise's magisterial tone and triumphalistic depiction of the peace and visible sanctity of church life that it was probably written after Athanasius became bishop and before his first exile, between 328 and 333. Correspondences between the contents of the treatise and the issues at play in the debate support this dating.[8]

A point of departure for reading this work as a discreet polemical engagement with Arius and his early supporters can be found in Alexander's letter to his namesake, Alexander of Byzantium.[9] Speaking of the exegetical strategy of Arius and his supporters, the author of this letter says, "They extract every passage which refers to the economy of the Savior, and to his humiliation for our sake . . . while they evade all those which proclaim his divinity which is from the beginning and the unceasing glory which he possesses with the Father. They maintain the ungodly doctrine entertained by the Greeks and the Jews concerning Jesus Christ."[10] Another passage that can throw light on Athanasius's implicit polemical intentions occurs in a treatise written in the 350s in defense of Nicene doctrine. In *On the Nicene Council* (*De decretis*), Athanasius likens the "Arians" to the Pharisees "who asked, 'Why do you, as a human being, make yourself to be God?' What they should have said, on the contrary, is: 'Why did you, being God, become a human being?'"[11]

The above passages suggest that Athanasius, following Alexander, believed that the heart of the "Arian" position was a particular construal of the nexus between what we would call "Christology" and "trinitarian theology." The "Arians" argued from the human limitations and suffering of Christ's humanity to the ontological inferiority (with respect to the Father) of his divinity. As evidenced by his comment in *On the Nicene Council*, Athanasius believed that the coherence of Christian faith depends centrally on the rationale for the self-emptying of the incarnation. The central Christian question, therefore, is: "Why did you, being God, become a human being?" That, of course, is the question of *On the Incarnation*. And Athanasius's response is that the proper understanding of the rationale for the incarnation would exalt rather than denigrate the status of the Son, "so that from the seeming devaluation of the Word, you may have all the greater and stronger piety towards him."[12] Moreover, Alexander's characterization of Arius's teaching as "the ungodly doctrine held by the Greeks and the Jews" gives us a further clue that we should understand Athanasius's treatise as a veiled attack on Arius and his supporters. Ostensibly, the positive exposition of the incarnation in this treatise is presented in

8. Anatolios, *Coherence*, 29.

9. See above, 79–80.

10. *Ep. Alex.*, Urk. 14.4–5 (ET: NPNF² 3:35, altered). Cf. 14.37: "Recalling all the words about the salvific suffering, humiliation, self-emptying, poverty, and other attributes that the Savior took on for our sake, they pile these up to impugn the supreme deity that was his from the start."

11. *Decr.* 1; Anatolios, *Athanasius*, 179.

12. *Inc.* 1.

polemical engagement with Greeks and Jews, both of whom reject the attribution of divinity to a crucified man. But it is likely that the "Jews" and "Greeks" Athanasius had in mind were really those Christians who were sympathetic to the doctrine of Arius. If, indeed, Athanasius found it politically expedient at this time to refrain from attacking Arius and his supporters publicly, the next best thing would be to establish the continuity between their doctrine and that of the prototypical non-Christian others, Greeks and Jews. By labeling as "Greek" and "Jewish" the notion that the human economy of Christ disproves the fullness of his divinity, Athanasius is thus able to make maximal usage of his calculated silence by portraying the issues in question as not merely constituting an abstruse and divisive intra-Christian debate (which would irritate Constantine) but as falling across the lines between Christianity and its cultural competitors.

We can further illuminate the dynamics of this text by observing the distinct similarities in terminology, imagery, and argument between this work and some of the works of Eusebius of Caesarea, especially the *Theophany* and the *Oration to Constantine*.[13] As we have noted, Eusebius of Caesarea, who had significant ties to the emperor, was an important early supporter of Arius. In taking over much of the framework set up by Eusebius while surgically altering and adjusting key points, Athanasius would be subverting the most coherent and articulate presentation of a subordinationist trinitarian theology from within. This is a typical and recurrent move in Athanasius's polemic. On the basis of the hypothesis that Athanasius's treatise is intended as a corrective to Eusebian theology, it is helpful to focus on key similarities and differences between this treatise and key motifs in Eusebius.

First, the overall narrative exposition of Christian faith is similar in *Against the Greeks–On the Incarnation* and Eusebius's work. Both narratives are to a considerable extent governed by an Origenian epistemological or "gnosiological" perspective. The goal of human existence, achieved in Christ, is true knowledge (*gnōsis*) of God.[14] Humanity, created in the image of the Word, has access to this knowledge from within its own being. The harmonious diversity of creation is witness to a transcendent rationality—the divine *Logos*—that guides it. But, through the misuse of free will, humanity has lost access to the knowledge of God and descended into a downward spiral of ignorance and moral depravity. More than Athanasius, Eusebius concedes some positive preparation for the appearance of Christ among both Jews and Greeks, but both he and Athanasius ultimately emphasize the inadequacies and distortions of both approaches. The Greeks are fundamentally mistaken about the nature of creation and its relation to the Creator, not to mention the perversities of Greek mythology, while the Jews ignore the Old Testament testimonies to the advent

13. I have noted some of the counter-Eusebian elements of this treatise in my "Influence of Irenaeus on Athanasius." See also Ernest, *Bible in Athanasius*, 49–50, 427–28. Other notable readings of this treatise as anti-Eusebian include Bienert, "Zur Logos-Christologie des Athanasius"; Mühlenburg, *Epochen der Kirchengeschichte*, 66; and Mühlenburg, "Vérité et Bonté de Dieu."

14. Athanasius, *C. gent.* 1; *Inc.* 8, 14–16; Eusebius, *Dem. ev.* 4.10; *Laud. Const.* 11.5; 14.5–12; *Theoph.* 1.75.

of Christ.[15] The demise of humanity presents a dilemma and a challenge for God's benevolent and compassionate omnipotence.[16] If he were to let humanity perish, his own benevolence would be defeated. God responds to this challenge by manifesting knowledge of himself through the human manifestation of the divine Word. Since humanity had become inescapably obsessed with sensible realities, the invisible Word and Image of God the Father has revealed himself in a sensible manner through the "temple" of his flesh.[17] Through his teachings and actions, Jesus manifests knowledge of the true God. Jesus's death is a redemptive sacrifice that atones for humanity's sins, and the manner of his violent death and three-day burial reveals both that he truly died and that his divine power is stronger than death.[18] His resurrection is manifest in the renewed knowledge of God and rehabilitated moral deportment evident in many people all over the world who profess faith in God through the name of Christ. There is a nuance of difference in the treatment of the last point, with Eusebius pointing principally to the new and peaceful world order under Constantine as evidence of the moral and religious regeneration of humanity, while Athanasius focuses exclusively on the holiness of the church.[19] Both, however, see the person of Christ as the active agent in this renewal and take such activity as evidence that its source is living and active, the risen Christ.

Furthermore, there is considerable overlap in the christological vocabulary of Eusebius and Athanasius throughout their respective expositions, not only with respect to widespread scriptural appellations, such as Image, Word, and Wisdom, but also in more idiosyncratic terminology that is prevalent in Eusebius's general corpus but largely restricted to this treatise among Athanasius's works. Examples would include referring to Christ as "our common Savior" and, adopting Eusebius's model of divine governance, naming Christ as ruler, governor, and king.[20]

Given this common narrative framework and shared vocabulary, Athanasius's originality and his polemical intent are manifested in the places where he makes significant changes to Eusebian motifs. The integrity of his theological vision, which is what makes this work a classic, is bound up with his success in reintegrating these changes into this shared narrative framework. We can elaborate on these significant alterations under three headings: the conception of divine transcendence; the divinity of the Word, in relation to both the Father and creation; and the understanding of redemption.

15. Eusebius, *Dem. ev.* 4.7–10.

16. Athanasius, *Inc.* 6, 13; Eusebius, *Dem. ev.* 4.10.

17. Eusebius, *Laud. Const.* 14.3.4; Athanasius, *Inc.* 26.

18. Eusebius, *Dem. ev.* 4.12; *Laud. Const.* 15.8–13; cf. Athanasius, *Inc.* 10, 15, 21–27.

19. Cf. Eusebius, *Laud. Const.* 16–18 and Athanasius, *Inc.* 29, 48, 51–52.

20. E.g., note the similarity in the usage of the phrase *ho koinos sōtēr* and *ho koinos pantōn sōtēr* in Eusebius, *Vit. Const.* 3.12; 4.64; *Laud. Const.* 9.4; 11.1; 14.4; *Com. Isa.* 2.16; Athanasius, *Inc.* 21, 30, 37. A TLG search attributed eleven out of thirteen occurrences of this phrase to the combination of Eusebius and Athanasius. All of the Athanasian occurrences are from *De incarnatione.* In addition, Athanasius appears to draw on Eusebius's collection of Old Testament *testimonia* to the Messiah. See Kannengiesser, "Les citations bibliques"; see also Ernest, *Bible in Athanasius*, 81–82.

Reconstructing Divine Transcendence

We saw earlier that Eusebius, like Asterius, posits that the highest level of divine transcendence is inaccessible to direct contact with creation. Also like Asterius, Eusebius refers to the necessity of a mediating being who can stand between creation and ultimate divine transcendence.[21] In this model, divine transcendence and divine immanence tend to be associated with the Father and the Son, respectively. The Father represents the extremity of divine transcendence; the Son, the attenuation of the Father's transcendence and the extremity of divine immanence. In order to place the Son on the same level of transcendence as the Father, Athanasius offers an alternative construal of the character of divine transcendence. Instead of assigning divine transcendence and immanence to Father and Son respectively, he construes them as attributes that belong to divine being as such and are harmonized through the category of *philanthrōpia*, God's love for humanity. While God is by nature inaccessible, he makes himself accessible to creation through his love.[22] No distinct mediating being is needed because the divine nature mediates its own transcendence through God's loving condescension. Simultaneously conceding that divine transcendence militates against direct contact with creation and integrating his theology of creation with his theology of incarnation, Athanasius characterizes the radical relation between God and creation, even in the very act of creation, as the expression of God's loving mercy.[23] The mercy of creation consisted in God's bestowing upon humans a participation in the Word through which they could attain knowledge of the Father. Characterizing God primarily in terms of *philanthrōpia* and mercy—attributes whereby God can transcend his own transcendence—explains both why no mediating being is needed and how the incarnation accords with the character of God's being and the divine deportment in the act of creation.

The Divinity of the Word

In keeping with the elasticity of the language of "divinity" at this time, both Athanasius and Eusebius portray the Son as "divine" and as exercising a creative and sustaining role with respect to creation. But subtle differences in their presentations manifest the differences in their respective conceptions of the kind and level of divinity which belong to the Word. For Eusebius, as for Asterius, the Son is a middle divine being who mediates between the inaccessible transcendence of the Father and the rest of creation. In *Against the Greeks–On the Incarnation*, Athanasius implicitly rejects the attribution of a middle divinity to the Word, instead conceiving of the Son's divinity as strictly correlative with that of the Father, in three ways:

1. Whereas Eusebius has a hierarchical chain of being, with the Son in the crucial middle position between the transcendent Unbegotten and the rest of creation,

21. *Dem. ev.* 4.6.
22. *Inc.* 2, 3.
23. *Inc.* 3.

Athanasius presents a strict ontological dialectic between a creation that comes to be from nonbeing and an uncreated divinity. This polarity is the oppositional yet relational difference between an inherently insecure and unstable creation and an ontologically secure and self-sufficient God, who lovingly and generously grants stable and secure being to what he creates from nothing. All that comes to be from nothing has the nothingness of its origin as an inherent gap in its attachment to being. But this gap is bridged by the creative, sustaining, and stabilizing power of the Word, who thus grants security to creation and protection from its ontological poverty.[24] In this way, the divinity of the Word is conceived both as being in strict ontological opposition to the realm of creatures and also as being in a fundamentally positive relation that grounds creation's being.

2. Athanasius also highlights the ontological correlativity between Father and Son by consistently naming one through the other. Thus, the Father is typically named "Father of the Word" or "Father of our Lord Jesus Christ," while the Son is "Word of God" or "Word of the Father." Other biblical titles of the Son also follow this pattern of correlativity: the Son and Word is also Wisdom, Power, Radiance, and Image *of the Father*.[25] Athanasius would later use *idios* as a technical term for the inseparable belonging of the Son to the Father; in this treatise *idios* already indicates the correlative relation between the two: "The Son is proper (*idios*) Word and Wisdom and Power from the Father."[26] Both Arius and Asterius explicitly deny that claim.[27] Athanasius implicitly counters their belief that the Son's existence originates from nonbeing, or from the Father's will, by asserting that the Son "proceeds (*proiōn*) from the Father."[28] The correlativity between the two is conceived along the lines of the mutual internality indicated by the declaration of the Johannine Jesus, "I am in the Father and the Father is in me" (John 14:10), which Athanasius interprets as signifying the eternal coexistence of Father and Son: "So necessarily, the Word is in his begetter and the begotten is eternally with the Father."[29]

3. A third distinguishing feature of Athanasius's depiction of the divinity of the Son is his understanding of the Son's gnosiological role, an important motif in the Origenian tradition. The permutations of this motif through this period illustrate different conceptions of the relative status of Father and Son. For Arius, the Son mediates a negative theology of the Father. The majesty that we know in the Son leads us to affirm the infinitely greater and ultimately unknowable majesty of the unbegotten Father. The Son himself does not know the Father's substance or even

24. On the significance of the motifs of "stability" and "security" in Athanasius, see Anatolios, *Athanasius*, 61–66.

25. Cf. *Inc.* 48. This pattern of co-naming is too pervasive to itemize; for detailed citations of the various titles of Jesus Christ in *Inc.*, see Kannengiesser, *Athanase d'Alexandrie*, 86–98.

26. *Inc.* 32. On the significance of this term for Athanasius, see Anatolios, *Coherence*, esp. 141–46, and Louth, "Use of the Term *IDIOS*," 198–202.

27. On Arius, see Williams, "Logic of Arianism." For Asterius's rejection of the claim that the preincarnate Christ is the "proper" (*idios*) Word and Wisdom of the Father, see Fr. 64 (Vinzent).

28. *C. gent.* 45; *Inc.* 32.

29. *C. gent.* 47.

his own. Arius, though reluctant, is biblically constrained to use "Image" language of the Son, but his theological vision as a whole makes him interpret it awkwardly: if the Son is Image, he is so precisely insofar as he is "unlike" the Father! But biblical usage and the utility of the term for explaining how the Son provides epistemic access to the Father led Arius's sympathizers to find a more positive interpretation. Asterius went so far as to speak of the Son as "exact Image of the substance of the Father," though he counterbalanced this concession by recalling that humanity, too, is in God's image.[30] When Eusebius designates the Son as "Image," he seems to mean primarily that the Son reflects the power and willful activity of the Father;[31] the Son as Image reveals knowledge less of the Father's person than of the Father's will and of the proper way to worship the Father.[32] In contrast, a pervasive motif throughout *Against the Greeks–On the Incarnation* is that the Son and Word reveals the Father directly: through him, we understand (*katanoeō*), perceive, and apprehend the Father.[33] Economically, there is an epistemological correlativity and mutual disclosure between Father and Son. From the human point of view, the Son reveals the Father to us; from God's point of view, as it were, the Father not only reveals himself through the Son, as if the Son were simply an instrument for the revelation of the Father, but also desires to reveal the Son to humanity: "Having such a Son, who is Creator and Good, from himself, the Father did not hide him and let him be unmanifest to his creatures. But every day he reveals him to all through the constitution and life of all things, which come about through him. In him and through him, he also reveals himself, as the Savior says, 'I am in the Father and the Father is in me' (John 14:10)."[34]

Trinitarian Salvation

With respect to soteriology, we find again many overlapping motifs between Athanasius and Eusebius. They both speak of salvation in a gnosiological vein; the Son renews and fulfills humanity's knowledge of God. But they also both speak of Christ's death as a sacrifice that repairs human sin, defeats death, and confers incorruptibility and immortality.[35] The language of deification is decidedly more prevalent in Athanasius but not absent from Eusebius.[36] But here also, the differences, while subtle, are decisive, and they have implications for the relationship between Father and Son. As we noted, the gnosiological aspect of Eusebius's soteriology depicts the incarnate Word as renewing and perfecting our knowledge of God's will and God's ways. By contrast, we find in Athanasius a rather more personalist emphasis on Christ's making knowledge of the Father himself accessible to humanity. Analogously, Eusebius tends

30. Fr. 10 (Vinzent, 86).
31. *Dem. ev.* 4.3.
32. Cf. *Laud. Const.* 11.5; 14.5–12; *Dem. ev.* 4.10.
33. *C. gent.* 29; *Inc*. 19, 31, 40, 43, 54.
34. *C. gent.* 47.
35. Cf. Eusebius, *Laud. Const.* 15.11–12; *Dem. ev.* 4.12; on the motif of sacrifice in Athanasius, see Anatolios, *Athanasius*, 57–61.
36. Cf. *Dem. ev.* 4.14: "He divinized humanity with himself."

to depict the redeemed state of humanity in terms of its intrinsic perfections, such as incorruptibility and immortality, and in terms of the perfection of its adherence to the divine law.[37] Athanasius's soteriology places much greater stress on participation in God and immediate ontological contact with the Word, which renders access to the Father. The trinitarian form of Christian salvation, as depicted in *Against the Greeks–On the Incarnation*, can be summed up in the Athanasian motif that the incarnate Word renders us present to the Father: "He brought all things over to himself and through himself to the Father."[38] Athanasius's articulation of how Jesus "brings us to the Father" has strong eucharistic overtones: Christ presents his own body as an "offering" (*prosphora*) and "sacrifice" (*thysia*) to the Father, and we are presented to the Father through association with Christ's body.[39]

A helpful way to synthesize the argument of *Against the Greeks–On the Incarnation* and to integrate it with Athanasius's later and more explicitly polemical work is to focus on the trinitarian-christological-anthropological nexus that forms the guiding motif of the work: only the One who is true Image can renew humanity's being according to the image (*kat' eikona*). The trinitarian ground of this nexus is the immediate relation (though we do not find the later technical vocabulary of "relation" in this treatise) whereby the Son is Image of the Father. The soteriological consequence of this immediacy is that the Son is uniquely able to grant direct and immediate access to the Father. The statement that humanity was created according to the Image is simultaneously anthropological and christological: to be created according to the Image is to be granted a participation in the one who is the true and full Image of the Father. When humanity lost its stability, which depended on remaining in the state of being according to the Image, the incarnate Word repaired the image of God in humanity by reuniting it with his own divine imaging of the Father. Jesus Christ is therefore both eternal divine Image and restored human image. The saving union of divine and human image in Christ is characterized by immediacy. One foundational principle of Athanasius's theological vision is this stress on the continuity of immediate connections between God and humanity and a corresponding abhorrence of obstacles and opaque mediations.[40] As perfect Image, the Son is immediately united to the Father and transparently reflects knowledge of the Father; anything short of this immediate and transparent relation would deconstruct our immediate connection with the Father through the Son from the divine side. Through his incarnation, the Son repairs our human participation in his imaging of the Father from within the human constitution; anything short of a full incarnation would leave humans disconnected from both Father and Son. Thus, incarnation and the full divinity of

---

37. *Laud. Const.* 14.11–12; 16–17, *passim*.

38. *Inc.* 37.

39. See Anatolios, *Athanasius*, 57–60. Later, in *C. Ar.* 2.74, Athanasius speaks of humanity's redemption being accomplished through being "co-bodied" (*syssōmoi*) with Christ's body, a term whose eucharistic connotations are explicit in Cyril of Jerusalem, *Mystagogy* 4 and elsewhere. See Anatolios, *Athanasius*, 250n162.

40. See Anatolios, *Coherence*.

the Son are both integral to the immediacy of our contact with the Father. Far from indicating inferior divinity, the human life and death of Jesus Christ extend the efficacy of his divine imaging of the Father in the face of humanity's loss of the state of being according to the image. It is a wonderful display of the loving-kindness that belongs to the divine nature as such, the *philanthrōpia* that is equally shared by Father and Son.

Constructing a Trinitarian Hermeneutics

One of the ironies of theological scholarship is that although Athanasius is generally regarded as the great "anti-Arian" theologian, his doctrine is usually read out of *On the Incarnation*, where he does not explicitly mention the Arians, while his *Orations against the Arians* are relatively neglected. This relative neglect partly explains why Athanasius's trinitarian theology tends to be reduced to the simple and relatively abstract soteriological position that Christ had to be fully divine in order to save us. In the *Orations*, we have a much more complex and wide-ranging trinitarian hermeneutics that certainly includes soteriological concerns but advances further into a broad reading of Scripture. Some of the key moves executed by Athanasius in this treatise will become paradigmatic for subsequent theological reasoning on behalf of Nicene theology.

The *Orations* were written between 339 and 343, while Athanasius was at Rome, during his second exile. There Athanasius encountered Marcellus and, through him, had access to the writings of Asterius. While Asterius, as a kind of *alter ego* to Arius, is the explicit target of much of Athanasius's polemic in the *Orations*, there is evidence that Athanasius also intended to distance himself subtly from Marcellus.[41] The most significant marker of this distance is that, throughout the *Orations*, Athanasius is content to argue with Asterius on the basis of the common ground of the preexistent Son as "Image" of the Father. In doing so, he decisively parts ways with Marcellus who, in his own debates with Asterius, firmly rejected the application of "Image" to the preexistent Christ.[42] Marcellus's rejection of a preexistent Image of the Father was consistent with a general strategy of denying any attribution of duality to the relation of Father and Son prior to the incarnation. But Athanasius is willing in the *Orations* to use a whole host of scriptural images and concepts that suggest duality and to say expressly, "They are two."[43] Moreover, Athanasius at one point charges that Asterius's doctrine of a primal Monad that produces an Image of itself amounts to a Trinity that comes into being through addition and is thus liable also to subtraction.[44] Now,

41. On Athanasius's preoccupation with Asterius's material in this treatise, see Kannengiesser, *Athanase d' Alexandrie*, 121–22, 151–58.

42. Fr. 51–56 (Vinzent). See Jon Robertson, "Divine Mediation in Marcellus of Ancyra."

43. *C. Ar.* 3.4. For a fuller exposition of the position that "Athanasius may have known and coopted something of the rhetoric by which Marcellus's trinitarian doctrine was criticized and corrected," see Spoerl, "Athanasius and the Anti-Marcellan Controversy," 41.

44. *C. Ar.* 1.17.

Asterius himself says nothing about expansion and contraction of the Trinity, but Marcellus notoriously did say something that was at least interpreted to that effect.[45] Athanasius's rejection of this notion suggests at least that he had no intention of trying to hide differences between himself and Marcellus. It would appear that, with the *Orations*, Athanasius strategically inserts himself into the debate between Marcellus and Asterius. He assumes the role of Asterius's chief debater, effectively replacing Marcellus in that role and discreetly putting aside the latter's distinctive emphasis on the undifferentiated oneness of God.

The main terrain of the debate in the *Orations* is the Scriptures. Athanasius's stance is generally defensive and reactive as he deals with one "Arian" proof-text after another.[46] These texts can be organized in two main categories. The first category consists of texts that were interpreted as directly indicating that the preexistent Christ's divine existence was caused, received, and had an origin, rather than being eternal. This group of texts included, most prominently, Proverbs 8:22 ("He created me as the beginning of his ways for his works"), as well as others in which the exaltation "given" to Christ was predicated of his preexistent divinity.[47] These texts are treated in the first two orations. The second category consisted of texts from which his opponents argued that the incarnate Word's human limitations indicated a lower level of divinity than that of the Unbegotten God. This was the strategy—alluded to in Alexander's letter, *Hē philarchos*—to which *On the Incarnation* was a preliminary response.[48] These texts are treated in the third oration, along with Athanasius's response to "Arian" interpretations of a dossier of Johannine texts which seem on the surface to affirm the oneness of Father and Son.[49]

Athanasius's *Orations against the Arians* can make for laborious and sometimes tiresome reading. Athanasius is not an elegant stylist; his argumentation is often diffuse and is liberally interspersed with outraged invective. I will not reconstruct the flow of the argument or inventory his counter-exegesis of his opponents' proof-texts. It seems more useful here to sketch the main structural elements of his trinitarian hermeneutics. Corresponding to the two main kinds of proof texts presented by his opponents—those interpreted as directly stating the originated divinity of the Son and those that infer a secondary divine status from his human limitations—Athanasius offers two approaches to a trinitarian reading of Scripture. The first approach tries to read the eternal coexistence of Father and Son out of the overlapping scriptural

---

45. Cf. Fr. 48 (Vinzent).

46. For a full list, see Ernest, *Bible in Athanasius*, 118–19 (tables 3–4).

47. E.g., Ps. 44:7 LXX (45:7): "You loved righteousness and hated wickedness. Therefore God, your God, has anointed you with the oil of gladness above your fellows"; Acts 2:36: "Let all the house of Israel therefore know assuredly that God has *made* him both Lord and Christ"; Phil. 2:9: "*Therefore* God has highly exalted him and *given* him the name which is above every name"; Heb. 1:4: "*Having become* as much superior to angels as the name he has obtained is more excellent than theirs" (my italics).

48. Urk. 14.37.

49. In the third oration, Athanasius treats John 14:10, "I am in the Father and the Father is in me," and John 10:30, "The Father and I are one," before proceeding to deal with "Arian" proof-texts that refer to Jesus's suffering, dereliction, ignorance of the day of judgment, and human weakness, in 3.26.

identifications of God and Christ. The second approach insists that the christological narrative is twofold, to be applied distinctly to the divine and human stages of
the incarnate Word; such a distinction is necessary to avoid attributing the human
self-humbling of the Word to an inferior divinity. With regard to negative polemical
applications, the first approach amounts to an argument that the "Arian" denial of the
eternal coexistence of Father and Son impermissibly violates the scriptural patterns
for naming both God and Christ. The second approach charges that the same "Arian"
position results in a faulty christological narrative. While analyzing Athanasius's positive construction and polemical application of a trinitarian way of reading Scripture,
we will also retrace the connections he draws between trinitarian doctrine and the
doctrines of creation, Christology, soteriology, and worship.

Trinitarian Identification of God through Scriptural Names

The background to Athanasius's biblical trinitarian theology of divine names lies in
the tradition of expressing the primacy of Christ through the exalted titles (*epinoiai*,
in Origen's language) attributed to him in Scripture, such as Word, Wisdom, Power,
Light, Life, and so on.[50] These titles generally represent New Testament applications to
Jesus of Old Testament characterizations of divine presence and activity in the world.
We have identified this maneuver as something to which all parties assented on the
eve of Nicaea. We have also seen how both Arius and Asterius were constrained by
their theological commitments to construct the notion of two Words/Wisdoms: an
innate Word and Wisdom, considered as an attribute of the Unbegotten God, and
the preexistent Christ, who is Word and Wisdom in a secondary sense, a creature
who enjoys a preeminent share in the Unbegotten's innate Word and Wisdom. For
Athanasius, these christological titles grant us genuine insight into divine being. He
refers to them as *paradeigmata*, which in this context is best translated as "symbols."[51]
While we cannot of ourselves conceive God's uncreated being, Scripture offers us these
symbols in order to structure our conception of the divine: "Since human nature is not
capable of the comprehension of God, Scripture has placed before us such symbols
(*paradeigmata*) and such images (*eikōnas*), so that we may understand from them,
however slightly and obscurely, as much as is accessible to us."[52]

SHARED NAMES, SHARED NATURE

Athanasius's theology of divine names, in its positive construction as well as in its
polemical application, has been both generally neglected and misunderstood. It is
something of a novelty even to find in it a strategy with an inherent logic rather than

50. See Antonio Orbe, *La* Epinoia.
51. On this aspect of Athanasius's exegesis, see Anatolios, *Athanasius*, 78–79; "When Was God
without Wisdom?" For a thorough treatment of Athanasius's exegesis, see the aforementioned excellent
study by Ernest, *Bible in Athanasius*, esp. 151–59. For further bibliography on Athanasius's exegesis, see
Anatolios, "When Was God without Wisdom?" 117n1.
52. *C. Ar.* 2.32 (ET: Anatolios, *Athanasius*, 126).

merely tendentious rhetoric.[53] The strategy usually takes the form of recurrent recitations of biblical titles applied to Christ, along with the accusation that the ur-"Arian" axiom that "there was once when the Son was not" amounts to asserting that God himself once lacked the characterizations depicted by these titles. And so the "Arian" position is reduced to the assertion that God was once without wisdom, power, life, and so on. It is easy enough to dismiss the logical force of Athanasius's rhetoric in such passages. Admittedly, he himself is more concerned with the rhetorical performance of recommending his own position and denigrating his opponents' in scriptural terms than with a sober exposition of the logic that underlies this performance. But I would hold that a certain logic does undergird and enable the rhetorical force of such passages; it is not, however, a logic of pure objective reason but a scriptural logic. Essentially, this logic presumes and demonstrates a correlation between, on the one hand, the scriptural intertextuality involved in the naming of God and Christ and, on the other hand, the ontological correlativity of Father and Son. To retrieve this logic, whose structure and movement Athanasius assumes rather than articulates, we have to empathize with the fundamental conviction that the Scriptures are really revelatory of God. Presumably, Christians in any age would have to hold to that conviction in some form. In our own time, one of the regnant forms of that conviction is the belief that the character of God is revealed in God's action in salvation history. In this modern framework, God is revealed in Scripture insofar as Scripture refers outside itself to the historical narrative of God's action in the world; hence, the modern motif of "the narrative identification of God."[54]

Athanasius would certainly assent to this aspect of the scriptural revelation of God, but this is not the aspect at work in his theology of divine names. Rather, the Egyptian bishop employs a fundamental principle of allegorical reasoning that stops short of producing standard allegorical exegesis. This principle is that the Scriptures are revelatory not only by their reference to external events in history but also by the mutual interrelatedness of biblical texts on a surface linguistic level. In standard allegorical technique, this principle of intertextuality enables one to construct a biblical meaning by connecting together related language from different parts of Scripture, seemingly overstepping the contextual distance between the different usages. The principle of the unity of Scripture is assumed to legitimate the meaningfulness of its intertextual relations. Athanasius's distinctly dogmatic application of this principle is found in his assumption that the intertextual patterns of the scriptural naming of God must mirror, in a way accommodated to human understanding, the being of God. The patterns of scriptural divine naming must correspond to the pattern of divine being. Athanasius's reiterated presentations of the *paradeigmata* presume this principle and then present these patterns as a demonstration of an implicit logic, as follows: (1) Scripture names the divine presence by reference to a delimited lexical

---

53. For the position that Athanasius is engaged in dubious logic for rhetorical effect, see Stead, "Rhetorical Method in Athanasius." For a response to Stead's criticisms along the lines offered here, see Anatolios, "When Was God without Wisdom?"

54. See, e.g., Jenson, *Systematic Theology*, 1:42, 46.

field: God is speaker of a Word, possessor of Wisdom and Power, manifest as Light, and so on; (2) Scripture names Christ by reference to the same lexical field: Christ is Word of God, Wisdom and Power of God, Radiance of the Light, and so on; therefore, (3) the biblically named God is the God whose being must be construed according to the mutual correlation of these lexical fields. Conversely, a god who is described or named in such a way as to disrupt this correlation is not the biblical God.

It could be objected that whatever intelligibility Athanasius's approach might have had in his own context, it no longer makes sense for us today. That objection, however, simply makes hermeneutical distance an excuse for not understanding rather than an invitation for a creative translation of his logic into categories that we *can* understand. Whether or not one ultimately agrees with Athanasius's way of interpreting Scripture, it is possible at least to discern its intelligibility even in our own terms. To begin with, as is often the case with allegorical exegesis, Athanasius is simply traveling along a hermeneutical trajectory delineated by the New Testament writers themselves. These "theologians," as Athanasius called them, had already made the crucial move of naming Christ through divine names, such as Word, Wisdom, and Power. In doing so, they were deliberately naming the identity of Christ through the names of the God of Israel. The basis of Athanasius's logic is that when the New Testament identifies Christ by having him share in the divine names of the God of Israel, it reveals that the preexistent Christ also shares in the divine nature. To reiterate his basic premise, the sharing of names indicates sharing of nature.

Shared Names and the Preeminence of Christ

This fundamental principle intersects with several other logical and polemical elements in Athanasius's interpretation of biblical intertextuality in support of his trinitarian theology. We can name three of these, all of which are used to regulate the proper signification of the intertextual naming of God and Christ.

1. Since the Scriptures as a whole (and for that matter all facets of Christian life) assert the unique preeminence of Christ, that preeminence must be applied to the interpretation of all of the christological titles in a way that maximizes their value to the point of associating him with the very being of God. We can see this principle at work in Athanasius's response to Asterius's infamous observation about the locust. Asterius is pursuing the hermeneutical strategy of devaluing the titles accorded to Christ in the Scriptures (in this case, "Christ the power of God" in 1 Cor. 1:24) by noting instances where the same names are applied to creatures (in Joel 2:25 LXX, God calls the locust "my great power"). Athanasius works in the opposite direction. Granting that the locust might have been referred to once as a manifestation of divine power, where has Scripture called the locust God's Word, Wisdom, Radiance, and so on? The fact that the Scriptures call Christ all of these things establishes his unique preeminence, and 1 Corinthians 1:24 must be read in accord with that whole pattern of preeminence—not upended on the basis of one stray text such as the verse Asterius has put on display. From this point of view, Athanasius expresses outrage at his opponents' violation of what he considers to be the scriptural logic of the presentation

of Christ: the Scriptures speak of Christ as "preeminent in all things" but the "Arians" liken him to a locust![55]

2. The second principle is a negative corollary of the first: the titles of Christ must not be interpreted in ways that extrapolate inappropriately from the creaturely characteristics of their literal referents. That is to say, once it is established that the christological titles in Scripture must be interpreted in accord with Christ's preeminence, it follows that the *paradeigmata* that express such titles in terms drawn from creation and from human experience must be interpreted in ways that take proper account of the difference between God and creation. The creaturely settings upon which the *paradeigmata* draw (material light, human speech, the human parent-child relationship, and so on) must not be interpreted in ways that inappropriately transfer creaturely attributes (the visibility of light, the compositeness of a human word, and so on) onto God and Christ. Most pertinently, the naming of God in terms of Father-Son cannot be understood according to categories of material generation but must be conceived in light of the Creator-creature difference. In general, Athanasius is not at all advocating the use of these biblical titles in a kind of imaging of or "picture-thinking" about divine being.[56] It is not the creaturely analogue of any of these names, taken by itself, that is significant for him but the overall formal logical pattern of correlation. In fact, Athanasius is not typically interested in the extratextual referent of any single one of the *paradeigmata* that designate this correlativity. It is a striking feature of his presentation that, unlike some of his predecessors whom he cites as precedents for his strategy for correlating biblical images, he never adds any non-biblical images to denote such correlativity. He is interested, rather, in the essential formal elements that underlie all the biblical *paradeigmata* taken together. Beyond that, all significations that attach to the creaturely referents of these names are to be shunned.[57]

3. As a positive corollary to the first principle, the divine names must be interpreted with a view to the perfection of divine nature. As a central example, the designation of the Son as "begotten" must be understood with reference to the eternity that befits the perfection of the divine nature: "It properly belongs to human beings to beget in time because of the imperfection of their nature, but the offspring (*gennēma*) of God is eternal because of the everlasting perfection of his nature."[58] Apart from the crucial exception of precisely the *paradeigmata* that indicate divine complexity by inserting the naming of Christ into the patterns of naming God, Athanasius assumes a fairly standard list of the constituent attributes of divine perfection: immateriality, immutability, impassibility, simplicity, and so on.[59] All biblical *paradeigmata* referring to the divine, including the correlative patterns that coordinate the names of Christ and God, must be interpreted consistently with these divine attributes.

55. *C. Ar.* 2.37.
56. The term is from Lonergan, "The Subject," 76.
57. *C. Ar.* 2.35–36.
58. *C. Ar.* 1.14; cf. *C. Ar.* 1.19; 1.23; *Decr.* 11.
59. Along with the references to God's eternity in the previous footnote, see, e.g., *C. Ar.* 1.28 on divine impassibility and simplicity; 1.17, 1.52 on divine immutability; 3.1 on immateriality; 3.48 on omniscience.

These three principles make sense of Athanasius's overall strategy for grounding the correlativity of Father and Son through the patterns of their scriptural naming. Athanasius insists that the conglomeration of divine epithets scripturally applied to Christ is altogether unique, and that those epithets indicate that he is other than creation, and that he shares in the name and being of the one God in a manner befitting all the criteria of divine perfection. So throughout the *Orations* he often repeats a litany of the exalted names of Christ, such as Son, Word, Wisdom, Image, Power, and Radiance.[60] For Athanasius, these biblical patterns whereby Christ has been named out of the names of God force us to see the ultimate ground of Christ's being as integral to the ground of divine being as such.

Scripture, Philosophy, and God as Creator

Athanasius's exegetical insistence that correlationality (between God and Christ) is integral to divine perfection complicates his acceptance of standard philosophical conceptions of divine perfection. In general, he takes these standard conceptions, such as simplicity, immateriality, and immutability, for granted. In fact Athanasius can often find scriptural warrants for them (for example, the description of God's immutability in James 1:17: "With whom there is no variation or shadow due to change"),[61] though he does not always find it necessary to do so: the "bare conception" of divinity is sufficient to indicate some of them, so that they are available to reason as well as to faith.[62] But when these standard conceptions conflict with the scriptural presentation of the preeminence of Christ as integral to the name and being of God, they must be set aside. Yet even then they are serviceable for interpreting what they originally cannot envision. Such is the case with the affirmation that correlationality belongs to the perfection of the divine essence. This affirmation, revealed in Scripture rather than disclosed by reason, requires a christological modification of the standard philosophical conceptions of God. But then it must itself be interpreted in light of the divine perfection of immutability: "The essence of the Father was never imperfect so that what was proper to it [i.e., the Son as Word, Radiance, Image of the Father] was added afterwards."[63]

We can cite three constituent elements in Athanasius's presentation of this conception of perfect divine correlationality. (1) Divine being has to be conceived as a dynamic outgoing movement, according to the scriptural imagery of the mind's self-extrapolation in word and expressed wisdom, light's outward radiance, a fountain pouring forth living water, and so on.[64] (2) Within that movement there is a logical (though not temporal) priority by which the source of the movement is

---

60. Cf. *C. Ar.* 1.12; 1.16; 1.20; 1.58; 2.32; 2.34; 3.4; 3.18; 3.29; 3.51; 3.59.
61. Cf. *Ep. Serap.* 1.26; *Ep. Afr.* 8.
62. Cf. *C. Ar.* 1:23.
63. *C. Ar.* 1.14.
64. Cf. John 1:1 (Word); Wis. 7:26 (Wisdom/Image); Heb. 1:3; Ps. 36:9 (Light): Jer. 2:13 (outflow from fountain).

distinguished from its term: the light is the source of radiance and not vice-versa.[65] (3) The relation between the source and its product is one of inseparable, though differentiated, unity: "They are two . . . but the nature is one."[66] These three formal elements are to be understood as agreeing with but also radically transforming the standard attributes of divine perfection. Divine perfection is dynamic simplicity, a source that communicates itself perfectly, such that its "product" is equal to it, priority and posteriority in perfect eternal simultaneity. Once again Athanasius dramatizes his opponents' failure to appropriate the biblical presentation of a dynamic movement of correlativity as integral to divine perfection: their monad god is a dry and barren fountain without outpouring, a light without radiance; he was once without word, reason, and wisdom.[67]

As a consequence of this christological reconception of divine perfection, Athanasius presents fecundity and generativity as integral to the perfection of divine being. Moreover, this generativity, even if not envisioned by standard accounts of divine perfection, is still answerable to these standards: it is to be characterized by simplicity, immutability, immateriality, and every other perfection. At the same time, for Athanasius, this trinitarian account of divine correlativity and dynamic generativity as integral to the divine essence also qualifies other Christian doctrines. For example, his understanding of creation is grounded in just such a trinitarian conception. As we have already noted, from the outbreak of the debates between Arius and Alexander onward, the question of the relation between Father and Son was bound up with that of the relation between both of them and creation. Different accounts of both sets of relations amounted to rival interpretations of the same biblical data. Those expecting to interpret the fourth-century debates in terms of the anachronistic categories of high and low Christology may be surprised to learn that all parties to the fourth-century debates unproblematically held to the biblical account that the preexistent Christ created the world. No one simply denied such texts as John 1:3 ("All things came into being through him") or Colossians 1:16 ("In him all things in heaven and on earth were created . . . all things have been created through him and for him") or contested the implication that in naming Jesus as divine Word and Wisdom, the Scriptures were attributing to him the creative agency of God as sung by the psalmist: "By the word of the LORD, the heavens were made" (Ps. 33:6). Thus, Arius, while safeguarding the unique uncreatedness of the one God by designating the Word as a creature, also taught that this Word created all that came to be after him. The preexistent Christ was thus a created Creator, a mediator of God's creative agency. Asterius further clarified this mediatorial function by characterizing it as an economic attenuation of the insupportable glory of the Unbegotten, since "creation could not withstand the immediate hand of God."[68] With Asterius's development of Arius's doctrine, we see the construction of a certain nexus between an account of the

65. *C. Ar.* 2.32; 3.15.
66. *C. Ar.* 3.4.
67. See Anatolios, "When Was God without Wisdom?"
68. Fr. 26 (Vinzent).

relation between Father and Son and the doctrines of creation, divine transcendence, and christological mediation.

In rejecting Asterius's version of this doctrinal nexus, Athanasius comes to the startling conclusion that to deny the Son a place within the divine essence is effectively to deny that God is Creator! His polemical deconstruction of his opponents' teaching, combined with the positive exposition of his own, constitutes a significant trinitarian interpretation of the doctrine of creation. Building on the foundation of the common scriptural ground shared with his opponents, which designates the preexistent Christ as Creator, Athanasius advances with syllogistic force to his conclusion: If the Word is Creator and the Word is extrinsic to the divine essence, then the creative agency of God is extrinsic to the divine essence and God cannot claim the title "Creator" as properly his own. To the exact extent that the creative Son is external to the divine essence, to that extent does God procure the title "Creator" from outside his proper being. The point is decisive in the framework of debate between trinitarian conceptions of unity of being versus those of unity of will. In this debate, common ground was delineated by the affirmation on both sides that creation was to be referred to divine willing. Athanasius insists that if the Son is the agent of the divine willing of creation, he must be integral to divine being in order for this willing to be properly owned by the divine being. In this way, he is striving to surpass the competing emphasis on the sovereignty of the divine will by insisting that such sovereignty is ultimately only affirmed by recognizing the Son's sharing in divine being:

> But if there is no Son, how then do you say that God is Creator, if indeed it is through the Word and in Wisdom that everything that is made comes to be and without which nothing comes to be, and yet, according to you, God does not possess that in which and through which he makes all things? (Cf. Ps. 104:20, 24; Wis 9:2; John 1:3.) But if, according to them, the divine essence itself is not fruitful but barren, like a light that does not shine and a fountain that is dry, how are they not ashamed to say that God has creative energy? Denying what is by nature, how can they not blush to wish to give precedence to what is by will? . . . Therefore, if that which is first, which is according to nature, does not exist, according to their mindlessness, how can that which is second, which is according to will, come to be? But what is first is the Word, and the creation is second.[69]

Athanasius is aware that his insistence on making the title "Creator" intrinsic to the divine essence raises certain problems of its own. Most crucially, it seems poised to make the eternal existence of creation a necessary corollary to the eternal existence of God. We have already noted that one element of the tense framework that motivated the eruption of the fourth-century doctrinal debates was Origen's speculation that the title "Almighty," as a designation of God's eternal being, implies that there was always a world over which God was "Almighty."[70] It was precisely that kind of speculation

69. *C. Ar.* 2.2 (ET: Anatolios, *Athanasius*, 111).
70. *Princ.* 1.2.10.

that inspired an intense focus on the absolute priority of the Unbegotten God over against a world that had a punctiliar origin "from nothing." Athanasius is treading dangerous ground in appearing to retrieve the very problematic that contributed, by way of reaction, to the stark differentiation between God and everything that derives from God, including even the Son. But Athanasius is careful not to repeat Origen's mistake. He seems aware that his task must comprise a careful balance of relating and distinguishing theology (the Father-Son relation) and economy (the God-world rela-tion) and of clarifying both the correspondences and the differences between the two relations. To the objection that his insistence on making the title "Creator" intrinsic to the divine essence effectively makes creation itself determinative of the divine nature, Athanasius responds by implicitly drawing a distinction between the active potency of God's creative act, which is coterminous with the Father-Son relation, and the term of that act. In order for the title "Creator" to be authentically predicated of the divine being, it is not necessary for the *term* of God's creative potency to be in existence but only for that active potency itself to be integral to the divine being. Since that active potency is biblically attributed to both Father and Son (leaving the Spirit out of consideration, for now), it can only be attributed to the divine being if both Father and Son are integral to the divine essence:

> Let me say once again that the work is external to the essence, whereas the Son is the proper offspring of the essence. Therefore it is not necessary for the work to always exist; the maker makes it when he wills. But the offspring is not subject to an act of will since he belongs to the essence. Someone can be and can be called a maker even when there is no work made as yet. But one cannot be called and cannot be a father unless a son exists. And if they exercise themselves with the question of why God does not always make if he always has the power to make (*dynamenos poiein*), let them receive the answer that God does always have the power of making but that the things that come into being do not have the power of being eternal. . . . It is not a diminishment of the Maker for creatures not to exist, inasmuch as he possesses the capacity for making when he wills it. But for the offspring not to be always with the Father would be a diminishment of the perfection of his essence. So the works were made when he willed it, through his Word, but the Son is always the proper offspring of the essence of the Father.[71]

Here Athanasius is not only revising Origen but also reworking Asterius's own revision of Arius's doctrine that God was not always Father. Drawing back from Arius's jettisoning of "Father" language, Asterius had explained that God is eternally Father despite the non-eternity of the Son because he always had the power to generate the Son. The significance of this particular difference between Asterius and Athanasius can perhaps be cast in terms of the formal relation of potency-actuality. For Asterius, the actuality that grounds God's generative and creative capacity resides in the one unbegotten; the begetting of the Son is consequent upon that actuality and is related

71. *C. Ar.* 1.29. See, further, Anatolios, "Theology and Economy"; Anatolios, *Coherence*, 116–25; Widdicombe, *Fatherhood of God.*

to that actuality as a mere potency. For Athanasius, however, the Father-Son relation, which is constitutive of the actuality of God's generative and creative capacity,
grounds, precedes, and supersedes the willed relation between God and the world.
The fecundity of the act of creation, which comes about through the working of divine
will, is grounded in the fecundity of the generation of the Son. This latter fecundity is
integral to and constitutive of the divine nature itself: "If God creates things that are
external [to the divine essence] and at first were not, by willing them to be, and thus
becomes their Maker, how much more is he first of all Father of an offspring from
his own proper essence? For if they grant to God the willing of what is not, why do
they not acknowledge of God what supersedes the willing? But what supersedes the
willing is his bringing-forth and his being Father, by nature, of his own Word. . . . So,
as I have said, God's creating is second to his begetting."[72]

The insistence that the creation of the world is grounded in the generation of the
Son is an aspect of Athanasius's trinitarian theology that has received remarkably
little attention. But it is not an incidental detail for Athanasius. What is at stake is
not only a certain vision of the fecundity of the divine nature, as a merely abstract
divine attribute. But it is also structural to Athanasius's vision that both in the original creation and in the renewed and redeemed creation, God's relation to the world
is enfolded by the Father's relation to the Son. Using the felicitous biblical image of
God's delight in Wisdom, Athanasius speaks of God's delight in the world as derivative
of and embraced within the intra-divine delight of the relation of Father and Son:

> Therefore all the earth is filled with his knowledge. For one is the knowledge of the
> Father, through the Son, and of the Son, from the Father, and the Father rejoices in the
> Son and in this same joy, the Son delights in the Father, saying, "I was beside him, his
> delight. Day by day, I rejoiced in his presence" (Prov 8:30). . . . When was it then that
> the Father did not rejoice? But if he has always rejoiced, then there was always the one
> in whom he rejoiced. In whom, then, does the Father rejoice (cf. Prov 8:30), except by
> seeing himself in his own image, which is his Word? Even though, as it is written in
> these same Proverbs, he also "delighted in the sons of people, having consummated the
> world" (Prov 8:31), yet this also has the same meaning. For he did not delight in this
> way by acquiring delight as an addition to himself, but it was upon seeing the works that
> were made according to his own image, so that the basis of this delight also is God's own
> Image. And how does the Son too rejoice, except by seeing himself in the Father? For
> to say this is the same as to say: "The one who has seen me has seen the Father" (John
> 14:9), and "I am in the Father and the Father is in me" (John 14:10).[73]

The Mediating Role of the Word

While Arius's and Asterius's theology of the preexistent Christ as created Creator
effectively deprived the Unbegotten God of owning in himself the title "Creator,"
it also involved, for Athanasius, a false account of the mediating role of the Word.

---

72. *C. Ar.* 2.2 (ET: Anatolios, *Athanasius*, 111).

73. *C. Ar.* 2.82 (ET: Anatolios, *Athanasius*, 174–75). For a modern treatment of the theme that the
world is created "within" the generation of the Son, see Balthasar, *Theo-Drama IV*, 317–81.

At this point, we rejoin the issue of the location of the christological *pro nobis*. According to Athanasius, the Arius-Asterius account of the mediating role of the Word simultaneously mislocates christological mediation and distorts divine transcendence. In Asterius's account, the rationale of the mediation of the Word, as created Creator, involves an account of the impossibility or unfittingness of direct contact between the supremely transcendent Unbegotten God and creation.[74] The mediation of the Son therefore involves a mitigation of the insupportable glory of the Unbegotten. Athanasius protests that such an account disfigures the biblical presentation of the character of God. A God who cannot be conceived as having direct contact with creation is either proud or weak, whereas the biblical God's creative power is matched by his loving-kindness.[75] He does not lack the power to create directly, as if in need of outsourcing his creative work, nor does he disdain to do so, as if direct contact with creation would be a taint to his glory. In Athanasius's account, a divine self-abasement is integral to the biblical character of God; this divine humility belongs to the divine nature directly, rather than to a separate mediating being, and enables direct contact between the transcendent God and his creation. Athanasius finally drives the point home by restructuring Asterius's notion that the attenuated transcendence of the Word was necessary to mediate "the untempered splendor" of the Unbegotten. Reworking the same vocabulary, he transfers the phrase "untempered splendor" to the Word himself, as an equal sharer in the divine nature. The Word's mediation consists not in an inferior and thus more accessible ontological status but rather precisely in the self-humbling love that the Word shares with the Father:

> For it is clear to all that he was called the "firstborn" of creation not as being of himself a creature nor because of any kinship of essence with all creation, but because the Word condescended to the things coming into being when he was creating them at the beginning so that they might be enabled to come into being. For they would not have withstood his nature, being that of the unmitigated splendor of the Father, if he had not condescended by the Father's love for humanity and supported, strengthened and carried them into being. Then, secondly, he was called "firstborn" because, by the Word's condescending, creation itself was made to be a "son" through him, so that he might become, as has been said, the firstborn of creation in every respect, both in creating it and in his being brought into this world itself for the sake of all.[76]

For Athanasius, only the attribute of God's loving self-abasement, which belongs to the divine nature itself, can bridge the distance between God and creation. This is a theme that was already present in *Against the Greeks–On the Incarnation*, where it was used to explain that the condescension of the incarnation does not indicate that the Word was lowly in his very nature but rather that the self-abasement was a manifestation of the *philanthrōpia* of the divine nature. The implicitly trinitarian content of that

74. Fr. 26 (Vinzent).
75. *C. Ar.* 2.25.
76. *C. Ar.* 2.64 (ET: Anatolios, *Athanasius*, 157–58).

argument becomes explicit at this stage, in Athanasius's direct polemical engagement with Asterius's account of the mediation of the Word. In the Alexandrian's estimation, Asterius's account is fatally flawed not only because it seems to portray a proud and inaccessible God but also because it presumes that the ontological distance between God and creation can be bridged on the side of creation—in this case, by a middle being, who is a created Creator. But Athanasius invokes a "middle-man" infinite regress argument used by Irenaeus against his "gnostic" opponents to make the point that such an apparent solution simply endlessly postpones the problem.[77] If a creature, by the very definition of its creaturehood, cannot withstand the immediate hand of God, then neither would the preexistent created Christ have been able to withstand it. But if he was able to withstand direct contact with the Unbegotten while being a creature, then so could other creatures. The whole point of his mediation would be evacuated.

HE FOR US OR WE FOR HIM?

While Athanasius thus finds Asterius's version of the mediating role of Christ to be problematic with respect to its depiction of both sides of the Creator-creation relation, he advances an even deeper criticism that strikes at the heart of the strategy of locating the mediatorial role of the preexistent Christ in the very rationale of his being. If, as both Arius and Asterius contend, the Word was created as an instrument of God's further creative activity, then humanity assumes a teleological priority over the Son, as if he was created for us, not we for him (cf. Col. 1:16).[78] In the interpretive categories that we have been employing, Athanasius is here asserting that the Arius-Asterius account distorts the proper relation between the primacy of Christ and his mediatorial work by reading his mediatorial work into the very *raison d'être* of the Son. Characteristically, Athanasius moves quickly from a logical statement of his argument to its rhetorical dramatization in scriptural idiom: To say that the Son is created for us, and not we for him, is to reverse the ratio of prototype and image in the relation between humanity and the Son. It amounts to saying, in other words, that it is the Son who is in our image and glory, and not the reverse. In that case, it is strange that the Word should enjoy the more intimate title "Son," since it seems that he was a mere functional accessory toward God's more primary motivation to create us.[79]

The proper location of the *pro nobis* thus cannot be placed within the Son's very being as merely a functional accessory to the end of humanity's being but rather in the economy of salvation. At the same time, however, the continuity between theology and economy is reestablished by the notion that the self-abasement of the economy of salvation "for us" is after all grounded in the divine nature. But it is grounded in the category of divine love, *philanthrōpia*, which is integral to the majesty of the divine nature, rather than through a secondary attenuated divinity. In this framework, the primacy of Christ has distinct aspects in the spheres of theology and economy, and

77. *C. Ar.* 2.26; cf. *Haer.* 2.1.3; see Anatolios, "Influence of Irenaeus on Athanasius."
78. *C. Ar.* 2.29.
79. *C. Ar.* 2.30.

according to the divine-human constitution of Christ. In the theological sphere, this primacy consists in the majesty and splendor of the divine nature as well as the divine *philanthrōpia*, which he shares equally with the Father; from that perspective, humanity and all creation exists both in him and "for him." In the economic sphere, however, this primacy consists in the demonstration of the divine *philanthrōpia* whereby he for whose sake creation exists became a creature "for us."

In this section, we have been looking at how Athanasius's trinitarian theology draws upon the biblical naming of God and Christ. We have seen that Athanasius's understanding of the revelatory dynamics of intertextuality within the biblical text enables him to affirm the ontological correlativity of Father and Son on the basis of the linguistic correlativity by which the two are biblically named. However, the proper interpretation of these biblical *paradeigmata* must take into account the unique and absolute preeminence of Christ as globally presented in the Scriptures as a whole and as performatively expressed in Christian life, as well as the difference between God and creatures and the generally accepted criteria of divine perfection. Dialectically, the attributes of divine perfection must be adjusted precisely by the christological modification whereby the divine naming is performed through the correlation of God and the preexistent Christ. Divine perfection must thus be thought anew in terms of dynamic simplicity, as a perfect and ordered outgoing self-communication. This complexification of the perfection of divine simplicity is given concrete doctrinal expression through a trinitarian conception of creation. The relation between God and the world is grounded in and ordered to the relation between the Father and the Son. The *pro nobis* of the Son is located in his economic self-abasement, which in turn is grounded in the *philanthrōpia* of the divine nature rather than in a putative secondary divinity.

Trinity, Christology, and Scriptural Narrative

We have already seen that the question of the proper construal of the christological scriptural narrative was a foundational one at the very outbreak of the controversy between Arius and Alexander. Alexander complains that Arius and his supporters use the scriptural account of Jesus's human career as evidence of his lower divinity, while they ignore his more exalted titles.[80] The previous section has dealt with Athanasius's efforts to demonstrate that the more exalted titles of Christ indicate a relationship of substantial correlativity with the Father. But Athanasius also had to deal with the scriptural christological material, pointedly cited by his opponents, that delineated Jesus's status and career as a human being who was limited, suffered, and died, as well as those texts that referred to his exaltation, while indicating the passive status of the Son with respect to the Father. Athanasius's principal strategy is to attribute texts depicting Christ's exaltation as passively received from the Father as referring to the Word's incarnation rather than to his preexistence. In most cases, this attribution

---

80. *Letter to Alexander of Byzantium*, Urk. 14.4, 37–38.

is more consistent with the plain sense of the text, as it would be discerned even by modern exegesis. In other cases, as in Proverbs 8:22, modern exegesis would find any application to Christ far-fetched.[81] But a common adherence to the principle of the intertextual unity of Scripture prevented participants in the fourth-century debates from taking that route. If Jesus Christ is scripturally identified as God's Wisdom (cf. 1 Cor. 1:24), then anything predicated of Wisdom anywhere in the Scriptures must be appropriately predicated of Christ. But the most interesting aspect of Athanasius's treatment is not that he simply adopted the strategy, perhaps from Marcellus of Ancyra, of restricting the signification of these texts to the incarnation. Rather, for our purposes, the crucial thing is to note how he takes the discussion to the level of the overall characterization of the person of Christ. In effect, he presents the rival interpretations as involving two different narrative identifications of the person of Christ and, once again, of the character of divinity itself.

Christology of Ascent or Christology of Descent?

In Athanasius's presentation, the "Arian" account presents the Word as the recipient of an exalted divinity as a grace from the Father. It interprets the scriptural texts describing the Word's incarnate life as indicating that the Son was granted this grace as a consequence of his human obedience. On the basis of Arius's original doctrine, the order of cause and consequence is not temporal but logical; the Son was granted the grace of divinity from the very beginning of his being on the basis of God's foreknowledge of the merits earned by his human obedience. Significantly, what is most objectionable about this picture for Athanasius seems to be that its overall presentation of Christ is that of an "ascending" god. It is true that he sometimes oversimplifies and distorts this picture into a straightforward adoptionism in which Christ is first human and then earns divinity. But the main trajectory of his logic does not strictly depend on whether there was an order of temporal succession from Christ's humanity to his exalted divine status. Rather, the more fundamental point is the "Arian" portrayal of Christ as an upwardly mobile god whose overall career is one of promotion, progress, and advance, regardless of the temporal order of merit and reward.[82]

Athanasius's objection to this version of the character of Christ's divinity becomes clearer when we contrast it with his own construction of Christ's scriptural narrative identity. Athanasius sees Christ as the descending, self-humbling God. The character of Christ's divinity is not to be delineated as a continuum of progress, advancement,

---

81. Hanson, *Search*, 825: "Had it occurred to Athanasius when he was writing the second book of his *Orations against the Arians*, most of which is devoted to this single text, to dismiss the whole debate as a storm in a teacup because the text does not refer to Christ, he would have been appalled, but the thought did not occur to him." In general, Hanson finds little salvageable in the exegetical strategies employed in these debates by all sides: "The last word on the appeal to the Bible during this crucial period in the history of Christian doctrine, however, must be of the impression made on a student of the period that the expounders of the text of the Bible are incompetent and ill-prepared to expound it" (848).

82. *C. Ar.* 1.38.

and the earning of grace but rather as an initial (divine) exaltation that is put aside and subsequently retrieved for the sake of humanity's exaltation:

> Therefore, if even before the world came to be, the Son possessed glory, and was both "Lord of Glory" (1 Cor 2:8) and "Most High," and descended from heaven, and is always to be worshiped, then he was not promoted on account of having descended but rather he himself promoted those things which were in need of advancement. And if he descended to accomplish the grace of their advancement, then he did not come to be called "Son" and "God" as a reward, but rather he himself made us sons for the Father and divinized human beings when he himself became a human being.[83]

In this way, Athanasius takes the debate beyond the questions *whether* Christ is divine and *to what extent* he is divine (fully? everlastingly?) to the question of the *character* of Christ's divinity. This character is specified in terms of *kenōsis*, self-humbling, in a way that makes the christological hymn of Philippians 2 a controlling hermeneutical key.[84] Such a characterization shows the consistency of Christ's divinity with the general character of God's self-humbling love for humanity (*philanthrōpia*) as portrayed in *Against the Greeks–On the Incarnation*. Once again, it is a matter of properly construing the dynamics of the *pro nobis* in the christological narrative. The whole story line of abasement-exaltation is *for us* in a way that delineates both the humanity and divinity of Christ. It delineates the humanity when we recognize that both the humiliation and subsequent exaltation are enacted by the Word through his humanity and thus are properly predicated of that humanity. But it also delineates the divinity inasmuch as it characterizes the kenotic movement as consistent with the divine attribute of *philanthrōpia*. Failure to acknowledge the natural unity of the Father and the Son thus involves distorting the christological narrative on both the human and divine levels of God's being "for us" in Christ, a point made explicit in Athanasius's Easter epistle of 338:

> O unthankful opponent of Christ. . . . If you had understood the Scriptures and listened to the saints . . . you would have known that the Lord did not descend for his own sake but for ours and so you would have admired his *philanthrōpia* all the more on that account. . . . If you had understood his work of loving-kindness toward us, you would not have alienated the Son from the Father.[85]

Such an interpretation of the christological narrative enables Athanasius also to deal with the second set of christological texts presented by his opponents and taken up in the third oration, those that deal with the human limitations of the incarnate Word. Those limitations are not indicative of an inferior divinity but are rather an extreme manifestation of the divine character of self-emptying that is manifested in Christ's humanity.

83. *C. Ar.* 1:38–39 (ET: Anatolios, *Athanasius*, 96).
84. Cf. *C. Ar.* 1.40.
85. *Ep. fest.* 10.9.

Athanasius's interpretation of the christological narrative presents the identity of Jesus Christ as dialectically dramatic. Eternally in possession of the fullness of divinity, the Word manifests the self-humbling divine love in the self-emptying of his humanity. The scriptural identity of Jesus Christ is the single subject of this twofold drama. The scriptural narrative that presents this drama thus presents a "twofold proclamation" of the Savior, one that refers us to the correlative sharing in the Father's being and another that delineates his self-humbling. To read the scriptural christological narrative correctly involves distinguishing between the two accounts while attributing both to the single subject of the Word incarnate. We have here not only the introduction of the crucial strategy of "partitive exegesis" into the fourth-century doctrinal debates,[86] but also a prototype of the Chalcedonian christological framework, inscribed in the framework of scriptural narrative. Grounding the later ontological vocabulary of two natures and one person, we have here the exegetical categories of two dimensions of the scriptural christological narrative and a single agent of whom this narrative is predicated:

> Therefore, as we have often said, the scope and character of Scripture is that there is in it a twofold proclamation about the Savior, that he was always God and is the Son, being Word and Radiance and Wisdom of the Father and that he later took flesh for our sake from the Virgin, Mary the *Theotokos*, and became human.[87]

> If we acknowledge what is proper to each [i.e., the humanity and the divinity] and see and understand that both are accomplished by one, then we will believe correctly (*orthōs*) and will never be led astray.[88]

THE TRINITARIAN TURN IN ATHANASIAN SOTERIOLOGY

We have already seen that the "exaltation" by which Christ acquired his divinity, according to the "Arians," is applied by Athanasius to the salvific work of Christ's humanity. In the *Orations*, we have the recurrence of the set of soteriological motifs introduced in *Against the Greeks–On the Incarnation*. These motifs attempt to represent the salvific value of the union of Christ's divinity with our humanity in both general terms (incorruptibility, knowledge of God) and, more specifically, in terms of the role played by Christ's death (repayment of debt, submitting to judgment on our behalf, sacrifice, offering to the Father, and so on). But Athanasius now introduces two further motifs that take his soteriology in a more comprehensively trinitarian direction. Both of these motifs depend on the christological narrative of loving self-abasement.

1. The first, essentially amounting to a Spirit Christology, is that the Word, who in his divinity is the giver of the Spirit, becomes the receiver of the Spirit in the kenotic self-humbling of his humanity. If humanity's original participation in divine life has

---

86. For this characterization of Athanasius's christological exegesis, see Behr, *Nicene Faith*, 1:208–15.
87. *C. Ar.* 3.29.
88. *C. Ar.* 3.35.

its origin from nothing and as such is a movement from nothing into the divine Word, its redeemed participation in divine life has its point of origin not in mere nothing but rather in the creatureliness of Christ: "Human beings now have the principle and origin of their receiving in him and through him."[89] But the content of the "receiving" in question is now specified beyond the merely generic divine attributes that we find in *On the Incarnation*, such as incorruptibility. Rather, what is received through Christ's humanity is the Holy Spirit, which is given and received by the incarnate Word. The fact that it is the same one who is giver of the Spirit in his divinity and perfect receiver of it in his humanity is what makes our sanctification and salvation ultimately secure, inasmuch as we become co-recipients of the Spirit, through Christ's humanity. Athanasius intimates that this event represents a qualitatively new state of affairs between God and humanity.[90]

2. Another significant motif is that the redeemed are enfolded into trinitarian life when they are "begotten by grace" through Christ. Here again, we are involved in the dialectic of the christological drama of the loving self-abasement of the Word. Athanasius expresses this drama through what can be called a "rhetoric of reversal."[91] The simplest expression of this rhetoric of reversal is the oft-quoted adage from *On the Incarnation*: he became human that we might become divine.[92] But the *Orations* offer a trinitarian extension of this rhetoric of reversal, intimating that the content of Christian salvation involves being enfolded in the inner life of the Trinity: the Word, who by nature is not made but begotten of the Father, is made a creature so that we, who by nature are creatures, can be begotten by grace. Thus we are enabled to call God "Father" rather than merely "our Maker." This motif of being enfolded into trinitarian life by being taken up into the position of the Son in relation to the Father is thoroughly integrated by Athanasius with the first motif of our perfect reception of the Spirit through the Son, which in turn is based on the christological dialectic of divine self-emptying:

> Yet the love of God for humanity is such that by grace he becomes Father of those in relation to whom he had previously only been Maker. He becomes their Father when created human beings receive "into their hearts the Spirit of the Son, crying out, 'Abba, Father'" (Gal. 4:6), as the apostle says. These are the ones who, by receiving the Word, receive authority from him "to become children of God" (John 1:12). Being creatures by nature, they would not become "sons" except by receiving the Spirit of the natural and true Son. So it was in order to bring this about and to make humanity receptive of divinity that "the Word became flesh" (John 1:14). . . . Accordingly, the Father calls "sons" those in whom he sees his own Son and he says "I begot" since "begetting" signifies "son," while "making" is indicative of the works. Therefore, we are not begotten first but made, for it is written, "Let us *make* humanity"

89. *C. Ar.* 1.48.
90. *C. Ar.* 1.50.
91. See Anatolios, *Coherence*, 133.
92. *Inc.* 54.

(Gen. 1:26). But when we later receive the grace of the Spirit, we are henceforth said to be also begotten.[93]

The salvific enfolding into trinitarian life also enables humans to achieve a loving unity among themselves that imitates the unity of trinitarian life. The oneness of Father and Son is "a prototype and lesson" of the bond of charity to which humanity should aspire. Athanasius conceives of this bond of charity as actualized by the Spirit and so interprets Jesus's high priestly prayer, "As you, Father, are in me and I in you, that they too may be one in us" (John 17:21) as a petition for humanity's reception of the Holy Spirit:

> When the Savior says about us, "As you, Father, are in me and I in you, that they too may be one in us," he does not mean that we will be the same as he. But it is an appeal to the Father, as John has written, that the Spirit be given through him to those who believe. Through the Spirit, we find that we have come to be in God and in this way we are joined together in him. For since the Word is in the Father and the Spirit is given from the Word, he wants us to receive the Spirit, so that when we receive him and thus have the Spirit of the Word who is in the Father, we may find ourselves also to have become one through the Spirit, in the Word, and through the Word, in the Father.[94]

We have seen that in the *Orations against the Arians* Athanasius constructs a trinitarian scriptural hermeneutics in response to his opponents' arsenal of proof-texts arguing from Christ's received exaltation and human limitations to his secondary divinity. Athanasius reads the Scriptures as providing an account of the correlativity of Father and Son by naming Christ through the titles of divine presence and activity. In keeping with these scriptural patterns, the divine being must be conceived as coextensive with the relation of Father and Son and not as prior to or separable from that relation. This conception of the divine nature requires positing the attributes of fecundity and generativity as integral to divine perfection in a way that re-situates the doctrine of God as Creator within trinitarian theology. The divine nature is creative *ad extra* because of the natural creativity *ad intra*, whereby the Father eternally generates the Son. Athanasius's trinitarian hermeneutics in the *Orations* also involves a particular construal of the biblical christological narrative. At the heart of this construal is the insistence that the lowliness of Christ's humanity be seen as not indicative of a lower divinity but rather of the self-humbling of divine *philanthrōpia*, which is considered to be an attribute of the divine nature. Finally, the *Orations* provide a trinitarian soteriology in which Christian salvation is interpreted as an enfoldment into the life of the Trinity, becoming "begotten by grace" in the Son by receiving the Spirit.

---

93. *C. Ar.* 2.59 (ET: Anatolios, *Athanasius*, 153); cf. *C. Ar.* 2.51: "Since we are servants, it was fitting that when he became as we are, he also calls the Father 'Lord,' just as we do. He did this out of his love for humanity, so that we who are servants by nature may receive the Spirit of the Son and so have the courage to call 'Father' by grace the one who is our Lord by nature" (cf. Gal 4:6) (ET: Anatolios, *Athanasius*, 144).
   94. *C. Ar.* 3.25.

Nicaea and the Dialectic of Scripture and Doctrine

Athanasius's *On the Nicene Council* (*De decretis*) marks a turning point in the doctrinal debates of the fourth century. Up to that point, the issues were debated for the most part without explicit reference to the council itself, but this treatise, which develops a theological argument on the relation between Scripture and doctrine, openly insists on the normative status of the Nicene council. The triggering historical circumstances were the ascent of Constantius after the death of his brother, the Western emperor Constans, and more particularly, a council held in Sirmium in 351. Constantius was sympathetic neither to Athanasius nor to the kind of doctrine propounded at Nicaea, and his ascendancy did not bode well for those who supported Alexander's position in the original Alexander-Arius dispute. Constantius himself presided at the council in Sirmium in 351, which rejected the Nicene *homoousios* as implying an "extension" of the Father's being, in the style of Marcellus and his Western disciple, Photinus. In defiant reaction, Athanasius's *On the Nicene Council* insists that the Nicene *homoousios* is an indispensable touchstone for the authentically Christian doctrine of God.

The Necessity of the Nicene Homoousios

In the *Orations*, Athanasius had elaborated a biblical trinitarian hermeneutics, demonstrating how Scripture, both in its patterns of naming Christ and in its christological narrative as a whole, presents Christ as correlatively sharing in the Father's being in his divinity and as enacting the Father's *philanthrōpia* in his kenotic appropriation of the human condition. In *On the Nicene Council*, Athanasius argues that Nicene doctrine is necessary precisely to safeguard this "ecclesial" reading of Scripture. The argument is waged defensively, in response to the charge that the Nicene *homoousios* should be rejected because it is not a scriptural term. The heart of Athanasius's response is that recourse to non-scriptural language is sometimes necessary precisely to stabilize and fix the "sense of Scripture" in the face of a conflict of interpretations. He dramatizes this point by narrating what happened at the Nicene council. According to his account, some attendees attempted to adjudicate the controversy by invoking scriptural language designating the uniquely intimate relation of the Son to the Father. Such language was derived from the set of exalted titles, or *epinoiai*, that we have already noted to be the scriptural storehouse, for all sides of these debates, from which the primacy of Christ can be designated. These titles, distinctly referred to by Athanasius as *paradeigmata*, included such names as Word, Wisdom, Power, and Image. But the supporters of Arius apparently were willing to accept these titles, while interpreting them consistently with the notion that the Son is a created and inferior divinity. In Athanasius's telling, each of the proposed designations of the Son was welcomed with nudges and winks, and explanations that such titles were also scripturally applied to creatures: human beings are also God's "image," God speaks many "words," and even the locust is called a "power" of God.[95] Language therefore had to be found to fix

95. *Decr.* 20.

the scriptural titles of the Son in a way that confirms one interpretation and rules out any other; the solution was the word *homoousios*. It is not itself a scriptural word, but it serves precisely to fix the meaning of scriptural words. Its signification, we can say, is meta-scriptural.[96]

Athanasius's account of the Nicene council and his justification of the doctrine of *homoousios* raise several important issues regarding how trinitarian doctrine signifies in Christian discourse, a question raised in the introductory chapter of this book. First, he clearly articulates the principle that the meaning of the Nicene *homoousios* is contained in its function as a guide to a certain way of reading Scripture. An immediate hermeneutical consequence of this principle is that efforts to understand this term primarily by recourse to secular usages of *ousia* and cognate terms are misguided. Neither the council fathers of Nicaea nor Athanasius himself were working with any determinate technical sense of *ousia* or *homoousios*. Moreover, they were not attempting to signify the divine essence by directly invoking an objective referent, whether the being of God or some creaturely analogue. The meaning of *homoousios* thus resides not in its inherent capacity to invoke an objective referent on its own, but rather in its assigned function of regulating how scriptural language as a whole refers to God and Christ. To say this is not to deny that the doctrine, in thus regulating scriptural language, successfully refers to God. In Athanasius's understanding, such reference succeeds when the Nicene *homoousios* is understood to regulate the reference of the whole nexus of scriptural *paradeigmata* in the direction of the radical ontological correlativity of Father and Son.

But granting that the function of trinitarian doctrine is to regulate the reference of scriptural language, we can still ask to what extent such regulation is an extrinsic imposition on Scripture. The question can be phrased thus: do the scriptural patterns of naming Christ and the scriptural way of telling the story of Christ equally permit two rival interpretations, so that endorsing one and rejecting the other amounts to a heteronomous determination of the meaning of Scripture? Athanasius says no. He argues that the Nicene *homoousios* provides the only correct interpretation of scriptural language; the doctrine that the Son is in any sense a creature is incorrect. The regulation of scriptural language provided by the *homoousios* arises *from within* scriptural language and narrative considered as a whole—not from without. The way Athanasius goes about this argument returns us to the notion of the primacy of Christ as a foundational question in these debates. Athanasius's radical premise, already elaborately expounded in the *Orations*, is that the Scriptures as a whole attribute an absolute and incomparable primacy to Christ. In *On the Nicene Council*, he reasserts this premise by structuring his narrative of the Nicene debate as a contest between rival accounts of the "precedence" (*pleon*) of the Son. The hermeneutical key to any biblical name of the Son is this overarching biblical principle of the Son's unique preeminence.

96. A similar point is made by Ayres when he interprets Athanasius as designating the *homoousios* to be a "cipher" for scriptural language about the relation between God and Christ. See his "Athanasius's Initial Defense."

Homoousios *and the Unique Priority of Christ*

In this treatise, the particular biblical term favored to express this overall scriptural designation of the unique precedence of Christ is "only-begotten Son." Athanasius imagines a conversation in which his interlocutors concede, and claim to meet, his standard of ascribing maximal signification to the absolute preeminence of Christ: "Perhaps they will respond . . . 'In this way we consider the Son to have precedence over the others and he is said to be only-begotten for this reason.'"[97] The "Arian" versions of the Son's preeminence are then presented, especially emphasizing Asterius's doctrine of the Son as the first creature, unique in his immediate contact with the one God and his role as minister of divine agency in the creation of other creatures. This version is rejected, as in the *Orations*, both for falsifying divine transcendence and for denying immediate contact between creation and the one God. But ultimately this account of Christ's preeminence fails, as do all the others, simply because it does not meet the standard of an absolutely unique preeminence, which is mandated by the Scriptures as a whole and expressed in the particular title "*only*-begotten." The rank of "first among creatures" represents only a qualitative precedence of honor and not the absolutely unique preeminence of his very nature that is mandated by the language and narrative of Scripture as a whole.[98] Only the *homoousios* finally succeeds in fixing the meaning of each and every biblical designation of Christ consistently with the pan-biblical standard of Christ's absolutely unique preeminence as the "only-begotten Son."

According to Athanasius, the "Arians" lack a satisfactorily maximal version of Christ's ontological preeminence and attempt to justify this lack by positing a standard of theistic primacy that excludes the Son. This standard is expressed by the title *agenētos*, which by now had been given a precise definition devised by Asterius and quoted by Athanasius: "that which does not have a cause for its being, but rather is itself the cause of the coming to be of what has come into being."[99] The reliance on this definition already brings us to the threshold of Eunomian doctrine, which was to flower by the end of this decade of the 350s, and its primary emphasis on the divine essence as defined by priority with respect to causality. Ultimately, the response to this line of argument will have to involve the inclusion of the attribute of being caused, in the special case of begetting, in the conception of divine essence. But this is not the thrust of Athanasius's response in this treatise. Rather, at this stage, he presents the differences between the two positions as different ways of relating christological primacy with theistic primacy. In doing so, he also expounds a theology of naming the divine.

Athanasius begins this discussion by criticizing the Arians for setting up a competition between theistic primacy and christological primacy. Rhetorically, this competition is dramatized as an intentional ploy to denigrate the status of the Son: "While pretending to speak well of God, they . . . harbor a hidden blasphemy against

97. *Decr.* 7. Translations are from Anatolios, *Athanasius.*
98. *Decr.* 9.
99. *Decr.* 29.

the Lord."[100] The debate is thus cast in terms of what is involved in "speaking well of God," a notion that comprises the proper understanding of the names of God. After making the counterpoint that *agenētos* is no more literally a scriptural name of God than *homoousios*, Athanasius states his fundamental principle of the inseparable correlativity of theistic and christological primacy. Speaking well of God is bound up with speaking well of Christ in a strictly correlative manner. The scriptural touchstone for this principle is John 5:23: "Anyone who does not honour the Son does not honour the Father who sent him."[101] This correlative speaking well of both God and Christ is to be distinguished from the naming of God in relation to creatures. The title "Unbegotten/Uncaused," as applied to God, derives its signification from its relation to creatures, and not to the Son: "Therefore, this title does not take anything away from the nature of the Word, nor does the designation of 'unoriginated' have its signification in relation to the Son, but in relation to the things which come to be through the Son."[102] Athanasius thus insists on two distinct categories of divine names: one set that belongs to God's relation to creatures and another set that belongs to God's relation to the Son. The rationale for distinguishing these two sets of divine names is based on the hermeneutical logic outlined in the *Orations*: the scriptural *paradeigmata* name Christ from within the divine names in a way that distinguishes him from mere creatures. The new development in *On the Nicene Council* is Athanasius's insistence, in the face of attempts to prioritize the name of "Unbegotten" as a key to interpreting other divine names, that naming God in reference to his relation to Christ is *superior* to naming him in reference to his relation to creation. In a typical strategy of co-opting his opponents' terrain, Athanasius makes his point by relying on the christological title "Image," which was accepted by Asterius. Inasmuch as that title clearly signifies likeness, the minimum yield of Athanasius's argument is that it is preferable to designate God from what is most like him rather than from what is less like him. But Athanasius wants to go further and reassert the priority of the hermeneutical principle that the names of Christ must always be understood as intrinsic to the names of God, even in the case of "Unbegotten":

> Furthermore, even if the Father is called "unoriginated," the Word is still also the Image of the Father and of one being (*homoousios*) with him. Being Image, he is other than originated things and other than all; for he has identity (*idiotēta*) and likeness (*homoiōsin*) with the One whose Image he is. Therefore, the one who calls the Father unoriginated (*agenēton*) and almighty perceives in the Unoriginated and Almighty his Word and Wisdom, which is the Son. But these amazing people, so reckless in their impiety, did not discover the title of "unoriginated" in their efforts to honor God, but on account of their maliciousness concerning the Savior. If they were concerned about honor and praise, then they should have acknowledged God as "Father" and called him so; that

100. *Decr.* 29.
101. *Decr.* 29.
102. *Decr.* 29.

would have been better than naming him "unoriginated." In calling God "unoriginated" they are speaking of him only as Maker, with reference to the things that have originated in being, as I said before, so that they can indicate the Son to be a work, according to their own fancy. But the one who calls God "Father" immediately signifies the Son also, who is in him, and is not ignorant that all things that came into being were created through the Son who is. Therefore, it would be more truthful to signify God by reference to the Son and call him Father than to call and name him "unoriginated," by reference only to his works. The latter title signifies the works which came into being from the will of God through his Word, whereas the title of "Father" acknowledges the integral (*idion*) offspring from his being. As much as the Word transcends the things which come into being, by so much and more does calling God "Father" surpass calling him "unoriginated."[103]

Admittedly, there is some question-begging in Athanasius's argument, especially when considered in its maximal form, which asserts that it is "more truthful" to name God from within the divine essence than by relation to his works. Clearly, this assertion has already assumed the Son to be "within the divine essence." But one also has to consider the integrity of Athanasius's hermeneutical circle, inasmuch as he exerts much energy precisely to argue that the sharing of names between Christ and God, considered within the christological narrative properly conceived, indicates a sharing of essence. Moreover, there are elements in Athanasius's argument that seize upon his opponents' own premises in order to force them closer to his own position of prioritizing Christ-related names of God. As we have already noted, Asterius's invocation of the christological title "Image" itself suggests that it is preferable to name God from what is most like him rather than from what is less like him. Indeed, forcing the "Arians" into a rhetorical debate about the relative merits of various versions of Christ's preeminence serves to reinforce the argument that, notwithstanding the differences between these versions, it is preferable to name God in relation to the preeminence of Christ rather than in relation to the lower status of lesser beings. Thus, even if the "Arians" fail to acknowledge that the Son is *homoousios* with the Father, Athanasius has succeeded in denigrating the value of *agenētos* as a divine name and asserting the priority of Christ-related names of God.

The Basis of Cataphatic Theology

Athanasius's argument, however, is not that *homoousios* rather than *agenētos* is the primary name of God. Rather, as we have indicated, *homoousios* is simply an interpretive key to the biblical names of God and the proper construal of the christological narrative of Scripture. But the prominence of the recourse to the title *agenētos* at this stage of the controversy pushes Athanasius to a clearer conception of just what is the primary divine name. His answer is that it is the name invoked at baptism:

103. *Decr.* 30–31.

It was his will also that the summit of our faith should have the same form, so he commanded us to be baptized not into the name of the unoriginated and the originated nor into the name of the uncreated and the created, but into the name of Father, Son and the Holy Spirit (Matt. 28:19). By this consecration, we too are truly made into sons, and saying the name of the Father, we also acknowledge through this name the Word who is in the Father.[104]

At this juncture, Athanasius anticipates Basil's argument, in *On the Holy Spirit*, that the baptismal formula is the primary touchstone for trinitarian reflection.[105] It is important, however, to delimit the precise function of invoking the baptismal formula. The mere use of it does not guarantee adherence to Nicene doctrine, and Athanasius is not in fact making the Nicene *homoousios* a direct and inevitable consequence of uttering the baptismal formula.[106] In *On the Nicene Council*, recourse to the trinitarian baptismal formula is part of a larger argument that the Christian God must be named primarily from his relation to Christ, and not otherwise. Thus the invocation of an attribute of divine transcendence that merely contrasts divine from creaturely being says less about the Christian God than the invocation of his relation to Christ. Once this principle is established, the logic that leads to *homoousios* is firmly anchored: the naming of Christ is constitutive of the divine name, and the baptismal formula is interpreted accordingly.

Ultimately, Athanasius's theology of the trinitarian naming of the divine strictly implies the priority of the cataphatic over the apophatic in the Christian vision of God. And he does not merely assert that positive statements about God are truer than negative statements. Over against negative statements that deny creaturely attributes to God, he prioritizes not merely a set of positive statements likening God to creatures but the immeasurably more awesome possibility that we can name God from within God's very being and self-naming. It is not we who name God thus. Rather, God is named from within God's self as Father, Son, and Holy Spirit, and we are enfolded into this intra-divine self-naming through the incarnation of the Word. This enfolding begins with baptism: "For the Father is called such by us on account of the Son. It is because the Word carried our body and came to be among us that God is called our Father, on account of the Word in us. The Spirit of the Word, in us and through us, names the Word's own Father as our Father, and this is the meaning of the apostle's saying, "God has sent forth the Spirit of his Son into our hearts, crying out, 'Abba, Father'" (Gal. 4:6).[107] Thus Athanasius's trinitarian theology involves interpreting Christian baptism as the event whereby human beings are assumed into intra-divine naming.

104. *Decr.* 31.
105. *Spir.* 26, 28, 68.
106. On the other side, the baptismal formula was interpreted as delineating the order of hierarchy between Father, Son, and Spirit. See Williams, "Baptism and the Arian Controversy."
107. *Decr.* 31.

Athanasius's invocation of the baptismal formula as a touchstone for trinitarian reasoning, which concludes *On the Nicene Council*, leads us back to his overarching concern in this treatise with the relation between Scripture and its actualization in Christian life. The fundamental motivation of this work is to defend the Nicene *homoousios* against the charge that it is unscriptural. Athanasius concedes that the word does not occur in Scripture but insists that it is necessary precisely to safeguard the sense of Scripture. We have thereby an understanding of doctrine as an interpretation and regulation of Scripture. Implicit in this understanding is a dialectic of Scripture and tradition and an assertion of the underlying continuity of tradition: "See, then, how we prove that this conception has been transmitted from fathers to fathers."[108] Whether Athanasius successfully proves that point in this treatise might be open to question, but the proper question might well be not whether the continuity of tradition is clear and obvious on a merely literal level (Athanasius himself seems to presume the contrary!) but whether it can be persuasively and coherently constructed at certain paradigmatic moments. At minimum, we should note his attempts to dramatize the Christian community's need to regulate the meaning of Scripture precisely to insure that it is faithful to that meaning, as well as his assumption that the church's interpretation of Scripture needs to locate itself within a historical continuity. Finally, his discussion of baptism suggests that the proper interpretation of Scripture, anchored in tradition, must have primary reference to the sacramental life of the church, whereby it is inserted into the life of the Triune God. Ultimately, the church can speak about God most truly by sharing in the mutual conversation within God of Father, Son, and Holy Spirit.[109]

Theology of the Holy Spirit

Some have explained the relative neglect of the Holy Spirit during the early stages of the post-Nicene controversy by saying that the question of the status of Christ's divinity had a logical priority and had to be settled first. But the aptness of that explanation is diminished by the fact that the Spirit was not totally neglected before the doctrinal debates of the fourth century. Irenaeus, Tertullian, and Origen, for example, had significant things to say about the Holy Spirit. Rather, the question of the status of Christ's divinity precipitated a certain forgetfulness of the Holy Spirit. This forgetting is all the more explicable if we consider that the question of Christ's divinity was wrapped up with how God and creation relate and how Jesus Christ, as somehow "divine" and Creator while also a human creature, mediates this relation. The framework structured by the Father-Son and God-world binaries did not readily extend itself to the consideration of the third of the Trinity, the Holy Spirit.

108. *Decr.* 27.
109. Jenson refers to Athanasius's *On the Nicene Council* to make this precise point. See his *Triune Identity*, 17–18.

The Orations against the Arians

Athanasius's *Against the Greeks–On the Incarnation* is a prime example of a christocentric forgetting of the Spirit; there are only isolated references to the Spirit as inspirer of Scripture. That neglect is perhaps another indication that this treatise was narrowly intended as a polemical demonstration that the human limitations associated with the incarnation are not indicative of an inferior divinity. By contrast, we have noted above that the *Orations against the Arians* contain a fully developed "Spirit Christology" to complement the "incarnation Christology" of *Against the Greeks–On the Incarnation*.[110] The christological framework for broaching the question of the Holy Spirit in the *Orations* is structured by the exegesis of Psalm 45:7, "You love righteousness and hate wickedness. Therefore God, your God, has anointed you with the oil of gladness beyond your companions." This text had already been applied to Christ in the Letter to the Hebrews, and Justin Martyr had seen the psalmist's dual reference to the enthroned Lord and the anointing God as a testimony to the numerical distinction between Father and Son.[111] Origen had taken the verse as indicating that the righteous (pre-incarnate) soul of Christ merited union with the *Logos*.[112] Asterius, perhaps following Arius himself, applied it to the future merits of the incarnate Word whereby he preveniently earned the grace of divinity, and pointed to the "therefore" as an indication that the Word is changeable by nature.[113] The subordinationist application of this verse was most simply articulated by Eusebius of Caesarea: "The Anointer, who is the Supreme God, is far superior to the Anointed, who is God in a different sense."[114]

Athanasius, following the New Testament, accepts that the referent of this verse is Christ; he takes the "anointing" as a reference to Christ's reception of the Holy Spirit (cf. Acts 2:33). He insists, however, that the text cannot be referred simply to the Word, as Word, but must be applied consistently with the christological dialectic of the union within distinction of divinity and humanity. The incarnate Word is conceived as having a double relation to the Spirit; he is giver of the Spirit according to his divinity and receiver of the Spirit in his humanity. The soteriological yield of this double transaction is that humanity becomes sanctified through its reception of the Spirit, which derives from the incarnate Word's human reception of it:

> The Savior . . . being God, and forever ruling the kingdom of the Father, and being himself the supplier of the Spirit, is nevertheless now said to be anointed by the Spirit, so that, being said to be anointed as a human being by the Spirit, he may provide us human beings with the indwelling and intimacy of the Holy Spirit, just as he provides

110. By characterizing the earlier treatise as an "incarnation Christology," I mean that the central motif is the humanization of the Word, which in Athanasius's treatment includes a primary emphasis on the soteriological value of Christ's death on the cross. See Anatolios, *Athanasius*, 56–61.

111. *Dial.* 56.14.

112. *Princ.* 2.6.4.

113. Fr. 45 (Vinzent).

114. *Dem. ev.* 4.15.

us with exaltation and resurrection. . . . For he is not sanctified by another, but he sanctifies himself, in order that we may be sanctified in the truth. But the one who sanctifies himself is the Lord of sanctification. How does this happen? How does he speak the way he does, except as if to say, "I, being the Word of the Father, give the Spirit to myself, having become a human being. And, in the Spirit, I sanctify myself, having become human, so that henceforth all may be sanctified in me by the truth, 'For your word is truth'" (John 17:17).[115]

This is a Christology in which the distinction of divinity and humanity is essentially defined in terms of the giving and receiving of the Holy Spirit. But, of course, the crucial soteriological factor is the unity of subject; there is a single agent who both gives and receives. It is this dialectical unity of the giving and receiving of the Spirit that provides the christological-trinitarian structure of human salvation:

> Therefore, "Jesus Christ is the same yesterday and today and forever" (Heb. 13:8), remaining and not changing. And he is the same, both giving and receiving, giving as the Word of God, receiving as a human being.[116]

> But through whom and from whom should the Spirit have been given, if not through the Son whose Spirit it is? And, then again, when were we empowered to receive, if not when the Word became a human being? Just as the apostle's words indicate that we would not have been freed and "highly exalted" if it were not that "he who is in the form of God took the form of a servant" (Phil. 2:6–7), so also David shows that in no other way would we have partaken of the Spirit and been sanctified if it were not that the Giver of the Spirit, the Word himself, spoke of himself as anointed by the Spirit for our sakes. Therefore we have received securely (*bebaiōs*) in that he is said to be anointed in the flesh. The flesh was first sanctified in him and he is spoken of as having received through it, as a human being, and so we have the Spirit's grace that follows from his reception, receiving from his fullness (John 1:16).[117]

The key soteriological term in this passage, as it is elsewhere in Athanasius, is "secure" (*bebaios*).[118] The usage of this term in Athanasius typically designates the qualitative redemptive difference inserted by the work of Christ into the human condition. The fundamental framework evoked by this terminology is that provided in *Against the Greeks–On the Incarnation*. There, insecurity and instability radically characterize human existence inasmuch as it has its origin, according to one polarity of its creatureliness, from nothing. The other polarity of the creaturely state, which is intensified in the case of human creatures, is the "grace" (*charis*) of participation in the Word. From the human side, free will mediates between the insecurity of creaturely nothingness and the grace of participation in divine life. Thus the proper

115. *C. Ar.* 1.46 (ET: Anatolios, *Athanasius*, 103–4).
116. *C. Ar.* 1.48 (ET: Anatolios, *Athanasius*, 106).
117. *C. Ar.* 1.50 (ET: Anatolios, *Athanasius*, 108).
118. See Anatolios, *Athanasius*, 61–63.

theocentric orientation of free will involves a self-overcoming that is oriented toward the transcending of creaturely nothingness in the mode of "remaining" in grace, with *menein* achieving in Athanasius a technical sense that has an analogous density to its Johannine usage.[119] However, the misshaping of the human will through sin reverses the direction of human "remaining" so that it becomes a fixed trajectory of reversion toward nothingness. In *On the Incarnation*, this trajectory is itself reversed through the humanization of the Word, which definitively establishes the security of remaining in grace. In that treatise, Athanasius depicts the structure of redemptive security in terms of a christological "Image theology." The Word, being the true divine Image of the Father, renews humanity's being-according-to-the-Image by redrawing it in his own humanity. He does this not only through the mere fact of incarnation, considered in a truncated punctiliar sense, but through his global stance of self-offering to the Father, which includes the offering of himself to death on the cross. Through our integration into Christ's self-offering, we too are presented to the Father and attain an intimate personal knowledge of the Father.

When Athanasius refutes the "Arian" contention that the Word is changeable by nature even if *de facto* rendered immutable by grace, he presupposes the innate instability of human creaturehood: "For the nature of things that come to be is changeable and not stable (*bebaia*). . . . Therefore there was a need for someone who was unchangeable, so that human beings might have that immutability as an image and archetype of virtue."[120] While in *Against the Greeks–On the Incarnation* the problem of radical human instability is resolved in the strictly binary terms of the incarnate Word's divine and human imaging of the Father, the *Orations* now presents a trinitarian account that sees "secure" salvation in terms of Christ's relation to the Spirit. Salvation is definitively secured when there is a perfect communication between the divine giving of the Spirit and the human receiving of the Spirit, as happens in Christ. In him, the giving is perfect because he is God, who is by nature the giver of the Spirit; the receiving is perfect because he is God in human form; and the perfect union of giving and receiving is established in that the same one is perfect giver and perfect receiver. For Asterius, the "therefore" of the psalm indicates the natural mutability of the Word, but for Athanasius it signifies the christological dialectic whereby the immutability of the Word underwrites humanity's perfect reception of the Spirit through its participation in Christ's human reception of the Spirit. Thus the *Orations* supplement the soteriological motif of Christ's "renewing the image," in *On the Incarnation*, with that of a new reception of the Spirit through Christ.

> But if, in order to suit their own wishes, they make a pretext for themselves because of the word "therefore," when the psalm says, "Therefore God, your God, has anointed you" (Ps. 45:7; Heb. 1:9), let these amateurs in Scripture and experts in impiety understand that there also the word "therefore" does not signify any reward for the virtue or conduct of the Word. Rather, it again refers to the reason for his descent to us, and for

---

119. See Hauck, "*Menō*," in *TDNT*, 4:574–76; Anatolios, *Athanasius*, 61–63.
120. *C. Ar.* 1.51 (ET: Anatolios, *Athanasius*, 108).

the anointing of the Spirit which took place in him for our sakes. For he does not say, "Therefore he has anointed you *to become* God or King or Son or Word"; for he was this before then and is so forever, as has been shown. But rather, "Since you are God and King, 'therefore' you were anointed—since there was no other to join humanity to the Holy Spirit except you who are the Image of the Father, and according to whose image we were made in the beginning; for the Spirit also is yours." The nature of things that come to be is not trustworthy for this task, for angels have transgressed, and human beings disobeyed. "Therefore" God was needed (and "the Word is God" John 1:1), so that he himself might free those who had come under the curse.[121]

Finally, this account of the secure salvation worked through Christ's divine and human receiving of the Spirit is integrated by Athanasius into his christological narrative, or *skopos*, of Scripture. Here again, the issue is the proper location and characterization of the christological *pro nobis*. While for Asterius and Eusebius the "anointing" or reception of the Spirit is read into the divinity of the Word, as indicative of an inferior divinity, it becomes for Athanasius a manifestation of the kenotic descent accomplished in the incarnation. Christ's reception of the Spirit must be interpreted in line with the overall christological plot of Scripture. This plot does not allow for an advancement of the Word, as Word. There is no scriptural drama of the advancement of the Word; all the drama is about the self-abasement of the Word for our advancement, and that is the meaning of Christ's reception of the Spirit.

What kind of progress, then, is it for the Immortal to assume the mortal? Or what kind of advancement is it for the Eternal to put on the temporal? What kind of reward could be greater than being the Eternal God and King, who is in the bosom of the Father (John 1:18)? Do you not see that this also took place and is written because of us and for our sakes (*di' hēmas kai hyper hēmōn*), so that the Lord, having become human, might grant immortality to us who are mortal and temporal and lead us into the everlasting kingdom of heaven? . . . To be sure, just as before his becoming human, he was the Word who granted to the saints the Spirit as his own (*idion*), so also, upon his becoming human, he sanctifies all by the Spirit, and says to the disciples: "Receive the Holy Spirit" (John 20:22).[122]

The Letters to Serapion

In the late 350s, while Athanasius was spending his third exile hiding among the monks of the Egyptian desert, he received word from Serapion of Thmuis that some Egyptian Christians were confessing the full divinity of the Son but denying the same confession to the Spirit. This group, derisively called *tropici* by Athanasius, presumably because of their allegorical construction of scriptural "tropes," cited biblical texts that referred to created spirit/wind (*pneuma*), as in Amos 4:13 ("I am the one who establishes thunder and creates spirit and declares to people his Christ" LXX), and that spoke of "ministering spirits"

---

121. *C. Ar.* 1.49 (ET: Anatolios, *Athanasius*, 106–7).
122. *C. Ar.* 1.48 (ET: Anatolios, *Athanasius*, 105).

(Heb. 1:14). It seems that they also accepted the notion of a full communication of being
from Father to Son in the act of generation but then wondered how that communication
could be extended to the Holy Spirit. It would appear that such is the reasoning behind
the seemingly facetious question as to whether the Spirit was the son of the Son or his
brother. Athanasius's response to this new challenge includes four significant features that
inform his mature trinitarian doctrine. First, he argues on behalf of the full divinity of
the Spirit, an argument whose essential components will be replicated in Cappadocian
rebuttals of "Macedonian" theology.[123] Second, he attempts to identify the distinction
of the person of the Spirit, manifesting the same careful attention to scriptural linguistic
patterns that we have seen him employ with respect to the Son. Third, his reflections
on the divinity and distinct role of the Spirit in the Godhead lead him now to a more
explicit consideration of the Trinity as a whole. And finally, this heightened attentiveness
to the trinitarian name leads him to an equally intensified focus on the event of baptism
as a privileged disclosure of the trinitarian being of God.

The Divinity of the Spirit

Athanasius argues on behalf of the divinity of the Spirit from his typical starting
point: positing the radical polarity of the Creator-creature distinction, he asks on
which side the Scriptures place the Spirit: "But let us finally look at the sayings about
the Spirit in the divine Scriptures, taking them one by one, and like expert investiga-
tors let us determine well whether the Spirit has anything that belongs to creatures or
whether it belongs to God. In this way, we will be able to say whether it is a creature
or whether it is other than creatures and belongs to and is one with the Godhead in
the Trinity."[124] Athanasius follows three lines of argument in asserting that the Spirit
belongs on the divine side of the Creator-creature distinction.

1. He uses scriptural texts to demonstrate that the Spirit is biblically characterized
in terms of divine attributes such as inalterability, incorruptibility, and omnipresence.
In order to reinforce the Creator-creature distinction that underlies his whole argument, Athanasius brings forward contrasting biblical texts that designate the opposing
attributes of creatures. Thus the Scriptures characterize the Spirit as belonging on the
divine side of the Creator-creature distinction.[125]

2. The second argument moves from the level of divine attributes to the level of
divine activity. At this level, the Creator-creature distinction is drawn in terms of
activity versus passivity and participation. The first has Stoic resonances and the
second Platonic connotations, but the overarching perspective is the biblical premise
that, in the relation between God and creation, God is active and creation receptive.[126]

123. On the possible dependence of Gregory of Nyssa on Athanasius's *Letters to Serapion*, see Meredith,
"Pneumatology of the Cappadocian Fathers," esp. 207–8. For the present purposes, I am not arguing for
direct dependence but merely noting that there are similarities in the basic elements of the argument.
    124. *Ep. Serap.* 1.21; translations are from Anatolios, *Athanasius*, throughout.
    125. *Ep. Serap.* 1.21–26.
    126. On Athanasius's use of the Stoic active-passive framework, see Anatolios, *Coherence*, 76–80; on
his use of the participation motif, see *Coherence*; Balás, *Metousia Theou*, 11–12.

Consequently, it is important not to sunder the active-passive distinction from the concrete framework of the God-world distinction and the biblical characterization of the particular set of acts that transpires between God and the world. Otherwise, Athanasius can be seen to be destabilizing his own argument when he goes on to characterize the Spirit as "receiving" from the Son. But Athanasius's argument is not concerned abstractly with activity and receptivity, as attributes considered purely in and of themselves, such that all activity indicates divinity and all receptivity denotes creaturehood. Rather, he has in view the activity, broadly considered, that transpires *between* God and creation, in the realms of creation and salvation. In Scripture, creatures are recipients of the divine creative and redemptive agency. Thus it is only with respect to the activities that pertain to creation and salvation that activity denotes divinity and receptivity characterizes creaturehood, not with respect to other "acts" that might take place between Father, Son, and Spirit.[127] The Spirit, however, is biblically represented as an agent of divine creative and redemptive activity directed toward the creation, not as the recipient of this activity; the Spirit vivifies and sanctifies and is not vivified or sanctified. Therefore, the Spirit is biblically placed on the divine side of the Creator-creature divide. The climactic moment of this argument from the Spirit's activity refers to the ultimate transaction between God and humanity, which is the communication of divine life to human beings at the maximal level of deification. If the Spirit is the agent rather than the recipient of such communication, then the Spirit is divine: "But if we become sharers in the divine nature through participation in the Spirit, one would have to be crazy to say that the Spirit is of a created nature and not of the nature of God, for that is how those in whom the Spirit is become divinized. But if the Spirit divinizes, it is not to be doubted that it is of the nature of God himself."[128]

3. Since his opponents acknowledge the full divinity of the Son, Athanasius transposes the analysis of the Spirit's activity from the perspective merely of his relation to creation to include that of his relation to the Son. If the Word is divine, and if the Spirit's activity is always coordinate with that of the Word, then the Spirit's divinity is also coordinate with that of the Word. This aspect of the argument therefore moves to the level of the trinitarian co-activity in relation to creation. Moreover, it presumes that such divine activity effects a union between God and creation—something only God can do. Athanasius then probes scriptural language and narrative, concluding that the Spirit unites us to the Son and that it is "in the Spirit" that the Word, in turn, unites us and "presents" us to the Father. Thus the Spirit's capacity to effect our union with the Son and the Father presupposes its own natural unity with them:

127. For this reason, Athanasius's arguments in this regard are not directly relevant to recent discussions about the appropriateness of positing receptivity as an inner-trinitarian category. For a significant modern treatment of this issue, see Balthasar, *Theo-Drama V*, esp. 85–91.

128. *Ep. Serap.* 1.24; cf. *Ep. Serap.* 1.25: "The one in whom creation is divinized cannot be extrinsic to the divinity of the Father."

Therefore, it is in the Spirit that the Word glorifies creation and presents it to the Father by divinizing it and granting it adoption. But the one who binds creation to the Word could not be among the creatures and the one who bestows sonship upon creation could not be foreign to the Son. Otherwise, it would be necessary to look for another spirit to unite this one to the Word.[129]

IDENTIFYING THE PERSON OF THE SPIRIT

The preceding arguments place the Spirit on the divine side of the Creator-creation distinction, but they do not yet specify the location of the Spirit within the Trinity, though the third line of argument stands at the threshold of this question. The question is thrust upon Athanasius by his opponents, who mocked the attribution of full divinity to the Spirit by asking whether the Spirit should then be considered a brother of the Son or a son of the Son. Athanasius's polemical rhetoric in turn derides the anthropomorphic cast of his opponents' argument: "For God is not as humans that we should dare to ask human questions about him."[130] But he clearly sees that the theological issue behind his opponents' mockery is the distinction of the Spirit with respect to the derivation from the Father and his relation to the Son. In his opponents' mind, the one who comes from the Father is called "Son"; if the Spirit is also "from the Father," is he another Son and therefore a brother of the Son? Or, if he is not directly from the Father so as to be a brother of the Son, does he emanate from the Son so as to be "grandson" of the Father? Behind the apparent silliness of articulating the issue in this way lie serious questions not only about the intra-trinitarian processions and relations but also about the integration of these questions with the biblical and liturgical forms of divine naming.

Athanasius's response to these questions consistently builds on the foundational principle of the primacy of scriptural language. Scriptural language employs the paternal-filial relation to name Father and Son, while the Spirit's name is cocoordinated with both Father and Son without being placed on either side of the paternal-filial framework. Each of the Trinity must be conceived consistently with the patterns by which the three are scripturally named. Moreover, each scriptural name is fully owned by its possessor in a strict and unqualified sense and is therefore not shareable. The non-communicability of the names of "Father" and "Son" is based both on the intractable givenness of the scriptural patterns of naming and on the understanding, consequent upon these patterns, that the act of generation to which these names refer does not partition the divine nature so that the name of "Father" is partially owned by the Son, and vice-versa:

God is not like a human being (Num. 23:19), nor does he have a partitioned nature. Therefore, he does not beget the Son by way of partition, so that the Son may also become father of another, since the Father himself is not from a father. Neither is the Son a part of the Father. Therefore, he does not beget as he himself was begotten, but

129. *Ep. Serap.* 1.25.
130. *Ep. Serap.* 1.15.

is whole image (*eikōn*) and radiance of the whole. It is only in the Godhead that the Father is properly (*kyriōs*) Father and the Son properly Son; in their case, the Father is always Father and the Son always Son. Just as the Father could never be Son, so also the Son could never be Father. And just as the Father will never cease to be uniquely Father, so also the Son will never cease to be uniquely Son. So it is madness to speak and even to think in any way of a brother of the Son, and to name the Father a grandfather. Neither is the Spirit called Son in the Scriptures, so as to be considered as a brother, nor is it called a son of the Son, lest the Father be conceived as a grandfather. But the Son is said to be Son of the Father, and the Spirit of the Son is said to be Spirit of the Father.[131]

Having ruled out any naming of the Spirit that is inconsistent with biblical patterns, Athanasius still must say how to speak positively of the Spirit's relation to Father and Son. His first concern is that this question not be treated as enquiring into the "composition" of God. Such an analysis of the inner composition of a being and the radical "how" of its existence is hardly possible in the case of creatures, much less that of the Creator. The "how" of God's act of existence cannot be the passive object of human scrutiny. Yet Athanasius does not simply reject enquiry into the relation of the Spirit to Father and Son. Rather, he relocates such enquiry from the realm of explanation and analysis to the realm of contemplating the scriptural disclosure of God. From the latter vantage point, the relevant data is given, as in the case of the Son, through the patterns of scriptural intertextuality: "Therefore, since such an attempt is futile and a surplus of madness, let no one ask such questions any more, or else learn only what is in the Scriptures. For the symbols (*paradeigmata*) in the Scriptures which pertain to these questions are sufficient and adequate."[132] Athanasius then proceeds to outline instances of the intertextual scriptural characterizations of Father, Son, and Spirit. In each case, he follows the distinct and co-related characterizations of the three with a reiteration of the co-relationality between Son and Spirit. It will prove instructive to rehearse some of his examples:

1. One is Father; the other is Son, and we are made "sons" when we receive the Spirit. The Spirit is thus the one who actualizes our adoption into Christ: "But when we are made sons by the Spirit, it is clearly in Christ that we receive the title 'children of God': 'For to those who did accept him, he gave power to become children of God' (John 1:12)."[133]

2. The Father is called light; the Son is radiance; the Spirit is the one in whom we are enlightened: "But when we are enlightened by the Spirit, it is Christ who in the Spirit enlightens us." [134]

3. The Father is called fountain; the Son is the outpouring from the fountain; and "we are given to drink of the Spirit": "But when we are given to drink of the Spirit, we drink Christ." [135]

131. *Ep. Serap.* 1.16.
132. *Ep. Serap.* 1.29.
133. *Ep. Serap.* 1.19.
134. *Ep. Serap.* 1.19.
135. *Ep. Serap.* 1.19.

4. The Father is wise; the Son is Wisdom; the Spirit is "the Spirit of Wisdom": "But, the Son being wisdom, when we receive the Spirit of wisdom, we attain Christ and become wise in him."[136]

5. The Father is the source of life (Athanasius does not say so, but the reader fills in the blanks); the Son is life (cf. John 14:6); and "we are said to be made alive in the Spirit": "But when we are made alive in the Spirit, Christ himself is said to live in us" (cf. Gal. 2:19–20).[137]

6. The Father works; the Son does the works of the Father; the works of Father and Son are accomplished "in the Spirit": "So also, Paul said that the works that he accomplished in the power of the Spirit were the works of Christ."[138]

Several significant points may be drawn from Athanasius's examples. (1) He reiterates the fundamental methodological principle that the correlation between Father, Son, and Spirit is being carefully read out of the intertextual patterns of Scripture. Once again, we see the direct translation from linguistic correlativity to ontological correlativity. So Athanasius concludes the section in which he analyzes the scriptural intertextual patterns of identifying Father, Son, and Spirit with a challenge: "Such being the correlation (*systoichia*) and the unity of the Holy Trinity, who would dare to separate the Son from the Father, or the Spirit from the Son or from the Father himself? Or who would be so presumptuous as to say that the Trinity is unlike (*anomoion*) and heterogeneous with respect to itself, or that the Son is of a different being (*allotrioousion*) than the Father, or that the Spirit is foreign to the Son?"[139] (2) Athanasius consistently concludes his characterizations of the interrelation of the three with a reprise of the co-relation of Son and Spirit. This strategy can be partly attributed to the fact that he is arguing against those who accept the full divinity of the Son but deny the same status to the Spirit, but it also represents the perspective of an Irenaean "two hands" theology in which the Son and Spirit are conceived as coordinate mediums between the Father and creation.[140] (3) Precisely through his careful attentiveness to the scriptural intertextual patterns, Athanasius is able to conceive a distinct and consistent "persona" of the Spirit. Characteristically, he is not concerned with conceptualizing this persona in abstract logical terms but is content simply to identify it within the biblical patterns. But if we look at his scriptural illustrations, we can readily see that an appropriate conceptualization of the distinct role of the Spirit would identify the Spirit as the one in whom the outward manifestation and activity of Father and Son is actualized in relation to us. In each case, the Spirit is thus characterized as the point of contact between God and creation.

To sum up the relations among the three according to Athanasius's presentation of the biblical patterns, we could say that in each case the Father is source, the Son is outgoing manifestation and imaged content of the source, and the Spirit is the

136. *Ep. Serap.* 1.19.
137. *Ep. Serap.* 1.19.
138. *Ep. Serap.* 1.19.
139. *Ep. Serap.* 1.20.
140. Irenaeus, *Haer.* 4, pref.

outward actualization of that content in and toward creation. Moreover, to repeat Athanasius's typical reprise, the actualization is precisely actualization of the content that is Christ. The characterization of the Spirit as actualization of the dynamism of divine life extends beyond these examples and is present throughout the *Letters to Serapion*. A striking demonstration of this conception is the fact that the same term (*energeia*) is used by Athanasius to depict both the outward activity of the Trinity as a whole and the specific role of the Spirit in relation to Father and Son. Thus, in the first instance, Athanasius can say that the Trinity is "identical with itself and indivisible in nature, and its activity (*energeia*) is one;"[141] here *energeia* denotes the outward activity of the Trinity. But, according to the second pattern, he typically identifies the Spirit as the "living energy" of the Son: "For where the light is, there is the radiance, and where the radiance is, there is its active energy (*energeia*) and luminous grace";[142] the Spirit "activates (*energoun*) everything that is worked by the Father through the Son."[143]

We can observe that the characterization of the Spirit in this way seems to be dependent on its connection with creation. If the Spirit is distinguished as the one in whom creation's participation in divine life is actualized, how does this distinction hold in the divine being, considered independently of creation? Suffice it to say that this is not the sort of question that Athanasius is motivated to ask. He only asks questions that presume the concrete reference of creation existing in relation to its Creator. Within that relation, the Spirit is the active agency by which divine life is actualized in us; that agency identifies both the Spirit's claim to the divine title and its specific role within the trinitarian divine agency in relation to creation. Augustine would later raise precisely this question, and we can here briefly anticipate his response in order to register its continuity with Athanasius's characterization. Augustine designates the Spirit's role as the outward actualization of divine life by referring to the Spirit's biblical name as "Gift." He asks what the eternal character of the Spirit as gift can be if considered independently of creation as the recipient of the gift. His response is that the Spirit eternally exists as "the Giveable God" (*Deus donabilis*) whose giveability is not strictly contingent on the existence of any recipients.[144] Athanasius's speculative ken does not stretch that far; he is content simply to clarify the scriptural designation of the Spirit as the one in whom divine life is given. Divine life has its source in the Father; its content is imaged in the Son; and it is outwardly given in the Spirit.

"The Trinity Is Complete in the Spirit"

Up to the time of the controversy with the *tropici* in the mid-350s, Athanasius's "trinitarian" theology had been largely centered on the relation between Father and Son. As we have seen, his reflections on this relation did take serious account of the Holy Spirit in the *Orations against the Arians*. In that treatise, Athanasius is also able

141. *Ep. Serap.* 1.28; cf. *Ep. Serap.* 1.31.
142. *Ep. Serap.* 1.30.
143. *Ep. Serap.* 1.30.
144. The character of the Spirit as gift is used as a description of the Spirit's procession by Augustine: "*Quia sic procedebat ut esset donabile . . .*" (*Trin.* 5.15.16).

to speak thematically about the "Trinity" as the proper and eternal identification of the Christian God,[145] though this language is infrequent. But in responding to the *tropici* with a thorough defense of the full divinity of the Spirit, the Alexandrian now makes much more prominent use of the language of trinity (*trias*). Now that the Holy Spirit has been strictly differentiated from creation and ontologically associated with the Father and the Son, Athanasius can speak summarily in terms of the coincident oneness and threeness of God: "Thus, there is one Godhead of the Holy Trinity";[146] "the Triad, the whole of which is one God."[147] The following passage is typical in its synthesis of explicit trinitarian language, its identification of the trinitarian God in terms of the Creator-creature distinction, and its simultaneous stress on the single co-activity and yet distinct positions of the three within that co-activity:

> The Trinity is holy and perfect, confessed as God in Father, Son, and Holy Spirit, having nothing foreign or extrinsic mingled with it, nor compounded of creator and created, but is wholly Creator and Maker. It is identical with itself and indivisible in nature, and its activity (*energeia*) is one. For the Father does all things through the Word and in the Holy Spirit. Thus the oneness of the Holy Trinity is preserved and thus is the one God "who is over all and through all and in all" (Eph. 4:6) preached in the Church—"over all," as Father, who is beginning (*archē*) and fountain; "through all," through the Son; and "in all" in the Holy Spirit."[148]

As this passage intimates, Athanasius's insistence on the "one Godhead of the Holy Trinity" cannot be understood as an endorsement of an undifferentiated unity. At this point, Athanasius seems intent on disassociating himself from the kind of modalism of which Marcellus was accused.[149] The following passage is striking in its incorporation of language traditionally associated with three-*hypostasis* theology and its explicit distancing from "Sabellianism":

> It is Trinity not only in name and linguistic expression, but Trinity in reality and truth. Just as the Father is the "One who is" (Exod. 3:14), so likewise is his Word the "One who is, God over all" (Rom. 9:5). Nor is the Holy Spirit nonexistent, but truly exists and subsists. The catholic church does not think of less than these three, lest it fall in with Sabellius and with the present-day Jews who follow Caiaphas, nor does it invent any more than these three, lest it be dragged into the polytheism of the Greeks.[150]

The insistence that the Trinity is really and truly so and not merely "in name" is startlingly redolent of the creed of the Council of Antioch in 341, which attempted to

145. Cf. *C. Ar.* 1.17.
146. *Ep. Serap.* 1.16.
147. *Ep. Serap.* 1.17.
148. *Ep. Serap.* 1.28.
149. See Spoerl, "Athanasius and the Anti-Marcellan Controversy," 34–55. Spoerl does not treat this particular passage.
150. *Ep. Serap.* 1.28.

replace the Nicene Creed and whose "*bête noire* [was] Sabellianism."[151] The Second Antiochian Creed had spoken in very similar terms of the necessity to believe in "the Father who is really Father and the Son who is really Son and the Holy Spirit who is really Holy Spirit, because the names are not given lightly or idly, but signify exactly the particular *hypostasis* and order and glory of each of those who are named, so that they are three in *hypostasis* but one in agreement."[152] Of course, Athanasius has not simply gone over to the position of the Antiochian Council of 341 at this point. That creed had insisted on the language of ontological diversity by speaking of three *hypostaseis* while reserving merely volitional language for the unity ("one in agreement"). But Athanasius assimilates the language of ontological distinction while also insisting throughout the treatise on the language of ontological unity as well. Thus, while he does not come up with the terse formula of "three *hypostaseis*, one *ousia*," with which the Cappadocians are traditionally said to have "resolved" the trinitarian debates, Athanasius nevertheless has all the component features of that logic in place in the *Letters to Serapion*: each of the three truly "exists and subsists," and yet "there is one Godhead of the Holy Trinity."[153] Finally, in this passage Athanasius once again uses "Jews" and "Greeks" to stand for opposing views with regard to an identity-marking tenet of Christian faith. In *Against the Greeks–On the Incarnation*, the Jew-Greek language dramatizes the point that it is essential and distinctive to Christian faith to believe that the one who suffered and died on the cross is fully God; here, it asserts that both the real unity and real distinction are integral to the Christian identification of God.

BAPTISM AND THE TRINITARIAN NAME

We have already noted that recourse to the baptismal invocation of the Trinity was *de rigueur* for all parties in the doctrinal debates of the fourth century. Arius, for whom the Trinity was "unlike in substance," used it, as did Marcellus, for whom the Trinity was an economic expansion of the Monad. Part of the legacy of the reception of Nicene-Constantinopolitan theology in the Christian tradition is the assumption that, as soon as we apply the foundational principle of *lex credendi lex orandi est*, the baptismal invocation supports a consubstantial Trinity as a matter of course. But the very fact that such different theologies as those of Arius and Marcellus should refer to the baptismal formula caution against such a simple view.[154] The Council of Antioch of 341, quoted above, used the baptismal formula precisely to emphasize the *difference* in being between Father, Son, and Spirit. Still far from the technical formula of Aetius and Eunomius, which stipulated that difference in names indicates difference in substance, that council nevertheless foreshadows their approach: "Just as our Lord Jesus Christ commanded his disciples, saying, 'Go, therefore, and make disciples of all the nations, baptizing them in the name of the Father, and the Son, and the Holy

---

151. Hanson, *Search*, 287.
152. Ibid., 286.
153. *Ep. Serap.* 1.16.
154. This point is ably argued by Williams, "Baptism and the Arian Controversy."

Spirit' (Matt. 28:19), . . . because the names are not given lightly . . . but signify exactly the particular *hypostasis* and order and glory of each of those who are named, so that they are three in *hypostasis* and one in agreement."[155] In this theological application of the baptismal trinitarian formula, the threefold name is used only to indicate the real difference among the three and not a unity of being. Within such a theology, the three names of the baptismal formula indicate a hierarchical structure of agency whereby the mediation of Son and Spirit enables humanity to worship and glorify the Father. The baptismal formula could thus be used to support a subordinationist theology that insists on the difference in being between Father, Son, and Spirit and does not establish any ontological unity beyond that of "agreement."

These observations show that the relation between the baptismal invocation and trinitarian theology is hermeneutically complex. Nicene theologies stipulated not merely a necessary continuity between the contents of worship and belief but also a particular interpretation of acts of worship—in this case, the baptismal rite. The understanding of Nicene trinitarian theology, therefore, involves an appreciation of the particularly Nicene interpretation of baptism. The essential elements of Athanasius's interpretation of baptism can already be found in the *Orations against the Arians*, but they find more thematic and consolidated expression in the *Letters to Serapion*. There we find, first of all, a reiteration of the general foundational principle, later espoused by Basil, that trinitarian faith is anchored in its performative expression in the event of baptism: "Let them learn that this is indeed the faith of the Church by considering how the Lord, when he sent the apostles, exhorted them to establish this as a foundation for the Church, saying: 'Go and make disciples of all nations, baptizing them in the name of the Father and the Son and the Holy Spirit' (Matt. 28:19)."[156] But, as we have noted, the mere acknowledgment of this principle does not of itself yield the kind of trinitarian theology espoused by Athanasius. Athanasius's construction of a distinctive interpretation of baptism enfolds the threefold name within an emphasis on the single divine agency, which he interprets as the content of the "oneness" of baptism. The biblical foundation of this move is provided by reference to the Letter to the Ephesians, which speaks of "one Lord, one faith, one baptism" (Eph. 4:5). Athanasius interprets "one baptism" as signifying not merely the fact that all Christians undergo the same external rite but, rather, in a strictly theological sense, as a description of the internal integrity of the divine agency by which it is efficacious in uniting the baptizand with divine life. From this perspective, the oneness of baptism, and the oneness of the faith that interprets it, both refer objectively to the oneness of the divine referent that is signified by both. The unity of the baptismal act is thus derivative from and a reflection of the unity of trinitarian agency.[157] Conversely, by breaking up the name cited in

155. Hanson, *Search*, 286.
156. *Ep. Serap.* 1.28.
157. Cf. *Ep. Serap.* 1.30: "For as the baptism given in the Father and the Son and the Holy Spirit is one and the faith in the Trinity is one, as the apostle says (Eph. 4:5), so the Holy Trinity, which is identical with itself and united with itself, has nothing of what is originated within it. This is the indivisible unity of the Trinity and faith in this Trinity is one."

the dominically mandated baptismal invocation into different ontological categories (Unoriginated God and originated creature), the *tropici* are breaking up the baptismal act into two acts, attributed to two very different kinds of agencies: "Then your faith is no longer one and neither is your baptism one but two—one of them being in the Father and the Son, and another in an angel who is a creature. But at this point nothing is left secure for you and nothing true. For what kind of communion can there be between an originated being and the Creator? Or what kind of oneness can there be between the creatures below and the Word who has made them?"[158]

We can distinguish two distinct yet related ways in which Athanasius interprets the baptismal formula and act, both necessitating an affirmation of the unity of the trinitarian agency. On the one hand, he interprets the trinitarian name of the formula as denoting the divine destination of the human subject of baptism. From that point of view, Athanasius sees baptism as entrance into divine life. If any of the three is a mere creature, the destination of baptism will be fragmented into a mixture of creation and Creator and the oneness of baptism will be destroyed. Thus he berates the *tropici*: "The baptismal consecration which you think that you are performing is not entirely an entrance into divinity, for you have appended a creature to the divinity."[159] This understanding of baptism involves an assumption that the act of baptism is, at least with regard to its final term, an act of deification; Father, Son, and Spirit together constitute the unified term of this act, the destination into which humanity "enters." But, of course, the act of baptism can be considered from another point of view, not so much with regard to its final term, but with regard to the dynamic process in which Father, Son, and Spirit are named as agents. Subordinationist theologies tended to interpret the baptismal trinitarian name as primarily denoting this hierarchical process, whose final term was a redeemed relation to the Father rather than union with Father, Son, and Spirit. Athanasius's trinitarian theology of baptism cannot finally tolerate such a disjunction between the term and the process of divine agency in the baptismal act; this disjunction would again represent the fragmentation of the "one baptism." His positive rationale for rejecting this disjunction is ultimately grounded in the fundamental principle that only God can join creation with God. Thus there can be no process that leads to God of which God himself is not always and immediately the agent. Athanasius's particular understanding of the oneness of baptism therefore involves the claim that the dynamic process that joins us to God, and of which Father, Son, and Spirit are co-agents, must be one with the term of this process, which is union with Father, Son, and Spirit. The oneness of baptism means that the one Trinity is both the goal and the way of our union with God. The trinitarian pattern of our entrance into divine life is described by Athanasius in terms of the Spirit facilitating the union of the Word with humanity, such that humanity is "presented" and "offered" to the Father through the Word. It is of course not incidental that such language of "offering" has eucharistic overtones: "Thus it was that when the Word

158. *Ep. Serap.* 1.30.
159. *Ep. Serap.* 1.28.

came to the holy Virgin Mary, the Spirit also entered with him (cf. Luke 1:35), and the Word, in the Spirit, fashioned and joined a body to himself, wishing to unite creation to the Father and to offer it to the Father through himself and to reconcile all things in his body, 'making peace among the things of heaven and the things of earth' (cf. Col. 1:20)."[160]

Christian Life in the Trinity

The above passage is a typical representation of Athanasius's way of conceiving the Trinity as the space in which Christian life takes place. The Spirit, as the actualization of the content of divine life for us, draws us to the Son and enables us to participate in Christ: "We will become partakers of Christ if we hold fast to the Spirit."[161] Reciprocally, the incarnate Word enables us to receive the Spirit through his own reception of the Spirit in his humanity. Through the correlated activity of Son and Spirit, we become "worded" and "sons" in the Son and thus are incorporated into the Son's stance of self-offering to the Father. Yet it is possible to imagine the literal components of such a scheme, constructed out of the narrative and intertextual patterns of Scripture, within a subordinationist trinitarian theology. Indeed, we can find these basic components in the theology of Eusebius of Caesarea, as one example. However, Athanasius's trinitarian theology is distinctive both in its negative preclusions and in its positive interpretation. Negatively, Athanasius denies that this pattern can be intelligible, in a Christian framework, apart from the consubstantiality of the Trinity. If the Spirit does not fully share the full divinity of the Son, then the Spirit cannot join us to the Son, and if the Son does not fully share the full divinity of the Father, the Son cannot join us to the Father. Conversely, Athanasius's positive interpretation of the trinitarian dynamics of Christian life is that this structure identifies the immediacy of our involvement in the fullness of divine life. If the scriptural narrative represents the Son and Spirit as mediators of divine life, they must both be in full possession of that life in order for their agency to effect the mediation of divine immediacy rather than its mere negation.[162]

Between Nothingness and Being

One way of retrieving Athanasius's conception of the trinitarian structuring of divine immediacy in humanity's sharing in divine life is to follow his usage of the language of "image," which we have already encountered as central to the conceptual structure of *On the Incarnation*. Much insight into the Alexandrian's theological vision can be gleaned by noting how the language of "image" is used to draw a series of immediate links between God and humanity. Humanity is made according to God's

160. *Ep. Serap.* 1.31; cf. *Ep. Serap.* 1.26.
161. *Ep. Fest.* 3.4. For other instances of the theme of partaking Christ, see 2.5, 5.5.
162. See Anatolios, "Immediately Triune God."

image, and its entrance into and perseverance in being is constituted through its participation in the divine Image, who is Word, Wisdom, and Son of the Father. The Son, in turn, is the true and perfect Image of the Father, who fully shares the being of the Father in himself and is only thus capable of sharing this being-with-the-Father with creation. The Spirit also is the Image of the Son, sharing the life of the Son in himself and enabling the life of the Son to be shared by creation.[163] Throughout this usage, "image" does not so much denote visibility or objective reproduction of a prototype but rather ontological sharing in the prototype. In the case of humanity, however, the being-according-to-the-image is not simply coincident with the entirety of its being, inasmuch as this being is also simultaneously a being-from-nothing. That is why the human being is not simply "image" of God, but "according to the Image."[164] Human being is thus a movement from nothing into God. When this movement became radically disrupted by sin, the divine Image, whose being is coincident with his sharing the life of the Father, repaired the human image through his own incarnate humanity. He did this by transferring humanity's movement-from-nothing into himself, such that we now have a new "point of origin" in Christ.[165] The human being's movement from nothing into God is now accomplished within Christ, who integrates this movement into his own imaging of the Father and the Spirit's imaging of himself. The salvific effect of the incarnation is precisely to transfer the potential obstruction of the starting point of nothingness, actualized and intensified by sin, into the free and unobstructed movement of Father, Son, and Spirit, through the new creatureliness of the incarnate Word.

For Athanasius, all this is catastrophically undone as soon as we introduce the notion that Son and Spirit are themselves creatures "from nothing." With the latter conception, the sting of nothingness, rendered deadly by sin but now safely enfolded in the radically unobstructed flow of divine life, is not only reintroduced into the movement of humanity into God but also reintroduced from the side of "divine" agency. If, even for subordinationist theologies, the Trinity structures our movement into God, then these theologies break down to the extent that they represent this movement as fragmented by abysses of nothingness not only between humanity and God but even between the Spirit and the Son and the Son and the Father. In the chain of relations between humanity and Father, Son, and Holy Spirit, Athanasius is prepared to admit only one gap of nothingness, and that has been filled in by the humanization of the true Image, who has enfolded our creation from nothing within his eternal generation, our being-according-to-the-Image within his perfect and whole imaging of the Father. By contrast, the attribution of creaturehood to Spirit and Son, for Athanasius, is a capitulation and return to the divisive potency of nothingness that is the paradigm of all sin and, like all sin, deconstructs our immediate involvement in divine life.

163. Cf. *Ep. Serap.* 1.24.
164. On the distinction between *eikōn* and *kat' eikona* in Athanasius, see Bernard, *L'Image de Dieu*, esp. 21–24.
165. *Inc.* 10; *C. Ar.* 1.48, 3.33.

I have been suggesting that the fundamental fault line in fourth-century approaches separates models that see the unity of the Trinity as a unity of will from models that posit a unity of being. Moreover, the question of the relation between divine will and divine being is bound up with how they interact with human being and human will. These issues all affect how Christian life is conceived in relation to the Trinity. We have seen that Athanasius's theological vision is radically structured by the framework of being and nothingness. God and creation are ontologically separated by nothingness; sin is the willful disorientation that makes nothingness the end of human being rather than the departure point of human participation in the divine; the divisions of nothingness and sin have been bridged within the interconnectedness of humanity and divinity in Christ and the interconnectedness of the Son with the Father and the Spirit. Athanasius insists on the radical reality of these patterns of interconnectedness, their rootedness in the realms of divine, created, and redeemed being. The Trinity's unity of being is thus fundamental to Athanasius's conception of how the ontological breach between God and creation, exacerbated by sin, has been overcome in the person and work of the incarnate Word.

An Essentialist Soteriology?

Does all this mean that Athanasius's account of humanity's relation to God can be appropriately characterized as "essentialist," in direct opposition to a "voluntarist" view? This was the position advocated by Gregg and Groh. [166] Gregg and Groh reject the traditional portrait of Arianism as motivated by cosmology and theistic monism and seek to replace it with an account in which soteriological concerns are primary. Early Arianism, by this account, is to be distinguished primarily by its "volitionist" understanding of Christian salvation. This understanding presents Christ as a creature "like us" who attains divinity by ethical striving and progress. It encourages human beings to claim equality with Christ and to imitate his exemplary attainment of salvation. This Arian volitionist soteriology is contrasted with Athanasius's essentialist and participationist account of salvation. In the latter perspective, the preexistent Christ is an unqualifiedly divine figure, and equality between him and humanity is strictly precluded. As Christ is God by nature and not through his own willful striving, human beings attain salvation and deification not by willful striving but by an utterly gratuitous participation in divine life. Thus, Gregg and Groh seem to render the trinitarian debates of the early fourth century largely through the framework of the dichotomy between salvation by works and salvation by "essentialist" grace. Their intriguing proposal raises the question of whether the differences between trinitarian unity-of-being and unity-of-will theologies can be correlated with essentialist and voluntarist soteriologies, respectively.

Gregg and Groh's account raises significant methodological issues. To begin with, they are to be commended for broaching the important issue of the *nexus* between

---

166. Gregg and Groh, *Early Arianism*, esp. 161–91.

what we would call the "trinitarian" question of the relation between Father and Son and questions of the character of human salvation and Christ's role in it. On the other hand, this broadening of the horizons of the significant content of the trinitarian debates is unfortunately counterbalanced by the re-constriction of these horizons by the claim that the early Arians were *not* concerned with cosmological questions and the oneness of God, but rather with a distinctive account of human salvation. This account strains against the evidence of the texts, which are plainly concerned with the oneness of God.[167] Moreover, the reflex to reduce a historical doctrinal position to a single primary insight or belief betrays a persistent disinclination to see the inherently systematic character of the Christian worldview that the trinitarian debates exemplified and developed. We should presuppose, rather, that any account of the Christian message would strive to present both God's character and the character of Christian salvation and Christ's role in it. Admittedly, that kind of coherence might often be lacking in particular cases. But when we do find connections between different doctrines in an individual theological position, it is more helpful, as a matter of principle, to note the intelligibility of these relations than to reduce the whole network of connections to one governing idea.

Gregg and Groh's accounts of the respective soteriologies of Athanasius and the "early Arians" are open to criticism on several counts.[168] The surviving texts certainly emphasize the oneness of God, a motif that Gregg and Groh dismiss. And the texts contradict, or fail to support, Gregg and Groh's thesis at several crucial points. The preexistent Christ, in fact, is not like us, since he created us. Even the incarnate Word is not like us, inasmuch as he does not possess a human soul. Moreover, we simply do not find the earning of human salvation by willful striving in these texts. But our concern, for the moment, is with Athanasius. Gregg and Groh's provocative thesis leads us to ask whether it is true that Athanasius's soteriology is so exclusively essentialist as to deny the interaction of divine and human volition. In Athanasius's account, is human involvement in trinitarian life an interpersonal drama of divine and human freedom, or is it merely an ontological given?

In fact, Athanasius's account of humanity's relation to the Trinity is not "essentialist" in a way that precludes volition, either from the divine or the human point of view.[169] Rather, Athanasius's account of this relation accommodates a certain synthesis between being and will, substance and action, with respect to both sides of the relation between God and humanity. We can begin with the divine side. Athanasius exploits every possible occasion to insist that the unity of Father, Son, and Spirit is one of being, and not merely of will. But to insist on unity of being is not to deny unity of will. While firmly anchored in the trajectory of a theology of trinitarian unity of being, Athanasius was not insensible to the challenge presented by the opposing trajectory, which insisted on the sovereign movement of divine

---

167. See the criticism of Stead, "Arius in Modern Research," 36.

168. For a summary of these criticisms, see Hanson, *Search*, 97–98.

169. For an earlier and more detailed response to Gregg and Groh's thesis, see Anatolios, *Coherence*, 167–77.

willing even in the generation of the Son. The Council of Serdica of 343, at which Athanasius was present along with mostly Western bishops (and Marcellus), reiterated the "unity of *hypostasis*" between the Father and the Son. On the other hand, the Eastern bishops, meeting separately, issued their own profession of faith (= the Fourth Creed of Antioch, 341) along with an added anathema directed against those who asserted that the "Father did not beget the Son by his counsel and will."[170] In the third oration, Athanasius deals with this problem by confronting his opponents' dilemma—either the Father wills the Son, or the Father begets the Son without volition. In response, the Alexandrian does not simply reassert his insistence on unity of being rather than unity of will. Instead, he rejects the dilemma altogether, with its presumption of a disjunction between divine being and divine will.[171] In fact, Athanasius can go so far as to assert that the relation between Father and Son is one of unity *and* will. He differs from his opponents not in denying the movement of will in God but in insisting that the relation between Father and Son belongs simultaneously to the structure of divine being and the internal movement of divine will. The conception that he is concerned to reject is that the being of the Son is the mere effect of the will of the Father, while the Father's being is intact prior to and independent of this willing of the Son. His own conception, fashioned in response to his opponents' provocation, is that Father and Son are together constitutive of divine being, and the volitional affirmation of this mutuality by Father and Son simply accompanies their coexistent being and is not in any way posterior to it. In a striking passage, Athanasius depicts the mutuality of being between Father and Son as also simultaneously a mutuality of willing:

> So then if the Son's existence is by nature (*physei*) and not from intention (*ek boulēseōs*), is he with the Father apart from willing and without the intention of the Father? Of course not! The Son is from the Father by will also, as he himself says, "The Father loves the Son and shows him all things" (John 5:20). For just as [the Father] did not begin to be good consequent upon [a prior] intention (*ek boulēseōs*), and yet is good not apart from intention and willing—for what he is, he is willingly—so also the Son's existence, while not having its beginning consequent upon an intention, is nevertheless not apart from willing or the Father's purpose. Just as [the Father's] own subsistence is willful (*thelētēs*), so also the Son, who is proper to his essence, is not without his willing. So let the Son be willed and loved by the Father, and thus may one piously (*eusebōs*) conceive of God's willing and of the Son's not being unwilled by God. For by the same willing by which the Son is from the Father (*para tou patros*), he also loves and wills and honors the Father and there is one will which is from the Father and in the Son, so that in this respect too we can contemplate the Son in the Father and the Father in the Son.[172]

170. The synodal letter and profession of faith of the Eastern bishops is found in Hilary, *Coll. Ant.* 4; for the above reference, see 4.2 (72); cf. Hilary, *De syn.* 34.
171. *C. Ar.* 3.62.
172. *C. Ar.* 3.66. In light of this passage, the contrast drawn by Meijering between Athanasius and Gregory of Nazianzus on intra-trinitarian will ("Gregory, in contrast to Athanasius, is quite ready to

Divine Personhood and Interpersonal Synergy

It has become fashionable to deny that early Christian theology conceived of divine "personhood" in terms anywhere resembling our contemporary understanding of this notion. Be that as it may, we should not overlook the ways in which a theology like Athanasius's, in its careful adherence to the narrative biblical patterns of identifying Father, Son, and Spirit, finds itself depicting the relation between Father and Son in terms that intersect with some aspects of our modern notion of personhood. Certainly, to be a subject of conscious intentionality is integral to our modern notion of personhood, and the interaction of subjects so that they become mutually subjects and objects of each other's intentionality and affirmation is integral to our modern conception of intersubjectivity.[173] But the attribution of conscious intentionality to the divine relations is precisely the point at issue in this passage, not because Athanasius has a presciently modern conception of divine or human personhood but simply because he is beholden to the patterns of biblical narrative and symbol. Drawing as he does on the Johannine motif of the mutual love of Father and Son in interpreting the characterization of Wisdom in the Old Testament, Athanasius affirms conscious intentionality by depicting the oneness of trinitarian being as a oneness of mutual love and reciprocal willing. While firmly anchored in the trajectory of unity of being, the Alexandrian bishop is here able to concede to the unity-of-will theologies that unity of being does not preclude but rather coincides with unity of willing.

If Athanasius can thus depict the relation between Father and Son in terms that can be appropriately styled as "interpersonal," it is not surprising that he can also depict the God-world relation as taking place within the interpersonal space between Father and Son. In the second *Oration against the Arians*, as he discusses the designation of the preexistent Christ as the Wisdom of the Father, Athanasius recalls Proverbs 8:30, "I was by him, daily his delight, rejoicing always before him." Consistently with his comprehensive strategy of reading the divine nature out of the intertextual scriptural patterns of identifying and relating God and Christ, Athanasius takes the mutual delight of Father and Son as intrinsic to divine being. Of course, another pervasive biblical motif is that God delights in creation. Athanasius alludes to an instance of this motif in the book of Proverbs, then locates God's delight in creation within the Father's delight in the Son. It is in and through the Father's delight in his own perfect Image that he also delights in the humanity that is "according to the Image." Thus God's delight in creation is not an "addition" to his being that disturbs divine immutability but an inclusion of creation into the eternal mutual delight of the being of Father and Son.[174] If we retroject his reasoning in the *Letters to Serapion* into this framework, we would have to say that the mutual delight of Father and Son is actualized and rendered available for us in the Spirit. This vision posits an integration of

---

concede that in the generation the Father wants the Son") seems overdrawn. See Meijering, "Doctrine of the Will and of the Trinity," 229.

173. For an excellent treatment of this theme, see Staniloae, *Experience of God*, 245–78.

174. *C. Ar.* 2.82; see above, 118.

divine being and willing in God's relation to the world. In terms of being, God's relation to the world is grounded in the mutuality of Father and Son. There is a place for
the world in God, and that place is the Word and Image of the Father, in which the
world comes to be, "according to the Image." In terms of will, God's loving-kindness
(*philanthrōpia*) toward the world is grounded in the mutual delight of Father and Son.

We can now approach the question from the human side: how does humanity
become incorporated into trinitarian life? Once again, we must disagree with Gregg
and Groh's reductionistic notion that such participation is merely "essentialist" in a
way that precludes human volition and striving. Rather, we find in this case also an
integration of the ontological and volitional aspects of humanity's redeemed relation to
God. We have already seen that, for Athanasius, Christ's redemptive work transforms
the ontological structure of humanity's relation to God. The original movement of
human being from nothing to God is reversed by sin into a movement back to nothingness. But when this movement is transferred into Christ, it becomes a movement
from Christ's human reception of the Spirit into the Word's imaging of the Father. But
all this does not happen automatically and without human volition. When Athanasius
is drawn to reflect on the dynamics of humanity's involvement in divine life, from the
human side, he expounds a vision that can be accurately articulated through what was
to become a classic motif of the Eastern Christian tradition: the co-working (*synergeia*)
between God and humanity. It is this motif, for example, that governs the exposition
of the *Life of Antony*: "Working with (*synergei*) [Antony] was the Lord who put on
flesh for us."[175] Throughout the *Life of Antony*, we find a dramatic dialectic of divine
intervention and Antony's willing response. An intriguing version of this dialectic is the
explanation that sometimes God withdraws the sense of his presence in order to give
Antony space to maximize his efforts. Invariably, Antony responds to the manifestation
of divine presence and activity by redoubling his own striving. This entire dialectic can
be summed up as the drama of Antony's willing appropriation of the reconstruction
of human being accomplished through the incarnate Word.[176]

We find the same dialectic dramatized throughout Athanasius's *Festal Letters*, his
annual Easter greeting to his flock in Alexandria. There he insists that human salvation
and transformation is grounded in the unqualifiedly divine being of the Son and his
salvific work, which reflect the *philanthrōpia* of divine being. Motivated by divine
philanthrōpia, the Son has appropriated and transformed the frailties of the human
condition, and the fruition of this transformation is contained in Christ's resurrection: "For he suffered to prepare freedom from suffering for those who suffer in him.
He descended that he might raise us up. He took upon himself the trial of being born
that we might love the one who is unbegotten."[177] Through his resurrection, Christ
has bestowed the Holy Spirit on humanity and incorporated humanity into his own
intimacy with the Father. All of this is grounded in the "eternal Godhead" of the Son

175. *Vit. Ant.* 5.
176. See Anatolios, *Coherence*, 177–95.
177. *Ep. fest.* 10.8 (ET: NPNF² 4:531, altered).

and his ontological kinship with the Spirit and the Father. The co-activity of Son and Spirit is constitutive of the "grace" of salvation, which is essentially the gift of the Spirit, given by Christ and enabling us to be conformed to Christ: "Therefore, the blessed Paul, when desirous that the grace of the Spirit given to us should not grow cold, exhorts, saying, 'Do not quench the Spirit.' For so we shall remain participants of Christ if we hold fast to the end the Spirit given at the beginning."[178] While the gift of the Spirit thus objectively consists in the life of Christ, which the Spirit renders shareable for us, the Spirit is himself the intentional object of transcendent joy: "To those who believe in the Lord, the coming of the Spirit is better than all refreshment and delight."[179]

All this does not simply happen automatically and without any human contribution. While carefully instructing his flock on the objective reality of the grace accomplished for humanity through Christ and the Spirit, Athanasius lays equal stress on the necessity of an intentional and active reception of such grace on the part of human beings. Active receptivity is a matter of both contemplation and ascetic action. It begins with a radical disposition of gratitude that arises from the understanding that all of Christ's self-humbling work was undertaken "for our sake" and out of the fullness of the divine love that he shares with the Father. The "Ariomaniacs" cannot have this gratitude because, in failing to acknowledge the equal divinity of Father and Son, they also fail to comprehend the mystery of divine self-abasement made manifest in the self-humbling of the Son.[180] Knowledge of the natural equality of the Son with the Father is correlative with a grateful appreciation of the Son's self-emptying in his laying aside that equality in his humanity. But this radical disposition of gratitude goes beyond a mere *gnōsis* of the Christian mystery and extends to a continual exertion to conform ourselves to the guidance of the Son and Spirit. Through adherence to the correct faith, contemplation, the sacramental incorporation into Christ, and the ascetical imitation of his life and death, we become enfolded in the redemptive co-activity of Christ and the Spirit. Athanasius's oft-voiced theme of the necessity of exertion in virtue and holiness can be summed up in his exhortation, "Our will should keep pace with the grace of God."[181] To lapse in our striving for Christlike virtue is "to despise the grace"; to exert ourselves in this holy enterprise is to live "in accordance with grace."[182] The heart of such striving is a willingness to be conformed to the death of Christ, while our identification with Christ's humanity in turn enables our reception of the Spirit: "For he who is made like him in his death is also diligent in virtuous practices, having mortified his members which are upon the earth. Crucifying the flesh with its affections and lusts, he lives in the Spirit and is conformed to the Spirit."[183]

178. *Ep. fest.* 3.4.
179. *Ep. fest.* 20.1.
180. *Ep. fest.* 10.9.
181. *Ep. fest.* 3.3.
182. *Ep. fest.* 3.3; 6.1; 6.4; 7.9; see Anatolios, *Coherence*, 175.
183. *Ep. fest.* 7.1.

※   ※

This book's introductory chapter claimed that "Nicene" theology involved a distinct account of the primacy of Christ. As we noted then, the issue in the fourth-century debates was not *whether* to accord primacy to Christ. Even Arius accorded primacy to Christ as "the firstborn of all creation," the created Creator, a kind of apophatic image of the Unbegotten One. It is true that the Athanasian account gives Christ greater primacy by making him a full sharer in the Father's being rather than ontologically subordinate. But the question that gets closer to the heart of the fourth-century debates is *how Christ's primacy informs the Christian faith as a whole*, and, in particular, the Christian understanding of absolute divine transcendence. With Athanasius, the answer is that two main scriptural routes lead us to see the very character of God as christological. The patterns of scriptural co-naming of God and Christ lead us to conceive of the God-Christ relation as intrinsically constitutive of God. Simultaneously, the salvific work of Christ, to the point of death on the cross, manifests the character of the divine nature as merciful *philanthrōpia*. Athanasius's reading of the Scriptures also identifies the Holy Spirit as constitutive of the scriptural naming of God and an agent of God's creative and salvific *philanthrōpia*. Athanasius's trinitarian theology is ultimately founded on the insistence that there is no divine "remainder" above or beyond or aside from the scriptural co-naming of God as Father, Son, and Spirit. God's creative and salvific agency is to be identified strictly within that divine interchange. Creation and redemption, and thus the fullness of Christian existence, take place within the generation of the Son by the Father, to which we have access through sharing in Christ's human reception of the Spirit that he divinely gives.

4

Gregory of Nyssa

The Infinite Perfection of Trinitarian Life

Gregory of Nyssa, the younger brother of Basil of Caesarea, was born sometime between 335 and 341. He probably studied rhetoric under Basil in Caesarea in the mid-350s and maintained a lifelong devotion to his elder brother, "our teacher Basil." Though ordained to the office of "reader" at an early age, he became a teacher of rhetoric and was married.[1] Under the influence of Basil, Gregory was drawn back to ecclesiastical life and was consecrated by his elder brother as bishop of Nyssa in 372. In 375, charges of misusing church funds and allegations of irregularities in his election to the episcopate were brought before a council in Ancyra composed of largely homoian bishops. Summoned to appear before the *vicarius* Demosthenes, Gregory was able to slip away from his escort and escape into exile. In 376, a council in Nyssa deposed him, and a non-Nicene bishop was appointed as his replacement. The last three years of the 370s was a time of great upheaval in Gregory's personal life. A letter of condolence from Gregory of Nazianzus on the untimely death of "the true consort of a priest," Theosebeia, might be referring to Gregory of Nyssa's wife, who died in 378.[2] Her death was followed in the next year by the death of his brother Basil on January 1, 379, and shortly afterward by the death of his sister, Macrina. Meanwhile, the death of the emperor Valens in 378 opened the way for Gregory to return to Nyssa and resume his ecclesial duties. Though we have no detailed accounts of Gregory's subsequent involvement in ecclesial affairs, there are indications of his

1. *De virg.* 3.
2. *Ep.* 197.6.

157

ascent to prominence. We hear that he was called to Ibora in Pontus to be consulted in the selection of a bishop; he was present at the Council of Constantinople in 381 and was invited to give the funeral oration of its presiding prelate, Melitius; and after the Council of Constantinople he is named by an imperial edict as one of eleven bishops whose teaching is to be considered normative for the interpretation of orthodoxy. He died sometime between 394 and 400. In modern times, many characterize Gregory of Nyssa as the most creative, original, and systematically coherent of the Cappadocians.[3]

This chapter presents Gregory of Nyssa as a second major exemplar of the systematic scope of trinitarian doctrine in the fourth century. It surveys his trinitarian doctrine under five headings: (1) the large polemical work *Against Eunomius*; (2) the *Catechetical Oration*; (3) Gregory's teaching on the Holy Spirit; (4) *hypostasis/ousia* and related language; and (5) Christian life in the Trinity.

The Doctrine of *Against Eunomius*

Until recently, discussion of Gregory of Nyssa's trinitarian theology has occupied itself with the smaller treatises such as *To Ablabius: On Not Three Gods*, but current scholarship increasingly emphasizes his large treatise *Against Eunomius*, intended to continue Basil's refutation of Eunomius (which bears the same title). Books 1 and 2 were composed just before the Council of Constantinople in 381, while book 3 was written after the council, sometime between 381 and 383. Gregory's anti-Eunomian polemic also finds expression in his *Refutation of the Confession of Eunomius*, penned in 383 when Theodosius summoned a council to bring about doctrinal consensus in the church.

Trinitarian Hermeneutics versus the Logocentrism of "Unbegotten"

In line with the contemporary emphasis on locating the main elements of Gregory of Nyssa's trinitarian theology in his explicitly anti-Eunomian polemic, I intend to discuss Gregory's trinitarian doctrine in *Against Eunomius* and the *Refutation* under three headings: (1) Gregory's trinitarian fundamental theology; (2) the Word of God and the primacy of Christ; and (3) the doctrine of God as three-personed Goodness.

GREGORY OF NYSSA'S TRINITARIAN FUNDAMENTAL THEOLOGY

In modern parlance, "fundamental theology" is concerned with delineating the parameters of the theological task and its *modus operandi*. Gregory of Nyssa's anti-Eunomian trinitarian theology offers not merely a different set of doctrinal assertions but first and foremost a different set of presuppositions as to how theology should be practiced. At the risk of mixing ancient and modern conceptual categories, I propose that Gregory's trinitarian fundamental theology is largely determined by his

---

3. For Gregory's biography, see May, "Die Chronologie," and Balás, "Gregor von Nyssa." For an English account dependent largely on May, see Hanson, *Search*, 715–19; see also Behr, *Nicene Faith*, 2:409–14.

reaction to Eunomius's unitarian "logocentrism." Of course, in referring to Eunomius's theology as "logocentric," I am not simply identifying Eunomius with Derrida's *bête noir*, much less attempting to portray the fourth-century bishop of Nyssa as fashionably postmodern.[4] But there are irresistible, if fragmentary, parallels at least with respect to the fundamental issue of how signs signify. Eunomius's doctrine of God had its immovable foundation in the premise that the word-sign "Unbegotten/unoriginate" (*agen[n]ētos*) renders the divine essence immediately present to the mind.[5] This presence is a dialectic between the term's privative signification (the unbegotten God is not caused in any way) and the affirmative apprehension of the reality that is uncaused. Denying that the term "unbegotten" is merely a negation, Eunomius claimed that it really makes present the divine essence, and the apprehension of that presence in turn enabled the denial that God is caused.

The Cappadocians saw that such an approach made unthinkable any claim that God is intrinsically trinitarian. Indeed, Eunomius's challenge is perennial and paradigmatic: a primary obstacle to accepting trinitarian doctrine will always be the premise of a direct and simple path from notions of divine simplicity, oneness, and causal priority to a definition of God's essence. This view implicitly or explicitly posits a more or less strict correlation between the singularity of the divine essence and the simplicity of the epistemological transaction that apprehends this essence. For Eunomius, the simplicity of this cognitive transaction is highlighted by the fact that it is all compacted into the one word "Unbegotten" (*agen[n]ētos*). On the other hand, the foundation of Gregory of Nyssa's trinitarian rebuttal of Eunomius is to subvert and replace Eunomius's version of this epistemological transaction. Before Gregory can argue for the specifically trinitarian complex simplicity of divine being, he must complicate the simplicity of Eunomius's account of how we can think and speak of the divine being. In retracing the logic of Gregory's trinitarian theology, we must therefore begin with his theological epistemology and move from there to his doctrine of God.

Gregory of Nyssa's trinitarian epistemology can be divided into its reactive and constructive aspects. Reactively, Gregory responds to Eunomius's narrow reliance on the immediate disclosure of the divine essence through the word "Unbegotten" in three ways, which we can style as scriptural, logical, and theological. The first two are taken over from Basil; the third represents Gregory's distinctive contribution to the debate. The scriptural argument insists that what is after all not literally a scriptural term cannot become the crucial touchstone for the Christian doctrine of God, supplanting the dominically authorized name of "Father, Son, and Holy Spirit."[6] On the

---

4. But for a bracing account of Gregory's theology as corresponding in important ways to the legitimate concerns and aspirations of postmodernism while avoiding its deficiencies, see Hart, *Beauty of the Infinite*. On the notion of "logocentrism" in Derrida, see esp. *Writing and Difference*, 197, and *Of Grammatology*, 10–15, 39–46.

5. See Vaggione, *Eunomius of Cyzicus*, 251–57. As Mortley puts it, "It is clear that Eunomius wants to establish a direct relationship between words and things. The word carries with it all the strength of being, or of the object it designates" (*From Word to Silence*, 2:186).

6. *C. Eun.* 1.156.

logical plane, Gregory challenges some key logical-linguistic assumptions made by Eunomius, insisting, for example, that plain common sense indicates that the word "Unbegotten" is a privative term, and a privative term cannot positively represent an essence.[7] Combining logical and scriptural arguments, he also fields a series of arguments that seeks to subvert Eunomius's position by applying his logical premises to scriptural language. For example, if names correspond directly to essences, and different names therefore indicate different essences, then the scriptural sharing of names between God and Christ would indicate sameness of essence.[8] Finally, on the level of theology proper, Gregory invokes the doctrine of divine infinity to conclude that the divine essence cannot be enclosed by language or thought, much less by one word; it is both irreverent and irrational to seek to "encompass by one title the infinite nature, confining the divine essence by the name of 'unbegotten.'"[9] But does Gregory's rebuttal of Eunomius's efforts to confine the conception of the divine essence to the notion of "Unbegotten" have the unintended consequence of disallowing any positive knowledge about the divine essence as such, thereby invalidating his own trinitarian theology? If we cannot say anything about the divine essence, how can we confidently identify the divine persons as sharers in that essence? These questions indicate how crucial it is to delineate the relationship in Gregory's thought between his apophatic rebuttal of Eunomius and his own cataphatic assertions about divine being. Ultimately, what is at stake is the proper correspondence between epistemological humility before the unfathomable mystery of God and the dogmatic affirmation that the divine essence is composed of no more and no less than the mutual relations of Father, Son, and Holy Spirit.

On Knowing and Not Knowing the Divine Essence

At the heart of Gregory of Nyssa's anti-Eunomian apophaticism is his conception of the infinity of the divine essence. Because the divine essence is infinite, it is incomprehensible: it cannot be fully encompassed or circumscribed by thought or word. But it would be erroneous to draw the conclusion from Gregory's premise that God as such is ultimately unknowable. In book 2 of *Against Eunomius*, Gregory deals directly with the question of what and how human beings can know of God. What has been too often overlooked is the extent to which language about the impossibility of "knowing the divine essence" is balanced by language that at least allows human knowing, through faith, to be in positive contact with the divine essence.[10] Gregory gives the biblical example of Abraham as one who "apprehended in the course of his

7. *C. Eun.* 2.600–604.
8. *C. Eun.* 2.554–57.
9. *C. Eun.* 2.125 (NPNF[2] 5:262, altered).
10. Recently, Martin Laird has emphasized this more cataphatic dimension of Gregory's thought in his *Gregory of Nyssa and the Grasp of Faith*. See also Canévet, *Grégoire de Nysse*, esp. 62–64. While Laird and Canévet are concerned with the epistemological capacities of faith, I am proposing here that underlying Gregory's approach is a more global ontological and epistemological vision, without denying that faith is necessary for the higher levels of knowledge of God.

reasoning (*tō logismō*)" what is "conceivable with respect to the divine nature (*peri tēs theian physin*)."[11] Abraham is a model for how faith "binds (*synaptousēs*) the seeking soul to the incomprehensible nature of God."[12] In general, Scripture efficaciously reveals God and makes him known to humanity, which is thus guided into "a union with the divine nature" (*synesin tēs theias physeōs*).[13] How then are we to reconcile statements in such close proximity apparently both denying knowledge of the divine essence and affirming such knowledge? To compound the dilemma, Gregory in this context also insists that we do not even know our own essences or those that constitute the external world around us.[14]

To have any hope of understanding how these various statements are coherent, at least for Gregory of Nyssa himself, we need to see that the heart of the matter is a particular vision of how being relates to thought. I think it is permissible in this regard to speak of a synthesis of trinitarian ontology and trinitarian epistemology. In neither case do I mean that Gregory is preoccupied with finding patterns of "triunity" in things. The issue is much more fundamental and has to do with the radical structure of an ontology-epistemology that opens up toward a pro-Nicene trinitarian confession over against that of Eunomius, which is radically closed to such a possibility. What we have called (taking some liberty) Eunomius's "logocentrism" allows for the knower to grasp the essence of God through one concept; Eunomius believes that concept grasps the divine essence sufficiently to make it the sole normative description of that essence. Gregory rules out the possibility of such a simple, commanding grasp of an essence not only in the case of God but even with creatures, indeed, even in relation to oneself. For Gregory, as a rule applicable not only to faith-knowledge but also to knowledge in general, the act of knowing is *not* an act of comprehension in the sense of enclosing a reality with the powers of the mind. Rather than the Stoic Zeno's image of comprehension (*katalēpsis*) as a hand closed tightly over an object that it grasps, knowing for Gregory is more dynamically conceived as "approaching," or "traveling" in the path projected by, the object of knowledge.[15] In the figure of Abraham, as in that of Moses in his later *Life of Moses*, Gregory's crucial metaphor for knowing is "journey." Abraham's faith-knowledge is characterized primarily by the dynamism of quest, wherein the luminosity of being and the receptivity of the mind to that inexhaustible luminosity animate a journey that leads upward from sensible things to the divine infinity:

This then was the secure path which guided him on the way to what he was seeking, that he did not let himself be guided by any of the things that were immediately at

11. *C. Eun.* 2.89.
12. *C. Eun.* 2.90.
13. *C. Eun.* 2.102.
14. *C. Eun.* 2.107.
15. Balthasar contrasts this Stoic image with Gregory's understanding of human knowledge, without citing Gregory's corresponding image of "journey": "Human knowledge is therefore true only to the degree it renounces by a perpetual effort its own nature, which is to 'seize' its prey" (*Presence and Thought*, 93).

hand for understanding the thoughts that pertain to God. Nor did he allow his mind to be deterred from its journey to what is beyond all that is known by any of the objects of sense. But having advanced beyond the wisdom of his land . . . and ascending high above what is knowable by sense perception, he proceeded from the beauty of what is beheld in contemplation and the harmony of the heavenly wonders to the desire of seeing Archetypal Beauty. Likewise, with all the other things which he apprehended in the course of his reasoning as he journeyed on, whether the power of God or his goodness, or his being without beginning, or his infinity, or whatever else is conceivable with respect to the divine nature, he made all of them into provisions and supplies for his upward journey. He was always transforming his discoveries into stepping stones along the way, and stretching forward to what lies ahead and placing in his heart, as the prophet says, each of these beautiful advances, and going beyond all that he had grasped by his own power as less than what he was seeking. When he had advanced beyond every hypothesis concerning the divine nature and purified his reasoning from such suppositions and arrived at an unalloyed faith pure from every imagining, he made this the fixed and manifest sign of the knowledge of God: to believe that he is greater and higher than every sign by which he is known.[16]

I propose that this metaphor of "journey" provides the most appropriate framework for synthesizing Gregory of Nyssa's seemingly contradictory language about knowing and not knowing God. In this framework, the unknowing indicates not a sheer otherness between God and the human mind but rather the infinite and thus inexhaustible plenitude of God, which offers a limitless horizon for human traversing. The human mind, when enlightened by faith, can journey endlessly within that plenitude, which nevertheless remains always greater. That is why Abraham's knowledge precisely of the inexhaustibility of the divine plenitude is the one sure indication that he authentically knew God. At the same time, Gregory seems to have in mind a very strict notion of what the act of "knowing the essence" contains. This becomes clear from the fact that Gregory demonstrates the unknowability of the divine essence by reference to the unknowability of "the essential nature" of creaturely realities—which in turn is demonstrated by a rhapsodic description of these very realities![17] It is indeed startling that Gregory would seek to elucidate the incomprehensiblity of the divine essence by comparison with mundane realities that are accessible to our sense experience and susceptible to lavish and detailed description. We should infer that for Gregory incomprehensibility of essence and inaccessibility are by no means equivalent categories. Creaturely realities are certainly accessible to us, and yet we can give no radical account of the fact and power of their being and of the act of self-bestowal whereby they become accessible to us. In this respect, Gregory's thought-world is somewhat akin to that of Plotinus, for whom each substance is "defined by its parent."[18] In Plotinus's scheme, the "parent" is the productive power that grants "form" to a lower reality and thus knows it from the stance of directing its

16. *C. Eun.* 2.89 (ET: NPNF² 5:259, altered).
17. *C. Eun.* 2.102–18.
18. *C. Eun.* 5.1.7.

act of existence. In Gregory's vision, the hierarchical chain of being is reduced to the polarity of the Creator-creation relationship. It is the unique Creator God, the sole radically productive power, who is the knower of all essences. But Gregory seems to have a similarly maximalist notion in which "knowing the essence" entails not merely registering the *effects* of a being, no matter how intimately one is engaged with these effects, but rather having a "God's-eye" view of its inner causality; in effect, the claim to know the essence is akin to naming oneself as the "parent" of a reality.

Closely aligned with this notion is the understanding of essences and natures as intrinsically productive: a nature manifests itself in its active effects.[19] Yet, for Gregory of Nyssa, encounter with the productive self-manifestation of a nature (*physis/ousia*) is not equivalent to knowing the nature as such. Knowing the nature, according to Gregory's maximalist sense, would mean reaching behind its self-presentation, thereby rendering it a merely passive object of the mind's act of comprehension. The knower would exhaustively grasp the nature's inner intelligibility and the root power of its existence. As a rule, Gregory's ontology precludes such an epistemology of "comprehension." Being, both divine and creaturely, is a dynamic of active self-announcement that cannot be superseded by the knower's grasp and announcement of it. Gregory definitively rules out that kind of knowing as a human possibility, with reference not only to God but to other creatures as well. Instead, knowing God—that is, endlessly journeying through the infinite plenitude of divine being—becomes a paradigm for knowing in general. We cannot know the essence even of creaturely realities; we cannot grasp the very origin of their causal power.[20] The operative image here is the sun and its radiance; one cannot reach behind the productive self-manifestation of the sun in its radiance to the essence that is the radical causal source of that self-manifestation. By Gregory's standards, then, we can register any number of true facts about a being and exhaustively analyze the connections between these facts and still be very far from "knowing the essence." That is how Gregory is able to say that we do not even know our own essences.[21]

It should be clear by now that all this is very far from denying that we have true knowledge of reality, or even a true encounter with creaturely natures and God's nature. Gregory of Nyssa clearly holds that both apophatic and cataphatic statements yield true knowledge of the essences of things human and divine. True affirmations say what truly belongs to the essence and true negations yield authentic knowledge of what does not belong to a given essence.[22] But neither true affirmations nor true negations can be so coextensive with the essence as to render further predication superfluous.[23] So Gregory allows that Eunomius's "unbegotten" truly describes God, but he denies that "unbegotten" exhaustively describes the divine essence such that any other word describing God ultimately signifies only by being reduced to that

19. See Barnes, *Dynamis*, 233–34.
20. *C. Eun.* 2.117–18.
21. *C. Eun.* 2.106–14. The same approach is taken by Gregory of Nazianzus; see *Or.* 28.
22. *C. Eun.* 2.146.
23. *C. Eun.* 2.177.

word. The distinctive character of Gregory's epistemology, therefore, lies not so much in delimiting the extent of information that can be gleaned by the mind (he insists there is no limit) as in locating the act of knowledge radically within the movement of receptivity and wonder. Those who fail to appreciate this distinction can misunderstand Gregory's notion of not knowing the essence as a quantitative statement. Rather, it is a qualitative statement about the nature of knowing as such and how knowing relates to the inexhaustibility of being. Authentic and understanding contact with reality accepts its own irreducible stance of receptivity with regard to the always prior self-presenting dynamism of the being that is known. Instead of claiming to supersede or overreach that dynamism, the one who seeks to know stretches herself out toward the unfathomable depths of the active source of a being's self-presenting dynamism or power (*dynamis*).

In a word, the kind of knowing that Gregory of Nyssa considers appropriate to an integral relation between the human mind and being is that which is permeated by wonder. He characterizes Eunomius's epistemology by the attitude of grasping and denuding being, while his own account receives being as gift in wonder:

> Though they see the power of God shining in upon their souls through the principles of his providence and the wonders in his creation . . . they do not marvel at the divine gift (*charis*) nor adore the one who is known through such things. But transgressing the limits of the soul's capabilities, they seek with their sophistical understanding to grasp what is intangible. . . . So pettily and so childishly do they labor in vain at impossibilities that they endeavor to include the inconceivable nature of God in the few syllables of the term "Unbegotten" and applaud their own foolishness and imagine God to be such that human reasoning can include him under one single term.[24]

If wonder is integral to the proper knowing of creaturely realities, proper knowing of God requires worship.[25] In the controversy with Eunomius, the relation between prayer and epistemology, between worship and the question of knowing the divine, was actually raised by Eunomius himself, who charged that Basil's stress on divine incomprehensibility made Christian worship void of intelligible content and susceptible to Jesus's rebuke of the Samaritan woman, "You worship what you do not know" (John 4:22). In his defense of the Basilian position, Gregory integrates reflection on the experience of Christian worship into his trinitarian epistemology. His position is more complex than a mere reiteration that God is simply unknowable. Rather, as we have been laboring to show, everything hinges on what kind of knowledge one seeks to attain of the divine. The crucial distinction is that between a comprehensive

---

24. *C. Eun.* 2.81–82 (ET: NPNF² 5:258, altered).

25. Cf. Balthasar: "The great eloquent passages in which Gregory demonstrates to Eunomius that we do not know the essence of any thing, of any element, not even of the smallest little shoot of a plant, have no agnostic flavor to them. Rather, they are atremble with the great mystery of the world and end in silent adoration . . . before the incomprehensible beauty of God" (*Presence and Thought*, 93). Equally apropos is Milbank's assessment: "Supremely, we *know* in praising God, in offering him glory which is his own, and not in *seeing* God, nor in manipulating men" (*Word Made Strange*, 197).

knowledge in which the mind masters its object and the doxological knowledge enacted in worship. The former claims to enclose the known object by the mind's grasp; the latter seeks to stretch out (*epekteinō*) into the infinitely open expanse of divine glory. God is simply not a fit object of the former epistemological stance but is the infinite horizon of the latter:

> Now if anyone should ask for some interpretation and description and explanation of the divine essence, we are not going to deny that we are untutored in that kind of wisdom. We confess only that what is by nature infinite cannot be comprehended in any conception expressed by words. . . . If then interpretation by means of names and words implies by its meaning some sort of comprehension of the subject (*to hypokeimenon*), and if on the other hand, that which is unlimited cannot be comprehended, no one could reasonably blame us for ignorance if we do not venture boldly into where no one should dare to tread.[26]

With this epistemological distinction in place, Gregory insists nevertheless that a pro-Nicene interpretation of Christian worship is not simply devoid of intelligible content. But the appropriate kind of knowing is precisely the knowing that has become utterly worship, the knowing-in-adoration of the transcendence of the glory perceived, traveled in, but not enclosed. Indeed, this doxological knowledge is possible only for those who admit that comprehensive knowledge is not possible:

> Therefore, we hold fast to the doctrine that they insult. We confess that we are indeed inferior to them in the knowledge of the things beyond knowledge. But we declare that we really worship what we know. We know the sublimity of the glory of the one we worship by the very fact that we are not able by reasoning to comprehend in our thoughts the incomprehensibility of his greatness.[27]

We will have occasion later to recall how Gregory of Nyssa's epistemological premises cohere with his better-known account of relation to God as limitless progress. For the moment, our task is to note that this conception of knowing as a journey of stretching receptivity and thankful wonder is the initial move that opens up an epistemological space for knowing God beyond the bare notion of unbegottenness. This space is not a mere vacuum of intelligibility, or it would not lead to trinitarian affirmations about God's being. If the divine infinity precludes comprehension through a single notion, it nevertheless invites a journey of wonder that is enabled by a multiplicity of notions. A key move in Gregory's trinitarian epistemology is thus the endorsement of multiplicity and difference as integral to our encounter with the divine infinite. If this characterization, like our allusions to the "logocentrism" of Eunomius's approach, has a suspiciously modern ring, we need to recall the original and concrete historical reference of Gregory's valuation of

26. *C. Eun.* 3.1.103–4 (ET: NPNF[2] 5:146–47, altered).
27. *C. Eun.* 3.1.108–9.

multiplicity. Gregory insists on the value of multiple approaches to the mystery of God because Scripture itself does not present any single, all-encompassing notion of God. Rather, Scripture describes God in many different ways and presents multiple descriptions of his varied attributes. For Eunomius, this linguistic multiplicity is logically reducible in each case to the equivalent of "unbegotten"; as Gregory reports, "the gist (*skopos*) of what he says is that there is no difference in the meaning of the different [divine] names."[28] In contrast, Gregory insists that each scriptural name and presentation of God has its distinct, irreducible meaning. Yet they all genuinely refer to the divine being, who "has something in common with all these notions."[29] Gregory's rejection of Eunomius's basic metaphysical presumptions that unity can only be monism and that difference denotes opposition thus refers concretely to scriptural language about God. The divine attributions are genuinely different and distinctly meaningful. They represent a coherent and harmonious complexity: "The meaning of each of the terms attributed to the divine nature is such that, even though it has a distinct significance of its own, it implies no opposition to the term associated with it. What opposition is there, for instance, between 'incorporeal' and 'just,' even though the words do not coincide in meaning; and what hostility is there between goodness and invisibility?"[30] At the same time, Gregory is clear that the epistemological validity of the multiplicity of divine names does not consist in directly mirroring differentiation within the divine essence. The divine essence is itself simple, but its infinite depths and riches can only be grasped by human creatures through complex predication.[31]

It is useful to remind ourselves again that Gregory of Nyssa's theological episte-mology is not "trinitarian" in the narrow sense of being grounded in patterns of "triunity." Nor can we reduce every aspect of his trinitarian epistemology to an ana-logue of how we understand God to be "three persons in one nature." For instance, his epistemological principle that divine simplicity must be approached through multiple predications does not mean that the divine essence in itself is simple while the differentiation of the persons pertains only to our apprehension of God. To avoid such errors, we have to respect the internal order of Gregory's logic. His understand-ing of the necessity and validity of multiple predications of the immanently simple divine essence does not give us a pattern as such for understanding the content of trinitarian confession. Rather, its proper place is simply to clear the way beyond the logocentric tyranny of the single word "unbegotten." The fundamental principle is that divine simplicity cannot be apprehended simply. The effect of this principle is to throw us back on the whole range of scriptural language and narrative, indeed, on the whole creation, as a complex manifestation of the Creator. This enlargement of the epistemological playing field does not yet amount to trinitarian doctrine *per se*, but it is an indispensable condition for getting there.

28. *C. Eun.* 2.480–81.
29. *C. Eun.* 2.477–78 (ET: NPNF[2] 5:298, altered).
30. *C. Eun.* 2.478–79 (ET: NPNF[2] 5:298, altered).
31. *C. Eun.* 2.475–76.

We are now at the threshold between Gregory of Nyssa's "fundamental" trinitarian theology, or theological epistemology at the level of general principles, and his positive scriptural arguments on behalf of Nicene doctrine. But one final consideration will bring us closer to seeing the organic continuity between his theological epistemology and his trinitarian and christological doctrinal commitments. We have seen that the stance of receptivity is crucial to Gregory's presentation of human knowing in general and, *a fortiori*, of human knowledge of God. We cannot supersede the radically self-presenting power of being, which is what the claim to "know the essence" amounts to for Gregory. Our only possibility for knowledge is to patiently attend to this self-presentation and receive it in wonder and thankfulness. In the case of God, as disclosed by Christian revelation, this self-presentation is primarily to be found in scriptural revelation and its complex presentation of the Divine. Thus the way to know God is to attend to the wholeness of this complex presentation, without any *a priori* reduction to a forced and monist simplicity. But this fundamental stance of receptivity, on which so much rides for Gregory, is claimed by Eunomius as well. Eunomius insists that it is his own epistemology that properly safeguards the appropriate relation between the priority of divine activity and the posteriority of human receptivity. In book 2 of *Against Eunomius*, Gregory presents Eunomius's counter-response to Basil's contention that the term "unbegotten" does not delineate the whole essence of God but conveys an aspect, or "concept" (*epinoia*) of human knowledge of God. Eunomius counters that this approach makes divine being posterior to our conception of God. In his view, Basil sunders the being of the divine from the naming of the divine and makes the naming of God's being merely the product of human activity. To assert his own strong conception of the epistemological sovereignty of God, Eunomius depicts the divine name as something like an emanation of the divine essence. Human beings simply receive this emanation, whose material expression is the word "unbegotten," and confess the reality which they passively receive and do not actively construct. Moreover, Eunomius relies on biblical testimony referring to God's speaking and God's naming the divisions of creation (Gen. 1:3–10) as evidence that all naming results from divine initiative. Human beings simply receive the names of things from God. Thus a battle is joined over which epistemological approach truly safeguards divine initiative and human receptivity in the act of knowledge of God. At stake in this battle are fundamental questions about how the divine-human interaction in the act of revelation is conditioned by and revelatory of the activity of the divine Trinity.

Knowing as Receptivity and Trinitarian Revelation

Gregory of Nyssa's rebuttal of Eunomius's complaint initiates a hermeneutical trajectory that makes significant connections with his positive trinitarian and christological commitments, even if he did not himself draw explicit attention to these continuities. The starting point for Gregory's counterargument is that human language is undeniably material and composite and conditioned by time and matter. The utterance of a word takes place through the temporal succession of conjoined vocables that require matter for their construction and transmission. Given these creaturely conditions of human language, Eunomius's efforts to associate the human naming of the divine directly and immediately with the divine essence and, even further, to attribute all human naming to divine speaking, succeed only in utterly anthropomorphizing God.[32] Gregory seems to have caught Eunomius here in a conundrum. By refusing to grant any place to human initiative in the construction of language and attributing it immediately to divine agency, he cannot logically avoid associating the divine essence directly with the conditions of creaturely and corruptible existence. Gregory is well aware that this is the very last thing that Eunomius wanted to say; his point is that there is no way to logically avoid saying this within Eunomius's framework.

In stating his own position, Gregory of Nyssa intends to press the converse paradox: that only by acknowledging the element of human agency can we maintain divine sovereignty and priority with respect to the human knowledge of God. In Gregory's framework, the initiative still belongs to God, and human knowing is still receptive. The divine initiative can be traced back to the very act of creation, which is the product of divine will. In their own proper voice, separated from the divine essence by the *diastēma* between creation and Creator, the elements of creation nevertheless speak to us of the ineffable beauty of the Creator in a way that "instills into our minds the knowledge of divine power more than if speech proclaimed it with a voice."[33]

Human knowing is thus responsive to the intelligible emanations of created beings that refer us to the dynamic power (*dynamis*) of their Creator. Moreover, even that radically receptive response of the intelligence to the intelligibility of beings has divine agency as its source, inasmuch as God is the Creator of human intelligence as well. Thus divine agency is maintained while the acknowledgment of human mediation avoids the error of involving the divine essence immediately with the corporeality of human language and knowing.

Gregory's argument comes to a climax when he considers the issue specifically in the context of scriptural language. Again, he reiterates his unassailably tautological point that human language is ineradicably human and that therefore attributing human naming of God directly to the divine essence anthropomorphizes God. Gregory savors the irony that Eunomius's privileged word for delineating the divine essence is actually nowhere to be found in the Word of God that is the Scriptures. He throws back the "unbegotten" at Eunomius as "your word"; but he can also claim ownership of it as "our word" inasmuch as it properly signifies an aspect of divine being. Gregory insists, however, that in neither case can it be equated directly and simply with God's Word. God's Word is given in much more mysterious and complex and multifaceted form in the Scriptures considered in their entirety, a form that is ultimately trinitarian in structure. The correspondence between the humanity of scriptural language and its divine origin and semiotic destination is effected by the power of God's self-humbling love. In this context, Gregory returns to the image of the sun and its radiance; we encounter the "sun" (the divine essence) not by reaching back behind its rays but

32. *C. Eun.* 2.198–200.
33. *C. Eun.* 2.224.

through the sun's own modulation of its rays in correspondence with the capacity of human receptivity. Ultimately, however, that image is left behind in favor of the more personal image of a mother speaking baby talk with her child:

> We hold that the reason why God allows himself to have conversation with human beings is his love for humanity (*philanthrōpian*). Because that which is finite by nature cannot rise above its own limits in order to lay hold of the transcendent nature of the Most High, he brings down to the level of our weakness his loving power (*tēn philanthrōpon dynamin*), as a gift and help to us, according to our capacity to receive it. Just as in the divine economy the sun modulates the intensity and directness of its rays through the intervening air and thus accommodates the bestowal of its light and heat to the capacity of its recipients while being itself inaccessible to the weakness of our nature, so the divine power (*dynamis*), consistently with this illustration, while being infinitely exalted above our nature and inaccessible to approach, is like a compassionate mother who joins in the inarticulate cries of her infants, and so grants to our human nature what it is capable of receiving. Thus, in the various divine manifestations to humanity, he presents himself in a form appropriate to human beings and speaks in human language and puts on the guise of anger and pity and such emotions, so that by everything that corresponds to our infantile life, we might be led by the hand by providential words and lay hold of the divine nature.[34]

We should note again, contrary to all assertions that Gregory of Nyssa denies the possibility of union with God or even of accessibility to the divine nature itself (keeping in mind the distinction between accessibility and comprehension), that Gregory here speaks boldly of laying hold of, or reaching, the divine nature (*tēs theias physeōs ephaptomenē*).[35] We should also be alert to the christological connotations of the description of divine revelation as an adaptation in the likeness of human form and human language. Ultimately, all of God's speaking is enfolded in the Word who was in the beginning and has become human in Jesus Christ. If the content of God's speaking is thus contained in Christ, it is the Holy Spirit who facilitates the translation of God's Word into human idiom, as well as the human appropriation and hearing of God's Word. In this way, Gregory arrives at an articulation of the trinitarian form of revelation; it is the trinitarian activity that ensures that despite its human element, scriptural language remains God's Word:

34. *C. Eun.* 2.417–20 (ET: NPNF² 5:292–93, altered); cf. *C. Eun.* 2.259.
35. For an account that denies the possibility of "union" with God in Gregory, see Mühlenburg, *Die Unendlichkeit Gottes*, 147–65. This judgment has been recently adopted by Heine in reference to Gregory's *Life of Moses*; see Heine, *Perfection in the Virtuous Life*, 107–14. I agree with Laird, who argues that Gregory countenanced the possibility of a dynamic union with God mediated by faith (*Gregory of Nyssa and the Grasp of Faith*). While valuable in itself, Laird's attempt to mitigate an overly apophatic assessment of Gregory's doctrine still leaves a lacuna for a detailed study respectful of the different nuances of Gregory's understanding of both "knowing" and "divine essence." Such a study, as intimated here, would show not only that it is possible to know God through faith but, more fundamentally, that the notion of "knowing the divine essence" is a category mistake from Gregory's perspective.

For our word is as nothing compared to the Word that truly is. Our word was not in the beginning but was created along with our nature, nor is it to be regarded as having its own subsistence (*hypostasin*). . . . But the word from God is God himself, the Word that is in the beginning and that remains for ever, through whom all things are and have their constitution . . . being Life, Truth and Righteousness, and Light, and all that is good and upholding all things in being. . . . If certain of our familiar expressions are ascribed by Holy Scripture to God as the speaker, we should remember that the Holy Spirit is addressing us in our own terms, as in the history of the Acts we are told that each person received the teaching of the disciples in his own native language, understanding the sense of the words by the language that he knew. . . . So, since human nature is in a sense deaf and insensible to sublime things, we hold that the grace of God which speaks in the prophets "in diverse forms and manner" (Heb. 1:1) and conforms the expressions of the holy prophets to our capacity and custom leads us in this way by the hand to the apprehension of sublime things.[36]

We are now in a position to summarize some basic features of a fundamental trinitarian epistemology in Gregory of Nyssa's *Against Eunomius*. The primary move is to reject the claim of simple epistemological access to divine simplicity. All human knowing must wait on the dynamic self-presentation of being, and this is *a fortiori* the case when it comes to knowing the infinite Divine. In creation and Scripture, the self-presentation of the infinite God takes a multiplicity of forms, and this multiplicity must be positively apprehended in the entirety and mutuality of its various relations. This multiplicity represents a complex mediation of the divine in human forms. Its integral apprehension is enabled by the divine loving condescension, which accommodates itself to the human condition.[37] The language of condescension, accommodation, and adaptation inevitably evokes christological resonances, while Gregory also points to the agency of the Spirit in this work of adaptation. Over against Eunomius's monist understanding of knowledge of God as the emanation of a simple apprehension of a singular divine essence, Gregory thus posits an epistemology that embraces multiplicity of data (ultimately all the contents of creation and Scripture in their integral diversity) as well as a christological synergy between divine adaptation and active human intellection that is enabled by the Holy Spirit. If we can join him, at least provisionally, in these fundamental presuppositions, we will be in good position to follow his account of the trinitarian structure of Christian faith.

THE WORD OF GOD AND THE PRIMACY OF CHRIST

At the heart of Gregory of Nyssa's trinitarian epistemology is the scripturally mediated affirmation of the absolute primacy of Jesus Christ. We have seen that his epistemology is determined by his opposition to what we have called Eunomius's logocentrism (i.e., his reliance on the single word "unbegotten" as mediating direct knowledge of God's essence). Following Basil, Gregory counters that this word signifies

---

36. *C. Eun.* 2.236–42 (ET: NPNF[2] 5:274–75, altered).
37. On the divine condescension in scriptural language, see Canévet, *Grégoire de Nysse*, 55–56.

a human conception (*epinoia*) representing one aspect of divine being; it is not an all-encompassing direct representation of the essence. But although Gregory insists on the cooperation of human agency in the knowledge of both God and creatures, the fundamental contrast that he draws between his own position and that of Eunomius is not that between unmediated knowledge of God and the inevitability of human interpretation. Far from conceding that his own position makes divine being a passive object of human intellective activity, Gregory says this objection applies more properly to the Eunomian position. He proposes that the right epistemological starting point is not the human word "unbegotten" but the trinitarian form of the Word of God as mediated in the economic dispensation summed up in Jesus Christ and adapted to human understanding by the Spirit. As we advance now from Gregory's fundamental theology to the actual contents of his trinitarian doctrine, we do well to recall his conception of the primacy of Christ. Gregory arrives at a trinitarian confession by way of the lordship of Christ in Scripture and worship and through a christologically conditioned conception of divine transcendence.

The Lordship of Christ in Scripture and Worship

Throughout *Against Eunomius*, Gregory of Nyssa does not simply dismiss the notion of "unbegotten" as a human concept (*epinoia*) but supplements it by the scriptural titles of Christ. Athanasius called these *paradeigmata*; Gregory calls them *epinoiai*. These christological *epinoiai* constitute the proper linguistic and conceptual starting point, for Gregory, in conceiving and articulating the Christian doctrine of God. That move ensures a radical paradigm shift from an abstract conception of divine transcendence to one that is christologically conditioned, thus opening up a path for a trinitarian reconception of divine transcendence. The strategy is equally determinative for the trinitarian scriptural logic of both Athanasius and Gregory. The premise in both cases is that authentic knowledge of God must follow the intertextual patterns of scriptural language, with central reference to how scriptural references to Christ figure in such language.

The explicitly epistemological turn taken by the debate with Eunomius enables Gregory of Nyssa to articulate Athanasius's implicit logic with considerably more directness and clarity. Eunomius's principle that different names signify different natures, which relies on the difference of the names of "Unbegotten" and "Only-begotten," is subverted through application to all the scriptural names shared by Father and Son: Light, Power, Truth, and the rest. If, as Eunomius holds, difference of names signifies difference of natures, then "the commonality of names surely manifests the communion of the essence."[38] Christian devotion and "piety" (*eusebeia*) attributes maximal meaning to the exalted titles of Christ because Scripture correlates the identity of the Son to that of the Father: "There is a long list of names through which the Son is co-named with the Father without variation of meaning—good, incorruptible, just, judge, long-suffering, merciful, eternal, everlasting, all of which manifest the sense of

38. *C. Eun.* 3.5.

majesty of nature and power—without any reservation being made in his case in any of the names with respect to the sublimity of the conception (*ennoias*)."[39]

Gregory chides Eunomius for overlooking "all those names supplied by Scripture for the glorification of God and predicated alike of the Father and the Son,"[40] but he knows that the real issue is not a mere oversight but a difference of interpretative perspective. Eunomius interprets all the exalted titles of Christ as qualified by his begotten and created nature; such terms are equivocal for him. Gregory's hermeneutic is dominated by the principle of the primacy of Christ. Like Athanasius, he reads the very nature of God out of the overlapping and correlative designations of God and Christ. A crucial philosophical-exegetical move on Gregory's part is the strict confla- tion of divinity and perfection: "With respect to the divine nature, every perfection pertaining to the good is connoted with the very name of God."[41] If they are taken to denote divine perfections, the divine titles scripturally applied in common to both Father and Son cannot admit of variance in quality. Thus they declare the co-equality of Father and Son. In line with this strategy, Gregory evokes certain Johannine texts not merely as direct testimony for the ontological equality of Father and Son but as hermeneutical keys for interpreting the overlapping scriptural linguistic fields in designating God and Christ. So, for instance, John 16:15, "All that the Father has is mine," is interpreted in the first place as an exegetical principle, as referring to the patterns of scriptural language itself and indicating that all the scriptural predications attributed to the Father are also descriptive of the Son.[42] The exegete who observes this principle will read the Scriptures in a way that is consistent with another Johannine saying, "that all may honor the Son just as they honor the Father" (John 5:23).[43] To pay this exegetical honor to the Son is a matter of interpreting every exalted christo- logical title "in the direction of greater majesty."[44]

Like Athanasius, Gregory of Nyssa also uses the rhetorical strategy of plugging Eu- nomius's statements into the scriptural linguistic patterns and trumpeting the results: if the Only-begotten is scripturally designated as Wisdom, Power, Truth, Life, and so on, then Eunomius's position, rendered within this scriptural idiom, amounts to saying that Wisdom is of a different essence than God and God is essentially without Wisdom, Power, and the rest![45] Gregory acknowledges Eunomius's counterargument that some of the exalted names of Christ are also scripturally applied to human be- ings and other creatures. (Incidentally, we can note here a tradition of argumentation on both sides, going back at least to Alexander and Arius, and continuing through Athanasius and Asterius, and onward.) Like Athanasius, Gregory responds to this

39. *C. Eun.* 3.5 (ET: NPNF² 5:195, altered).
40. *C. Eun.* 2.15 (ET: NPNF² 5:251, altered).
41. *C. Eun.* 1.334.
42. *C. Eun.* 1.594.
43. *C. Eun.* 1.333.
44. *C. Eun.* 3.1.138.
45. E.g., *C. Eun.* 1.584; 3.1.48–49; 3.6.49.

challenge by reiterating that consideration of the Scriptures as a whole shows that no mere creature is so decorated with exalted language as Christ.[46]

If Gregory invokes a hermeneutical circle between the presumption of Christ's absolute primacy and a reading of Scripture that substantiates this primacy, he expands that circle to include the dialectic of scriptural meaning and Christian worship. In book 2 of *Against Eunomius*, this dialectic is broached when Gregory discusses the proper interpretation of such exalted scriptural titles as Truth, Light, Power, and Life. The difference between him and Eunomius hinges on whether such titles apply to Christ in a strict maximal sense, denoting true divinity, or "homonymously," in an attenuated creaturely sense. That Christian faith consists in the maximal and strict interpretation of these titles can finally be settled by recourse to the fact that Christians worship Christ.

> This then is the chief point of Christian piety: to believe that the only-begotten of God, who is Truth, and true Light and Power of God and Life, truly is what he is said to be, above all especially in that he is God and Truth, which is to say, God in truth, always being what he is conceived to be and what he is called. . . . Such is the understanding that prevails among all Christians, . . . those who have been taught by the Law to worship nothing that is not truly God and by that worship to confess that the only Begotten is God in truth and not a God falsely so called.[47]

Christian worship expresses distinct exegetical commitments and a global interpretation of Scripture. If the scriptural titles of Christ are not integrally constitutive of the biblical presentation of God and thus do not denote the genuine divinity of the Son, "it follows that he is not rightly the object of worship and adoration or, in fact, of any of the honors that are paid to God."[48] In the context of worship, the strict ontological opposition of Creator-creation is not an abstract metaphysical notion but a practical and existential principle in the doxological and devotional performance of Christian faith. The notion of a creature whose qualified divinity earns him a measure of worship is disallowed by the scriptural prohibition of idolatry. If the Only-begotten is a creature to be worshiped, then other creatures could also garner attributions of qualified divinity and worship. Eunomians must either forbid worship of Christ or justify such worship of a created deity at the cost of opening the door to pagan pantheism: "For either the elements of the world must be divine, according to the foolish belief of the Greeks, or the Son must not be worshiped."[49]

Gregory of Nyssa's accusation that Eunomius's position dismantles the logic of Christian worship extends to a more general claim that Eunomian doctrine distorts the notion of Christ's lordship. In his exposition of this critique, Gregory also extends his trinitarian theology in the direction of a political theology that decisively

---

46. *C. Eun.* 3.6.64–65.
47. *C. Eun.* 2.12–14 (ET: NPNF² 5:251, altered).
48. *C. Eun.* 2.59.
49. *C. Eun.* 3.2.35.

qualifies the notion of intercreaturely authority and leads ultimately to a denunciation of slavery. In this context, the Creator-creature opposition is cast in political language that plays off biblical motifs in response to Eunomius's own characterization of the Son as "subject" to the Father. Gregory invokes the scriptural designation of creation as "subject" to God, a designation which Eunomius also presumes in making the created divinity of Christ subject to the Father. But Gregory contrasts this designation with the scriptural characterization of Christ as "Lord of creation" and of creation as "in bondage" and "enslaved," awaiting liberation from its bounteous Master. Thus, in asserting the creaturehood of the Son, Eunomius has abrogated the scriptural attestation to Christ's preeminence as Master and consigned him to the slavery of creatures: "I hear Paul cry aloud, 'There is one Lord Jesus Christ' (cf. 1 Cor. 8:6), but Eunomius shouts against Paul, calling Christ a slave."[50] Gregory concedes that Eunomius's doctrine contains the significant nuance that although the divinity of Christ is not absolute but originated, he is nevertheless the Lord of the rest of creation. But Gregory rejects outright the notion of a Lord who is also ontologically a "fellow servant" along with the rest of the creation. Christian worship interpreted along these lines would entail worship of a fellow servant and ultimately a kind of self-worship; the worshiper would be "seeing himself in the one that he worships."[51] Gregory's own interpretation of the lordship of Christ uses the Master-slave framework as merely a starting point for designating the relationship of God to the world; he then transposes it entirely in line with its inversion in the christological narrative. Far from being merely a "fellow servant" in his very nature, Christ is entirely Lord in his divine nature but indeed takes our slavery upon himself in order to eradicate it by the power of his own lordly nature:

> At the urging of divine teaching, I boldly state that the Divine Word does not want even us to be slaves, now that our nature has been transformed. He who has taken all that was ours in such a way that he has given us in return all that is his took our slavery also, just as he took our disease, death, curse, and sin. He took all this in such a way as not to have what he took but rather to purge our nature of all such things so that they may be extinguished in his stainless nature. Just as there will be no disease nor curse nor sin nor death in the life we hope for, so slavery also will vanish away along with these. And I call the Truth himself to witness that what I say is true, he who said, "I call you no more servants but friends" (John 15:15). If then our nature will in the end be free from the disgrace of slavery, how is the Lord of all enslaved by the frenzy and madness of these deranged people?[52]

Gregory of Nyssa's affirmation of the primacy of Christ thus insists that only a maximalist understanding of the exalted scriptural titles of Christ is consistent with Christian worship and with an authentic interpretation of the "lordship of Christ."

50. *C. Eun.* 3.8.43–44.
51. *C. Eun.* 3.8.53.
52. *C. Eun.* 3.8.54–55 (ET: NPNF² 5:227, altered).

Christ's divinity fully shares in the Father's sovereignty and has ontologically nothing in common with the bondage and slavery to which creation is subject. The manifestation of the lordship of Christ has a trinitarian shape. It is authentically confessed in the acknowledgment that he "reigns over all things not by an arbitrary act of capricious power but has authority over all by superiority of nature . . . so the principle (*archē*) of all things is the Lord, who shines in our souls through the Holy Spirit, since it is impossible for the Lord Jesus to be contemplated except in the Holy Spirit, as the apostle says (1 Cor. 12:3). And then the principle which transcends every principle, the God over all, is discovered through the Lord, for it is also impossible to come to know the Archetypal Good except as it appears in the Image of the Invisible."[53]

At the same time, Christ's lordship is manifest in his abrogating the conditions of bondage and slavery to which creation is subject. However, Gregory is well aware that the Scriptures not only name Christ through the inventory of divine names but also apply to him the names and conditions of creatures. In scriptural terms, Jesus Christ is both "Lord" and "slave," a problematic already broached by Gregory in the passage cited above. If one part of Gregory's task is to explain how the lordship of Jesus is unqualified divinity, with nothing slavish about it, another part is to explain how Jesus's creaturely servanthood can be consistent with such absolute divinity. As in the case of Athanasius, therefore, the trinitarian identification of Jesus Christ necessarily involves an interpretation of the scriptural christological narrative, to which we now turn.

The Trinity and Christological Narrative

In *Against Eunomius*, the question of precisely how the christological narrative identifies Christ in his humanity and divinity is broached when Gregory of Nyssa takes up the debate between Eunomius and Basil on the proper interpretation of Acts 2:36, "God has made him both Lord and Christ."[54] Eunomius, following a tradition of interpretation that goes back at least to Asterius, interprets this to mean that the divinity of Christ was "made" and is not co-eternal with the Father.[55] Basil had insisted that the verse refers not to Christ's divinity but to the humanity that he assumed when he took upon himself "the form of a servant." Gregory dramatically casts this debate as a scuffle over which party is "ashamed of the cross."[56] Eunomius had charged that Basil is ashamed of the cross because it is the humiliation of the cross that repels him from referring the created condition and the "form of the servant" to the very essence of the Son. Moreover, this refusal to ascribe a created "servant" nature to the Son fragments the integrity of Christ by positing two distinct subjects, "two Lords." Finally, according to Eunomius, this conception enervates any intelligible notion of *kenōsis*, or self-emptying. If the subject of the humiliation is simply the humanity, then what sense does it make to say that the human being emptied himself to become a

---

53. *C. Eun.* 1.530–32 (ET: NPNF[2] 5:84, altered).
54. Basil, *C. Eun.* 2.2.
55. Athanasius, *C. Ar.* 2.1.
56. *C. Eun.* 3.3.15.

human being, and the one whose nature was in the form of a servant took the form of a servant?[57]

Given our own predilection for the plain and immediately contextual meaning of a scriptural text, we may think that the issue can be adequately disposed of (in Gregory's favor) by simply asserting that the text clearly refers to the humanity and not to the original generation of the Son. But while that assertion might sunder the link between Eunomius's critique and this particular verse, it would not dispose of the issues he raises. These issues are structurally attached to the problematic of identifying Jesus, through the scriptural narrative, as both human and divine. Both parties in these debates share common ground in accepting crucial elements of this problematic while offering different resolutions to it. Both are dealing ultimately with questions about divine transcendence and how it relates to human suffering: How can Christ suffer and yet be God? How can the "self-emptying" be predicated of Jesus Christ? Does it belong essentially to his divinity or merely to his humanity? And if the latter, then how is the divine Word the subject of this self-emptying? All these questions directly anticipate the "christological" debates of the fifth century, and their appearance here demonstrates a substantive continuity in the key problematics of both sets of debates. Of course, Eunomius's global response to these questions presumes that Christ's divinity is a lesser, created divinity. For Eunomius, presumably, the self-emptying describes the transition from Jesus's divine state to his human state, but the basis for that self-emptying is his created, and thus passible, divinity. For Basil, Christ's suffering and passibility belong to his humanity. As with Eunomius, the self-emptying also occurs in the assumption of humanity, but, according to Basil, this self-emptying is not grounded in a lower divinity but in the willful transition from an unqualifiedly transcendent divinity to the condition of humanity. Both Eunomius and Basil are thus presuming that self-emptying is a global characterization of the person of Christ in some way, though they differ in trying to understand how it can be applied to both his humanity and divinity as well as to the relation between them.

As a first move, Gregory of Nyssa follows Basil in attending to the context of the passage in order to demonstrate that the biblical author's reference is actually to the incarnate state of the Word and not to his original generation. But Gregory recognizes that the underlying problematic is not thereby adequately addressed. He proceeds to deal with the structural theological issues involved in the question of how to attribute the human life, suffering, and death of Jesus to the divine-human incarnate Word. Gregory begins his response by joining the rhetorical battle over which doctrine reflects a mindset that is ashamed of the cross. Echoing a structural motif of Athanasius's *On the Incarnation*, Gregory represents Basil's position as one of "honoring the one manifested on the cross as God."[58] It is rather Eunomius who is ashamed of the cross because he considers it unbefitting of the Father's absolute

57. *C. Eun.* 3.3.17–18.
58. *C. Eun.* 3.3.30.

impassibility to be ontologically associated with the suffering Christ and so relegates the possibility of the Son to his inferior created nature:

> For if the economy of the Passion is integral to the faith of both parties, while we say that the God who was manifested through the cross must be honored in the same way as the Father is honored while they consider the Passion as an obstacle to glorifying the only-Begotten God equally with the God who begot him, then our sophist's accusations fall back on himself. . . . For it is obvious that the reason why he places the Father above the Son and exalts him with superior honor is that the shame of the cross does not pertain to him. And the reason why he insists that the nature of the Son is different and inferior is that the disgrace of the cross is attributed to him alone and does not pertain to the Father. . . . So then who is ashamed of the cross? The one who even after the Passion worships the Son equally with the Father or the one who even before the Passion degrades him, not only by counting him among the creation but by asserting that his nature is passible on the premise that he could not have come to experience his sufferings if he did not possess a nature susceptible to such sufferings?[59]

Gregory here touches on the complexity of an anti-Nicene position that has been characterized as advocating "a suffering God."[60] As Gregory points out, the price that Eunomius pays for linking Christ's suffering to his divinity is precisely to relegate that divinity to a secondary and created level; the only way to have a suffering God, in Eunomius's terms, is to have a lesser "god." On the other side, it must be admitted that Eunomius poses a formidable critique that still resonates in contemporary appraisals of patristic Christology. If the suffering can be ascribed only to the humanity of Christ, while his divinity remains impassible, then where is the self-emptying?[61] Implicit in this question is also the question of the integrity of Jesus Christ as a single subject, since Eunomius interprets Basil's position (which Gregory adopts) as logically positing two subjects in the incarnate Word, one to whom the passion can be attributed and another to whom it cannot.

Gregory's response to these challenges involves some key moves that anticipate the Chalcedonian logic of predicating human and divine properties to the single subject of the incarnate Word. Retracing these moves provides a valuable demonstration of the organic continuity between "Nicene" trinitarian theology and "Chalcedonian" Christology. But the best starting point for appropriating Gregory's logic is to begin with a theme that is not generally treated in appraisals of his Christology but which, I hope to demonstrate, is foundational. That theme is the reconstruction of the notion of divine transcendence, which Gregory perceives to be at the heart of these questions. In treating this theme, Gregory is following and developing the project undertaken by Athanasius in *On the Incarnation*. In that work, Athanasius's efforts to demonstrate that the one who died on the cross is fully God involve integrating

59. *C. Eun.* 3.3.30–34 (ET: NPNF[2] 5:176, altered).
60. Hanson, *Search*, 109–16.
61. See, for example, Moltmann's critique of patristic Christology in *Crucified God*, 227–31.

Christ's human work and suffering with the divine attribute of *philanthrōpia*.[62] If the divine nature is defined primarily in terms of generous and beneficent love, then the cross is an appropriate demonstration of divine transcendence, not evidence of a lack of transcendence. Elsewhere, Athanasius insists that divine transcendence, biblically conceived, aligns more with God's immediate contact with and providential care for creation than with a distance that would necessitate semi-divine intermediaries.[63] For his part, Gregory begins his own revision of the notion of divine transcendence by the startlingly bold declaration that the divine greatness is manifested preeminently in God's overcoming the "limitations" of divine nature. Eunomius's downfall is that he

> fails to perceive the fact that, while nothing which moves according to its own nature (*physin*) is marveled at in wonder, everything that goes beyond the limits of its nature becomes especially an object of wonder for all, and to it every ear is turned, every mind is attentive in wonder at the marvel.... And so all who preach the Word advert to the wonder of the mystery at this very point—that God was manifested in the flesh, that the Word became flesh, that the Light shone in darkness, that Life tasted of death, and all such expressions which the heralds of the Word proclaim, through which our wonder is magnified at the One who manifested the superabundance of his power through what is external to his nature (*tou dia tōn exō tēs physeōs to perion tēs dynameōs heautou phanerōsantes*).[64]

The bold rhetoric of this passage reminds one of certain modern Orthodox theologians who apply to God the modern existentialist motif of personal existence as the overcoming of "nature."[65] But without dissipating the rhetorical force of this passage, we must attend carefully to its dialectical presentation of the divine character through the interplay of the categories of nature (*physis*), power (*dynamis*), and manifestation (*phaneroō*). The crucial point is that for Gregory divine "power" (*dynamis*) means the manifestation in act of the divine nature as such.[66] Thus, to say that God manifests the superabundance of his power by "what is external to his nature" is an intensely dialectical statement. Therefore, the "boundaries" of the divine nature as alluded to in this passage—that outside of which God manifests his power—cannot refer to *the limitations of God's natural power*, but rather, we can say, to the natural conditions of divine existence. Reading the passage strictly in context, the conditions in view entail God's not being in direct contact with human limitations. To go beyond the boundaries of the "habitat" of the divine nature, in its native condition of being distant from human vulnerabilities, is a supreme manifestation of divine power.

62. See above, 104.
63. See Anatolios, *Coherence*.
64. *C. Eun.* 3.3.34–35 (ET: NPNF[2] 5:176, altered).
65. Zizioulas, for example, tends to associate "substance" with necessity: "Therefore, as a result of love, the ontology of God is not subject to the necessity of the substance" (*Being as Communion*, 46). The scope of the present work does not allow for an evaluation of the complex interaction of the motifs of nature, person, freedom, and communion in Zizioulas's work. The immediate concern is simply to signal that Gregory should not be assimilated to that framework.
66. See Holl, *Amphilochius*, 209–11; this is the central thesis of Barnes, *Dynamis*, 260–307.

It would be unwise to force a kind of scholastic parsing of Gregory of Nyssa's rhetorical gambit beyond what we have already done. We must simply register the cumulative effect of his rhetoric, which seeks to redefine divine greatness away from an essentialist conception of what it cannot do toward a receptivity to the surprise of the gospel *kērygma*. In the *kērygma*, God's power is startlingly manifest when he shows up where he is not supposed to be, in conditions "external to his own nature." Again following a structual motif of Athanasius's *On the Incarnation*, Gregory continues to re-vision divine transcendence in the christological narrative by dialectically applying the terminology of strength and weakness to the cross. Eunomius's mistake is to interpret the cross as a sign of weakness rather than as "a superabounding activity of power,"[67] "an unspeakable and majestic power."[68] While Athanasius had elaborated on the "power of the cross" mostly in soteriological consequentialist terms, referring to the salvation that resulted from it, Gregory pays more concrete and explicit attention to the "power of the cross" as the supreme manifestation of a divine power that is absolutely unrestricted, even by any preconceived canons of transcendence.

Given our exposition so far, it might seem that Gregory is willing to re-conceive the divine nature so as to allow divine passibility as consistent with God's greatness and power. But, in fact, Gregory clearly rejects that notion and insists that the divine nature is not susceptible to suffering and mortality.[69] Here again we encounter the seeming inconsistency of patristic Christology. Gregory seems to be making some significant headway in redefining divine transcendence in terms of the christological narrative but then falls short of making the crucial move of allowing passibility. The question of divine suffering and its attribution to the divinity and humanity of Christ is a complex one and perhaps finally inscrutable; at least, we cannot claim to have resolved it in our own time.[70] Our present object is simply to clarify how Gregory went about dealing with the question, not so much in order to demonstrate how he "solved" it but in order to show how his dealing with it constitutes a distinctive arrangement of the internal structure of Christian faith. In embarking on this task, the primary distinction to note in Gregory's own framework is between divine passibility (*pathos*) and divine "contact" with creaturely realities, the latter typically verbalized in the Stoic language of "mingling" (*krasis*).[71] Gregory does not compare and contrast the two categories thematically, but he does so performatively. All Gregory's efforts to redefine divine transcendence aim to show that, while the divine nature remains impassible, it is nevertheless a fitting and supreme manifestation of both

67. *C. Eun.* 3.3.34.
68. *C. Eun.* 3.3.40.
69. *C. Eun.* 3.4.6.
70. Among recent notable presentations of patristic doctrine on Christ's suffering and divine impassibility, in light of modern objections, see Weinandy, *Does God Suffer?*; Gavrilyuk, *The Suffering of the Impassible God*; Hart, "No Shadow of Turning"; and Marshall, "Dereliction of Christ."
71. For a good overview of Gregory's use of this language and its philosophical and theological provenance, see Bouchet, "Le Vocabulaire de l'union et du rapport des natures," esp. 547–60.

divine *philanthrōpia* and power (*dynamis*) to have contact and enter into "combination" or "mixture" with human conditions. But the all-important question remains: why is this mingling not passibility?

We can discern two responses to this question in *Against Eunomius*. The first implicitly applies the Stoic distinction of activity-passivity/passibility (*to poioun/to paschon*) to the transformative soteriological dynamism of the unity of humanity and divinity in Christ.[72] Such a framework is evoked, for instance, in the following statements: "For truly the divinity is active (*energei*) in working the salvation of the world through the body that enveloped it. In this way, the passibility (*to pathos*) belonged to the body, but the activity (*energeia*) belonged to God";[73] "The flesh is of a passible nature (*pathētikēn physeōs*), but the Word is active (*energētikēs*)."[74] The "activity" of the divinity and the "passibility" of the humanity are equally constitutive of the mingling of humanity with God. Therefore, divine activity, while not passibility, is also not disconnectedness. If the distinction between the categories of "activity" and "passibility" is enfolded within the overarching divine-human action of "mingling" and contact, then "activity" and "passibility" must be conceived as two different modalities of contact. "Activity" is a mode of contact in which the divine maintains and does not relinquish its sovereign mode of operation, while "passibility" involves the reception or "suffering" of such activity. To complete the picture, we must also keep in mind that the essential content of this mingling is the salvific transformation of humanity.[75] Thus the divinity of Christ is in contact with human limitations in a way that *actively transforms* these limitations while the human nature is in contact with them in a way that *undergoes* that transformation. The fact that the divine comes into "contact" with human passibilities while persevering in the active stance of divine power simultaneously effects human transformation and maintains divine impassibility:

> We do not say that in passing through those sufferings in the flesh of which we are talking, he was subject to passion. Rather, just as we say that He is the cause of all things that exist, that he holds the universe in his grasp, that he directs all that moves and maintains on a stable foundation all that is stationary by the unspeakable power of his own majesty, so we say also that He was born among us in order to cure the disease of sin, adapting the exercise of his healing power in a manner corresponding to the suffering, applying the healing in the manner which he considered to be for the benefit of that part of the creation which he knew to be infirm. As it was expedient that He healed our sufferings by touch, he healed it in that way. Yet he should not be considered passible himself because he is the healer of our infirmity.[76]

72. I note the importance of the active-passive framework in Athanasius's Christology in *Coherence*, 76–84. For its Stoic provenance, see Diogenes, *Vita* 7.134; Seneca, *Ep.* 65; Spanneut, *Le stoïcisme des pères de l'église*, 90–91.

73. *C. Eun.* 3.4.9.

74. *C. Eun.* 3.3.64.

75. That the soteriological yield of human transformation is the key to Gregory's Christology had already been suggested by Daley's insightful article, "Divine Transcendence."

76. *C. Eun.* 3.4.30 (ET: NPNF[2] 5:186, altered).

This dynamic of transformation is Gregory of Nyssa's soteriological expression of themes Chalcedonian Christology would later delineate in terms of the distinction of natures, the communication of properties, and the unity of Christ's person. While Christ's humanity and divinity each have their distinctive properties, globally characterized in terms of activity and passivity, the properties of each condition are also shared by the other: "because of the connection and intertwining (*symphuian*), what particularly belongs to each becomes common to both."[77] Yet the union of humanity and divinity maintains the distinction between them insofar as the asymmetrical structure of activity-passivity is preserved, such that the divinity actively transforms the humanity with which it comes into contact and the humanity passively accepts that transformation. Thus God keeps on actively being God while humanity is divinized:

> The lowliness of the one who was crucified in weakness, because of its mingling (*anakraseōs*) with the infinity and limitlessness of the Good, no longer remained in its own proportions and properties but the Right Hand of God raised it up together with itself so that instead of a servant it became Lord, instead of a subject, Christ the King, instead of lowly, Most High, instead of a human being, God.[78]

Only against the background of this entire dialectic can we see how Gregory can insist that the Word underwent a real self-emptying and yet did not become passible. He mocks the Eunomian notion of a self-emptying that means merely transferring from one condition of creaturehood to another. From Gregory's point of view, Eunomius's version of christological *kenōsis* is "not that the master was mingled with servants but that a servant came to be among servants."[79] For his part, Gregory not only insists that his doctrine properly attributes self-emptying to the Word but goes so far as to allow for the proper use of the language of change for the incarnation, using a Septuagint version of Psalm 76:11, "the change of the right hand of the Most High."[80] This "change" (*alloiōsis*), however, consisted in the immediate and transformative contact of divine activity with the conditions of human passibility and not in the reversal of this divine activity to passivity. What was reversed was the negativity of human limitations through their newfound participation in divinity.

Nevertheless, Gregory perceives that there will still be a stigma attached to the notion of divinity being in such immediate contact with human "passions." We have traced some of his efforts to deal with this problematic from the perspective of Christ's divinity, both by re-conceiving divine transcendence as *philanthrōpia* and by insisting on the perseverance of divine active agency in its union with Christ's humanity. But Gregory also complements his reconstruction of the category of divine transcendence with a revised notion of human passions. In the Hellenistic worldview shared by his contemporaries, the notion of "the passions" conflates ontological and

77. *C. Eun.* 3.3.66.
78. *C. Eun.* 3.3.46 (ET: NPNF² 5:178, altered).
79. *C. Eun.* 3.3.55.
80. *C. Eun.* 3.4.24; cf. *Vit. Mos.* 2.28.

moral connotations. "The passions" (*ta pathē*) was a category that designated both disordered affections, such as excessive anger or lust, and the conditions of finite material existence that rendered a nature passive to external forces. Moreover, there was a causal relationship between the two significations of the term: the weakness and passivity that besets materiality and finitude gives rise to the disordered affections of the soul. But, complementing his strategy of redefining divine transcendence in terms that would make it compatible with the christological narrative, Gregory now makes the correlative move of redefining human existence so as to make its union with the divine more intelligible. To this end, he sunders the conflation of ontological and moral connotations attached to the language of "passions," a conflation that tended to assign negative moral value to the very structure of corporeal human existence. His strategy is to propose that the language of "passion," with its then negative connotations, should be reserved only for willful moral failure: "nothing is truly passion which is not conducive to sin . . . only the diseased condition of the will is truly passion."[81] He insists therefore that the language of *pathos* should not be applied to "the necessary routine of nature" or to "the distinctive attributes of our nature."[82] Inasmuch as the incarnate Word was sinless, he did not partake of "passions" in the sense of moral failure, but he did partake of all the structural conditions of finite corporeal human existence, including the emotions that arise naturally and faultlessly from these conditions. Gregory elaborates his rehabilitation of the concept of human nature more extensively later in his *Catechetical Oration*, as we will see. For the moment, we are content to conclude that his efforts to relate Christ's divinity to the Father in light of the biblical christological narrative have led Gregory to affirm the lordship of Christ in scriptural language and in Christian worship; to stress the relative equality of all creatures as subject to that lordship and released from creaturely slavery through Christ's lordship; to re-conceive divine transcendence; to analyze the dynamics of soteriological transformation in relation to the diverse natures and unified subject in Christ; and finally to reevaluate human nature itself in light of the incarnation.

DOCTRINE OF GOD: THREE-PERSONED GOODNESS

The previous sections have already disclosed some key features of Gregory of Nyssa's doctrine of God in *Against Eunomius*. We have shown that, for Gregory, the essence of God is incomprehensible in the precise sense that it cannot be passively enclosed by the human intellect. At the same time, we can have both affirmative and negative knowledge of God and are able to speak truly of what really pertains to God and what does not. The nature of the relation between the infinite God and finite humanity is such that knowledge of God can only take place in the modality of receptivity, awe, and worship. Ultimately, "the only name that signifies the divine nature is the wonder that arises ineffably in our souls concerning it."[83] The fact that we cannot have any

81. *C. Eun.* 3.4.27–29 (ET: NPNF² 5:186, altered). Cf. *Cat. or.* 16.
82. *C. Eun.* 3.4.27–29.
83. *C. Eun.* 3.6.4.

simple and immediate grasp of the divine essence means not that we cannot know God altogether but that genuine knowledge of God is only possible by receptively engaging the complex totality of divine self-disclosure. The center and apex of this complex totality is the christological narrative of the Word of God that was manifest in the humanity of Jesus through the work of the Spirit.[84] We have also seen that the christological narrative leads Gregory toward a re-conception of the notion of divine transcendence. In light of the humanity and suffering of Christ, divine majesty cannot be interpreted exclusively as abstraction from conditions of materiality and finitude but rather in terms of the power and freedom of the divine nature to perdure in conditions "external to its nature" in order to manifest the divine *philanthrōpia*. Indeed, the human suffering and passibility of Jesus disclose not that the divine nature is itself passible, since the divinity was active in its transformative contact with the possibilities of the flesh, but rather that the mark of the divine nature is love for humanity: "What took place was not passion but *philanthrōpia*."[85]

One of the manifestations of the propositionalist fixation in trinitarian theology is the tendency to interpret Gregory's trinitarian theology principally from the perspective of the language of *hypostasis* and *ousia*, or at least of the mystery of three-in-oneness. While the general intent of this study is to recommend a more comprehensive and systematic view of what constitutes trinitarian doctrine, the present section will propose that, even with respect to questions of unity, equality, and distinction in the Trinity, a more intelligible starting point for understanding Gregory's trinitarian theology can be found elsewhere. Gregory's elucidation of Basil's distinction between *hypostasis* and *ousia* is one important feature of his doctrine of God, but it is largely derivative of his brother's treatment and does not in itself capture the distinctive perspective of the Nyssan. A more profitable starting point for gauging Gregory's distinctive approach is to focus on his understanding of the relation between Father and Son (and to a lesser extent, as far as this treatise is concerned, the Spirit) in terms of the category of divine goodness, an identification of the divine which enabled Gregory to assimilate Platonic characterizations of the good to the biblical narrative of the God of Israel and Jesus Christ.[86] Approaching Gregory's doctrine from the perspective of this key theme has the further merit of uncovering a foundational treatment of an issue with which modern theology has become once again engaged, that of giving a properly trinitarian account of divine attributes.[87]

We have already noted that one of the significant features that constituted common ground among all parties in the fourth-century doctrinal controversies was a radical

---

84. *C. Eun.* 2.236–42.

85. *C. Eun.* 3.4.

86. For Plato, the good is the supreme form and archetypal beauty (cf. *Rep.* 6.509b; *Crat.* 439c; *Phaedr.* 100b). Plotinus identifies the good with the One (*Enn.* 5.5.13). On this background, see Balás, *Metousia*, 94.

87. Thus Pannenberg considers it crucial for a renewed understanding of trinitarian theology to supplant an older treatment that separates consideration of the divine attributes from the doctrine of the Trinity (cf. *Systematic Theology*, 1:282).

distinction between the Uncreated and the created. Even those theologians who considered the preexistent Christ to be a created creator preserved that distinction precisely by insisting that even if Christ was creator, he himself was not uncreated. We have seen that Athanasius insisted on strictly conflating the categories of "uncreated" and "Creator," thus rejecting the possibility that "creator" can be a middle term that could be aligned with "created." This process of dismantling the ontological ladder and replacing it with a strictly binary framework of uncreated Creator versus creation achieves a leap in comprehensive conceptualization in the case of Gregory of Nyssa. With Gregory, the category of uncreated Creator becomes aligned with a series of biblical and philosophical categories that radicalize the distinction between the Creator and creation, without allowing for any ontological hierarchy with respect to the divine side of the polarity. The Uncreated is the first existent, whose name is "I am who I am" and whose possession of existence is complete and unvaried: what fluctuates in being is not God.[88] This being is infinite because his perfection and goodness are utterly without limits. Thus the uncreated Creator is also the first existent, the infinite, the perfect, the good, the one and only God. What essentially characterizes all these categories is a simplicity that does not allow for variation in degree. The various characterizations of the divine represent distinct conceptions of the one God, which bear mutual reference to one another, and so the whole set can be treated from the perspective of any one of the terms. In *Against Eunomius*, it is the category of the good that has pride of place.[89]

The simplicity of the good can be grasped precisely through its reference to the other categories that refer to the transcendent being of God. The good is wholly perfect and as such must be infinite, because it is inexhaustible in its essential goodness and not bounded by its contrary. It is therefore not susceptible to limit, diminution, or increase. Since nothing better than perfect goodness can be conceived, the term "God" must denote "the Highest Nature, the First Good";[90] "lacking nothing conceivable as pertaining to the good."[91] Variation in goodness is only thinkable on the level of creation, as distinct levels of participation in perfect goodness, whereas that essence that is goodness itself cannot admit of degrees.[92] All this seems self-evidently logical for Gregory, but he also applies biblical texts that speak of the uniqueness of God as confirmation of his doctrine of divine simplicity, of the lack of "priority and posteriority" within the divine being.[93]

Thus Gregory of Nyssa constructs a synthesis of biblical testimony and philosophical reasoning to present the notion of God as perfect and simple goodness,

---

88. *C. Eun.* 3.6.3–4.

89. See Balás, *Metousia*, 54–75. Balás remarks that "among the divine perfections ... it is doubtlessly Goodness which occupies the most important place in the works of Gregory" (54); cf. Holl, *Amphilochius*, 201–3.

90. *C. Eun.* 1.274.

91. *C. Eun.* 3.6.74.

92. *C. Eun.* 1.334; 1.276; 3.6.74.

93. *C. Eun.* 3.3.8, where he refers to Isaiah 44:6.

thereby dismantling the notion of a graded hierarchy of divinity as both irrational and non-biblical.

It must be kept in mind, however, that the complexity and inner tension of Eunomius's theology is such that it too is involved in the project of dismantling a graded hierarchy of divinity. That, after all, is the whole point of insisting that the Son is not, in the full and strict sense, God. With reference to the category of the good, Eunomius can agree with Gregory's principle of the simplicity of essential goodness while insisting that only the Unbegotten God possesses perfect essential goodness. Indeed, he can cite Jesus's rejoinder to the rich young man ("Why do you call me good. No one is good but God alone," Luke 18:19) as testimony that the title "Good" belongs uniquely to the Unbegotten, "the one who is the cause of his own goodness and of all goodness."[94] Gregory's distinct challenge therefore is to advance from an affirmation of the simplicity of divine goodness to a properly trinitarian conception of this simplicity, and he does this by way of reinterpreting the category of divine goodness with reference to the christological narrative.

As for Jesus's response to the rich young man, Gregory maintains that it was intended to underline precisely the conflation of the categories of divinity and goodness; Jesus was reprimanding the young man not simply for calling him good but for calling him good without recognizing his divinity. More generally, Gregory argues that the Scriptures, taken as a whole and as interpreted by common Christian experience, designate both Son and Spirit by the qualities of divine goodness and perfection: "Everyone knows that the *hypostasis* of the Son and that of the Spirit do not lack anything of perfect goodness, perfect power, and every such quality."[95] If Son and Spirit are essentially good, then this biblical datum must be understood in a way that does not disturb the non-hierarchical simplicity of perfect and infinite goodness, thereby making them co-equal sharers in the divine goodness. Mirroring Eunomius's direction of argument, Gregory elaborates his own theology of divine goodness largely with reference to the Son, occasionally extending the results of his argumentation to the Spirit as well. The exalted scriptural names of Christ (*epinoiai*) come to the fore. Such scriptural identifications of Christ as King, Judge, Creator, Life, Light, Power, and Wisdom reveal the Son as "equal in every operative and conceivable conception (*epinoian*) of the good to the majesty of the Father's goodness."[96] In short, Christ is "the fullness of all good."[97] Once again Johannine sayings about the mutual reference of Father and Son are employed as global hermeneutical keys for the scriptural sharing of divine titles between Father and Son, prescribing equality of goodness and honor between them:

> With reference to the divine nature, every perfection that pertains to goodness is connoted with the very name of God. Consequently, there can be no grounds for our minds

94. *C. Eun.* 3.9.1.
95. *C. Eun.* 1.167.
96. *C. Eun.* 1.339.
97. *C. Eun.* 3.6.7.

to discover modulations in honor. Where there is no greater and smaller in power or glory or wisdom or love or any other conception (*ennoias*) that pertains to good, but the good which the Son has is the Father's also and all that is the Father's is seen in the Son, what possible condition of mind can lead us to show more reverence to the Father? If we think of royal power and worth, the Son is King; if of a judge, "all judgment is committed to the Son" (John 5:22); if of the magnificence of the office of creation, "all things were made by him" (John 1:3); if of the author of our life, we know the true Life came down as far as our nature; if of our being taken out of darkness, we know he is the true Light who releases us from darkness (John 1:9); if wisdom is precious to anyone, Christ is God's power and Wisdom (1 Cor. 1:24).[98]

Like Athanasius, Gregory of Nyssa takes the scriptural sharing of names and titles between God and Christ as constitutive of divine goodness. If we are to speak of God *from within scriptural language*, we must say that God's goodness is his wisdom, power, light, and so on. But these are also the titles of the Son. Consequently, we must say that it is good for God to be Father of the Son, just as it is good for God to be wise and powerful. To remove the Son from the essential definition of God is thus to dismantle the specifically scriptural construction of divine goodness. That is the logic behind Gregory's refrain, echoing Origen and Athanasius before him: to say that God was ever without the Son is tantamount to saying that God was at some point "devoid of good." As we said in the case of Athanasius, it is a mistake to dismiss such statements on strictly abstract logical terms. Their proper import derives most directly from their implicit insistence that properly theological statements about divine being are strictly accountable to scriptural linguistic patterns. One must speak of God from within the patterns of scriptural language. If God's goodness, in its various delineations, is scripturally associated with the figure of Christ, that association cannot be broken. To attempt to break it might still result in a doctrine of God that is rational in its internal coherence, on strictly objective logical grounds. But, for those who subscribe to the scriptural identification of God, the break in this association can be judged precisely in terms of its disturbance of scriptural linguistic associations. Within the framework of these associations, to say that the radical being of Christ, in his divinity, is external to the being of the Father must be translated into statements that the Father's being is intrinsically devoid of goodness.

If one level of Gregory's argument is to construct a doctrine of divine goodness out of the scriptural patterns of naming God and Christ, another polemical posture is to press the distinction between uncreated essential goodness, in which no variation can be posited, and creaturely, participated goodness.[99] As we have noted, only the latter admits variance of degree. But Gregory argues that placing the divinity of Christ in this latter category again distorts and contradicts the standard Christian estimation of Christ as "the fullness of all good" and giver of goodness. A creaturely being who does not possess essential goodness and only acquires it by partial participation is not

98. *C. Eun.* 1.334–35 (ET:NPNF² 5:66, altered).
99. *C. Eun.* 1.273; 3.6.75.

capable of imparting goodness but is continually seeking goodness. Here we can see the polemical trinitarian background to Gregory's notion of the creatures' infinite growth and "stretching" toward the fullness of infinite divine perfection.[100] If Christ is not himself, in his divinity, possessor of this essential goodness, then he will be always stretching toward the fullness of this goodness. To conceive of Christ in this way would again result in a performative self-contradiction in Christian devotion.

A significant example of such performative self-contradiction would be the practice of baptism. Gregory sees the event of baptism as an entrance into divine "life-giving power" (*hē zōopoios dynamis*).[101] The recipient of baptism is engaged with Father, Son, and Spirit as a united agency that grants the limitless goodness of divine life. The sacramental event of baptism opens up to a pattern of exchange in which the recipient embarks on an unceasing participation in the limitless divine goodness. But the failure to attribute essential goodness to the Son and Spirit who are named with the Father as agents of the baptismal impartation subverts the integrity of that impartation and thus evacuates the salvific meaning of Christian baptism:

> If we concede the impious notion that goodness does not essentially reside in the life-giving power but is acquired by participation, then it can no longer be properly named "the Good." . . . And if this is granted, then the divine nature cannot be conceived as causative of goodness but rather as itself in need of goodness. How can one provide another with what one does not have? In such a state, one will not benefit an inferior but will strive to fill up what is lacking to oneself. Thus, according to them, the notion of providence would be a lie as well as that of judgment and of the economy of the only-Begotten and all the things that we believe have been done and are always done by him, since he is apparently preoccupied with concern for his own goodness and neglecting oversight of the universe. . . . If this is so, then our faith is empty and our preaching is vain and our hopes, which derive their substance from faith, are insubstantial. So why then are they baptized into Christ, if he has no power of goodness of his own? May such blasphemy be far from my mouth! Why do they believe in the Holy Spirit if they think the same about him too? How are they going to be regenerated by baptism if, according to them, the Power that is supposed to grant the new birth does not possess indefectibility and self-sufficiency in its own nature?[102]

We have seen thus far that Gregory of Nyssa defines divine goodness in terms of the intertextual scriptural identifications of God and Christ and in terms of the trinitarian name of the "Life-giving Power" invoked in baptism. These strategies insert the identities of the Son and the Spirit into the non-hierarchical simplicity of essential, perfect, infinite, life-giving goodness. However, the maximal christological transformation of the category of divine goodness is realized through Gregory's insistence that it is precisely the salvific, kenotic self-humbling of the Son, by which he became

100. See below; for a treatment of the later *Life of Moses* as bound to Gregory's anti-Eunomian polemic, see Heine, *Perfection in the Virtuous Life*.
101. On the crucial significance of this title for Gregory, see Holl, *Amphilochius*, 209–11.
102. *C. Eun.* 1.285–89 (ET: NPNF² 5:61–62, altered).

a sin and a curse, that constitutes the supreme manifestation of divine goodness and thereby manifests the Son as a co-sharer of essential divine goodness. In this regard, Gregory depicts Eunomius's doctrine as manifesting a grotesque failure of Christian piety precisely by refusing to see the self-humbling of Christ as a manifestation of divine goodness: "What more bitter malice can one find than to deny that he is good who 'being in the form of God did not regard equality with God as something to be exploited' (Phil. 2:6) but lowered himself to the abasement of the human nature and did so only for the love of humanity?"[103] Read strictly out of the christological narrative, the divine goodness is manifest as the kenotic love for humanity and the power to impart that goodness to fallen humanity. Gregory depicts Eunomius as someone who is uninitiated into the paradoxical logic of the christological narrative to the extent that he interprets the weakness of Christ as simply weakness rather than as a manifestation of the strength of divine love: "He does not think that it was by his almighty divinity that the Son proved strong for such a form of loving-kindness but that it was by being of a nature subject to passion that he was susceptible to suffering on the cross."[104]

Having initiated his reader into the paradoxical christological rhetoric of weakness-as-strength and the redefinition of divine power in terms of the efficacy of salvation, Gregory mocks Eunomius's implicit standard of transcendence as merely distance and disinvolvement from human affairs. At this juncture in the debate, Eunomius's conception of the height of divine transcendence in the Unbegotten as prior to and independent of all activity is brought into direct confrontation with Gregory's efforts simultaneously to safeguard divine transcendence as "activity," within the Stoic active-passive framework, and to define that activity according to the christological narrative as the "power" (*dynamis*) of self-humbling love. In reaction to Basil's argument that the sharing of scriptural titles, such as Light, indicated a continuity of nature, Eunomius had insisted that the Begotten Light, who "activated" (*enērgēsen*) the economy of love for humanity, was still inferior to the Unbegotten Light, who was "inactive (*anenergēton*) with respect to that grace."[105] Eunomius's position is perfectly consistent with his fundamental conviction that all activity is separable and ontologically inferior to the divine essence as such. Insisting on soteriological activity as the supreme mark of transcendence, Gregory pours scorn on this conception of an "inactive" transcendence: "A new way of evaluating precedence in honor! They judge what is inert in *philanthrōpia* as superior to what is active (*energēsantos*)!"[106] Thus Gregory arrives at the point of replacing "being uncaused" as the primary designation of divine transcendence with the power to act in order to bring about good: "The one who is powerful to accomplish the good is greater than the one who is impotent in accomplishing good."[107]

103. *C. Eun.* 3.9.8.
104. *C. Eun.* 3.10.39.
105. *C. Eun.* 3.10.36.
106. *C. Eun.* 3.10.36.
107. *C. Eun.* 3.10.44.

Applying this christological reconstruction of divine goodness to the affective texture of Christian piety, Gregory of Nyssa insinuates that Eunomius's doctrine of God gives no ground for the fundamental Christian disposition of thanksgiving.[108] Humanity need not be thankful to Christ if his suffering represents not divine self-humbling but the natural consequence of an attenuated and passible divinity. And it need not be thankful to the Father if his superior dignity is defined merely in terms of an impassibility that distanced him from the salvific work of Christ. Gregory gives a final acerbic evaluation of Eunomius's account of the higher dignity of the Father's impassibility with respect to the Son's salvific involvement in the human condition: According to Eunomius, if the Son were as great as the Father, we would not be saved![109] But if the Son saves us because he is not as great as the Father, then we should really honor him more than the Father, and not less. Of course, Eunomius himself did not draw these conclusions, and we need not detain ourselves from exploring whether they necessarily follow from his doctrine. Our immediate purpose is the positive exposition of Gregory's trinitarian theology. From that perspective, the salient point is that for Gregory, as for Athanasius, the ultimate motive for human thanksgiving is the self-humbling of the Son from a fully divine state to a condition that shares and reverses human suffering. Rather than let the narrative of Christ's self-humbling detract from the Son's full divinity, Gregory defines divine goodness itself by that very narrative. Father, Son, and Holy Spirit are co-agents of the narrative of the manifestation of divine goodness and are thus co-equal sharers in the simple perfection of that goodness.

Gregory's application of the christological narrative to a redefinition of divine goodness can thus be seen as constructing a logic that moves from the christological economy to a trinitarian doctrine of God by way of a christological transmutation of divine attributes. A culminating step in this logic is the application of christologically re-conceived notions of divine power, goodness, activity, and causality to what later theology calls the "relations of origin" between the trinitarian persons, particularly with respect to the status of Father as cause of Son and Spirit. Eunomius understands that relation quite simply in terms of the superiority of cause to effect, and he posits the causal activity of the Father as extrinsic and posterior to the integrity of his essence.[110] The productivity of divine generation does not belong to the self-sufficient simplicity of the divine essence but to the external (*ad extra*) works of the Unbegotten. Eunomius's theology thus involves a strict separation of divine being and act; there can be no act within the divine being. Every divine act (*energeia*) results in a work, or an effect, that is inferior to its cause. The Son is the first of such created causes, and his being is bounded by the divine act that produced him. For his part, Gregory does not dispute that the Father is cause of the Son; he interprets the Johannine "the Father and I are one" (John 10:30) as indicating that "the Lord is from a cause (*ex*

---

108. Cf. a similar motif in Athanasius, see above, 155.

109. *C. Eun.* 3.10.44.

110. For a clear and thorough exposition of how Eunomius conceives causal activity as secondary and exterior to divine essence, see Barnes, *Dynamis*, esp. 190–91.

aitiou)" in such a way that precludes differentiation in the nature (*kata physin*) but safeguards the distinction of *hypostaseis*.[111]

The root of Gregory of Nyssa's difference from Eunomius with respect to conceiving the causal relation between Father and Son is the former's rejection of the notions that divine activity *per se* is posterior to divine being and that the simplicity of the divine essence excludes activity.[112] We have already seen that Gregory's notion of divine simplicity is determined by his characterization of divine goodness, which is in turn determined by the christological narrative as involving "the power to act" for the sake of the impartation of goodness. It is no surprise, then, that Gregory constructs a notion of inner-divine causality that is determined by the categories of goodness, perfection, and maximal power of action. He mocks Eunomius's fundamental premise of the inferiority of effect to cause, which Eunomius shares with the Neoplatonic tradition, as amounting to the principle that "the meagerness of the work achieved is demonstrative of greater power. . . . But who would assent to the notion that a great and powerful cause is manifested in meagerness of results?"[113] Gregory suggests that just the opposite must be true. The greater the cause, the greater the effect; a perfect cause would suitably manifest itself in a perfect effect. In arguing this point, Gregory takes over Eunomius's premise that the Son is a "work" (*ergon*) and transforms it by insisting that it is still possible to think of a perfect "work" of the Father that would reduplicate the Father's perfection. Such a transmission of perfection from the Father to the Son would be in keeping with the divine goodness, a point that Gregory implies by invoking the Platonic motif that God is not "envious." The effect of the privileging of the category of divine goodness is here evident in that whereas Eunomius considers that introducing activity into the divine essence attributes "passion" to God, Gregory insists that "passion" is introduced by ascribing to God the envy that would be implied in his withholding the sharing of divine perfection:

> Is he telling us that the notion of perfection is not applied to the one who is begotten from [God] so that the honor and glory of the one who is honored for his superiority may not be lessened? But who is so abject as not to acquit the divine and blessed nature of any imputation of the passion of envy? What appropriate reason, then, is there for the God of the universe to arrange things in such an order with respect to the Only-Begotten and the Spirit?[114]

Gregory thus integrates into his doctrine of divine perfection and goodness a conception of a perfect self-communication of the Father to the Son as constitutive and demonstrative of a perfect intra-divine causality. While he is able to articulate this

111. *C. Eun.* 1.503.
112. Balás remarks that for Greogry "the divine life, though perfectly unchangeable and eternal in the strictest sense, is nevertheless conceived as an activity." He further notes that in *On the Soul and Resurrection*, "this *energeia* is described as that of love (*agapē*)" (*Metousia*, 84).
113. *C. Eun.* 1.417.
114. *C. Eun.* 1.418.

conception in Eunomius's language of being, causality, and activity, he also relates it to biblical language denoting the mutual indwelling of Christ and the Father, as in John 10:38 ("The Father is in me and I am in the Father"), as well as to the christological *epinoiai* that delineate the shared goodness of Father and Son. While the Father is cause, he is also in the Son as the beauty of the prototype is in the image.[115] Because of this perfect act of causality in which the cause indwells its perfect effect, there is no "interval" (*diastēma*) or "separation" in the movement of self-communication from Father to Son: "It is impossible to separate the one from the other, as the apostle says, neither the expression from the reality (*hypostasis*) nor the radiance from the divine glory, nor the image from the goodness."[116] It is this perfect communication of goodness from Father to Son and Spirit that constitutes their "community of essence." This perfect causality establishes both the homogeneity of divine life among Father, Son, and Spirit and the distinctions that pertain to the very structure of causality by which the three *hypostaseis* share in divine goodness: "Apart from the notion of cause, the Holy Trinity has no discrepancy in itself whatsoever."[117]

Yet, even with regard to causality, Gregory of Nyssa wants to differentiate himself from Eunomius's reduction of the Father-Son relation to a matter of cause and effect. It is true that he had made use of Eunomius's notion of the Son as a "work" of the Father in order to suggest that even such a starting point can pass through a proper conception of divine perfect goodness and yield the notion of a perfect effect of a perfect cause. But such a perfect effect would ultimately need to be distinguished from a mere "work." Once again, the framework of activity-passivity seems determinative. The crucial distinction is one between an "effect" in which the active power of the cause is extended and reproduced and one that is merely acted upon, constituted as the passive recipient of the activity of the cause: "The one who designates the Son as the effect of an activity (*energeias*) posits him as one of those passible things (*tōn pathētōn*) which are produced by an action."[118] This notion Gregory summarily dismisses as blatant "impiety" inasmuch as the scriptural account of Christ's primacy rules out a notion of Christ as merely passive. His perfect relation of derivation from the Father is such that, in his divinity, he is "not passive and thus not the result of an action but certainly true God, radiating and shining forth from the true God and Father."[119] Because the generation of the Son constitutes a perfect manifestation of the power of divine causality and because in this particular case the cause indwells the "effect," the Son is not in the last analysis adequately conceived as merely a passive effect of the Father. Though he can be said to be "caused" by the Father, the Son is more appropriately designated by the scriptural idiom, as "radiance" of the cause, than through the binary framework of active cause–passive effect.

---

115. *C. Eun.* 1.636.
116. *C. Eun.* 1.636.
117. *C. Eun.* 1.691.
118. *C. Eun.* 2.376.
119. *C. Eun.* 2.377.

Like Athanasius, Gregory of Nyssa is eventually led to compare and contrast this conception of the unity of nature between Father and Son to that of a mere unity of will, rejecting a simple contrast in which unity of nature precludes activity of the will in the transmission of divine goodness from Father to Son. What is unacceptable to him is not the involvement of divine will in the act of the Father's generation of the Son but an understanding of that involvement that would make the Son extrinsic and posterior to the being of (the Unbegotten) God. There was no God whose nature was intact apart from the generation of the Son and then became Father by willing it, as Eunomius would have it. Rather, the Father's being eternally involves his generation of the Son, which is the perfect act of "willing the good." The following passage demonstrates Gregory's pointed and seemingly quite deliberate efforts to offer a synthesis of the doctrines of trinitarian "unity of nature" and "unity of will" by way of his distinctive emphasis on the category of divine goodness:

> As for those who say that the Father first willed and then became a Father and thereby assert posteriority in existence as regards the Word, we would like to persuade them to turn to the orthodox (*eusebes*) understanding by whatever illustration would make this possible. The immediate conjunction [of Father and Son] does not exclude the willing of the Father (*tēn boulēsin tou patros*) as if He had a Son without choice by some necessity of his nature. But neither does the willing separate the Son from the Father, coming in between them as a kind of interval. So we neither reject from our doctrine the willing of the Begetter in reference to the Son as if it were forced out, as it were, by the conjunction of the Son's unity with the Father, nor do we in any way break that inseparable connection when we regard willing as involved in the generation. For it properly belongs to our heavy and inert nature that the willing and the possession of a thing are not often present with us at the same moment.... But in the case of the simple and omnipotent nature, all things are conceived together simultaneously, both the willing of the good and the possession of what it wills. For the good and eternal will is contemplated as always active (*energon*), indwelling (*enousion*) and existing in (*enypostaton*) the eternal nature, not arising in it from any separate principle, nor capable of being conceived apart from what is willed. In reference to God, it is not possible either for the good will not to exist or for what is willed not to accompany the willing, for no cause can bring it about that what is suitable for the Father should not always exist or that there should be any impediment to the possession of what is willed. Since, then, the only-begotten God is by nature the good (or rather beyond all good!), and since the good never fails to be willed by the Father, it is clearly shown both that the conjunction of the Son with the Father is without any intermediary and also that the will, which is always present in the good nature, is not forced out or excluded by this inseparable conjunction.[120]

The identification of God's very being in terms of "willing the good" thus conceives the act of generation within the divine essence in a way that synthesizes the doctrine of trinitarian inseparability of being with that of trinitarian unity of will. God exists precisely through willing the good of the existence of the Son (and, by implication, the

---

120. *C. Eun.* 3.6.16–18 (ET: NPNF² 5:202, altered).

Spirit). Gregory is here giving larger and more systematic expression to Basil's previous synthesis of intentionality and unity of being in the Father's generation of the Son: the Father "always possessed the Son by reason of his always willing what is good."[121] But, in reaction to Basil, Eunomius had objected that the introduction of the activity of "willing the good" into the very nature of God is a slippery slope that lies within the terrain of pagan philosophy, leading from the conception of eternal generation to that of eternal creation. Once again, the specter of Origen lurks in the background, and we have seen that the same anti-Origenian argument was directed against Athanasius.[122] Since creation is also good, and scripturally designated as such, does God also need to be eternally creating in order to be eternally good? In response, Gregory invokes the fundamental distinction between Creator and creation, now read through the lens of the category of goodness. In this framework, the Creator-creation distinction is rendered in terms of the difference between what is good in itself and what is good by participation. The Son belongs to God's natural goodness, which constitutes what it is to be God: "It is irreverent to believe that what is good by nature was not always in God."[123] But the goodness of creation is extrinsic to the divine being and constituted by creation's participation in God's goodness. The demonstration that the Son belongs to the inherent goodness of God's nature is once again composed of a recitation of the exalted scriptural names of Christ; thus biblical christological language is made to define the boundary line of the God-world distinction. While creation is scripturally designated as good, it is not correlated with the scriptural naming of God as Christ is:

> For creation was not in the beginning and was not with God and was not God nor life nor light nor resurrection nor the rest of the divine names, such as truth, righteousness, sanctification, judge, just, maker of all things, existing before the ages, forever and ever. The creation is not the brightness of the glory, nor the express image of the reality, nor the likeness of the goodness; nor is it grace or power or salvation or redemption. Nor do we find any one at all of those names which are employed by Scripture for the glory of the only-Begotten either belonging to the creation or employed concerning it. . . . But if all these conceptions and names involve communion with the Father, while they transcend our notions of the creation, is not our wise and clever friend ashamed to discuss the nature of the Lord of creation by reference to what he sees in creation?[124]

As involving both the good willing of the Father and the inseparably eternal good fruit of that willing, the divine generation of the Son is the eternal actualization of divine goodness, whose perfection can be shared by creation but is not itself susceptible to diminution, increase, or degree of variation:

> To say of [the divine nature] that it does not always possess what is good but afterwards chooses to have something which it did not choose before belongs to a wisdom that

---

121. Gregory thus renders Basil's position in *C. Eun.* 3.6.56; cf. Basil, *C. Eun.* 2.12.
122. See above, 70–71.
123. *C. Eun.* 3.6.60 (ET: NPNF[2] 5:208, altered).
124. *C. Eun.* 3.6.64–65 (ET: NPNF[2] 5:208, altered).

exceeds ours. For we were taught that the divine nature is at all times full of all good, or rather is itself the fullness of all good, seeing that it needs no addition for its perfecting, but is itself, by its own nature, the perfection of good. Now that which is perfect is equally remote from addition and from diminution; and therefore we say that that perfection of goods that we behold in the divine nature remains the same.... The divine nature, then, is never void of good. But the Son is the fullness of all good, and so he is at all times contemplated in the Father, whose nature is perfection in all good.[125]

Our efforts to reconstruct some of the main lines of Gregory of Nyssa's trinitarian vision in *Against Eunomius* can now be summarized. Gregory's trinitarian theology begins with a categorical rejection of the notion that the simplicity of the divine essence can be apprehended through a simple epistemological encounter with that essence, as is presumed by Eunomius's theology of the "Unbegotten." Rather, we have access to divine self-manifestation only through the multiplicity of scriptural language and narrative and the manifold variety of creation. Our knowing of God can never comprehend the divine essence as if it were an inert object; our knowing succeeds in being in touch with the reality of God only when it reacts to the divine self-manifestation in wonder and worship. Our naming of God encapsulates a synergy between the divine self-disclosure and our active response to it. This synergy finds its maximal expression in scriptural revelation, which represents a christological "condescension" or self-humbling of God by which the divine is accommodated to human perception and understanding by the power of the Spirit. Genuine knowledge of God is to be looked for through these scriptural notions (*epinoiai/ennoiai*) of God, in which the relation of Christ to God is seen to be constitutive of divine self-disclosure and of the divine nature itself. The lordship of Christ thus disclosed and performatively expressed through Christian worship leads to a reconstruction of divine transcendence as the power of kenotic love (*philanthrōpia*). Conceiving the divine through this christological lens, we see divine transcendence not from the point of view of an abstract apophaticism, as being uncaused, but positively, as divine power efficacious for doing good. The original movement of this supremely efficacious benevolence is the Father's impartation of his goodness to the Son, making him a co-equal sharer in that goodness. Father, Son, and Holy Spirit share equally in the goodness that constitutes the divine nature in a way that does not preclude the movement of willing. We now turn to a shorter treatise of Gregory's in which he seems to be deliberately constructing a coherent account of Christian faith centered on the vision of God as self-communicating trinitarian goodness.

The Trinitarian Systematic Theology of the *Catechetical Oration*

Gregory of Nyssa's *Catechetical Oration*, composed after the Council of Constantinople in the early 380s, appears to be intended not so much for catechumens directly as for

125. *C. Eun.* 3.6.19–21 (ET: NPNF² 5:213, altered).

catechists.[126] In view of modern ideas of the proper contents of "trinitarian doctrine," it might seem odd to refer to this work as a trinitarian systematic theology. After all, apart from some preliminary remarks at the beginning of the treatise, the theme of "how the three are one" is not prominent in this work. Indeed, the bulk of the treatise is concerned with the incarnation, inducing its placement in the modern compartment of "Christology." Yet Gregory explicitly states at various points that his purpose is to argue that the Christian revelation proclaims a "fitting conception of God."[127] Does Gregory simply forget his trinitarian commitments once he gets past his opening remarks on the Word and the Spirit? If we insist on our preconceptions regarding the proper domain of trinitarian doctrine, we will be tempted to think so. An alternative approach, however, is to at least temporarily put aside these presuppositions and allow Gregory's exposition of the Christian doctrine of God to suggest to us a different way of conceiving what is involved in "trinitarian doctrine." I cannot here provide a detailed analysis of this treatise. Instead, I will trace the development of a key motif that is in continuity with the earlier *Against Eunomius*: Gregory's christologically determined conceptions of trinitarian divine perfection and goodness. In my analysis of *Against Eunomius*, I have tried to show how these motifs inform a doctrine of God that is determined by the christological narrative. If we had to pinpoint the key trinitarian move of *Against Eunomius*, it would not be Gregory's use of *hypostasis* and *ousia* but his insistence on the christological determination of the doctrine of God. This key move, re-performed in a more integral catechetical setting in the *Oration*, entitles us to see it as a classic exposition of trinitarian doctrine.

Gregory begins his treatise by defending the intelligibility of the Christian doctrine of God against its main cultural competitors: Greeks and Jews. The Greeks are made to represent two competing views: atheism and polytheism. Atheism is unintelligible in light of the intelligent design of creation, which indicates "some power (*dynamin*) which is manifested by it and which transcends the universe."[128] Polytheism is equally untenable in light of the principle of the simplicity of absolute perfection. Gregory challenges an imaginary polytheist: "Does he think the divine is perfect or imperfect?"[129] If this interlocutor acknowledges that the divine nature is perfect, then he must logically concur that absolute perfection cannot admit of variation or difference. Different gods are as inconceivable as different perfections. These putative differences will either entail a variation of greater and lesser, in which case the lesser is not perfect and thus not God, or there will be no "distinguishing marks" to identify the differences, in which case there is no real plurality. Thus, there can be only one perfect and divine nature.

Gregory immediately follows this argument with a trinitarian qualification: "Our religious teaching, however, is able to discern some distinction of persons (*hypostaseis*)

126. Balás, "Gregor von Nyssa," 176; Hanson, *Search*, 718.
127. E.g., *Cat. or.* 5, 9, 20.
128. *Cat. or.* prol. Translations are from Hardy, *Christology*.
129. *Cat. or.* prol.

in the unity."[130] He identifies these *hypostaseis* as Word-Reason (*Logos*) and Spirit (*Pneuma*). He argues for the plausibility of this conception of the divine nature in imagined dialogue with both Greek and Jewish audiences. Speaking first to his imagined Greek interlocutor, he asks him to concede that God must have *logos*, which is to say, reason, intelligence, consciousness. God's *logos* can be contemplated by analogy with human nature, qualified by an anagogical ascent toward the perfection of divine nature. Human reason is unstable, so the word that expresses this reason is transient and perishable, mirroring the imperfection of human nature. However, God's reason must be conceived consistently with the perfection of the divine nature as informed by and interpreted through the christological scriptural narrative, and thus we must attribute to it eternal subsistence, simplicity, the faculty of will (*tēn proairesin*), "the power to act," and a consistent intentionality and power to do the good. Just as the human word is distinct from the mind in its dynamic derivation from it and yet is "one in nature" with the mind as its expression and reflection, so the divine Word is "distinct from him from whom it derives its subsistence (*hypostasin*)" and yet "identical in nature (*kata tēn physin*) with him," in sharing and expressing the same divine attributes.[131]

Gregory continues along this trajectory of analogical-anagogical reasoning in his presentation of the Spirit. Our human word is vivified and its utterance actualized by an underlying breath (*pneuma*). Since God does not lack anything that we enjoy, God's Word is also breathed forth: "God has a Spirit, which accompanies his Word and manifests his activity."[132] But, again, God's Spirit must be conceived in line with the divine perfections: "Like God's Word, it has its own subsistence, is capable of willing, and is self-moved and active. It always chooses the good and possesses the power corresponding to its will in fulfilling every intention."[133]

In the middle of his presentation of trinitarian doctrine to Greeks and Jews, Gregory points out that this teaching is indeed a "middle way" between Hellenism and Judaism. It contains what is right and useful from each, while rejecting the distortions and errors of both. It retains the Jewish notion of the oneness of God as well as the Greek conception of distinctions in the realm of the divine, while rejecting both polytheism and the denial of God's Word and Spirit. Of course, the "ineffable depth of the mystery" of the Christian conception of God remains transcendent to explanation: "how the same thing is subject to number and yet escapes it; how it is observed to have distinctions and is yet grasped as a unity; how it admits distinctions according to *hypostasis*, and yet is not divided with respect to the underlying [nature] (*tō hypokeimenō*)."[134] After this middle interlude on the golden mean of the Christian doctrine of God, Gregory summons forth his hypothetical Jewish interlocutor. His argument is that the Scriptures clearly demonstrate that God has a Word and a Spirit. His evidence for this claim is a single verse from the Psalms: "By the Word (*logos*) of

130. *Cat. or.* 1.
131. *Cat. or.* 2.
132. *Cat. or.* 2.
133. *Cat. or.* 2 (altered).
134. *Cat. or.* 3 (altered).

the Lord the heavens were established and all their power by the breath (*pneuma*) of his mouth" (Ps. 33:6). Again, an implicit recourse to the criterion of divine perfection leads to the conclusion that the perfect utterance of God must involve a Word and a Spirit with essential being and subsistence. Somewhat surprisingly, Gregory concludes this section by expressing confidence that this ineffable mystery of the complex unity of the divine being will not prove to be much of a stumbling block to either Greeks or Jews: "Neither Greek nor Jew, perhaps, will contest the existence of God's Word and Spirit—the one depending on his innate ideas, the other on the Scriptures."[135] An important transition is signaled when he asserts that the real difficulty will be encountered in relation to the doctrine of the incarnation, which then takes up most of the remainder of the treatise.

In trying to interpret the movement of Gregory of Nyssa's logic in this treatise, it is helpful to make explicit the "fusion of horizons," or perhaps rather "clash of horizons," between this logic and our own presuppositions and standards of judgment. It seems to a modern reader that Gregory demonstrates the doctrine of the Trinity by recourse to a mixture of a "psychological analogy" and an analogy of the spoken word, what Augustine would refer to as "inner word" and "outer word," respectively. He then invokes a single scriptural verse from the psalm to demonstrate that God has both a Word and Spirit. He appears to signal that the matter of "trinitarian doctrine" has been fairly settled at this point and then proceeds to matters of Christology. In sum, Gregory seems to be trying to prove the existence of the Trinity by recourse to the analogy of the human word and then to move to an examination of the doctrine of the incarnation. But such a description of Gregory's approach presupposes both a notion of theological reasoning as offering objective "proof" and a compartmentalization and division of theological themes into separable categories of "trinitarian doctrine" and Christology. We need to interrogate our own presuppositions; we need to ask whether the text corresponds to our categories of interpretation. Does the fact that we are not impressed by Gregory's "proofs" for the Trinity on the basis of the analogues of the human word and breath perhaps indicate not that his proof fails but that he was not attempting any such proof? Does our sense that he has prematurely closed the discussion of the Trinity perhaps indicate the inadequacy of our own categories, which break up the organic continuity of Gregory's logic?

If we follow the immanent logic of the text itself, we find that the unifying theme is neither "trinitarian doctrine" nor "Christology," according to our modern divisions, but rather simply the Christian doctrine of God ("a fitting conception of God"), which seamlessly encompasses both. The whole text must be read as a sustained and organically unified rational reflection on this subject rather than as a series of proofs for distinct elements of Christian faith. Keeping this unified perspective firmly in view, the relative emphases manifested in the text must be seen as themselves revelatory of the structure and logic and relative pressure points of the argument. The fact that Gregory begins with an exposition of trinitarian monotheism demonstrates that he

135. *Cat. or.* 5.

considers the trinitarian identification of God to be the starting point of Christian doctrine. But the fact that he spends relatively little time on the ineffable combination of distinction and unity in the Christian conception of God shows that he does *not* consider this to be the central matter of Christian theological reflection. Gregory could surely have greatly expanded his brief arguments demonstrating the distinct existences of the Word and the Spirit, but it is significant that he does not. These arguments seem much rather like token suggestions of the plausibility of a trinitarian identification of God rather than an attempt to prove the Trinity. Once this identification is in place, Gregory moves on to what he clearly believes to be the central task of Christian theology, that of meditating on the revelation of God through the life, death, and resurrection of Jesus Christ. The point is not that for Gregory the concept of the Trinity is less important or more marginal than Christology; that way of looking at it would be simply a reversion to divisive categories that break up Gregory's holistic vision of the Christian "conception of God." Rather, the point is that, for Gregory, what needs to be centrally communicated in the exposition of Christian theology is not an account of unity-within-distinction but an account of how our notion of who God is becomes determined by the christological narrative. Once the latter is accepted, the trinitarian identification of God follows from the structure and dynamics of the christological narrative itself and is to be interpreted from within the framework of that narrative. Therefore, Gregory's strategy is merely to suggest some preliminary ways of allowing for the possibility of a trinitarian identification of God before he proceeds to his central argument on behalf of the intelligibility of the christological narrative, which is what ultimately substantiates that identification.

The English theologian Colin Gunton has proposed that the doctrine of divine attributes needs to be rethought from the perspective of the "economic Trinity." Gunton contends that while the "tradition" has gone wrong in defining divine attributes by a mere negation of the characteristics of the material world, the required revision would trace "what happens when the doctrine of the divine attributes takes shape in the light of the economy of God's actions—of creation, reconciliation and redemption . . . a trinitarian construction will begin with the implications of the Son's involvement in the material world."[136] I suggest that Gunton's articulation of this necessary revision of the tradition serves very well as a summary of the contents of Gregory of Nyssa's *Oration*, which endeavors to present the divine attributes in light of the christological narrative. Disproportionate attention to what seems like a bizarre theology of atonement in which the devil is tricked by Christ's veiling his divinity in his humanity has distracted from Gregory's central demonstration that the christological narrative represents a superior dramatic presentation of divine perfection and goodness.

As we have noted, after his preliminary remarks on the Christian doctrine of God as including the confession of the divinity of Son and Spirit, Gregory turns to the Christian teaching on the incarnation. He acknowledges that the Christian account of the

136. Gunton, *Act and Being*, 76.

economy of the Word's becoming flesh will strike non-initiates as "unbefitting to say of God."[137] Like Athanasius, Gregory begins his systematic response to this objection with the doctrine of creation. Also like Athanasius, his purpose is to present a Christian account of reality that is christologically determined at every point. As we follow Gregory's representation of different aspects of Christian doctrine, the key to seeing the consistent logic of the whole is to note how each of these aspects is made to refer to the doctrine of the incarnate Word as the supreme and supremely unanticipated manifestation of divine goodness. We have seen that in *Against Eunomius*, a prominent theme was the characterization of God as the good and the presentation of the incarnate Word as an equal sharer of the divine goodness in his divinity and an enactor of the divine goodness through the salvific activity of his humanity. The presentation of the Word as the one who shares the substantial goodness of the Father and who communicates this goodness to humanity is radically opposed to Eunomius's monistic conception of divine substance and goodness as incommunicable. This fundamental opposition transcends later distinctions between "trinitarian theology" and "Christology." Throughout his *Catechetical Oration*, Gregory is consistently preoccupied with the characterization of the goodness of God as shared and communicated both within the divine trinitarian life and to humanity through the incarnation.

Gregory of Nyssa begins his systematic presentation with a doctrine of creation. The world is presented in the first place as a manifestation of the goodness of the Word, who is "a power existing in its own right, able to will all good and having the power to do everything it wills. Since the world is good, this power which prefers and creates the good is the cause of it."[138] The Word created the world not out of necessity but because of his "abundant love," in order that every aspect of the divine nature might be shared: "For it was not right that light should remain unseen or glory unwitnessed or goodness unenjoyed, or that any other aspect we observe of the divine nature should be idle with no one to share or enjoy it."[139] We can note again how the preceding statement implicitly evokes a trinitarian logic, which is then applied to a doctrine of creation. Against Eunomius's insistence that the divine nature is not shareable, the opposite principle of the fittingness of the "shareability" of God is here applied to the divine nature in a way that is consistent with Gregory's trinitarian commitments; by contrast, an unshareable god is dismissed as an "idle" god.

The communicability of the divine nature also becomes the determinative principle for Gregory's anthropology, which is centrally determined by the notion of humanity's participation in divine goodness: "If then, humanity came into being in order to participate in the divine goodness, it had to be fashioned in such a way as to fit it to share in this goodness."[140] Although Gregory does not yet make the connection explicit, such an anthropology is clearly christologically determined. An anthropology predicated on humanity's aptitude to share in the divine is not shy of finding a

137. *Cat. or.* 5.
138. *Cat. or.* 5.
139. *Cat. or.* 5.
140. *Cat. or.* 5. On the importance of the category of participation for Gregory, see Balás, *Metousia*.

divine-human union inherent in the very constitution of the human being: "For just as the eye shares in light through having by nature an inherent brightness in it, and by this innate power attracts what is akin to itself, so something akin to the divine had to be mingled with human nature. In this way its desire would correspond to something native to it."[141] Gregory concludes his section on creation with a reprise of the theme that the nature of the world manifests the shareablity of divine goodness: "Our nature in its origin was good and set in the midst of goodness."[142]

In the context of defending human goodness, Gregory is forced to deal with evil, inasmuch as the present human condition belies humanity's nature as ordained to participate in divine goodness. But even Gregory's treatment of evil irresistibly veers toward a reaffirmation of original human goodness and humanity's radical and ontological relatedness to divine goodness. Humanity's capacity to turn away from divine goodness is a tragic distortion of free will, which itself, however, is a faculty that enables humanity to own its participation in the good, "so that participation in the good may be the reward of virtue."[143] Moreover, following an Irenaean rather than Athanasian tradition, Gregory depicts humanity more as the victim than as the original perpetuator of the evil that now afflicts it. Gregory's explication of humanity's moral victimization by the devil again involves a subtle evocation of key christological motifs, which are perhaps all the more effective for being unvoiced and, as it were, almost subliminal. So we are told that the devil was motivated by envy on account of the union of divine and human aspects in human nature.[144] It seems that the devil resented precisely the christological dimension of the human being. Similarly, Gregory's articulation of the distortion of human nature through sin uses the language of "mingling," which he typically employs in reference to the union of humanity and divinity of Christ, to designate this distortion as an anti-image of humanity's christological likeness. Whereas the original human condition represented a "blending" (*synanakrasis, migma*)[145] of earthly and heavenly aspects, the adversary of humanity has "mingled" (*emmixas*)[146] evil with human nature and so brought about an anti-christological "unexpected union between what is our own and what is foreign to us."[147] Humanity's original created state is thus contrasted with its fallen condition in terms of the different unions and minglings; the former, a christological blending that inclines to the good; the latter, an anti-christological union with sin and death.

According to the Christian story, however, humanity's tragic demise provides the occasion for a dramatic presentation of God's "exceeding goodness."[148] Of course, this dramatic presentation is the event of the Word's humanization, comprising both

141. *Cat. or.* 5.
142. *Cat. or.* 5.
143. *Cat. or.* 5.
144. *Cat. or.* 6.
145. *Cat. or.* 6.
146. *Cat. or.* 6.
147. *Cat. or.* 8.
148. *Cat. or.* 8.

his life and his death. Gregory again concedes that it is particularly this element of Christian faith that appears to be "unbefitting a right conception of God."[149] His response to this challenge includes both a radical critique of prevalent conceptions of divine transcendence and a positive christological reconstruction of these conceptions. On the side of critique, Gregory insinuates that those who believe the incarnation to be unworthy of God have been misled by misanthropic self-loathing into a distorted notion of the good. Fundamental to Gregory's critique of this misguided conception of transcendence is his further development of the distinction between ontological hierarchy and moral polarity, which we have already seen in *Against Eunomius*.[150] Those who mock the notion of a divine incarnation strictly conflate the two, as if the union of the divine nature with a lower level of being constitutes a detraction from the good. Gregory insists, however, that the polarity of good and evil cannot be simply superimposed on the hierarchy of being. The key, he insists, is "to consider what real goodness and its contrary are, and by what distinctive marks each is known. . . . One thing alone in the universe is by nature shameful and that is the malady of evil, while no shame at all attaches to what is alien to evil."[151] In effect, Gregory insists that the discussion of the divine fittingness of the incarnation must take place on the level of the moral polarity between good and evil, rather than between the ontological hierarchy of intelligible and sensible. Within the framework of this strictly moral polarity, he challenges his opponents either to declare that human nature is intrinsically evil or to admit that it is good. If human nature is good, the incarnation will not be unfitting for God, since "everything we see included in the good is fitting to God."[152]

His posing of this dilemma in these particular terms exposes Gregory of Nyssa's ulterior motive in dwelling upon the goodness of human nature earlier in the treatise. Defending the goodness of human nature prepares for a presentation of the incarnation as "befitting of God." The correlation between the two doctrines is made explicit when Gregory turns from anthropology to the incarnation itself. At this juncture he characterizes as misanthropic those who reject the incarnation because they consider it unfitting for God: "But our opponents ridicule human nature . . . as if it were unbecoming for God to share in and to have contact with human life by entering it in such a way."[153] In the course of asserting the fittingness of the incarnation, Gregory's rehabilitation of a devalued estimation of human nature even includes an insistence that the sexual organs are not only not shameful, but indeed are more honorable than the other organs, since they perpetuate life and "war against death." Therefore, it is not unfitting for God to be united with human sexual organs: "What unfitting notion, then, does our religion contain, if God was united with human life by the very means by which our nature wars on death?"[154] Gregory's defense of human genitalia

---

149. *Cat. or.* 9.
150. See above, 181–82.
151. *Cat. or.* 9.
152. *Cat. or.* 9.
153. *Cat. or.* 28.
154. *Cat. or.* 28.

represents a maximal application of his strategy of dismantling the conflation of moral polarity and ontological hierarchy. Not only is the opposition between good and evil not reducible to that between the intelligible and the sensible, but the rejection of the union of intelligible and sensible in human nature is literally demonic. It was the devil who first took offense at this christological dimension of human being and was thus motivated to deceive humanity. In its union of intelligible and sensible aspects, human nature is entirely good insofar as it is constructed with an innate capacity to share in divine goodness and with the power to intentionally and freely participate in this goodness. The opposite of goodness is thus not any level of the ontological hierarchy but the willful rejection of the opportunity to participate in divine goodness. The communicability of divine goodness, in both its trinitarian and christological aspects, and its anthropological correlative, humanity's structural capacity to share in that goodness, are central to this whole vision.

"But, they object, is not human nature paltry and circumscribed, while the divinity is infinite?"[155] In confronting this objection, Gregory moves from dismantling the conflation of moral polarity and ontological hierarchy to exploring the appropriateness of the incarnation strictly from within the framework of ontological hierarchy. He has tried to persuade his readers that there is nothing about the incarnation that detracts from divine goodness. The opposite of good is only evil, and there is nothing evil about the union of divinity with human nature. The present objection, however, asks whether, apart from the moral framework of good and evil, there is still something unbecoming and finally unintelligible in the christological collapsing of the ontological hierarchy. We are no longer dealing within the framework of good and evil but of infinite and finite, the uncircumscribable majesty of the divine nature as contrasted with the enclosed littleness of human nature.

Gregory presents two responses to this challenge. The first retrieves a motif that we saw him use earlier in *Against Eunomius*, and which was also prominent in Athanasius. This is the construction of an ontology based on the God-creation polarity as conceived in terms of the Stoic framework of activity-passivity.[156] Repeating the gist of Athanasius's argument in *On the Incarnation*, Gregory contends that the incarnation does not mitigate the stance of divine activity but simply manifests it in the language of the human condition. The divinity of Christ is manifest in his "activities" (*tas energeias*), "the wonders evident in his actions" (*ta kata tas energeias thaumata*).[157] The second response also transposes the logic of *On the Incarnation* but uses that logic to articulate a more explicit christological redefinition of divine nature. Athanasius had also contended against the notion that it was unfitting to attribute absolute divinity to one who became human and suffered humiliation on the cross. He countered that critique by presenting the central characterization of the divine nature as love for humanity, *philanthrōpia*. The cross is a genuine sign of true divinity because it is a

---

155. *Cat. or.* 10.
156. See above, 180.
157. *Cat. or.* 12.

manifestation of the salvific power of this divine *philanthrōpia*, which overcomes the weakness of human sin and death. Gregory retrieves both Athanasius's logic and its rhetorical framework of the seeming weakness of the cross manifesting the strength of divine love. He poses the question of the correspondence between the majesty of divine nature and the "humiliation" of the cross in this way: "Why, then, they ask, did the divine stoop to such humiliation? Our faith falters when we think that God, the infinite, incomprehensible, ineffable reality, transcending all glory and majesty, should be defiled by associating with human nature, and his sublime powers no less debased by their contact with what is abject."[158] It is the recurring question of how the christological narrative can be compatible with a respectable notion of divine primacy and transcendence. Gregory begins his response to this question by recalling the Athanasian motif of *philanthrōpia*: "If the love of humanity is a proper mark of the divine nature, here is the explanation you are looking for, here is the reason for God's presence among human beings."[159] But he continues with a more explicit and focused critique and reconstruction of categories of divine transcendence. Explicating divine "power" as the communicability of divine goodness, he now emphasizes the christological-soteriological manifestation of that goodness.[160] Divine power should not be construed negatively, in terms of God's incapacity to extend his act of existence to the inferior ontological realm. It is not even primarily manifest in the divine work of creation and preservation, whereby divine majesty presides over these lower realms from a safe distance, as it were. Rather, the supreme manifestation of divine power is the loving self-abasement of God in choosing to share the lowliness of the human condition. This claim brings to its culmination Gregory's project of a christological reconstruction of divine transcendence:

> In the first place, that the omnipotent nature was capable of descending to man's lowly position is a clearer evidence of power than great and supernatural miracles. For it somehow accords with God's nature and is consistent with it, to do great and sublime things by divine power. It does not startle us to hear it said that the whole creation, including the invisible world, exists by God's power, and is the realization of his will. But descent to man's lowly position is a supreme example of power, a power that is not bounded by circumstances contrary to its nature. . . . God's transcendent power is not so much displayed in the vastness of the heavens, or the luster of the stars, or the orderly arrangement of the universe or his perpetual oversight of it, as in his condescension to our weak nature. We marvel at the way the Godhead was entwined in human nature and, while becoming man, did not cease to be God.[161]

158. *Cat. or.* 14.
159. *Cat. or.* 15 (altered).
160. Barnes's analysis of the theme of divine power, *dynamis*, gives a magisterial account of the significance of this notion for Gregory's understanding of Trinitarian relations and divine creativity—thus elucidating the connections between these two themes—but largely leaves out of account this christological-soteriological dimension. See Barnes, *Dynamis*.
161. *Cat. or.* 24. This passage has a mutually illuminating relationship to *C. Eun.* 3.3.34–35, discussed above, 177–79.

In *Against Eunomius*, we noted the primacy of the characterization of God as the Absolute Good. In his *Catechetical Oration*, Gregory defends the Christian faith as revelatory of "a fitting conception of God" by insisting on the communicability of divine goodness both within the divine being and outwardly. This then encompasses modern categories of both trinitarian doctrine and Christology, as well as soteriology and anthropology. At the heart of the Christian conception of God is the christological narrative, wherein divine goodness and power are revealed in a startlingly unexpected fashion, not in the first place in the work of creative and providential causality but in the manifestation of God's loving condescension in solidarity with human weakness. At the same time, the systematic effort to rationalize such an act of loving self-humbling as "worthy of God" involves a radical linking of creation and especially humanity with the goodness of God. Just as divine goodness is interpreted christologically, so is human goodness interpreted as the human aptitude for "mingling" with the divine, a mingling that achieves its consummation in sacramental communion with Christ.[162] The appearance of Christ thus represents the intersection of both divine and human goodness and the fulfillment of the latter. The fact that Gregory spends most of his argument on this christological manifestation shows that he considers this to be the center of the distinctly Christian conception of God. But he began his exposition of the Christian doctrine of God by insisting on the distinct *hypostaseis* within the one divine nature. There is a certain givenness about this trinitarian identification of God that simply arises from the christological narrative. Significantly, Gregory's efforts at explanation are focused not so much on the three-in-oneness of divine being but on the goodness of God as distinctly interpreted by the christological manifestation. Anticipating this exposition in his opening presentation of the doctrine of the three *hypostaseis*, Gregory identifies both Son and Spirit with divine goodness: the Word is identified as a subsistent agent who wills whatever is good and whose good work is this world,[163] and the Spirit as the one who "always chooses the good and has the power corresponding to its will in fulfilling every purpose."[164]

Theology of the Holy Spirit

In his explicitly anti-Eunomian works, as well as in the *Catechetical Oration*, Gregory of Nyssa's focus is centered on the divine-human identity of Jesus Christ as determining the Christian conception of God. But in the early 380s, roughly contemporaneously with the composition of both *Against Eunomius* and the *Oration*, Gregory responds to the Macedonian doctrine that acknowledged the full divinity of the Son but denied the same status to the Spirit. Gregory's anti-Macedonian treatment of the Holy Spirit may be considered intermediately between his consideration of the Spirit in *Against Eunomius* and in his treatises dealing with practical spirituality, which were written

---

162. *Cat. or.* 33–37; see below, 235–39 ("Christian Life in the Trinity").
163. *Cat. or.* 1.
164. *Cat. or.* 2.

during the last decades of his life. Each of these contexts brings out a different aspect of Gregory's understanding of the character of the Spirit and his role in Christian life.

In *Against Eunomius*, Gregory reactively follows Eunomius's own preoccupation with the doctrine of God in general terms, and specifically with the relation between Father and Son. We have seen that in reacting against Eunomius's theology, Gregory pursues a conception of God that allows for a complex simplicity and dismantles Eunomius's association of the passibility of the incarnate Word with an attenuated divinity. So the treatise focuses on the Father-Son relation. But Gregory does sound several key themes in this treatise that will be elaborated in his more developed teaching on the Spirit.[165] Like the Father and the Son, the Spirit is perfect in his goodness and power, as well as other attributes of the divine nature, and so shares in the simplicity of the divine essence.[166] Consequently, Gregory rejects as blasphemous Eunomius's conception of the Spirit as "subordinate" to Father and Son.[167] If the Spirit's possession of goodness is not substantial and perfect, then he will be always in need of goodness and not the dispenser of goodness. In that case, the invocation of the Spirit in baptism could not effect the regeneration that comes from participation in divine goodness.[168]

Also like Father and Son, the Spirit is a distinct subsistence (*hypostasis*), and the distinction of his being is constituted by the order of causality within the divine essence. In large part, Gregory is content to delineate this distinction merely by contrast with the Father and the Son: "His most particular characteristic is that he is neither of those things which we contemplate in the Father and the Son respectively. He is simply, neither as unbegotten nor as only-begotten; this is what constitutes his chief particularity."[169] More positively, the Spirit can be distinguished as the one who "is manifested by means of the Son" (*dia tou huiou pephēnenai*).[170] The Son seems to have a causal role in the procession of the Spirit, such that it can be said that the Son is prior to the Spirit in terms of the order of causation.[171] The nature of that priority is not explained any more precisely, but Gregory insists that it does not amount to an ontological inferiority of the Spirit. On the other hand, the coordination of the being and operations of the Son and Spirit is manifest in the co-presencing of Son and Spirit in believers: Christ "shines in souls by means of the Holy Spirit."[172] The latter notion is glossed by a reference to 1 Corinthians 12:3, an important text for Gregory's insistence on the co-activity of Christ and the Spirit as indicative of their coexistence: "No one can say 'Jesus is Lord' except by the Holy Spirit." The Spirit is

---

165. For a detailed exposition of Gregory's treatment of the Spirit in *C. Eun*, see further Pottier, *Dieu et le Christ*, 313–77.

166. *C. Eun*. 1.161.

167. *C. Eun*. 1.196.

168. *C. Eun*. 1.288.

169. *C. Eun*. 1.279–80 (ET: NPNF[2] 5:61, altered).

170. *C. Eun*. 1.280.

171. *C. Eun*. 1.690. Given the lack of clear definition applied to that causal priority in Gregory, one should hesitate to designate him anachronistically as a proponent of the *filioque*; see the balanced discussion of this point in Pottier, *Dieu et le Christ*, 362.

172. *C. Eun*. 1.531.

further characterized as the one who inspires the Scriptures, and this inspiration is associated with the Spirit's mediating to humanity the relationship ("the supercelestial dialogue") of Father and Son.[173] The life of Christian virtue can be globally characterized as "the life which is indicated by the Spirit."[174]

While Eunomian theology was predicated on a strict unitarianism, the "Macedonians" acknowledged the full and equal divinity of both Father and Son while denying that status to the Holy Spirit.[175] Like the *tropici* with whom Athanasius argued, the Macedonians contended that the Scriptures do not explicitly attribute the title "God" to the Spirit and cited scriptural texts that seemed to impute a creaturely status to the Spirit, principally among them Amos 4:13 (LXX), "I am the one who establishes thunder and creates *pneuma* and declares to people his Christ." As we indicated in the case of the *tropici*, the Macedonians gave maximal significance to the scriptural attribution of divinity to the Son and were able to conceive of the relation of generation between Father and Son as constitutive of a shared divinity, but they could not go further to conceive of a relation between the Spirit and the Father that would communicate full divinity to the Spirit, while not being simply another generation. Gregory's response to the Macedonians involved him in retrieving some of his fundamental points on the Spirit's sharing in the simplicity of the divine essence. But given the common ground with the Macedonians on the point of the full divinity of the Son, he was led to extend his reflections on the Spirit to a more focused treatment of the Spirit's relation to the Son.

Gregory of Nyssa's defense of the full divinity of the Spirit against the Macedonians is articulated in two short treatises dating from the early 380s: *Against the Macedonians on the Holy Spirit* and *To Eustathius*. As in *Against Eunomius*, the foundational premise of Gregory's conception of the full divinity of the Spirit is the reiteration of the principle that variations in divinity are logically inconceivable. As we have already noted, this principle follows upon the strict conflation of the categories of divinity and perfection, such that divine simplicity is defined in turn as non-variability with regard to perfection: "Once our minds have grasped the idea of divinity, we accept by the implication of that very name the perfection in it of every conceivable thing that befits the divinity. For divinity possesses perfection in every way that pertains to the conception of the good. If it fails and comes short of perfection in any single point, in that point the conception of divinity will be impaired, so that it cannot in that case be or be called divinity at all."[176] Armed with this conception of the simplicity of divine perfection, Gregory presents his opponents with an ultimatum: the Spirit either is not divine at all or is perfectly and thus fully divine. Gregory simply asserts that "the Scriptures and the fathers" ascribe divinity to the Spirit, though he

---

173. *C. Eun.* 3.5.14.

174. *C. Eun.* 3.5.10. In general, *C. Eun.* 3.5.1–31 represents a notable qualification to Pottier's observation that "the theme of Christian life in the Spirit is less developed" in Gregrory's treatise against Eunomius (my translation). See Pottier, *Dieu et le Christ*, 377.

175. On Macedonian theology, see, further, Hanson, *Search*, 760–72; Simonetti, *La crisi*, 480–85.

176. *Spir.*; GNO 3.1.91 (ET: NPNF² 5:316, altered).

does not refer to specific scriptural texts. His main strategy is rather to rely on the all-or-nothing ultimatum that comes with his conception of divine perfection, and he seems confident that his opponents will shrink from agreeing to strip the Spirit of all divine attributes. This strategy indicates that Gregory sees the essential issue in the debate about the Spirit's divinity to be not scriptural proof-texting but the logical impossibility of ascribing some divine titles to the Spirit while withholding the attribution of full and perfect divinity. Positively, Gregory characterizes the Spirit as fully, and thus infinitely, sharing all the divine attributes: "His perfection in everything good is absolutely infinite and uncircumscribed."[177]

In *To Eustathius*, Gregory of Nyssa also cites the principle that the unity of nature among the trinitarian persons is deducible from the identity of operations or activities (*dia tōn energeiōn*).[178] But it is interesting that when he faces the objection, in *Against the Macedonians*, that the Scriptures refer the title "Creator" to both Father and Son but not to the Spirit, he does not try to argue directly that the Scriptures ascribe creative activity to the Spirit. Instead, he argues from the theoretical principle of the inseparability of the divine persons and their common agency and tries to embarrass his opponents with the question: "What was the Holy Spirit doing when the Father was at work with the Son upon creation?"[179] It might seem that there is a certain circularity here between positing the unity of nature on the basis of the identity of operations and then basing the identity of operations on the inseparability of the persons. But Gregory does in fact go on to argue for the identity of operations. Perhaps in keeping with an Origenian tradition, Gregory's insertion of the Spirit into the trinitarian identity of operations tends to take its point of departure not so much from scriptural accounts of creation but rather in the trinitarian pattern of the Christian believer's relation to God: "As it is impossible to rise to the Father, unless our thoughts are lifted up there through the Son, so it is impossible also to say that Jesus is Lord except by the Spirit."[180] The unity of operations in the order of sanctification is thus read back into the order of creation. So only after reciting the trinitarian order of humanity's redeemed relation to God does Gregory return to the assertion of the trinitarian pattern of divine creative activity: "The fountain of power is the Father and the power of the Father is the Son and the spirit of that power is the Holy Spirit and creation is entirely ... the achievement of the divine power."[181] Creation is then conceived as "a transmission of power beginning from the Father, advancing through the Son, and completed in the Spirit."[182]

If Gregory of Nyssa gives a certain priority to the order of redemption in revealing the divine creative agency of the Spirit, it is specifically the sacramental event of baptism that his anti-Macedonian writings treat most extensively as a manifestation of

177. *Spir.*; GNO 3.1.94 (ET: NPNF[2] 5:318, altered).
178. *Eus.*; GNO 3.1.11.
179. *Eus.*; GNO 3.1.98.
180. *Eus.*; GNO 3.1.98 (ET: NPNF[2] 5:319, altered).
181. *Eus.*; GNO 3.1.100 (ET: NPNF[2] 5:320, altered).
182. *Eus.*; GNO 3.1.100.

the inseparable operations of Father, Son, and Spirit. It stands to reason that baptism should be so especially emphasized in this particular polemical context. The Macedonians assented to the mutual correlativity, in both theological and logical terms, of the Father-Son relation. From a logical-linguistic point of view, the very name "Spirit" seemed to indicate that his connection to the Father-Son relation was extrinsic. The baptismal formula, however, included all three names in the same invocation and thus provided a sacramentally authorized logic, sanctioned by dominical command, of the connection of all three names. The assertion of such a sacramental logic includes foundationally an insistence on the epistemological primacy of the baptismal formula itself. It was Basil who had developed this sacramental epistemology in the course of his treatise *On the Holy Spirit*.[183] The fundamental principle of this approach is to insist on a chain of continuity between knowledge of God, participation in divine life, and the material form of the sacramental event that initiates and actualizes that participation (i.e., the baptismal formula of the triune name). The form of the baptismal formula is thus interpreted as directly indicating the "form" of divine life, which is communicated through the rite. The baptismal invocation reliably names the divine life that is communicated to the baptizand through a single divine agency: "The grace flows down in an unbroken stream from the Father, through the Son and Spirit, upon the persons worthy of it."[184] If the Spirit is a co-agent in this life-giving power, the Spirit must share fully in the perfect divinity of Father and Son.

Gregory's reflections on the Spirit's identity from the point of view of the baptismal rite lead him to two further characterizations. Both approach the Spirit's identity from the perspective of his relation to Christ. The first takes up a motif originally constructed by Irenaeus, that the very name of "Christ" designates his relation to the Spirit. For Irenaeus, this designation of Jesus referred to the whole Trinity: the one who is anointed (the Christ), the one who anoints (the Father), and the anointing itself (the Spirit).[185] As would be expected in a post-Nicene setting, Gregory offers a more extensive and precise analysis of how this title indicates the ontological immediacy between Son and Spirit, an analysis that involves a paradigmatic exposition of the move from trinitarian economy to trinitarian theology. Gregory begins by exegeting the title "Christ" as referring specifically to the anointing of Jesus by the Holy Spirit, invoking Acts 10:38, "God anointed Jesus of Nazareth with the Holy Spirit." He goes on to draw out the biblical symbolism of "anointing" as indicating appointment to kingship. In the case of Christ, this kingship is not merely provisional and functional but must be understood ontologically, as a reference to his absolute "kingly nature," his divinity. But if Christ's divine kingship thus involves the anointing by the Spirit, then the lordship of the Spirit is constitutive of the lordship of Christ. The anointing by the Spirit would not make Christ a king if the Spirit itself were not of a kingly nature. The title "Christ" is thus interpreted by Gregory as indicative of

183. Basil, *Spir.* 68.
184. *Spir.*; GNO 3.1.106.
185. *Haer.* 3.18.3.

the unbroken unity of the kingly nature among Father, Son, and Spirit: "For the Son is king and his living, substantial (*ousiōdēs*) and personal (*enypostatos*) kingship is the Holy Spirit, by whom the only-begotten Christ is christened as king of all. So if the Father is king and the only-begotten is king and the Holy Spirit is the kingship, the definition of the kingship of the Trinity is entirely one. The conception of anointing or christening thus intimates in an ineffable manner that there is no intervening gap (*diastēma*) between the Son and the Holy Spirit."[186] From the perspective of the baptizand, this means that incorporation into the kingdom of Christ necessarily involves a participation also in the "kingship" of the Spirit. The co-relation between Christ and the Spirit is ineluctably manifest in the relation between the believer and Christ: "Therefore the confession of the lordship of Christ comes about in those who attain to it by means of the Holy Spirit; on all sides, those who approach [Christ] through faith encounter the Spirit."[187]

A second and related characterization of the Spirit that we find in Gregory of Nyssa's anti-Macedonian writings, also derived from Basil, is that of the Spirit as the one who "glorifies" Father and Son.[188] In *On the Holy Spirit*, Gregory refers to the Johannine texts that speak of the mutual glorification of Father, Son, and Spirit (John 12:28; 17:4–5) and links these texts with the general scriptural portrait of the Spirit as the one who enables relation to Christ. The Spirit glorifies Christ both because he is co-constitutive of Christ's kingly nature and because he enables human recognition of Christ's lordship. In this particular context, Gregory refers specifically to the scriptural designation of the Spirit as the one who receives from the Son and "searches the deep things of God" (John 16:14; 1 Cor. 2:10). Assuming that his characterization of the Spirit's role as glorifying Father and Son will be granted, Gregory then argues that the one who glorifies must himself "possess superabundant glory."[189] There follows a characterization of the divine Trinity as a "circle" of mutual glorification: "Do you see the circle of glory revolving among those who are alike? The Son is glorified by the Spirit; the Father is glorified by the Son; again the Son has his glory from the Father and the only-begotten thus becomes the glory of the Spirit. For with what shall the Father be glorified but with the true glory of the Son, and with what shall the Son be glorified but with the majesty of the Spirit?"[190]

The characterization of the Trinity as a circle of mutual glorification is a conception that has been reintroduced into modern theology, without reference to Gregory of Nyssa, by Hans Urs von Balthasar, Wolfhart Pannenberg, and Jürgen Moltmann.[191] In the case of Gregory, this conception of intra-trinitarian glory contains within it also a theology of Christian worship and an analysis of the notions of "honoring" and

186. *Spir.*; GNO 3.1.102–3.
187. *Spir.*; GNO 3.1.103 (ET: NPNF² 5:321, altered).
188. Basil, *Spir.* 46.
189. *Spir.*; GNO 3.1.108.
190. *Spir.*; GNO 3.1.109 (ET: NPNF² 5:324, altered).
191. Balthasar, *Glory VII*, esp. 264–317; Pannenberg, *Systematic Theology*, 1:308–19; Moltmann, *Trinity and the Kingdom*, 176.

"glorifying" God. Just prior to this depiction of trinitarian mutual glorification in his *Against the Macedonians*, Gregory had stressed the divergence between the ascribing of honor among human beings and the human honoring of the divine. In immanently human transactions of honor, the one who bestows the honor in some sense adds value to the recipient of the honor, and this gesture depends on the goodwill of the one who bestows the honor. The human honoring of God, however, does not add value to the divine being but simply expresses the human acknowledgment of the intrinsic worth of the divine being. This analysis is taken a decisive step further in the conception of divine glory as an immanently intra-trinitarian event in which the human honoring of God is enfolded. The human glorification of God is not merely an acknowledgment of the intrinsic worth of the divine being but rather a participation in the mutually self-glorifying being of the Trinity. Christian worship is thus a matter of being included within "the circle" of the mutual glorification of Father, Son, and Spirit.

Gregory of Nyssa is sometimes chastised for his lack of attention to the Spirit in his treatises of practical spirituality, such as the *Commentary on the Song of Songs* and the *Life of Moses*.[192] It is largely true that in these treatises we do not find doctrinal expositions of the full divinity of the Spirit or its role in Christian salvation. But it is also true that, in keeping with the largely non-analytical tenor of these works, we do find various evocative characterizations of the Spirit *en passant*. In the *Life of Moses*, the economic co-activity of Son and Spirit is vividly evoked when the Spirit is pictured as "the divine finger" that carved the flesh of the Word.[193] Divine grace "flourishes through the Spirit,"[194] and the grace of the Spirit is what guides the worthy toward the Good.[195] But it is especially in the *Commentary on the Song of Songs* that we find the Spirit portrayed in a richly pluriform set of motifs, as the divine agent of revelation, adoption, and human purification. The Spirit reveals "the hidden mysteries in our Lord Jesus Christ."[196] Those who turn to the true God and receive "the properties of the divine nature" are "warmed by the Spirit and by the beams of the Word."[197] The Spirit inspires the scriptural word and enables the transformative contemplation of Scripture so that "the living Word" might penetrate the prayerful reader of Scripture[198] and the divine law might be written into the human heart.[199] The characterization of the Spirit as "Spirit of adoption" continues the theme of the co-presencing of Christ and the Spirit in the believer. The bride/soul becomes a sister of the Son when she is "adopted into this kinship by the Spirit of sonship and delivered from communion with the daughters of the false father."[200] A related motif is that of divine "begetting,"

192. Meredith, "Pneumatology of the Cappadocians," 208.
193. *Vit. Mos.* 2.216.
194. *Vit. Mos.* 2.187.
195. *Vit. Mos.* 2.121.
196. *Comm. Cant.* 4.
197. *Comm. Cant.* 5.
198. *Comm. Cant.* 12.
199. *Comm. Cant.* 14.
200. *Comm. Cant.* 4. On the complex gender characterizations in Gregory's *Commentary*, as illustrated in this passage, see Coakley, "Re-Thinking Gregory of Nyssa."

which Gregory directly attributes to the Spirit.[201] A model disciple becomes "a child of the Holy Spirit" who "pours out the wine of the Word" and exudes, through her virtues, "the fragrance of Christ."[202] Gregory typically associates the Spirit especially with purity and the self-transcendence of orienting human desire to God.[203] The Spirit enables the believer to be conformed to the purity of Christ, the bridegroom. While purity of life is thus especially appropriated to the Spirit, it is still an activity in which the Spirit acts with the Father and the Son.[204] The spiritual life is globally characterized as life in the Spirit; the spiritual person is one who "lives by the Spirit, is conformed to the Spirit, and by the Spirit puts to death the works of the body."[205] On the collective level, the Spirit's gifts constitute the body of the church.[206]

At the conclusion of the *Commentary on the Song of Songs*, we find an important representation of the Spirit that both retrieves and significantly develops earlier motifs. The exegetical occasion is provided by Song of Songs 6:9, "My dove is one, my perfect one; she is the one of her mother, chosen by the one who bore her." Gregory interprets the reference to the oneness of the dove as the unity of the church, which is "united into one and single good by the unity of the Holy Spirit."[207] He then combines this characterization of the Spirit with the motif of the trinitarian "circle of glory," which we saw earlier in *Against the Macedonians*. But now the representation of the mutual glorification of Christ and the Spirit is integrated with a kind of "Spirit Christology" such as we saw in Athanasius. In Gregory's version, the mutual glorification of Christ and the Spirit is extended through the incarnation to include Christ's human disciples. Thus Gregory understands the Spirit to be the glory of which the Johannine Jesus speaks when he prays to the Father on behalf of his disciples, "The glory that you have given me, I have given them" (John 17:22). Gregory explains that this glory was given to the disciples when Christ gave them the Holy Spirit. In this way, Christ's eternal divine glorification by the Spirit was extended to humanity through his own human reception of this glorification: "He received this glory which he always had prior to the existence of the world when he put on the human nature. Since that human nature was glorified by the Spirit, the distribution of the glory of the Spirit came upon all who had kinship with him, beginning with the disciples. Therefore, he says, 'The glory which you have given me I have given to them, that they may be one even as we are one, I in them and you in me, that they may become perfectly one' (John 17:22–23)."[208]

While not claiming to provide an exhaustive analysis of Gregory of Nyssa's theology of the Holy Spirit, the preceding section highlights some of Gregory's key notions

201. *Comm. Cant.* 7.
202. *Comm. Cant.* 14.
203. Cf. *Comm. Cant.* 12–13.
204. *Comm. Cant.* 10.
205. *Comm. Cant.* 4.
206. *Comm. Cant.* 7.
207. *Comm. Cant.* 15.
208. *Comm. Cant.* 15.

regarding the Spirit. In his anti-Eunomian polemic, he associates the Spirit with the simplicity of the divine attributes and the unity of divine activity. In his anti-Macedonian polemics, he stresses the co-agency of Christ and the Spirit in the life of sanctification that begins with baptism and in the divine work of creation. Especially distinctive is his emphasis on the Spirit as constitutive of the "kingship" of Christ and as integral to the inner-trinitarian circle of glory into which the baptized are initiated. His later works of practical spirituality portray the Spirit as an agent of revelation, the granter of adoption, and the guide and enabler of human purification. Finally, the humanity of the incarnate Word, inasmuch as it shares through the unity of Christ in the eternal glorification of the Word by the Spirit, enables humanity to share in that glory.

Defining the Trinity? Three *Hypostaseis*, One *Ousia*

It has been my premise throughout this study that the language of *hypostasis* and *ousia* has been saddled with a disproportionate share in the burden of carrying the intelligibility of trinitarian doctrine. This language has been traditionally vaunted as the "Cappadocian resolution," which ushered in the close of the "Arian" controversies by positing distinct terminology for what is one and what is three in God. Recent accounts have qualified this picture by adverting to the broader set of terms by which the Cappadocians denoted divine unity and distinction.[209] But even this valuable corrective can perpetuate the perception that the Cappadocian settlement consisted principally in the creation of distinct sets of vocabulary for threeness and unity in God, though admittedly containing more terms than the *hypostasis-ousia* pairing. Such an approach makes it seem almost as if this terminological organization itself enabled trinitarian belief, as if everyone agreed that God was both three and one but just needed to find the appropriate terminology in order to subscribe to this belief. But, of course, *hypostasis-ousia* language and other terms denoting unity and distinction did not make it possible to believe that God is triune nor even to concretely conceptualize that belief. They were simply *a posteriori* logical-linguistic maneuvers that followed upon the belief concerning Father, Son, and Spirit that each is fully God and together they are one God. Linguistic frameworks demarcating unity and distinction are not the inner shrine of the meaning of trinitarian doctrine but a set of logical regulators that safeguard the contents of that meaning. The proper signification of *hypostasis-ousia* and kindred language is not to be found in its references to abstract logical categories of unity and difference but in its connections with the scriptural, liturgical, and soteriological conceptions and performances of how Father, Son, and Spirit are each fully God and together one God. In order to arrive at such a contextual and systematic understanding of Gregory's account of trinitarian unity and

209. See especially Lienhard, "*Ousia* and *Hypostasis*." Barnes (*Dynamis*) has successfully demonstrated the centrality of *dynamis* language in Gregory's trinitarian theology, and his insights have been presumed at various points in the present account.

distinction, we need to follow his presentation of this issue through several writings bearing distinct emphases: his account of trinitarian unity and distinction in *Against Eunomius*, his discussion of the notion of *hypostasis* in the *Catechetical Oration*; his exposition of nature/person language in *Epistle* 38; and, finally, his rebuttal of the charge of tritheism in *To Ablabius*.

Against Eunomius *1.267–94*

An important example of Gregory of Nyssa's systematic treatment of *ousia-hypostasis* language occurs in the first book of *Against Eunomius*.[210] In this context, Gregory's point of departure is Eunomius's insistence on the differences between Father, Son, and Spirit as constituting different substances and occupying different levels in the hierarchy of being. The meaning of Gregory's use of *hypostasis-ousia* language in this context is strictly dependent on this problematic and is generated by Gregory's efforts to locate the differences between Father, Son, and Spirit within the differentiations of the hierarchy of being considered comprehensively. Thus the character of trinitarian hypostatic difference is designated in light of an ontology centered on three themes: the identification of God as the Absolute Good; the difference and relation between God and creation; and the content of differences at various levels of the hierarchy of being. The goal is to demonstrate the validity of his own account of trinitarian differences of *hypostaseis* within a common nature over against the Eunomian account of a difference of nature between Father, Son, and Spirit. The ultimate verification that Gregory provides for his own account of trinitarian difference is a soteriological one: only this account provides for authentic hope in a baptismal regeneration that binds the human being to the divine.

The first structural difference cited by Gregory in his account of the hierarchy of being is that between the intelligible and the sensible. He then immediately proceeds to clarify the character of difference within each of these levels of being respectively. Purely material differences come about through variation in physical properties such as quantity and quality; though he does not mention Aristotle by name, these are the Aristotelian "accidents."[211] In the intelligible world, the ultimate content of all difference is variation according to degree of intentional participation in the First Good, who is God. In fact, creation's participation in the First Good is really the ultimate content of the God-world relation as such: "The source and origin and supply of every good is regarded in the uncreated nature and the whole creation inclines toward it, clinging to and participating in the supreme nature by sharing in the First Good."[212] In the realm of the intelligible, differences arise with respect to the quality and depth of such participation as the result of the exercise of free will. The uncreated nature, however, inasmuch as it is strictly defined as the Good itself, cannot admit of any such difference with respect to the possession of goodness. At this point, Gregory is

---

210. This is equivalent to section 22 in the translation in NPNF[2] 5.
211. Cf. Aristotle, *Cat.* 4b–6a.
212. *C. Eun.* 1.274 (ET: NPNF[2] 5:60, altered).

careful to enlist Eunomius's own agreement as to the coincidence of the categories of uncreated nature, the absolute good, and absolute simplicity: "The uncreated nature is far from such difference [with respect to the good] since it does not possess the good by acquiring it nor receive into itself the beautiful (*to kalon*) by participating in a higher Beauty. In its own nature it is and is perceived as good and is attested even by our opponents to be the source of goodness, simple, uniform, and uncompounded."[213]

Having come to this common agreement with his opponents on the simplicity of the uncreated nature and its coextensiveness with the Good, Gregory can now frame the question of trinitarian difference as a choice between two alternatives: either these are differences *within* the uncreated nature that do not harm the simple goodness of that nature or they are differences that straddle the Creator-creature divide and thus represent variation in goodness. In the latter case, such variation would necessarily entail an admixture of the good and its opposite, thereby introducing the privation of goodness into the Trinity itself! Rhetorically, Gregory relies in part on the shock value of his bald assertion that the Eunomian position amounts to positing a privation of goodness within the Trinity. But he also extends the argument in a soteriological direction, echoing Athanasius's assertion that if the Son is not essentially divine then he cannot impart the divine aid of salvation inasmuch as he himself would be the recipient rather than the giver of such aid. If Son and Spirit are not essentially good, then they will lack the capacity to impart goodness to creatures.[214] For his own part, Gregory concludes this section of his argument by insisting that trinitarian differences of *hypostasis* must be located within the common goodness of the uncreated nature, which is to be "conceived as utterly perfect and incomprehensibly transcendent, while possessing unconfused and clear differentiation with respect to each of the *hypostaseis* according to their inherent properties (*idiōmasin*)."[215] Thus only the Father is unbegotten (*agen[n]ētos*); only the Son is only-begotten; while the Spirit is distinguished apophatically as neither unbegotten nor only-begotten, but "simply is," deriving his existence from the Father and being manifested through the Son. These characteristics are incommunicable and particular to the *hypostaseis*, who nevertheless share equally in being uncreated, essentially good, and thus "independent of all external goodness."[216]

A close reading of *Against Eunomius* 1.267–94 reveals the impoverishment of a non-contextual analysis of the purely logical relations of the language of distinction and unity or an approach that privileges analogical sites abstracted from the overarching theological arguments that surround and condition them. Moreover, contrary to the notion that the Greek fathers "start with the persons," we see here that the logical point of departure for Gregory is very much the divine nature. Indeed, far from denigrating the logic of natures in general in the style of some modern existentialism, Gregory begins with a comprehensive taxonomy of the fundamental differences of nature within the hierarchy of being, of which the most radical is the

213. *C. Eun.* 1.276 (ET: NPNF² 5:60–61, altered).
214. *C. Eun.* 1.285–89.
215. *C. Eun.* 1.277 (ET: NPNF² 5:61, altered).
216. *C. Eun.* 1.278–80 (ET: NPNF² 5:61, altered).

difference between the uncreated nature, conceived as the first and essential Good, and created natures, whose being and well-being depend on participation in essential goodness. Since the biblical narrative provides Christians with the different names of Father, Son, and Spirit, Gregory endeavors to locate these differences within his comprehensive framework of differences of nature. Moving from ontological to soteriological frameworks, he argues that the differences between Father, Son, and Spirit must stand according to the specific designations provided by the biblical narrative (unbegotten, only-begotten, neither unbegotten nor only-begotten) but must be located within the simplicity of the uncreated and essential goodness. The meaning of *hypostasis-ousia* language in this passage is generated and conditioned by this whole framework. God's nature is to be understood as essential goodness, causative of the participated goodness by which creation subsists and thrives and by which human beings are created, sustained, and granted new birth through baptismal life. The divine persons (*hypostaseis*), who are agents of the imparting of divine goodness in the sacramental event of baptism, constitute differences *within* the essential divine goodness yet not differences of goodness itself.

The Catechetical Oration

We have seen that the *Catechetical Oration* claims to present an account of the Christian conception of God as an alternative to the deficiencies and misconceptions of both Hellenism and Judaim. A Hellenistic view differs from Christianity in its proclivities toward both atheism and polytheism. Atheism is unintelligible in light of the orderly arrangement of creation, and polytheism is untenable in light of the logically necessary conflation of the categories of "divinity" and "perfection." "For if he grants that perfection is to be entirely attributed to the subject of our discussion, and yet claims that there are many perfect beings with the same characteristics, this follows: In the case of things marked by no differences but considered to have identical attributes, it is absolutely essential for him to show the particularity (*to idion*) of each. Or else, if the mind cannot conceive differentiation in cases where there is no variation of distinction, he must give up the idea of distinction (*diakrisin*). . . . Indeed, because the idea of God is one and the same and no particularity (*idiotētos*) can reasonably be discovered in any respect, the erroneous notion of a plurality of gods must necessarily give way to the acknowledgment of a single deity."[217] The reader of the *Catechetical Oration* might be won over by this simple logical argument but is likely to be jolted when Gregory uses the same vocabulary he has just used to refute the notion of many gods in order to proclaim a few sentences later that Christian faith discerns a "distinction of persons (*diakrisin hypostaseōn*) in the unity."[218] But the use of the same terminology to assert that difference (*diakrisin*) is both nonapplicable and applicable to the notion of the Divine actually highlights a crucial emphasis in Gregory's exposition of the conception of divinity. It is not difference

217. *Cat. or.* prol.
218. *Cat. or.* 1.

as such that is non-applicable to the divine; it is precisely difference *with respect to perfection*. What Gregory is again insisting is the conflation of the categories of divinity and perfection, such that the oneness of God is to be construed as a single perfection. Whatever differences can then be properly attributed to God, whether differences in the distinct notions involved in the different attributes or differences in persons, are not differences that fall outside the single perfection of divinity. In other words, the only differences that cross the boundary between what God is and what is not God are differences that pertain to perfection and its cognate notions, such as the Absolute Good. Thus the conflation of the categories of divinity and perfection means that the oneness of God requires only non-difference in perfection and not non-difference *tout court*. Ultimately, the essential difference that separates divinity and the created realm is not the classic Platonic difference between the one and the many but that between infinite perfection and participation in infinite perfection. Herein lies Gregory's Christian transformation of Platonic metaphysics, enabling the confession of the difference of persons in God within unity. The Christian distinction of persons does not amount to a non-intelligible difference of perfections and therefore constitutes difference *within* God and not a difference of multiple gods.

Having thus set the framework for the distinction between the untenable notion of different perfections (polytheism) and that of differentiations within a single perfection, Gregory advances to a presentation of the *hypostaseis* of the *Logos* and the Spirit. He begins his presentation of the distinct status of the *Logos* within God by asking his interlocutor to concede that God is *logikos*. Identifying God as *logikos*, in effect, would correspond both to Greek conceptions of divine rationality and Jewish conceptions of God as speaking. Gregory's next step is to anagogically differentiate the conception of God as *logikos* from human reason and speech. The primary difference is that human *logos* is manifested in temporary instances that do not have a self-standing substantiality, whereas the divine *Logos* is eternal, subsistent, and endowed with life; the divine *Logos* is a *hypostasis*. What it means to say that the *Logos* is a divine *hypostasis* is explicated by Gregory through a series of logical connections. As a divine *hypostasis*, the *Logos* is simple. In this particular instance, simplicity is not a numerical notion but a function of the framework of participation that separates God as participated from creation as participating.[219] As simple, the *Logos* possesses subsistence and life without participation. Since the *Logos* is living, he possesses will (*proairetikēn*); his will is matched by his power (*dynamis*) to act, which translates his will into activity (*energeian*); he always wills the good, and the goodness of the world is his "work" (*ergon*); the living *Logos* is active (*energon*) and creative (*poiētikon*). The Word is other than the Father, as deriving his *hypostasis* from the Father, but manifests all the attributes of divine perfection that exist in the Father: "In whatever way one indicates the conception of the Father, whether by goodness, or power, or wisdom, or eternal being, or freedom from evil, death,

219. See Balás, *Metousia*, 121–30.

and corruption, or complete perfection, by the same attributes he will recognize the Word derived from him."[220]

Gregory of Nyssa's presentation of the *hypostasis* of the *Logos* is a paragdigmatic instance of the causal series emphasized by Barnes, of *dynamis-energeia-ergon*. Gregory speaks of the "power of the Word" (*tou logou tēn dynamin*),[221] which enables his activity (*energeian*),[222] resulting in the "works" (*erga*) of creation.[223] But this causal series is embedded in and contextualized by other significant conceptions that should not be neglected. Gregory starts his depiction of the Word not with his characterization as *dynamis* nor indeed with God as productive, but with the notion of divine perfection. It is part of the logic of divine perfection, for Gregory, that God's Word should not be "unsubstantial" but "hypostatic." It should be well noted that here the very notion of *hypostasis* is seen to be integral to divine perfection, a motif that would become thematic in later Western medieval theology.[224] The point is a significant one, because while Eunomius himself might have shied, for the most part but not always, from referring to the divinity of Jesus Christ as divine "power," an earlier generation of anti-Nicenes (including Arius and Asterius) was willing to allow that scriptural designation, provided that this christic "Power" and *Logos* was differentiated from the innate divine power and *logos* that was not hypostatic.[225] These anti-Nicenes would have been able to acknowledge that God has a power intrinsic to his nature but not that this power is hypostatic. Gregory here pointedly makes the hypostatization of divine power/ word part of the anagogical ascent from creatures to the Creator. The non-hypostatic character of human rationality/speech/power is seen to reflect the weakness of the created state: "For since our nature is corruptible and weak, for this reason our life is fleeting, our power unsubstantial (*anypostatos*) and our reason unstable."[226] While the *hypostasis* of the Son is designated by a variety of descriptions (Life, Power, *Logos*, Wisdom), the most prominent term is *Logos*, and the most prominent sense of that term is spoken speech. God is characterized as a speaker (*phthengomenos*), and the perfection of God requires that his speech have hypostatic existence: "If then we attribute *logos* to God, it will not be thought to derive its subsistence from the impulse of the speaker and like our speech to pass into nonexistence. But just as our nature, by being perishable, has a *logos* that is perishable, so the incorruptible and eternal nature has a *logos* that is eternal and substantial."[227]

Closely associated with the characterization of the Word as hypostatic is the attribution to the *Logos* of the faculty of will (*proairesis*). Already, in *Against Eunomius*,

220. *Cat. or.* 1.
221. *Cat. or.* 1.
222. *Cat. or.* 1.
223. *Cat. or.* 1.
224. Cf. Aquinas, *Summa Theologiae* Iae.29.3, resp. Here Aquinas argues that the word *persona* is fittingly used of God, because "*persona* signifies what is most perfect in all of nature."
225. On Eunomius's avoidance of *dynamis* language, see Barnes, *Dynamis*, 190. On Arius and Asterius's insistence that the innate *logos* and *dynamis* of God was not hypostatic, see above, 42–59.
226. *Cat. or.* 1.
227. *Cat. or.* 1 (ET: Hardy, *Christology*, 270–71, altered).

Gregory was preoccupied with inserting a conception of will into the causal sequence of power-activity-work. He thus found it necessary to alter the standard example of the unity of a nature with its productive capacity, that of fire and its heat, by speaking of a fire that wills its own heat![228] In the *Catechetical Oration*, the emphasis on will is even more pronounced and pervasive. The characterization of the *Logos* as possessing will precedes the attribution to him of *dynamis*, and the latter qualifies the former: "If, then, the Word has life because it is life, it certainly has the faculty of will; for no living thing is without it. It is religious then to conclude that this will is potent (*dynatēn*)."[229] The mutual qualification of the categories of will and *dynamis* is further reinforced and then bound together with the characterization of God as the Good by Gregory's assertion that the Word always wills the good and is powerful to bring about an appropriate effect of his will and power, which is the good creation. In summary, Gregory's depiction of the *Logos* as a *hypostasis* in the *Catechetical Oration* begins with the characterization of God as speaking; being perfect, his speech enjoys the perfection of owning existence and life in itself and without participation; it pertains to such a self-standing existence to have its own will, which is potent, and it exercises its will and potency in producing what is good. In the *Catechetical Oration*, the category of will is decisively inserted into the causal sequence of essence-power-activity-work and closely associated with the category of *hypostasis*.

Gregory of Nyssa's depiction of the *hypostasis* of the Spirit also follows the characterization of God as speaking, drawn anagogically by reference to the analogy of human speaking. Just as the human word becomes outwardly audible by being accompanied by breath, *pneuma*, so is God's *Logos* inseparably accompanied by *Pneuma*. The perfection of God's speaking is such that the breath by which his Word is uttered is "not extraneous or alien" to him but belongs intrinsically to his being. The Spirit accompanies and "manifests the activity (*energeian*)" of the Word and is inseparable from both God the speaker and God's spoken Word. As belonging to the divine realm, the Spirit also enjoys the divine dignity of hypostatic existence. The characteristics of that existence are those we have already seen with regard to the Word: self-subsistence, faculty of will, and a power that is active and always efficaciously wills the good. "It is not dissipated into nonexistence, but like God's Word it exists in its own subsistence (*kath' hypostasin ousan*), has will (*proairetikēn*), and is self-moved and active (*energon*). It always chooses the good; and to fulfill every purpose, it has the power (*dynamin*) that corresponds to its will."[230] Once again, we find the causal sequence of *dynamis-energeia-ergon*, albeit with the latter item present only by implication. Nevertheless, this sequence is embedded in a larger framework, which notably includes the elements of will and the characterization of the whole sequence with reference to the Good.

Summarizing Gregory's characterization of divine unity and distinction in the *Catechetical Oration*, we can make the following observations. First, the unity of God

228. On this passage (*C. Eun* 2.192), see Barnes, *Dynamis*, 286–87.
229. *Cat. or.* 1 (ET: Hardy, *Christology*, 271, altered).
230. *Cat. or.* 1 (ET: Hardy, *Christology*, 273, altered).

is conceived not so much in terms of a numerical unity but primarily in terms of the characterization of the perfection of God. To say that there is one God is to designate one perfection, which can be conceived in diverse notions, such as infinite goodness, wisdom, power, and so on. Christian monotheism is first of all belief in a single divine perfection, which does not admit of variance or multiplicity *in itself*, such that there can never be more than one perfection, or greater and lesser perfection. This much Gregory argues against the polytheism of the Greeks. But, in contradistinction to the Jews, Christians believe in distinctions within divine being. These are not variations with regard to perfection itself, but distinctions within the simplicity of a single perfection. Gregory depicts these distinctions within a characterization of God as speaker. This characterization has not achieved the attention it deserves, particularly in light of modern attempts to link the Trinity to biblical notions of God speaking his Word. The most comprehensive such project is Karl Barth's attempt to image the Trinity in terms of God's revelation of himself in his Word and the accomplishment of this event in the "revealedness" of the Spirit.[231] Barth's approach cannot be simply assimilated to Gregory's terse treatment of the Word and Spirit as manifestations of divine speech. But there is also a fundamental link that becomes evident when we realize that Gregory presents the distinctions of divine being with reference to Christianity's dialogue with Judaism. At the outset of his treatise, Gregory remarks that theological exposition must be tailored to the presuppositions of one's interlocutor, "so that the truth may finally emerge from what is admitted to both sides."[232] Gregory's depiction of the *hypostaseis* of Word and Spirit in relation to human speech seems both forced and facile if this presupposition of the scriptural background is not kept in mind. Thus students routinely complain that they are unconvinced that Gregory has "proven" the Trinity by contriving such an analogy. But it must be remembered that the fundamental presupposition that Gregory is adopting in recommending divine distinctions to his imagined Jewish interlocutor is the biblical God who speaks his word in the spirit, and it is this image of the biblical, speaking God that determines the choice of the analogue of human speech. The conception of such a God in just these terms is presupposed as a given; it is not something to be proved.

As to what Gregory of Nyssa means by *hypostasis*, this passage should alert us, on the one hand, against a too facile assimilation of Gregory to a so-called "social model" of the Trinity and, on the other hand, a categorical rejection of all "personalist" elements in Gregory's conception of the divine *hypostaseis*. The analogue that Gregory chooses here is not that of "three people" but of a single speaking person. At the same time, Gregory draws the analogy only to qualify it immediately, and these qualifications emphasize the conceptions of self-subsistence, intentionality, and volition as closely associated with the notion of *hypostasis*. While Gregory clarifies elsewhere that there is one movement of will that encompasses divine being, he is equally clear here and elsewhere that this one movement is appropriated by all three *hypostaseis* such that

---

231. *Church Dogmatics* I/1, 295–347.
232. *Cat. or.* prol.

each becomes the subject of the divine will, agency, and power.[233] This might not amount to "modern conceptions of personhood," but neither does it utterly exclude some of these conceptions.[234]

Epistle 38

Epistle 38, *On the Difference between Ousia and Hypostasis*, is identified by different manuscript traditions as written by Basil and addressed to his brother Gregory of Nyssa, or as written by Gregory and addressed to his brother Peter. The overwhelming if not unanimous consensus among modern scholars sides with the latter attribution, which is presumed here.[235] With this letter and the epistle *To Ablabius: On Not Three Gods*, to be treated in the next section, we now finally arrive, it seems, at the holy grail of trinitarian doctrine, a focused and extended treatment of the language of three-in-oneness! In modern scholarship, the regnant questions regarding Gregory's appropriation of this linguistic and logical edifice are whether they indicate a merely generic unity that is vulnerable to the charge of tritheism, and what if any content they ascribe to notions of divine personhood and "communion."[236] While such questions are certainly worthy of treatment, it needs to be asked whether their dominant status in interpretations of Gregory's use of *ousia-hypostasis* language is due to a narrowly propositionalistic preconception of trinitarian doctrine. As stated at the outset of this work, one of the principal hermeneutical principles of the approach undertaken here is that doctrines truly signify the realities of divine things not directly and autonomously in their bare propositional form but precisely through the regulation of Christian discourse and action as a whole. This synthesis of effecting an objective reference (the

---

233. Cf. *Ad Ablabium*; GNO 3.1.51.

234. For an excellent treatment of the centrality of the category of will in Gregory's conception of the divine *hypostaseis*, see Barnes, "Divine Unity." I am less dismissive than Barnes of the suggestion that this conception has any common ground with modern conceptions of personhood, and I would balance his assessment that "there is nothing in Gregory's writings which require that the wills of each of the Three be conceived as separate wills" (59), which is quite correct, with the observation that there does seem to be distinct inflections of the one divine will belonging distinctly to the three *hypostaseis*. It also seems to go too much against the grain of the plain sense of the relevant passages in *Cat. or.*, as discussed above, to say that Gregory "does not use the term [*hypostasis*] to refer to or to name a subject of cognition *or volition*" (52, my italics). Along similar lines, I would qualify Ayres's assertion that Gregory "present[s] the three not as possessing distinct actions, but as together constituting *just one distinct action* (because they are one power)" (*Nicaea*, 358). Such a judgment leaves out of account statements in which Gregory distributes the one divine action distinctly among the *hypostaseis* by using different verbs, as in the passage discussed above wherein the one divine *energeia* "originates in the Father, proceeds through the Son, and is completed in the Holy Spirit" (*Ad Ablabium*; GNO 3.1.47).

235. For the arguments on behalf of Gregory's authorship, see Fedwick, "Commentary on Gregory of Nyssa."

236. On the alleged tritheism of Nyssa's understanding of the *hypostasis-ousia* framework, see Stead, "Why Not Three Gods?" Turcescu argues that Gregory is articulating a conception of communion between the divine persons; see Turcescu, "Concept of Divine Persons." This interpretation is contested by Behr (*Nicene Faith*, 2:420–22). Both Ayres (*Nicaea*, 363) and Barnes ("Divine Unity") deny that a conception of "divine personhood" can be gleaned from Gregory's thought.

reality of what is signified) and regulating the act of signification is perhaps most clearly evident in the case of *ousia-hypostasis* language. The evidence for this properly synthetic function of such language becomes manifest as soon as we take account of what happens when we neglect the distinction between these two aspects by which the doctrine achieves its meaning. When Gregory says in this epistle, "We shall not include in our evaluation of the differentiation [which delineates the distinction of *hypostaseis*] what is seen to be common, such as the attribute . . . ,"[237] he is making a regulative statement about the categorization of Christian *language* that structures the act of signification itself. He is saying in effect: let *x* (*hypostasis* language) be distinguished from *y* (*ousia* language, such as the attributes) such that *x* and *y* constitute two distinct sets of words. But the same statement cannot be understood as directly and immediately referring to the divine *being*, in which case Gregory would be saying that the *hypostaseis* of Father, Son, and Spirit *in reality* do not contain the attributes they have in common—which, of course, is nonsensical. Rather, in reality, the exact opposite is true: everything that is common to the *hypostaseis* is common precisely because it is "included" in the reality of each *hypostasis*, albeit distinctly inflected in each case.

The methodological point of the foregoing remarks is that our appropriation of Gregory of Nyssa's *ousia-hypostasis* language is misguided to the extent that we are exclusively concerned with the objective ontological "information" content of this language (i.e., does it delineate a generic unity? what exactly is the content of the category *hypostasis*?) without paying equal attention to how Gregory is actually using it to regulate the act of signifying God as Father, Son, and Spirit in the comprehensive utterance and performance of Christian faith. As it happens, if we approach the matter in the first place from a strictly literary perspective, Gregory's sentences for the most part are not objective statements of the form, "God is . . ." but rather directives about how to organize and structure our speaking and thinking of God. Our analysis of *Epistle* 38 will therefore try to follow closely that pattern in which the recommendation of *ousia-hypostasis* language is articulated not primarily in terms of *what* it means but rather in terms of *how* it regulates our speaking of God. Of course, the former is not excluded but only comes into view by proper appropriation of the latter.

There is a threefold structure discernible in this epistle. The first part (sections 1–4) notes the confusion generated by some in speaking of God as both one *ousia* and one *hypostasis* and explains Basil's principle that language of *ousia* and *hypostasis* denote respectively what is common among Father, Son, and Spirit and what is particular to each. The second part (5) presents the example of the rainbow as a creaturely illustration of unity-in-distinction. The last part (6–8) deals with the objection that Gregory's explanation of the *ousia-hypostasis* distinction does not seem to correspond to Hebrews 1:3, where Christ is called the Image of the Father's *hypostasis*. We will now briefly draw out the highlights of the argument in order to appreciate what role *ousia-hypostasis* language played in informing the meaning of trinitarian doctrine for Gregory.

237. *Ep.* 38.3.

The first part begins with a linguistic analysis, noting that the structure of language provides for distinct delineations for universals ("the common nature") and the particulars in which the common nature is individuated. The example is given of "humanity" as a word denoting the common nature (*ousia*) and "Peter, Andrew, John, or James" as words denoting individual subsistents (*hypostaseis*). Gregory then recommends applying this strategy of linguistic differentiation between what is common and what is particular to language about God. It should be immediately noted that it misses the point to speak over-hastily of "the social analogy" in this context. The analogy is not really being drawn between human "persons" and divine "persons" and human "nature" and divine "nature." Rather, the point is that just as there is a relation of common to particular in the human sphere, so is there a relation of common to particular in the divine sphere. There is no indication there that the relation of common to particular in the human sphere is proportional to the relation of common to particular in the divine sphere. Consequently, the work that this language is intended to do theologically does not reside in probing relations among human persons with reference to their common nature. Moreover, immediately after recommending that *ousia-hypostasis* language be applied theologically, Gregory goes on not to an analysis of human relationality but to generating rules for thinking and talking about Father, Son, and Spirit. The first rule is this: "Whatever conception you have about the being (*to einai*) of the Father and however you conceive that . . . you are to have the same conception about the Son and likewise about the Holy Spirit."[238] This directive again underscores the complexity of the dual aspects in the functioning of *ousia-hypostasis* language, inasmuch as this language is meant both to organize speech about God and to actually refer to God. With regard to the first function, it can be said that *ousia* language does not apply to the persons (i.e., we do not say that there are three *ousiai*). But with regard to the second function, it is obviously not the case that we deny that Father, Son, and Spirit possess being. Rather, the way that *ousia* language actually functions in referring to God as Father, Son, and Spirit is successfully indicated by Gregory's rule: all the attributes ascribed in common to Father, Son, and Spirit are indicative of the "common nature" and are thereby attributed equally to each of them; each is equally "uncreated" and "incomprehensible," for example.

As to the differentiations among the divine *hypostaseis*, once again we must notice that Gregory does not return us to the "social analogy" but prescribes another set of rules generated by the application of the *ousia-hypostasis* framework to scriptural contemplation. Here also, the characterization of the Trinity as a unity of potent Goodness is foundational. The Christian is to have in view all the work of divine benevolence under the general rubric of "everything good which comes to us from divine power."[239] Gregory then pointedly and repeatedly refers to "the Scripture" as indicating that the divine source for these good things is threefold. For the identification of the Spirit as the source of divine benevolence, Gregory cites 1 Corinthians 12:11, "But all these

238. *Ep.* 38.3.
239. *Ep.* 38.4.

things are the work of one and the same Spirit." As to the Son, "we are again guided by Scripture to the faith that the only-begotten God is the origin and cause of the supply of good things accomplished in us through the Spirit. For we have been taught by Holy Scripture that all things were made through him (John 1:3) and are constituted in him (Col. 1:17)."[240] Ascending through this scriptural contemplation, we are led to the conception of the Father as "a certain power subsisting without begetting and without beginning, who is the cause of the cause of all beings."[241] Ultimately this scriptural contemplation is what yields the "distinguishing marks" (*idiōmata*) of each *hypostasis*, which are manifest in their mutual relations. The Son "alone shines forth from the unbegotten Light as the only-begotten"[242] and "makes known the Spirit through himself and with himself."[243] The Spirit is "linked with the Son," since no one can have an appropriate conception of the Son apart from the Spirit; thus the "distinguishing mark" of the Spirit is that "he is made known after the Son and with the Son and subsists from the Father."[244] Finally, the Father's "distinguishing mark" is that "he alone subsists from no other cause."[245]

In Gregory's presentation in this epistle, the "distinguishing marks" of each of the persons are thus to be encountered through scriptural contemplation, with an implicit understanding that the order of the economic manifestation of Father, Son, and Spirit is revelatory of their immanent order. At the same time, their "common nature" is manifest in the scriptural narration of the economy of divine goodness, which is attributable to all three *hypostaseis* and thus pertains to what they have in common. It cannot be overemphasized that throughout this epistle, Gregory's perspective remains practical and epistemological. It is a "how-to" manual for trinitarian contemplation rather than merely a set of objective "information" statements about the *ousia* and the *hypostaseis*. Thus the first part of the letter ends with an extended prescription for the rules of trinitarian contemplation, wherein what came to be called the *perichōrēsis* of the persons is treated not objectively but rather subjectively in terms of the "perichoretic" structure of human contemplation of the Trinity. As in his treatment of the ontological unity of the divine *hypostasis*, so in his prescriptions for a perichoretic epistemology for the apprehension of the divine Trinity Gregory offers his characteristic caution: beware the gap (*diastēma*)! Some snippets of this little manual of the rules of trinitarian contemplation will perhaps indicate the flavor of the whole:

> However one perceives the majesty of any one of those whom faith holds to be in the Blessed Trinity, he will advance without any variation by the same thoughts to seeing the glory in the Father and the Son and in the Holy Spirit, since the mind does not traverse

240. *Ep.* 38.4.
241. *Ep.* 38.4.17–19.
242. *Ep.* 38.4.31–32.
243. *Ep.* 38.4.30–31.
244. *Ep.* 38.4.28–29.
245. *Ep.* 38.4.36–37.

any interval between the Father and the Son and the Holy Spirit. For there is nothing intruding between them ... nor is there any empty un-*hypostatic* gap that causes the harmony of the divine essence to be broken by a chasm. But the one who perceives the Father both perceives him by Himself and includes the Son in the same conception. And the one who receives the Son does not separate him from the Spirit. ... And the one who mentions only the Spirit still includes within that confession the One whose Spirit He is. ... For it is not possible in any way to conceive of a separation or division such that the Son can be thought without the Father or the Spirit severed from the Son. Rather, there is apprehended among them a certain ineffable and inconceivable communion and distinction. The distinction of *hypostaseis* does not break apart the continuity of nature nor does the communion of nature dissolve the particularities by which each is distinctly known.[246]

Having thus translated the dogmatic formulations of trinitarian doctrine into practical rules for trinitarian contemplation, Gregory proceeds in the second part of his argument (section 5) to offer the analogy of the rainbow. In light of the comments above on how the reduction of the contents of trinitarian doctrine to analogies subverts rather than enables its appropriation, it is important to identify the precise role of this analogical reasoning within Gregory's argument as a whole. To begin with, we must note its location in the sequence of the argument. It is of the highest significance that the rules for trinitarian contemplation have already been established; the reader has already been instructed on how to "think," to the degree possible for human beings, about the common essence and personal distinctions among Father, Son, and Holy Spirit. The analogy offered, then, is not meant to be itself an object of contemplation that simply replaces contemplation of the reality of Father, Son, and Spirit. Gregory begins this part of the argument with a disclaimer that dissociates the "truth" of trinitarian being from the shadow of analogy: "Receive what I say as a token and shadow of the truth, not as if it were the truth itself of these matters."[247] He then goes on to identify the specific contents of analogical correspondence in the phenomenon of the simultaneity of distinction and unity. The example he offers is that of the rainbow, and the specific aspect of correspondence is the coincidence of continuity and distinction, inasmuch as the common "essence" of the sunlight is refracted into different colors of "mutual combination" that intermingle without intervening spaces. But following this exposition of a certain objective correspondence between the "shadow" of the creaturely illustration and the "truth" of trinitarian being, Gregory proceeds to draw out an epistemological correspondence, one that pertains to the structure of the act of knowing itself. In the latter perspective, the element of correspondence lies in the relation between experienced facts and their analysis by understanding. We can be dazzled by the intermingling of colors in the rainbow without being able to analyze or rationally account for the phenomenon

246. *Ep.* 38.4.50–87.
247. *Ep.* 38.5.1–2.

that we in fact apprehend. Similarly, the experience of faith is the basis for acceptance of trinitarian doctrine and not the rational explanation of how this can be:

> This account teaches us not to be distraught with regard to matters of doctrine when we encounter what is difficult to understand and become disoriented in giving our assent to what is proposed. Just as in the realm of what is visible to the eyes, experience of a thing is manifestly greater than an account of its causation, so in the case of transcendent doctrines the faith that teaches us both the distinction according to *hypostasis* and the unity of essence is greater than comprehension by reasoning.[248]

Our tendency is to locate the analogical correspondence in Gregory of Nyssa's account exclusively in the objective aspect of the unity-within-distinction of the colors of the rainbow and to relegate the above-quoted exhortation to the level of pious admonition. However, if we simply follow the argument of the text as it stands, we should see that Gregory is identifying two equally important ways in which creaturely analogies help orient us to the truth of trinitarian doctrine. There is an objective or ontological aspect, in which a creaturely example of unity-within-distinction confirms our orientation to the real unity-within-distinction of the Trinity. Equally, too, there is an epistemological aspect, in which the transcendence of rational analysis by the sheer givenness of experience confirms us in the disposition to transcend our rational difficulties by recourse to the givenness of the experience of faith. Both these aspects together constitute an appropriate creaturely "token or shadow" of the experience of apprehending the reality of trinitarian being.

We have already seen that Gregory's depiction of a creaturely analogue for trinitarian being follows upon a set of guidelines for direct contemplation of Father, Son, and Holy Spirit. On the other side of this analogy, there follows a reinsertion of trinitarian contemplation into the realm of Scripture. This reinsertion occurs in section 6, where Gregory deals with the objection that the account he has given of the terms *hypostasis* and *ousia* seems to conflict with scriptural usage in Hebrews 1:3, where Christ is described as "the brightness of his glory and the image of his *hypostasis*." This passage seems to contradict the signification of *hypostasis* as delineating the unique characteristics of each person of the Trinity by referring to the Son as the image of the Father's *hypostasis*. Gregory responds that the apostle Paul, whom he takes to be the author of this passage, was being consistent with his intent (*skopos*) to signify "the genuine and inseparable and unified relationship of the Son with the Father"[249] and the lack of any gap intervening between them. Gregory effectively employs the biblical text as a cipher for his own exposition of the simultaneous unity and distinction between Father and Son:

> And so the Apostle considers that even though the word of faith teaches the unconfused and distinct difference of *hypostaseis* he is nevertheless compelled through these words

248. *Ep.* 38.5.52–55.
249. *Ep.* 38.7.9–10.

to present also the continuity and as it were congenital relation of the Son to the Father. This is not to deny that the Only-Begotten exists hypostatically but to affirm that he does not admit any intervention in his union with the Father. Consequently, the one who gazes with the eyes of his soul on the expressed image (*charactēr*) of the only-begotten comes to a perception also of the *hypostasis* of the Father.[250]

From our vantage point, we can query Gregory's assumptions about the biblical author's knowledge of future doctrinal formulations. But our present concern is not with Gregory's presuppositions about the nature of biblical inspiration and its relation to doctrinal development but with how he sees *hypostasis-ousia* and kindred trinitarian doctrinal language as functioning within the Christian's relation to the Triune God. *Epistle* 38 offers a valuable entry into Gregory's vision in this regard, but only if we do not isolate certain aspects of his argument (specifically, the objective "definition" of these terms) from the entirety of his presentation and the structural interrelations of its parts. The overarching thesis proposed by the present reading is that the argument as a whole is concerned not primarily with how *hypostasis-ousia* language defines the divine Trinity but rather how it functions within a scriptural program of contemplating the Trinity. The three parts of the argument that we have identified contribute individually and together to this overall intent, or in Gregory's terms, *skopos*.

In the first part, Gregory does offer a definition of the objective content of *hypostasis-ousia* language as signifying the relation of the particular to the common, or universal. However, in applying such language to God, he immediately turns to the practical rules that such linguistic precision provides for scriptural trinitarian contemplation. Successful practical application of these linguistic rules requires a distinction between how these terms regulate other trinitarian language and how they norm the practice of trinitarian contemplation. We noted the example that the rule, "Let what is held in common be referred to the category of *ousia* and not applied to that of *hypostasis*" in fact translates quite otherwise as a rule for trinitarian contemplation, "Let what is held in common within the category of *ousia* language be applied equally to each of the persons." The second rule is by no means a logical contradiction of the first but the successful application of the linguistic norm to the practical one of direct trinitarian contemplation. Facilitating that transition is Gregory's central preoccupation in this treatise, and to neglect or underestimate the significance of that strategy is to miss the fundamental thrust of the argument. Only after he has placed the reader in the milieu of direct contemplation of the Trinity does Gregory pause, in the second part of this epistle, to offer encouragement by referring to a creaturely analogue. This analogue is meant to offer a suggestion for the plausibility of trinitarian contemplation from the realm of quotidian experience both by attending to a natural phenomenon that exhibits a coincidence of unity and distinction (the rainbow) and by attending to the regular epistemological phenomenon whereby

250. *Ep.* 38.7.33–42.

we experience in fact a reality that transcends our powers of analysis. It would be a mistake to interpret Gregory's injunction to trust faith rather than rational analysis in terms of a modern conception of faith as an individual subjective disposition to accept as true what cannot be rationally justified. Rather, the faith alluded to in this context is the concrete experience of a Christian life informed and nourished by the Scriptures and performed within the ecclesial community. It makes eminently good sense, then, that the last step in Gregory's program for trinitarian contemplation, in the third part of this epistle, is to read trinitarian doctrine back into the Scriptures and to be concerned with harmonizing scriptural language with the language of doctrinal formulation.

To Ablabius: On Not Three Gods

The short treatise *To Ablabius* has received considerable attention in recent scholarship, much of it centered on whether it represents Gregory of Nyssa's acceptance or disavowal of "the social analogy" and whether it contains a "dense account of divine personhood."[251] While these questions are important from the point of view of later developments, they must be appropriately situated within the stated "scope" (*skopos*) and "sequence" (*akolouthia*) of the text itself, to borrow the key terms of Gregory's own hermeneutics. The stated aim of this piece is to deal with a dilemma that poses an abiding challenge to the proclamation and reception of trinitarian doctrine: we must either say that there are three gods or deny divinity to Son and Spirit. Gregory sees this dilemma as the crux of the criticisms made by the opponents of Nicene doctrine, as reported to him by his younger contemporary, the bishop Ablabius. These criticisms are rhetorically based on the Cappadocian doctrinal formulations that distinguish between what is common and what is particular in God by language such as *ousia-hypostasis* and other kindred pairings. In the case of human persons who share a common nature, we still speak of three "men"; why not then three gods? It has been correctly pointed out that this apparent recourse to the "social analogy" is thereby introduced by Gregory's opponents and not spontaneously by Gregory himself.[252] But we must concede that Gregory does elsewhere directly refer to the example of distinction of persons and unity of nature among humanity, either of his own initiative or in defense of Basil.[253] Indeed, the most plausible supposition is that the force of his opponents' argument resides precisely in producing a *reductio ad absurdum* based on Gregory's (and Basil's) own formulations: since Gregory himself uses the example of three human individuals

251. On the predominance of the first themes in interpreting this treatise, and Gregory's trinitarian theology in general, see Coakley, "Re-Thinking Gregory of Nyssa," 2–4. The phrase quoted above is from Ayres, *Nicaea*, 363. Ayres's treatment of Nyssa, however, tries to situate Gregory's theology more broadly within the problematic of an emerging "pro-Nicene" grammar of divinity and is thus complementary to the methodology executed here, despite some differences in our interpretations, which will be duly noted.

252. Ayres, *Nicaea*, 345.

253. E.g., *C. Eun.* 1.497; 3.5.21; *Ep.* 38.2.

sharing equally in human nature, then he must reckon with the objection that in the case of human beings we speak of "three men," and consequently his formulation leads to the positing of "three gods."

Several times in the opening paragraphs of this treatise, Gregory acknowledges the difficulty of this challenge. His guidelines for negotiating this challenge really amount to another installment in his overarching program of providing a practical epistemological strategy for appropriating the positive contents of trinitarian doctrine and dealing with the objections of its critics. The first step prescribed in this instance is to insist that the givens of faith, as received by the church as a whole, are not vulnerable to the outcome of efforts to provide a rational explanation for such faith. Gregory embraces the challenge of "fortifying the mind in its doubt," but even if the exertions of rational explication should prove inadequate, "we must guard the tradition we have received from the fathers as always secure and immovable."[254] If we follow the scholarly consensus in dating this treatise ca. 375, it is most likely that "the tradition we have received from the fathers" is a reference to the Nicene Council. Gregory's next step, constituting another element in his trinitarian "fundamental" theology, is that conventional habits of thought and expression cannot norm theological language. Indeed, the reverse movement can throw light on the fallacies of customary patterns of thought and language. This happens to be the case in this instance, inasmuch as the expression "three men" taken completely literally seems to signify a plurality of human natures. However, what is multiple in the case of "Peter, James, and John" is not the human nature ("the humanity in them all is one") but rather the individual *hypostaseis*. The expression "three men" is therefore strictly speaking incorrect, an illogical abuse of language hallowed by custom, which cannot seriously challenge the logic of theological formulation. It should be noted that nowhere in the course of this ingenious response does Gregory simply repudiate altogether the example of three human individuals sharing a common nature as supplying a logical analogy for the formal relation of common-particular in *ousia-hypostasis* and kindred analogies. Rather, Gregory assumes the validity of the comparison and indeed validates trinitarian language by reference to it. Whether that amounts to "a social analogy" is a larger question that depends on exactly what one means by the term. All that can be safely said is that Gregory accepts a certain likeness between the distinctions among human individuals within a common human nature and the distinctions among the trinitarian *hypostaseis* within the common divine nature. As we shall see, he is equally clear that there is also a great unlikeness between the two.

However we evaluate the adequacy of Gregory's counterargument, the relatively brief space allotted to it in this short essay seems to indicate that Gregory himself considered it as merely a minor engagement in a side-skirmish to more radical questions about how we name and know God. These are the questions that Gregory apparently considers to be at the heart of differences between him and his opponents, since he devotes the larger part of his treatise to treating them. Gregory's account of

254. *Ad Ablabium*; GNO 3.1.257.

how a proper conception of the naming and knowing of God leads to a pro-Nicene trinitarian confession is not difficult to reconstruct. But it does involve the dialectic of apophatic and cataphatic elements (which we encountered previously in *Against Eunomius*) whose subtle balance is so easy to distort, partly because the modern reception of them has been bedeviled by imprecise and sometimes misleading interpretive categories. It is essential therefore to reproduce verbatim some of the categories used by Gregory himself to construct his trinitarian epistemology.

The foundational principle of Gregory of Nyssa's account is that, contrary to a common misperception, the attribution of "divinity" does not actually name the divine nature (*physis*) in the same way that other "names" signify a subject (*hypokeimenon*).[255] According to Gregory, it is the Scriptures that reveal to us that the divine nature is ineffable and cannot be named. All names that successfully refer to God, either by scriptural inspiration or human custom, are "explanatory of our conceptions (*nooumenōn*) regarding the divine nature (*peri tēn theian physin*)" but do not encompass (*periechein*) the nature itself. Attributes that are customarily considered as identifying the divine nature *tout court* can be successful in attaining appropriate significations concerning the divine nature (*peri tēs theias physeōs*) but do not signify what that nature (*physis*) essentially (*kat' ousian*) is.[256] Our knowledge of God, therefore, is gained not from our capacity to identify and noetically "encompass" the divine nature but rather from our perception of the "activities" (*energeiai*) of the transcendent divine "power" (*dynamis*). Gregory proposes that the term *theotēs* or "divinity" indicates the activity of "beholding" or "overseeing," which he takes as encompassing all the activity by which God manifests his lordship over creation. He offers some token scriptural passages as evidence that Scripture attributes the divine activity of overseeing creation to Father, Son, and Holy Spirit. Each is therefore equally "God," an affirmation that we make not on the basis of a comprehensive perusal of the divine nature but on the basis of identifying the scriptural naming of the activities (*energeiai*) that constitute God's own self-manifestation.

What is essential in getting a handle on the trinitarian apophatic epistemology proposed here is that we avoid interpretive frameworks that see the issue within polarities of knowing–not knowing or direct knowledge–indirect knowledge or direct perception–inference.[257] As interpretive categories, these are themselves often ill-defined, and they do not succeed in following the contours and nuances of Gregory's own more precise thought structure. Most crucially, it must be noted that Gregory speaks positively in this treatise of the human capacity to attain knowledge of God, even if such knowledge is not an "encompassing" of the divine nature itself, and he does not denigrate such knowledge as "indirect" or "hidden" or by any such qualifiers

---

255. *Ad Ablabium*; GNO 3.1.42.

256. *Ad Ablabium*; GNO 3.1.43.

257. By way of example, one of the differences I have with Ayres's interpretation is a tendency to overplay the apophatic element by filtering Gregory's epistemological schema through his own "direct-hidden" framework, which is not properly Gregory's: "From the act of mental dissection that is *epinoia* we may acquire a sense of an object that remains *hidden* from *direct* perception" (*Nicaea*, 253; my italics).

that suggest diminution. So the critical question is what it means for Gregory to speak of the impossibility of knowing the divine nature in light of his positive affirmations of the human capacity to know God. As with *Against Eunomius*, everything depends on how we interpret the category of "knowing the divine nature"; and the framework of nature (*physis*)–activity (*energeia*), which is much more prominent in this treatise, sheds significant light on this question. Along these lines, we can interpret the core of Gregory's theological epistemology at this stage as encapsulated in the following proposition: we can only encounter the divine nature in its active outwardness, but we cannot supplant its own innermost act of self-standing, which is the source of its active self-presencing. We can justify the preceding statement by demonstrating its consistency with Gregory's key motifs as noted above. We can speak of "encountering the divine nature," despite Gregory's strictures against "knowing the divine nature," because he himself allows for a knowing that concerns or is "around" the divine nature. The crucial qualification of this kind of knowing is not that it is hidden or indirect but that it can only be reactive to the prior activity (*energeia*) and outward self-presencing of God. God is not some inert object that can be passively spied on and encompassed by a creaturely knowing but an active subject who can only be encountered in relation to his own self-presencing. Given the definition of "the divine nature" as the "subject" (*hypokeimenon*) that underlies this active self-presencing, the claim to know the divine nature would amount to the claim that one can transcend or in some way go behind the effected self-presencing of God and reach to the very innermost cause of that effect. Clearly, such a claim involves a supplanting of God's very self-standing, and that is why Gregory sees it as blasphemy. Positively, however, to know God through God's self-presencing is in no way a matter of a lack of knowledge of God or a lack of directness but rather of knowing God as a God who is always lord of his own self-presencing, which is the only way to know God as God.[258] Perhaps more profoundly than any modern theologian, Gregory of Nyssa offers the most thoroughgoing explanation of why it must be that we only encounter the Trinity through the trinitarian economy. It is a necessity of the divine nature itself and of the structure of the God-creature relationship that we have no access to the immanence of God apart from God's economic self-presencing. To go further with Gregory, the divine economy is never left behind as we enter into a sphere of the absolute immanence of God. Ultimately, the only immanence of God to which we have access is God's self-economized immanence.

Having reconfigured the notion of "knowing the divine nature" into that of a knowing concerning (*peri*) the divine nature from a stance of receptivity to the self-manifesting dynamic activity (*energeia*) of that nature, Gregory finds himself even more vulnerable to the rhetorical charge that his way of conceiving the Trinity inescapably leads to positing "three gods." If the language of "three men" can be repudiated on the basis that what is multiplied in the case of three individuals is not the nature, it now returns with the seemingly stronger justification that we refer to three individuals

---

258. The admittedly Barthian overtones of this interpretation should not disqualify it, given its recourse to the key motifs of Gregory himself.

sharing a common activity in the plural; thus, we speak of "three farmers" or "three orators." Why then, again, not three gods? As we noted, the first time that Gregory confronted this problematic conclusion based on distinction and unity in the human sphere, he left the comparison between the human and the divine intact. Rather than repudiating it altogether, he proposed that in the human sphere (and, thus, presuming the "analogy," in the divine sphere also) multiple individuals do not constitute a multiplication of natures. In this case, however, Gregory does repudiate the appropriateness of the comparison. Human co-activity and divine co-activity are radically and structurally different. When human beings cooperate, "each one acts separately and by himself," and thus contributes a distinct action within a field of cooperation.[259] However, "with regard to the divine nature (*epi tēs theias physeōs*), we do not learn that the Father does something by himself, without the Son taking part [in that very action], nor again that the Son distinctly does something without the Spirit. Rather, every activity (*energeia*) reaching from God to creation and named according to our various conceptions (*ennoias*) originates in the Father, proceeds through the Son, and is completed in the Holy Spirit. The exertion of each in any act whatsoever is not separated and owned distinctly. But whatever happens in the course of the providence towards us or the management and constitution of the universe happens through the Three and yet does not result in three happenings."[260]

Clearly, Gregory of Nyssa is here reaching for a conception of a *perichōrēsis* of divine co-activity, such that each of the persons participates in the agency of the others. The notion of separate agencies resulting in distinct actions, however intimately co-operative (as in a symphony, for example, where each player creates a distinct sound that is joined with the others in a unified sound), is ruled out (the violinst does not participate in the particular sound that the cellist makes). But the notion of an altogether undifferentiated agency in which each of the persons partakes in exactly the same manner is also implicitly but very clearly ruled out by Gregory's consistent strategy of using three different verbs to distribute the common action distinctly to the three persons. As we have seen in the passage quoted above, the typical pattern for that distribution is that every action issues from the Father, is actualized through the Son, and is completed by the Spirit. There is thus an ineffable distinction within unity in divine co-activity such that the one divine activity is completely effected by each of the persons and yet is distinctly inflected between them. Every activity that is originated by the Father is equally yet distinctly owned by Son and Spirit. Once again, the notion of "no interval" plays a key role in Gregory's conceptualization of the trinitarian distinction-within-unity: "There is no delay that exists or can be conceived in the motion of the divine will from the Father through the Son to the Spirit."[261]

Once again, in light of the assertion that the Greek fathers begin with the persons rather than the common nature, it should be noted that only at the conclusion of this

259. *Ad Ablabium*; GNO 3.1.47.
260. *Ad Ablabium*; GNO 3.1.47.
261. *Ad Ablabium*; GNO 3.1.51.

treatise does Gregory turn his attention to emphasizing the distinction of *hypostaseis* and only in rebuttal of the anticipated charge that his emphasis on the common nature thus far leads to a confusion of the persons. His response to this accusation is that the confession of the invariability of nature does not amount to a negation of "one from another" in the Trinity with respect to causality. Only the Father is uncaused, while the Son is immediately (*prosechōs*) from the Father and the Spirit is "through" the mediation of the Son.[262] Some currents in modern theology have manifested dissatisfaction with this Cappadocian "reduction" of the distinction of trinitarian persons to the order of causality.[263] However, such criticism is based on an artificial abstraction of condensed doctrinal formulations such as the one above from the larger context of these theologians' engagement with the biblical narrative as a whole. The statement that the only ontological ground for the distinction of *hypostaseis* is the order of causality is not equivalent to the statement that the only *characterization* we can make of the trinitarian persons is that of correctly naming their location in the order of causality. The very motifs that later critics have latched onto in order to attain a thicker description of the distinctions and relations between the *hypostaseis*, such as *kenōsis* and mutual glorification, are already anticipated in Gregory, as we have shown.

We can conclude our exposition of Gregory of Nyssa's *To Ablabius* by applying this reading to two significant issues in recent scholarship: the question of the "social analogy" and that of Gregory's account of divine personhood. With regard to the former, it must be conceded that we do not find an extended and focused discussion of the likeness between the unity-in-distinction in the human realm and that in the divine realm as a central theme in Gregory's theology, certainly not to the extent that we find in modern proponents of this approach or even in Richard of St. Victor. However, the tendency to dismiss scattered allusions to such a likeness takes the matter too far in the other direction. As we noted, the observation that in this treatise the comparison is treated in light of opponents' objections does not nullify the instances where it is invoked spontaneously; he is probably reacting against his opponents' objections to his own prior invocation of that comparison. Lewis Ayres's argument that the core of Gregory's comparison resides in a cosmological conception of the indivisibility of natures in general, rather than having a particular reference to human nature and persons, is more applicable to Gregory's insistence that communication or "production" within a nature does not result in a diminution of the nature.[264] The argument from the indivisibility of natures is distinct from the framework of *ousia-hypostasis*, while obviously not unrelated to the former. Thus, to use Ayres's own example, there is a "community of nature" between the vine and its moisture and the resultant wine. However, this more general conception of the "indivisibility of natures" tends not to involve the particularly intense evocation of unity-within-distinction articulated by the combination of *ousia-hypostasis* and kindred pairings. To my knowledge, Gregory

---

262. *Ad Ablabium*; GNO 3.1.56.
263. E.g., Pannenberg, *Systematic Theology*, 1:320–32; Jenson, *Systematic Theology*, 1:108.
264. For Ayres's argument, see *Nicaea*, 348–51.

does not speak of the vine, its moisture, and wine as *hypostaseis* within the nature of the grape! The language of *hypostasis* and *prosōpon* does seem to connote an intentional ownership of a nature in a way that goes beyond merely general cosmological conceptions of the continuity of natures and thus to be particularly fitted to the distinctly human realm. Moreover, categorical dismissals of Gregory's adverting to some likeness between the unity of the divine *hypostaseis* in the one nature and the communion of human nature among individuals have to take account of Gregory's distinct sense of the unity of human nature.[265] Finally, the consideration that Gregory explicitly contrasts human and divine types of co-activity does not render the likeness between human communion and trinitarian unity a "disanalogy," since an aspect of unlikeness is inherent to the notion of analogy. An analogy does not simply do away with the radical otherness between God and creation but functions to illuminate a certain likeness within that radical unlikeness. All that being said, we do in fact find elsewhere in Gregory a significant counterpoint to the disavowal of the likeness between human and divine co-activity. In his *Homily 15 on the Song of Songs*, Gregory evokes an eschatological vision wherein the diversity of human action will be harmonized by the Holy Spirit into a unified clinging to the good that is imitative of the mutual indwelling of Father and Son:

> If love perfectly casts out fear, according to what is written (cf. 1 John 4:18), and fear becomes transformed into love, then unity will be found as a result of salvation, inasmuch as all have been united to each other in their attachment (*symphuia*) to the one Good through the perfection of the dove [i.e, the Spirit]. . . . What the Lord says in the gospel explains this more clearly. When he blesses his disciples by granting them every power, he grants to the holy ones the other good things through his words addressed to the Father. And as the summit of all good things, he adds this: that they may no longer differ in their purposes nor be divided by any variance in their discernment as to the beautiful, but that all should be one, united by the one and only Good through the unity of the Holy Spirit. Accordingly, the apostle says, "Bound together by the bond of peace, that all might become one body and one spirit through the one hope into which they have been called" (Eph. 4:3–4). But it is even better to state the divine words of the gospels themselves: "That all may be one, just as you, Father, are in me and I am in you, that they also may be in us" (John 17:21).[266]

The question of whether Gregory of Nyssa endorses a "social analogy" is tied to the second issue identified above, that of Gregory's account of divine personhood. Those who deny that Gregory countenances a "social analogy" tend to resort to an extreme apophaticism wherein "not only can we not name the divine nature but

265. On the unity of human nature in Gregory, see Zachuber, *Human Nature*, and Balás, "*Plenitudo Veritatis.*" For an account of *Ad Ablabium* that does insist on some analogical correspondence between human and trinitarian communion, see now Maspero, *Trinity and Man*. Against the notion that Gregory held to a Platonic conception of universal human nature contributing to a "physcial" conception of salvation, see Hübner, *Die Einheit*.

266. *Comm. Cant.* 15.

we do not even know what a divine person is."[267] This way of stating the matter is not incorrect, but it needs to be carefully nuanced in light of the entire apophatic-cataphatic framework in Gregory, which, as we have noted, operates not with a fundamental polarity of knowing–not knowing but within subtle distinctions between knowing and "encompassing" the nature and knowing "about" or "around" (*peri*) the nature through that nature's self-presencing *energeia*. If we neglect to take all these nuances and distinctions into account and settle for a blanket apophaticism, we are apt to return to the kind of "notional" triniarianism without any intelligible content that Rahner cites as a root cause of the decline of trinitarian doctrine in the lived experience of Christians.[268] We may not know what a divine person is in the sense of reaching behind the self-presencing activity of the divine nature by which the persons are manifested. But we do know the divine persons as manifest precisely by that activity. Indeed, the heart of the argument in this treatise, namely, that we know the divine persons to be equally God as manifested by the divine *energeia*, necessarily presumes that the divine persons are distinctly manifested by the divine *energeia*.

We are now in a position to draw together our conclusions as to what can be gleaned from Gregory's use of *hypostasis-ousia* and kindred language. The first affirmation signified by Gregory's *hypostasis-ousia* language is that Father, Son, and Spirit are each fully God. Whatever the term "God" signifies can be attributed without qualification to each of the three, individually. The great preponderance of Gregory's writings that can be construed as dealing, in a narrow sense, with "trinitiarian theology" is preoccupied with nothing less than establishing this point with reference to either the divinity of Christ or the Holy Spirit. Concretely, to say that each is God, for Gregory, is to say that each shares fully in all the divine perfections, especially as these are delineated by scriptural terminology. It is also to say that each is Creator and agent of salvation. All this is concretely signified by Gregory when he denotes each of Father, Son, and Spirit as a divine *hypostasis*, who co-owns the divine *ousia*.

A second signification, attaching especially to Gregory's application of the term *hypostasis* to Father, Son, and Spirit, is what we might call an account of individual simplicity. For Gregory, to say that Father, Son, and Spirit are each fully God is to say that each has self-possession of the divine perfections by virtue of his own being and not by acquisition. There is no "composition" in each of the persons between their being and their attainment of divine qualities. In his attribution of the language of *hypostasis*, Gregory lays special stress on the perfection of agency and will. His conception of divine perfection includes an emphasis on God as willing subject, in no way willed by another and himself willing the existence of created beings. Both Son and Spirit are *hypostaseis* in the sense of being fully subjects of divine agency.

A third signification in Gregory's application of *hypostasis* language is that Father, Son, and Spirit are distinguishable through the order of their causality, as read from

267. Behr, *Nicene Faith*, 1:432; this view is also consonant with that of Ayres (*Nicaea*, 359, 363).
268. Rahner, *Trinity*, 14–15.

their distinct characterizations within the scriptural narrative. Thus, the hypostatic identifier of the Father is that he is the sole origin of both Son and Spirit; that of the Son is that he is generated from the Father; and that of the Spirit is that he proceeds from the Father somehow through the mediation of the Son.

Thus, to say that each is a divine *hypostasis* is to say that each is fully God, that each owns divine being "in himself" without any interval between his being and any of the divine qualities, that each exists as a willing subject, and that each is distinguishable from the other through an integral movement of the communication of divine being from the Father to the Son and from the Father to the Spirit, through the Son. To say that Father, Son, and Spirit are one being or nature (*ousia/physis*) is to say principally that the distinctions between them are enfolded in the simplicity of divine perfection. These distinctions do not amount to a difference in perfection, which, as we have seen, Gregory considers to be a nonsensical notion. Father, Son, and Spirit are equally perfect and are thus one in being. But we should not forget other supplementary accounts of divine unity in Gregory's writings. To say that Father, Son, and Spirit are one in being is also to say that they constitute one integral and unbroken "circle of glory" into which human beings are enfolded; it is also to say that they constitute a single unified agency, "one life-giving power" that effects the creation, salvation, and perfection of creatures.

Christian Life in the Trinity

Arguably, the most distinctive and characteristic aspect of Gregory of Nyssa's account of Christian life is expressed in the notion of *epektasis*, the "stretching forward" toward an ever deeper contemplation of and participation in the divine life.[269] For Gregory, the dominant note of Christian life is that of ceaseless desire, exertion, and upward progress. The dynamic kineticism of Gregory's spirituality has an attractive ring in our own time. But it is crucial not to abstract this aspect of his vision from its moorings in the whole nexus of trinitarian faith, as if it referred to the ascent of the lone individual to the Infinite alone. An integral understanding of Gregory's notion of *epektasis* involves seeing how it is predicated both on a conception of the human being's involvement in the trinitarian salvific economy and on a particular apprehension of the nature of trinitarian life. This is to say, in modern terminology, that the notion of *epektasis* involves Gregory in accounts of both the economic and immanent Trinity. In order to round out our retrieval of Gregory's trinitarian theology, we need to clarify its connections with this central aspect of his Christian vision.

269. The still indispensable treatment of this theme in light of Gregory's practical spirituality as a whole is Daniélou, *Platonisme et théologie mystique*, 309–26. Daniélou uses this theme as a central reference point for recapitulating "the synthesis of Gregorian spirituality" (309). More recent treatments have engaged the question of the relation between this theme in Gregory and Origen's notion of the possibility of aseity in humanity's relationship with God: cf. Mühlenberg, *Die Unendlichkeit Gottes*, 26–27; Heine, *Perfection in the Virtuous Life*, 63–114, esp. 76–97; Laird, *Gregory of Nyssa*, 96.

We find a synthetic account of the constituent elements of the notion of *epektasis* in the prologue of the *Life of Moses*. Once again, the conception of God as infinite goodness is fundamental; correlatively, human virtue is conceived as limitless progress in participating in God's infinite goodness:

The Divine One is himself the Good (in the primary and proper sense of the word) whose very nature is goodness. This he is and is so named and is known by this nature. Since, then, it has not been demonstrated that there is any limit to virtue except evil, and since the Divine does not admit of an opposite, we hold the divine nature to be unlimited and infinite. Certainly whoever pursues true virtue participates in nothing other than God, because he is himself absolute virtue. Since, then, those who know what is good by nature desire participation in it, and since this good has no limit, the participant's desire itself necessarily has no stopping place but stretches out (*symparateinousa*) with the limitless.[270]

Elsewhere in Gregory's writing, it is clear that the middle term for this relation between the infinite divine goodness and human participation in it is Jesus Christ, the incarnate Word. Consequently, Gregory's conception of *epektasis* includes coordinate conceptions of Christ's union of divinity and humanity, his presence in the church and the sacraments, and Christian ethical life.

The fact that Christian discipleship constitutes a limitless journey into the infinite perfection of the divine nature is predicated on the union of genuine divinity and humanity in Christ. Because the divinity of Christ is a full co-owner of the infinite divine goodness, "he who finds any good finds it in Christ who contains all good."[271] In the *Life of Moses*, Gregory interprets the divine instructions to Moses ("there is a place beside me where you shall stand on the rock" [Exod. 33:21]) as a reference to Christ. Christ is the place and the rock in which the infinite progress within divine life takes place.[272] Gregory explains that, as a result, our union with God is "both a standing still and a moving."[273] It is a standing still because the union with Christ constitutes "stability in the good,"[274] inasmuch as the divinity of Christ contains the unchangeable Good, which is the divine nature. But it is also a moving, precisely because of the inexhaustible plenitude of this unchanging Good.

If the divinity of Christ contains the inexhaustible Good, which accounts for the limitlessness of the life of holiness, the humanity of Christ makes our participation in this infinite divine life possible. In his *Commentary on the Song of Songs*, Gregory explains that the Song refers to mystical realities through bodily images "because our mind does not reach the incomprehensible and invisible unless faith first grasps the visible, and it is the nature of the flesh that is visible."[275] In this context, Gregory

270. *Vit. Mos.* prol. 7. Translations are from Malherbe and Ferguson, *Gregory*.
271. *Vit. Mos.* 2.248.
272. Cf. Daniélou, *Platonisme et théologie mystique*, 325.
273. *Vit. Mos.* 2.243.
274. *Vit. Mos.* 2.244.
275. *Comm. Cant.* 13.

is speaking specifically of the flesh of Christ, which mediates between the incomprehensibility of the divine nature and its inexhaustible accessibility: "Since he is uncreated and pretemporal and eternal, he remains entirely incomprehensible and ineffable with respect to his nature. But what was manifested to us through the flesh enabled him to become known in some way. I am speaking of the great mystery of faith (1 Tim. 3:16) through which God was manifested in the flesh."[276] Gregory can speak of the Christian's union with God through Christ as attaining "a knowledge directed toward the infinite" (*gnōsin pros to achōriston*).[277] Such a knowledge still does not amount to an enclosing of the divine nature by the human mind but is rather a conscious participation in the divine infinite.

This participation in God through Christ is mediated by the church: "The one who looks to the Church is directly looking to Christ."[278] In the *Catechetical Oration*, Gregory of Nyssa focuses on the sacraments of baptism and Eucharist as primary means of effecting union with Christ. He is concerned that baptism be not viewed as mere "teaching" but as representing "what he who entered into communion with humanity accomplished in fact."[279] Baptism is interpreted as a sharing, through mimetic representation, in the death and resurrection of Christ. This union with Christ is also a rebirth into trinitarian life: "We are taught in the gospel that there are three Persons and Names through whom believers come to be born. He who is born of the Trinity is born equally of Father, Son, and Holy Spirit."[280] The Eucharist is the means by which Christ "implants himself in all believers" and "unites himself with their bodies."[281] Yet sacramental union with Christ is not magic. The efficacy of the sacraments is dependent upon both faith and conduct. A proper baptismal faith is one that interprets the sacrament as an entrance into the one uncreated life of the Trinity, which becomes the source of the Christian's own life. Conversely, a doctrine that posits the Trinity itself to be a mixture of created and uncreated leaves the baptizand outside the simplicity of divine life.[282] Finally, even correct faith does not guarantee the efficacy of the sacraments if it is not accompanied by appropriate action and ethical deportment. When Gregory asks how baptism transforms and renews human nature, his response is that it does not actually produce any structural changes in human nature itself: "Neither reason nor understanding nor capacity for knowledge, nor anything else that marks human nature, undergoes a change."[283] But baptism does offer the possibility of regeneration by accomplishing a cleansing of the will, which itself has to be willfully appropriated. Without this willing reception of the grace of the sacrament, Gregory does not hesitate to say that its efficacy is annulled: "But if the washing

276. *Comm. Cant.* 13.
277. *Comm. Cant.* 13.
278. *Comm. Cant.* 13.
279. *Cat. or.* 35.
280. *Cat. or.* 38.
281. *Cat. or.* 37.
282. *Cat. or.* 39.
283. *Cat. or.* 40.

has only affected the body, and the soul has failed to wash off the stains of passion, and the life after initiation is identical with that before, despite the boldness of my assertion, I will say without shrinking that in such a case the water is only water, and the gift of the Holy Spirit is nowhere evident in the action."[284] Gregory pointedly remarks that the transformation that comes from a willing reception of the grace of the sacrament is not only something interior and consisting of an exalted spiritual state but needs to be manifested and recognizable in social relations. The person who shows no outward signs of conversion and assimilation to the divine life has not appropriated the grace of the sacrament: "Those who are wronged, defrauded, and deprived of their property observe, for their part, no change when a man like this is baptized. . . . Make it clear who your Father is."[285]

If the *epektasis* of endless progress in the union of God takes place within the divine-human unity of Christ, it thus also transpires within the co-presencing of the Son and the Spirit. As we have seen earlier, Gregory speaks of the Spirit as being "manifested through the Son" and of Christ as "shining in our hearts by means of the Holy Spirit."[286] We have also seen that the Spirit is especially associated with cleansing and perpetuating the upward ascent of human desire. Gregory thus views the *epektasis* of Christian life as a participation in the salvific activities of Son and Spirit by which Christians are adopted in the Spirit into the eternal mutual glorification of the Trinity. Even more emphatically than Athanasius, Gregory specifies that this participation is not automatic or "substantialist" in the sense of precluding volition and action, but rather a continuous exertion in the union with Christ in the Spirit.

While Gregory thus structures his depiction of Christian life in terms of the economic activity of the Trinity, there are also significant, albeit unthematized, correspondences between this depiction and his account of God's trinitarian being. Two such correspondences come into view when we consider, first, what we might call the "kineticism" of Gregory's anthropology and practical spirituality and, second, his insistence on the all-encompassing range of Christian commitment. For Gregory, human existence is constituted by movement, and the perfection of human existence is not a static state but a limitless movement of participation in the divine Good. It is true that Gregory sometimes contrasts the inherent kineticism of human nature with the unchanging being of the divine. But while Gregory insists that the divine does not change, his trinitarian doctrine impels him to acknowledge that there is nevertheless active movement in God. This point can best be appreciated by contrast with Eunomius. At the heart of Eunomius's doctrine is the insistence that all activity (including the generation of the Son from the Father) must be external to the divine essence; failure to adhere to this principle would result in the attribution of "passion" to God. Gregory's conception of divine nature, however, involves the notion of a perfect productive activity that is internal to the divine essence; God's being is not

284. *Cat. or.* 40.
285. *Cat. or.* 40.
286. *C. Eun.* 1.280.

only active but is even constituted by dynamic interrelated activity. The kineticism of this doctrine of God is more explicit in Gregory of Nazianzus's direct attribution of the language of motion to the trinitarian processions. The older Gregory speaks of the "identity of motion" among the persons and describes the trinitarian processions directly in the language of motion (*kinēsis*).[287] Nevertheless, the Nyssan's account of divine productive activity as integral to the essence also presumes such a kinetic conception of God. His distinct contribution is to mirror this kineticism in his account of human existence and its ultimate fulfillment. As God's trinitarian being is perfect interrelated activity, human being consists in relating itself to the activity of divine being through its own unceasing active participation. Human existence is composed of acting into and out of inner-trinitarian activity (*energeia*).

This interpretation can help us to reconsider why Gregory of Nyssa seems to regard the whole notion of "knowing the divine essence" as a category mistake. When Gregory considers this issue, he typically insists that what can be known are the operations and not the essence. Exactly the wrong way to understand this point is to posit some kind of unbridgeable chasm between the divine operations and the divine essence, which the human mind can never pass over. Foundational to this distortion is a conception of the essence precisely as a static object that is uninvolved in divine activity. But that is the Eunomian view, not Gregory's. The divine essence is unknowable in itself—which is to say, apart from its active operations—precisely because it is irreducibly and infinitely active. The operations, as it were, actively announce the essence, and the essence thus cannot be grasped apart from that active self-announcement. This foundational insight, which we have found it necessary to reiterate throughout this exposition, can also be directly linked with Gregory's emphasis on the comprehensive and radically open-ended scope of Christian commitment. We have noted that stance in his scriptural hermeneutics, exemplified in his frequent insistence that the whole range of the Scriptures needs to be taken into account in the identifying of Christ, over against Eunomius's reduction of knowledge of the divine essence to the single concept of *agen*[*n*]*ētos*. The same posture of comprehensiveness is evident in his efforts to link scriptural understanding with worship and correct faith with appropriate ethical deportment. The ultimate expression of this stance is Gregory's vision of eschatological union with God as unrestricted progress.

※ ※

Underlying all these various strands of Gregory's theological vision is the conception of a God who is irreducibly active within the dynamism of the trinitarian life and who actively announces himself through his benevolent and loving activities. If the relation between the human being and God could be encompassed by an immediate transaction between the divine essence—itself conceived as a static point, as it were—and the cognitive representation of that essence in the human intellect, then that relation would tend to be always focused upon that punctiliar moment of

---

287. Gregory of Nazianzus, *Or.* 29.2.

encounter, however evasive and fleeting, as in the Plotinian ascent of the alone to the Alone. But if the trinitarian God is radically active in his own being and inaccessible apart from his self-presencing activities, then the encounter with God must stretch out toward an infinite embrace, beyond any pretensions of a comprehensive and exhaustive grasp. The proper human stance, rather, is to ceaselessly act into the infinite trinitarian divine activity, never encompassing, always traveling. The systematic scope of trinitarian doctrine, for Gregory, is literally infinite.

5

Augustine's *De Trinitate*

Trinitarian Contemplation as Christological Quest

The two preceding chapters have presented the theological vision of Athanasius and that of Gregory of Nyssa as exemplars of the systematic scope of trinitarian doctrine in the fourth century, from the perspective that affirmed the trinitarian unity of being. Such an approach could certainly be applied with good effect to the greatest Western representative of early Christian theology, Augustine. This chapter, however, focuses on a theme that came to the fore in our treatment of Gregory of Nyssa: theological epistemology. In my introduction I suggested that two fundamental principles that underlay the development of "Nicene" trinitarian theology were the christological reconstruction of divine transcendence and a theological espistemology that was able to affirm both divine incomprehensibility and the possibility of being related to the trinitarian being of God. A comprehensive treatment of Augustine's trinitarian theology would include an analysis of his application of the first principle, particularly in his conception of Jesus as revealing divine humility.[1] But the focus of this chapter will be primarily his application of the second principle. In order to suggest some broad contours for the retrieval of Nicene theology, our study will show that for Augustine the knowledge of the Triune God is a matter less of grasping certain propositions or using certain analogies than of structuring one's whole perception and existence through the entirety of Christian faith so as to successfully "refer oneself" to

---

1. "Furthermore, the only thing to cleanse the wicked and the proud is the blood of the just man and the humility of God" (*Trin.* 4.2.4; translations are from Hill, *Trinity*). On this theme, which pervades Augustine's thought, see the excellent treatment of Daley, "Humble Mediator."

the God who is Father, Son, and Holy Spirit. To put the matter thus is once again to retrieve the theme of the "systematic scope of trinitarian doctrine," as thought through from the particular lens of theological epistemology. In order to pursue this theme in some detail in a way that is solidly anchored in Augustine's own writing, this chapter will be exclusively concerned with his classic work *De Trinitate*. This work has been both praised and blamed for locating the meaning of trinitarian doctrine in the so-called psychological analogy, but I hope to show that it is actually a demonstration of how a christocentric way of life enables the appropriation of trinitarian doctrine.

Augustine's Trinitarian Epistemology

Augustine's *De Trinitate*, composed over a period of two decades, follows and furthers the epistemological turn of the trinitarian debates of the second half of the fourth century.[2] In this work, Augustine takes up the task of establishing that the Scriptures and Christian experience require the confession of Nicene trinitarianism. The entire project asks how we can know the reality of God.[3] He does not begin with treatments of divine unity and diversity but with questions of faith, reason, and revelation. Once again we can speak of a trinitarian fundamental theology.

Reason, Faith, and Trinitarian Epistemology

The very first sentence in *De Trinitate* intimates that trinitarian faith requires a very particular resolution to the question of faith and reason: "The reader of these reflections of mine on the Trinity should bear in mind that my pen is on the watch against the sophistries of those who scorn the starting-point of faith and allow themselves to be deceived through an unseasonable and misguided love of reason."[4] The modern reader, in turn, needs to be on guard not to read medieval and post-Enlightenment concepts into Augustine's "faith" and "reason." For Augustine the distinction here invoked between faith and reason is not ultimately about two separable modes of consciousness or cognition but rather about from which side the chasm between Creator and creation is to be bridged. So Augustine's further categorization of those who are deceived by a misguided reason does not describe people who try to understand too much and to make sense of unfathomable mysteries; rather, it refers to human strategies for attaining to the divine from the starting point of human initiative: they "strive to climb above the created

2. Augustine embarked on the composition of this work in 399 and completed it, after pirated copies of it began to circulate without his permission, in the 420s. For treatments of the dating of *De Trinitate*, see LaBonnardière, *Recherches de chronologie augustinienne*, 165–77; Teselle, *Augustine the Theologian*, 223–37, 294–309; Hendrickx, "La Date de composition."
3. I have already treated the necessity of framing *De Trinitate* within the overarching theme of theological epistemology in my "Oppositional Pairs." For a thorough treatment of *De Trinitate* from that perspective, see now Gioia, *Theological Epistemology of Augustine's* De Trinitate.
4. *Trin.* 1.1.1.

universe, so ineluctably subject to change, and raise their regard to the unchanging substance which is God."[5] Augustine describes three such strategies, embracing both cataphatic and apophatic postures. A misguided reason can manifest itself as: (1) the projection of human corporeal notions onto God; (2) the projection of incorporeal and spiritual notions that are nevertheless still human; (3) the positing of assertions about God that are not projections from created realities but are sheer contrivances of human thinking, applicable neither to human experience nor to the reality of the divine; these assertions amount to an apophaticism that simply has no real referent. So it turns out that a misguided reason is simply the project of trying to cross the God-world divide through human initiative by either projecting or abstracting from created realities. While Augustine does not explicitly name the parties guilty of such misuse of reason, it is probably the "Arians," who project created conceptions onto the divine Son, and the Platonists, who attempt to reach God merely by abstracting from creaturely realities.

By contrast, Augustine describes the "starting point of faith" (*initio fidei*) as a fundamental assent to the divine project of crossing the God-world divide by divine initiative. In fact, both projection and understanding are also involved in the enterprise of faith. But the projection in question is a *divine self-projection*: God uses creaturely realities to project knowledge of himself in scriptural revelation. This divine self-projection nourishes human understanding and raises it through sensible and created realities to the reality of God. Faith, which is assent to the downward movement of divine self-adaptation, purifies human attachment to created realities and empowers an ascent to true knowledge of God. The dialectic of descending divine "adaptation," on the one side, and ascending human "purification," on the other, is constitutive of Augustine's presentation of the posture of faith:

> It was therefore to purify (*purgaretur*) the human spirit of such falsehoods that holy Scripture, adapting (*congruens*) itself to babes, did not shun any words, proper to any kind of thing whatever, that might nourish our understanding and enable it to rise (*assurgeret*) to the sublimities of divine things. Thus it would use words taken from corporeal things to speak about God ... and from the sphere of created spirit it has transposed many words to signify (*significaret*) what was in fact not like that but had to be expressed like that.... The divine Scriptures then are in the habit of making something like children's toys out of things that occur in creation, by which to entice our sickly gaze and get us step by step to seek as best as we can the things that are above and to forsake the things that are below.[6]

Already in the first few paragraphs of *De Trinitate*, Augustine has thus presented the whole enterprise of knowing God as a dynamic ascent and a path of purification. This presentation puts the accent not on the objective contents of knowledge of God as "comprehensible" in the sense impugned by Gregory of Nyssa but rather on the

5. *Trin.* 1.1.1.
6. *Trin.* 1.1.2.

purificatory process of knowing God. Knowledge of God is presented as a way (*via*) rather than a thing (*res*). More to the point, it takes place within the way-in-person, Jesus Christ, "in whom are hidden all the treasures of wisdom and knowledge" (Col. 2:3). Consequently, different stages of human spiritual development correspond to different aspects of Christ's disclosure of the divine, a disclosure whose content is safeguarded by both christological and trinitarian doctrine. Christ grants access to the full vision of God through his equality to the Father, and he can also cater to weaker spiritual palates through the milk of his crucified humanity. Until we can attain to the full vision of the equality of Christ and the Father, our knowledge of God is largely a matter of purification, of appropriating created realities in a way that gestures beyond them toward the divine.

"When some people are told this they get angry and think they are being insulted."[7] Who are these people? In the *City of God*, Augustine identifies Porphyry as rejecting the regimen of purification provided by the incarnation and presuming a continuity between the human soul and the divine.[8] It is likely that Augustine has in mind such a philosophical mindset that rejects the principle that knowledge of God is only coextensive with the path of purification through Christ. But since Augustine does not specifically identify those who get angry in this way, we should follow the text in its broad and general reference. Indeed, Augustine here touches on a crucial and perennial moment in the task of approaching trinitarian faith, and he presents this dramatic interjection as crucial to the rationale of his whole project in this work. The anger that Augustine reports expresses frustration, resentment, and suspicion with regard to the notion that trinitarian faith is lacking in "reasons." Presumably, the anger is caused by Augustine's insistence on the epistemological gap between humanity and God that persists even in the mode of faith. Trinitarian faith does not erase this gap but rather enfolds it in Christ, who makes of the gap a way toward the full vision of God. Augustine rather acerbically responds that he is prepared to give them "reasons," yet reasons that would only demonstrate this gap rather than annul it: "And sometimes we give them reasons—not indeed the ones they ask for when they inquire about God, since they are not capable of taking them, nor perhaps are we of mastering or presenting them—but reasons to show how unfit they are, how little suited to receiving what they demand."[9] Augustine here discounts the possibility of theological "reasons" that would simply abolish or render superfluous the christological distance, which is also a way, between humanity and God. Authentic theological "reasons" for trinitarian faith are only those that correctly propose the orientation for a full vision of God along with the distance between humanity and God that can only be traversed in Christ. The project of Augustine's trinitarian theology in this treatise is to provide precisely and only those kinds of "reasons":

7. *Trin.* 1.1.3.

8. *Civ.* 10.24–31. The centrality of the theme of purification in *On the Trinity*, in relation to the complementary discussion in *City of God*, is masterfully analyzed in Cavadini, "Trinity and Apologetics."

9. *Trin.* 1.1.3.

That is why with the help of the Lord our God, we shall undertake to the best of our ability to give them the reasons they clamor for, and to account for the one and only and true God being a trinity, and for the rightness of saying, believing, understanding that the Father and the Son and the Holy Spirit are of one and the same substance or essence. In this way, instead of feeling that they have been fobbed off by my excuses, they may actually come to realize that that supreme goodness does exist which only the most purified minds can gaze upon (*cernitur*), and also that they are themselves unable to gaze upon it and grasp it for the good reason that the human mind with its weak eyesight cannot concentrate on so overwhelming a light, unless it has been nursed back to full vigor on the justice of faith.[10]

We have now arrived at a vantage point from which we can discern the overall thrust and shape of Augustine's theological project in this work, as well as the inadequacy of certain interpretations. Too many interpretations of *De Trinitate* hang up on the question of whether the "psychological analogy" that is described in the latter half of the book succeeds or fails as a "picture" of the Trinity.[11] Those who reduce the scope of this work to that question miss the christodramatic center of Augustine's trinitarian epistemology, as clearly expressed in the opening passages of book 1. According to this epistemology, there can be no question of the human "picturing" of the divine; there can be no static and non-dialectical vision of the God who is Trinity. Rather, knowledge of God, and so knowledge of the God who is Trinity, is a matter of on the one hand discerning the "reasons" of faith, which allow us to glimpse something of the vision of God's adaptive self-disclosure, and on the other hand acknowledging the broken path between humanity and the full enjoyment of this vision. To acknowledge this broken path is not to retreat into agnosticism or even apophatic quietism but rather to recommit to the purificatory christological "regimen of faith," which renders the broken path an ascending way. This is what Augustine promises to attempt in *De Trinitate*:

> But first we must establish by the authority of the holy Scriptures whether the faith is in fact like that. Only then shall we go on, if God so wills and gives his help, to accommodate these talkative reason-mongers who have more conceit than capacity, which makes the disease they suffer from all the more dangerous. We shall do them such a service, perhaps, that they are able to discover reasons they can have no doubt about, and so in cases where they are unable to discover any they will sooner find fault with their own minds than with the truth itself of our arguments. In this way if there is a particle of the love or fear of God in them, they may return to the beginning and right order of faith, realizing at least what a wholesome regimen is provided for the faithful in holy Church, whereby the due observance of piety makes the ailing mind well for the perception of unchanging truth.[12]

10. *Trin.* 1.2.4.

11. For bibliography on how this approach has determined discussion of *De Trinitate*, see Anatolios, "Oppositional Pairs," 231n2.

12. *Trin.* 1.2.4.

As we can see from this passage, Augustine makes no overtures of promising to "show" his readers the Trinity. He wants to demonstrate (1) that the Scriptures tell us that God is Trinity; (2) that we can attain some experience of certainty regarding the trinitarian being of God ("We shall do them such a service, perhaps, that they are able to discover reasons *they can have no doubt about* [*ut inveniant aliquid unde dubitare non possint*]");[13] (3) that contained within that experience of certainty will be a realization of the inadequacy of the human mind to attain a full vision of the Trinity; and (4) that this realization will lead the inquirer to the christological "regimen of faith," which heals the human spirit toward the fullness of this vision. These four foci can be intelligibly synthesized into two: to demonstrate from the Scriptures that God is in fact Trinity, and to inculcate with regard to that truth an experience of certainty that contains a knowledge of one's incapacity to apprehend that truth apart from the mediation of Christ. As with Gregory of Nyssa, we have here a reconception of the kind of knowledge that we are looking for with regard to God. While Gregory typically conceived of knowledge of God as "journey," it is a recurring motif throughout *De Trinitate* that such knowledge has the character of quest; Augustine goes on in the next paragraph to cite Psalm 105:4, "Seek his face always." Trinitarian theology is primarily and ultimately a christological quest; the goal is to learn, in Christ, why and how to seek God as Trinity.

Scriptural Revelation and Human Knowledge of God

In the second section of book 1 of *De Trinitate* (beginning with 1.4.7), Augustine presents what he considers to be the trinitarian self-manifestation of God in scriptural revelation and attendant problems of interpretation. Contrary to some misrepresentations, Augustine begins not with God *in se*, or divine substance as such, but with the scriptural revelation of the one God who acts under three names.[14] The question of the distinction and unity of the Trinity is posed in terms of divine activity; Scripture depicts Father, Son, and Spirit as distinct agents. It was not the Trinity as such that became incarnate but only the Son; it was only the Father to whom the voice from heaven can be attributed, which said, "You are my Son"; and only the Spirit descended upon the apostles in the form of tongues of fire. Augustine locates a central problematic in the appropriation of trinitarian faith in the difficulty of understanding how divine agency is distinctly attributed to three different names while Scripture and "Catholic commentators" still maintain that one God works inseparably in all divine activity.[15] An alternative reading of Scripture, which would bypass this difficulty, is of course available in anti-Nicene versions that locate the oneness of God only in the Father and ascribe a lower rank of divinity to Son and Spirit. Augustine quickly runs

13. *Trin*. 1.2.4.
14. The motif, until recently regnant in modern systematic theology, that Augustine and the West begin with the one substance while the Greek fathers begin with the three persons has been famously debunked by Barnes, "*De Regnon* Reconsidered."
15. A similar treatment is found in his *Serm*. 52; cf. Ayres, "'Remember That You Are Catholic.'"

through a dossier of scriptural texts that attribute divine status to both Son and Spirit. But he specifies as the primary cause of anti-Nicene scriptural misreading the failure to take account of the christological plot of scriptural narrative. Overlooking the christodramatic character of scriptural narrative, anti-Nicenes simply apply scriptural depictions of the human Jesus onto his divinity. A properly trinitarian account of the self-manifesting activity of God, as narrated by Scripture, can only occur when the dramatic and dialectical character of the scriptural presentation of Christ is consistently in view. Certain scriptural texts that depict this dramatic and dialectical presentation of Christ must be taken as hermeneutically determinative for the whole reading of Scripture.[16] A central such instance is the kenotic hymn of Philippians 2:6–8, "Though he was in the form of God, [he] did not regard equality with God as something to be exploited, but emptied himself, taking the form of a slave, being born in human likeness. And being found in human form, he humbled himself and became obedient to the point of death, even death on a cross." Thus, for Augustine, a scriptural account of the manifestation of God as Trinity is one that simultaneously has in view at least three things: (1) scriptural affirmations of the oneness of God's being and activity; (2) the three distinct names under which such activity is depicted in the climax of God's salvific intervention through Christ; and (3) the dialectical and kenotic character of the scriptural presentation of Christ such that part of this presentation applies to Christ's divinity and another part to his humanity. The latter principle echoes the treatments of both Athanasius and Gregory in delineating a distinct christological narrative that grounds a trinitarian reading of Scripture.

Augustine's emphasis on the christological determination of a properly trinitarian reading of Scripture must be placed in the context of his earlier discussion on the dynamics of human knowledge of God. At the heart of this discussion is a complex rhetorical play of the scriptural motifs of faith and sight; this motif pervades the entire work and illuminates especially its christocentric logic.[17] The scriptural source for this rhetorical play is the Pauline exhortation, "We walk by faith, not by sight" (*per fidem enim ambulamus, non per speciem*, 2 Cor. 5:7). This verse is a recurring motif in many of Augustine's writings throughout his career. Most globally and fundamentally, it expresses his radically eschatological orientation, his conception of human existence as essentially a pilgrimage toward the full vision of God. But in *De Trinitate* it is put to more complex use to articulate precisely the epistemological principles that we have already outlined. According to these principles, the way of faith is an assent to the divine program of symbolic self-disclosure as narrated by biblical revelation. Within this assent, the dialectic of faith and sight is not in fact a simple contrast between apprehending what is seen and what is unseen. Nor is it merely a distinction between cognitive apprehension (sight) and assent of the will (faith) such that faith is

16. See Pelikan, "*Canonica Regula.*"

17. See Anatolios, "Oppositional Pairs," esp. 243–47. In speaking of the rhetorical play of the motifs of faith/sight, I am including under "sight" Augustine's references both to the activity (*visio, species*) and object (*visum*) of seeing. Where there is some doubt as to which sense is intended, I have used "sighting" to refer to the objects of vision.

understood to be the assent of the will to what is unseen and unknown. Rather, there is a distinction within unity between two kinds of seeing: that which apprehends historical sightings (*visa*) or symbols (*similitudines*) and eschatological vision of the full reality (*res*) of trinitarian being. Faith provides a semiotic continuity between these two kinds of sight; it is assent precisely to the referentiality of the sightings of divine self-disclosure, thus enabling the ascent from the historical sightings of divine self-revelation to the full eschatological sight of God's trinitarian being. In book 1 of *De Trinitate*, Augustine sets up a rich rhetorical interplay of motifs that depict Christian life within this fundamental dialectic of historical revelation and eschatological vision. Christian life in the world is a stance of faith, hope, purification, quest, and the use (*uti*) of the mediating signs of divine self-revelation in order to enjoy (*frui*) the full vision and contemplation of the truth of divine being.

An integral reading of *De Trinitate* must consequently begin by registering Augustine's foundational epistemological insight that human existence, as radically determined by its relation to God, is a semiotic existence.[18] God and creation are radically different; what mediates between them are the signs and symbols, the *similitudines*, provided by God to refer humanity to the full vision and contemplation of his being. As we have noted, this semiotic structure of the God-world relation is, of course, first and foremost christological. The person of Christ ultimately represents both the supreme historical sighting (*visum*) that orients faith and the ultimate eschatological object of the vision of contemplation. Following his preliminary statement of the trinitarian form of the scriptural revelation of God and its distortion through inattentiveness to the dialectical presentation of Christ, Augustine returns to the theme of the christological structure of humanity's appropriation of divine revelation. Using the *kenōsis* hymn of Philippians 2, he provides an account of both the human/divine difference as well as the personal unity of Christ in terms of this epistemological framework. In the form of God (*forma dei*), Christ is the object of eschatological vision in his unity with the Father and the Spirit; in the form of the servant (*forma servi*), he is the object of seeing by faith. Because of the unity of his person, Christ is the secure and perfectly efficacious link between the vision of faith and eschatological vision: "The fact is that 'the man Christ Jesus, mediator of God and men' (1 Tim. 2:5), now reigning for all the just who live by faith (Hab. 2:4), is going to bring them to direct sight (*ad speciem*) of God, to the 'face to face' vision (*visionem*), as the apostle calls it (1 Cor. 13:12)."[19]

Moreover, Augustine points to a particular event in the life of Christ that signals his role as mediator between the historical seeing oriented to the sightings (*visa*) of adaptive divine self-manifestations and eschatological vision of the divine being. The ascension is the event that signifies that the visible, historical manifestation of Christ does not fully disclose his identity but is meant rather to lead to the

18. See Anatolios, "Divine Semiotics."
19. *Trin.* 1.8.16.

ultimate vision of the invisible Christ in his relation of equality to the Father: "So it was necessary for the form of a servant to be removed from their sight (*ab oculis eorum*) since as long as they could observe it they would think that Christ was this only which they had before their eyes (*quod videbant*). . . . His ascension to the Father signified his being seen (*videre*) in his equality with the Father, that being the ultimate vision (*finis visionis*) that suffices for us."[20] This ultimate vision will be the contemplation and indwelling of the Trinity: "For the fullness of our happiness, beyond which there is none else, is this: to enjoy God the Trinity in whose image we were made."[21]

In analyzing some of the key motifs of Augustine's introduction to his own work in book 1 of *De Trinitate*, we already have access to the guiding logic of the whole. The central tenet of this logic is the christological mediation of the vision of the Triune God. The whole of Augustine's argument is structured by the premise that God is disclosed as Trinity through Christ and that the way from this disclosure in the mode of historical encounter, the "sightings" of divine self-manifestations, to its eschatological fulfillment is to be found only in Christ. Before we launch into further analysis of this treatise in search of Augustine's "trinitarian theology," we must now re-conceive that enterprise on his own terms. On the basis of our analysis to this point, "trinitarian theology" cannot mean, for Augustine, an analysis or description of the vision of the Triune God. He could not be any clearer that such a vision is not possible in this world. But neither does trinitarian theology simply do without vision altogether. Like all theology from the standpoint of faith, trinitarian theology is a matter of referential, or symbolic, vision; it is a matter of seeing the realities of divine self-disclosure in this world in the mode of their referential capacity in signifying the reality of God. Trinitarian theology, like all theology, is much rather a matter of properly learning to signify God than of encompassing the object of that signifying activity. The discourse of faith partakes of the radical pilgrim stance of human existence; it is the discourse of seeking. And, of course, this seeking, this pilgrimage of signifying God through God's own self-symbolizations, is completely enfolded in and enabled by the person of Jesus Christ. Trinitarian theology, conceived in Augustine's own terms, is thus the activity of properly seeking and signifying the God who is Trinity in such a way as to effect our approach toward full recognition of and union with what we are signifying. This way is Christ.

Scriptural Exposition of God as Trinity

After establishing in book 1 the christological epistemology that governs knowledge of the Trinity, Augustine proceeds, in books 2 and 3, to an exposition of the trinitarian disclosure of God as revealed in Scripture. The particular perspective of this exposition is determined by Augustine's polemical context. He wants to counter

20. *Trin.* 1.8.18.
21. *Trin.* 1.8.18.

the arguments of anti-Nicenes that since the Father sends the Son and the Spirit, they must be ontologically inferior to the Father.[22] This Western "homoian" conception characterized the humanity of Jesus in terms of visibility and passibility and associated these characteristics with the attenuated and subordinate divinity of the Son, in contrast to the utterly transcendent invisible and impassible Father. Reading this logic back from the incarnation, the homoians saw all the Old Testament instances of divine visibility as manifestations of the secondary divinity of the Son. In this polemical context, Augustine's program of demonstrating the trinitarian self-disclosure of God is preoccupied with the categories of visibility and invisibility as applied to the biblical theophanies. His object is to complicate and deconstruct the anti-Nicene presentation of a subordinationist dialectic between the invisibility of a supreme divine transcendence and the visible manifestation in Christ of a secondary divinity. He proposes to replace it with a trinitarian-christological framework in which the visible manifestation of God in Christ is both properly related to and properly differentiated from the invisible divine nature that Jesus shares fully with the Father and the Spirit.

The Old Testament Theophanies

As we have pointed out, Augustine's christological epistemology operates within the foundational premise of the difference between God and world. For Augustine, this difference means that the God who is being revealed cannot be generally equated with the features of his appearances in creaturely forms. Seeing the divine self-disclosure in the created realm (historical sightings, *visa*) is not simply equivalent to seeing the divine being (eschatological vision), but neither are the two kinds of sight simply discontinuous. The distance between the two is always mediated by Christ. On the basis of this christological epistemology, Augustine will proceed to demonstrate the scriptural disclosure of the Trinity from the perspective of a semiotic analysis. We find the basic elements of this framework outlined in *De doctrina christiana*.[23] There Augustine tells us that a sign is a thing (*res*) that functions to refer to another thing. The ultimate *res*, in relation to which every other thing is a sign, is the Trinity itself.[24] Conceiving the theophanies as symbols (*similitudines*) and thus as signs (*signa*), Augustine seems to be applying to them two questions that must be asked in relation to any sign: (1) what *res* is signified? and (2) what is the nature of the *res* that is the sign? These questions give us the key to the structure of Augustine's treatment of the Old Testament theophanies in books 2–3.

First, he asks about the reference of these signs. Did the Old Testament theophanies mediate the personal presence of Father, of Son, or of Spirit? Or of each, alternately? Or of all together, as the one God? On exegetical grounds, Augustine insists that

22. See Barnes, "Visible Christ."
23. *Doctr. chr.* 1.4. See Anatolios, "Divine Semiotics."
24. *Doctr. chr.* 1.5.

we cannot be certain about the answers to these questions. Besides demonstrating hermeneutical prudence, Augustine's agnosticism in this regard bespeaks his prior and overriding commitment to emphasizing the discontinuity between the being of God and these creaturely manifestations. The anti-Nicene logic sees a direct correspondence between the character of the divine manifestation in the humanity of Christ and the attributes of Christ's putatively secondary divine nature. For his part, Augustine wants to allow for the possibility of divine manifestation of all three persons while categorically denying any strict correspondence between the nature of the divine signified and that of the created sign:

> An examination of what seems a sufficient number of scriptural passages, and a modest and careful consideration of the divine symbols or "sacraments" (*divinorum sacramentorum*) they contain, all served to teach us, I think, one lesson; that we should not be dogmatic in deciding which person of the three appeared in any bodily form or likeness . . . unless the whole context of the narrative provides us with probable indications. In any case, that nature, or substance, or essence, or whatever else you may call that which God is, whatever it may be, cannot be physically seen, but on the other hand we must believe that by means of the creature who is subject to him, the Father, as well as the Son and the Holy Spirit, could offer the senses of mortal men a token representation of himself in a bodily sight or likeness.[25]

That is to say, the reference of the Old Testament theophanies varies according to context and in any case cannot be determined with certainty. The essential point is the discontinuity between sign and signified, which renders the reference indeterminate. It follows that the disclosure of God as Trinity cannot be read in any clear way out of the Old Testament.

As to the second question, that of the nature of the thing that the sign itself is, Augustine answers that, in his opinion, it was most likely angels who appeared in order to signify the divine presence. But Augustine's demythologization of the Old Testament theophanies only serves to set in greater relief his emphasis on the incarnation as the supreme event of divine self-disclosure. Over against anti-Nicene attempts to collapse the self-disclosure of the Son/Word into a more or less continuous trajectory of a visible and passible subordinate divinity, Augustine insists on the discontinuities not only between any visible manifestation of the divine and its real referent but also between any foreshadowings of the incarnation in the Old Testament theophanies and the appearance of Jesus in the new dispensation. To make this point, Augustine typically recalls Galatians 4:4, which speaks of the sending of the Son as occurring "in the fullness of time."[26] The fullness of trinitarian disclosure only comes about through the sendings of the Son and the Spirit that are narrated in the New Testament. Augustine proceeds to this theme in book 4.

25. *Trin.* 2.18.35 (altered).
26. Cf. *Trin.* 4.26. For a list of these citations, see the scriptural index for Galatians 4:4 in Hill, *Trinity*, 451.

The Incarnation as Climactic Sign

Following the analysis of divine self-disclosure in the Old Testament appearances in books 1–3, book 4 treats the incarnation as the climax and recapitulation of the whole "dispensation of symbols" (*dispensatio similitudinum*)[27] by which divine presence was signified up to that point: "This sacrament, this sacrifice, this high priest, this God, before he was sent and came, 'made of woman' (Gal. 4:4)—all the sacred and mysterious things that were shown to our fathers by angelic miracles, or that they themselves performed, were likenesses of him (*similitudines huius*), so that all creation might in some fashion utter the one who was to come and be the savior of all who needed to be restored from death."[28] On the face of it, this statement directly seems to contradict Augustine's previous repudiation of precisely the notion that the Old Testament theophanies all referred to the Son. Augustine does not explicitly treat this apparent contradiction, but a closer scrutiny of his logic resolves the issue. Once again, the distinctions involved in Augustine's semiotic analysis are crucial. Previous divine symbolizations in the Old Testament were likenesses of Christ not because their signified referent was Christ but precisely in their character of being signs. All previous signifying of divine presence achieves a fulfillment in the supremely signifying activity of the humanity of Christ and can thus retroactively be seen as a foreshadowing of this supreme signifying activity.

While there is thus an element of continuity between the Old Testament theophanies and the appearance of Christ, inasmuch as they all represent instances of divine self-symbolization, there is also a great qualitative leap. In all self-symbolizations of God apart from Christ, the difference between God and the world insinuates itself into the very structure of divine self-disclosure. God, who is signified, remains utterly other than the creaturely mode, which signifies. In Christ, however, this difference is maintained in the otherness between his humanity and divinity yet also bridged in his personal unity. The person of Jesus Christ, therefore, not only brings to climactic fulfillment the history of divine self-disclosure but ontologically restructures humanity's access to that self-disclosure. To reengage some of the rhetorical resonances of Augustine's conception, we should again retrieve the dialectic of faith and sight set out at the beginning of *De Trinitate* and now reemployed by Augustine to speak of the fulfillment of the mission of the Son in book 4. We can recall that Augustine described the way of faith as a compliance with the regimen of divine self-symbolization. This regimen provided purificatory sightings, which faith accepts precisely in the mode of their capacity to refer to the divine. Only in Christ, however, is the sight that is the object of faith (his humanity) structurally united with eschatological sight (his divinity in its unity with the Father and the Spirit). Thus the entire dialectic of faith and sight, which constitutes authentic knowledge of God, is enfolded in Christ. This point is rhetorically magnified by Augustine's applying the entire repertoire of motifs associated with faith and sight to his description of Christ as the supreme

27. *Trin.* 1.8.16.
28. *Trin.* 4.7.11.

sign and sacrament of divine presence. Divine adaptation to human sensibilities and human purification, temporal faith and eschatological sight, and contemplation of the truth of God are all united in Christ. The "clash" between our creaturely mode of knowing and the divine truth we seek to know is overcome in Christ. A key passage in *De Trinitate* 4 displays Augustine's rendering of the role of Christ in securing and completing human access to the divine self-disclosure:

> To sum up then: we were incapable of grasping eternal things, and weighed down by the accumulated dirt of our sins, which we had collected by our love of temporal things . . . so we needed purifying. But we could only be purified for adaptation to eternal things by temporal means like those we were already bound to in a servile adaptation. . . . Now just as the rational mind is meant, once purified, to contemplate eternal things, so it is meant while still needing purification to give faith to temporal things. . . . So now we accord faith to the things done in time for our sakes, and are purified by it, in order that when we come to sight and truth succeeds to faith, eternity might likewise succeed to mortality. Our faith will then become truth . . . therefore when our faith becomes truth by seeing, our mortality will be transformed into a fixed and firm eternity. Now until this happens and in order that it may happen, and to prevent the faith which we accord with all trust in this mortal life to things "that have originated" from clashing with the truth of contemplating eternal things which we hope for in eternal life, truth itself, co-eternal with the Father, "originated from the earth" (Ps. 85:12) when the Son of God came in order to become the Son of man and to capture our faith and draw it to himself, and by means of it to lead us on to his truth; for he took our mortality in such a way that he did not lose his own eternity. . . . So it was proper for us to be puri-fied in such a way that he who remained eternal should become for us "originated"; it would not do for there to be one person for us in faith, another in truth. Nor, on the other hand, could we pass from being among the things originated to eternal things, unless the eternal allied himself to us in our originated condition, and so provided us with a bridge to his eternity.[29]

While Augustine's depiction of the christological structure of divine revelation and humanity's access to God is pervasively cast in the epistemological categories of faith and sight, we should not interpret these categories in narrowly cognitive or gnosiological terms.[30] We have noted that, given the polemical context in which he is engaged, Augustine is treating the content of Christian faith from the perspective of revelation, as manifestation, disclosure, and representation, in keeping with the controverted framework of visibility-invisibility. But this does not mean that he is losing sight of the soteriological and dramatic aspects of divine intervention. The "sight" of Christ's humanity, which leads by faith to the sight of the trinitarian being of God, in the context of the entire presentation of book 4, encompasses the extent of the self-manifestation of Christ in his life, death, and resurrection. We can advert

29. *Trin.* 4.18.24.
30. On the "gnosiological" or, one could also say, "sapiential" aspect of Augustine's soteriology, see Anatolios and Clifford, "Christian Salvation."

to at least five distinct aspects of the "sight" of Christ, as presented by Augustine, in this crucial stage of *De Trinitate*:

1. The first is that our salvation by God through Christ manifests the extremity of God's love. That God's salvific love in Christ should be directed toward a sinful humanity is a cure for both human pride and despair; it heals our pride through the recognition that our salvation was utterly unmerited by our sinful state, and it heals our despair by displaying that our sinfulness is not an obstacle to the power of divine love.[31]

2. The second motif, which is the one most comprehensively treated by Augustine, is that Christ's death and resurrection each represent a sacrament (*sacramentum*) and exemplar (*exemplum*) of our own death and resurrection.[32] Here we see that the existential and dramatic categories of death and resurrection are depicted in the language of semiotic representation and manifestation, in keeping with the governing motifs of the work as a whole. By "sacrament" Augustine means a visible representation that symbolizes an invisible reality; "exemplar" means a visible representation that is meant to evoke a mimetic response. The bodily death of Christ is a sacrament of the death of the human soul by sin; thus Christ's cry of dereliction upon the cross is a representation of our sin (*figuram peccati nostri*).[33] Christ's death is an exemplar of the witness of martyrdom, which must be imitated by the disciple of Christ should need arise. Christ's resurrection is also both sacrament and exemplar. It is a sacrament insofar as it outwardly represents our inner resurrection, which is our orientation toward "the things that are above, where Christ is seated at the right hand of God" (Col. 3:1–2); and it is an exemplar of our future bodily resurrection.

3. A third aspect of Christ's salvific manifestation is that he intercedes for humanity with the Father, introducing his disciples into the unity that he enjoys with the Father. Augustine comments on Jesus's Johannine prayer "that they may all be one. As you, Father, are in me and I am in you, may they also be in us" (John 17:21). The unity of the church, always a passionate theme for Augustine, is here presented as a reflection of trinitarian life effected by the salvific intercession of Christ—"that just as Father and Son are one not only by equality of substance but also by identity of will, so these people, for whom the Son is mediator with God, might be one not only by being of the same nature, but also by being bound in the fellowship of the same love."[34] This is one instance in which the trinitarian unity or identity of will is treated productively by Augustine.

4. A fourth aspect of Christ's salvific manifestation is the display of divine humility, another theme writ large over much of Augustine's work.[35] The condescension of God in assuming humanity in Christ and undergoing suffering and death on our behalf represents an antidote and counter-witness to humanity's overweening pride.

31. *Trin.* 4.1.2.
32. *Trin.* 4.3.6.
33. *Trin.* 4.8.16.
34. *Trin.* 4.8.12.
35. See Daley, "Humble Mediator."

5. Finally, a fifth aspect of Christ's salvific manifestation is that Christ has become our high priest, who offers the perfect sacrifice in expiation of human sin. Christ is the perfect offerer, as the sinless Son of God; and he makes a perfect offering of his sinless humanity on behalf of kindred humanity.[36] This sacrificial-liturgical account manifests the connections between Augustine's trinitarian theology, Christology, and eucharistic theology.

All these aspects, taken together, constitute Augustine's presentation of Christ as bringing to fulfillment the "regimen of symbols" through the "sight" of his own incarnate humanity. It will be noted that each of these aspects has resonances with other foci of Augustinian theology, such as ecclesiology, ethics, and eucharistic theology. In book 4 of *De Trinitate*, they are brought together to demonstrate that the manifestation of Christ is the supreme "sight" of historical faith, which leads to the eternal sight of the contemplation of the divine Trinity. While all previous divine sightings foreshadowed this supreme self-manifestation of God, only in the person of the incarnate Son and Word is the historical visible manifestation of God continuous with the eternal truth of God's trinitarian being. Precisely this continuity constitutes the "mission" of the Son. For human beings to receive the "sending" of the Son is to be so oriented toward the "sight" of Christ's humanity as to be referred toward his eternal being, which is both from and equal to the Father. Therefore, the temporal mission of the Son brings about knowledge of his eternal being: "And just as being born means for the Son his being from the Father, so his being sent means his being known to be from him."[37] The directionality of the sending, the fact that it is the Son who is sent by the Father, is revelatory of the eternal relation by which the Father is begetter of the Son. But Augustine insists that the order of the relation between Father and Son does not mitigate scriptural testimony to their oneness; the two aspects of divine disclosure must be accepted in tandem: "But just as the begetter and the begotten are one, so are the sender and the sent, because the Father and the Son are one (cf. John 10:30); so too the Holy Spirit is one with them, because 'these three are one.'"[38]

The Mission of the Spirit

The fulfillment of the mission of the Son in the Christ event is paralleled by that of the mission of the Spirit. Augustine comments on the Johannine saying, "The Spirit was not yet given because Jesus was not yet glorified" (John 7:39), with the qualifying explanation that, in fact, the Spirit was in some sense given and sent throughout the history of divine self-manifestation, as in the inspiration of prophecy. But the correct interpretation of the Johannine saying is that the Spirit was about to be given in an unprecedented manner, so that, properly speaking, the fullness of the sending of the Spirit occurs only in conjunction with the fulfillment of the mission of the Son. The unique quality of this consummate sending of the Spirit is attested by the fact

36. *Trin.* 4.14.19.
37. *Trin.* 4.20.29.
38. *Trin.* 4.20.29.

that it was accompanied by the remarkable sign of the disciples' speaking in many languages: "For then his coming needed to be demonstrated by perceptible signs (*signis sensibilibus*), to show that the whole world and all nations with their variety of languages were going to believe in Christ by the gift of the Holy Spirit."[39] Augustine notes that while the mission of the Son is accomplished at the point when his visible human manifestation is joined in a unity with his eternal being, such that the "sight" of the humanity of Christ directly signifies his divine relation to the Father, there is no such unity between the visible manifestation of the Spirit and his eternal being. The "perceptible signs" of the Spirit's presence, manifest in the speaking in tongues, do not indicate an "incarnation" of the Spirit. Rather, these signs refer to the Spirit's work in enabling the manifestation of Christ. The fulfillment of the mission of the Spirit is accomplished in the Spirit's role in bringing about the universal reign of Christ.

Just as the temporal manifestation and mission of the Son indicate his eternal being, so does the mission of the Spirit. The Holy Spirit is scripturally described as "the gift of God" who proceeds from the Father (cf. John 15:26), and his mission is received precisely in the knowing of this divine relation to the Father: "And just as for the Holy Spirit his being the gift of God means his proceeding from the Father, so his being sent means his being known to proceed from him."[40] Augustine concludes that the Spirit also proceeds from the Son by applying the principle of the correlation between the structural order of the temporal missions of Son and Spirit and their eternal relations. Continuing the language of signification and divine self-symbolization, he explains that Christ's breathing of the Holy Spirit upon the disciples was "a convenient symbolic demonstration," which signified (*demonstratio per congruam significationem*) "that the Holy Spirit proceeds from the Son as well as the Father."[41] However, Jesus's promise that he will send the Holy Spirit "from the Father" indicates that the Father is the "source of all divinity" (*totius divinitatis vel si melius dicitur deitatis principium pater est*).[42] The Spirit's procession from the Son keeps intact the order of the Son's own generation from the Father such that the Father's ultimate priority as unique source of the deity remains intact: "So the Spirit who proceeds from the Father and the Son is traced back, on both counts, to him of whom the Son is born."[43]

The Structure of De Trinitate

Putting aside typical divisions of *De Trinitate* into a scriptural half and a reasoning half, it is more helpful to see book 4 as the center of its complex movement.[44] By book 4, Augustine has resolved the history of divine self-symbolization into the

39. *Trin.* 4.20.29.
40. *Trin.* 4.20.29.
41. *Trin.* 4.20.29.
42. *Trin.* 4.20.29.
43. *Trin.* 4.20.29.
44. For incisive criticisms of the faith/reason division of the contents of *De Trinitate*, see especially Cavadini, "Structure and Intention," 103–4, 111.

consummating events of the coordinated missions of the Son and the Spirit, what we would refer to as "the economic Trinity." Dividing the book into halves through the scriptural faith/reasoned (Platonic) ascent framework does not take into account Augustine's explicit statements in book 1 that the whole ascent to God is scripturally mediated. Augustine clearly intends the scriptural presentation of trinitarian faith as part of the ascent, indeed its very ground and foundation, inasmuch as the Scriptures narrate God's adaptive self-disclosure by which humanity is led upward from creaturely experience to the vision of God. By book 4, we have seen that this divine self-disclosure finds its consummation in the supreme self-symbolization of trinitarian being through the incarnation of the Son and the witness to this event by the Spirit. Book 5 negotiates the correlation between this scriptural disclosure of the trinitarian God and ecclesial conciliar formulations in terms of substance, person, and relation, while books 6 and 7 take up the exegesis of 1 Corinthians 1:24 ("Christ the power of God and the wisdom of God") in light of the consubstantiality and distinction of persons between the Father and the Son.[45]

The movement from books 1–4 to books 5–7 can thus be seen as delineating a transition from the scriptural exposition of "the economic Trinity" to the doctrinal formulations pertaining to "the immanent Trinity." This transition is scripturally informed throughout, as is evidenced by Augustine's concern for the exegesis of 1 Corinthians 1:24 in books 6–7.

If we were to divide *De Trinitate* into two parts, inasmuch as at least books 1–4 do seem to be preoccupied with a distinct task from that pursued in books 8–15, we should take our cue from Augustine's stated intentions in book 1. As we analyzed it at the beginning of this chapter, Augustine's task can be reduced to two main trajectories: to provide a scriptural account of trinitarian faith, and then to inculcate a dialectical experience that comprises both a kind of certainty that inclines us toward the contents of this faith as well as an awareness of the need for a christological bridging of the distance between our broken capacity for knowing God and the full vision of the Trinity. Toward the end of book 7, Augustine again adverts to this double task: "For it is known with complete certainty from the Scriptures (*certissime . . . de scripturis congnoscitur*) and is thus to be devoutly believed and grasped by the mind's eye with an indubitable perception (*indubitata perceptione*), that the Father exists as well as the Son and the Holy Spirit and that the Son is not the same as the Father nor is the Holy Spirit the same as the Father or the Son."[46] I suggest that the best way to conceptually frame Augustine's discussion of the trinitarian image in the human being is to locate it within this dialectic, to which Augustine refers at key junctures of this extended

45. Barnes, "*De Trinitate* VI and VII."
46. *Trin.* 7.4.9 (altered). Hill takes some liberties with the translation here, interjecting his own editorial gloss, "and the mind's eye can also achieve a *faint* but undoubted glimpse of the truth, that the Father is and the Son is and the Holy Spirit is . . ." (my italics). In fact, there is nothing about faintness in Augustine's text, which reads: "*Certissime quippe et de scripturis congnoscitur quod pie credendum est, et aspectu mentis indubitata perceptione perstringitur et patrem esse et filium esse et spiritum sanctum, nec eundem filium esse qui pater est nec spiritum sanctum eundem patrem esse vel filium.*"

meditation on coming to knowledge of the Triune God. The goal of adverting to this inner-trinitarian likeness is neither simply to "picture" God nor to demonstrate that knowledge of the Trinity is inaccessible to "reason" but rather "to give a reasonable account" (*reddere rationem*)[47] for trinitarian faith through a dialectical experience of certainty that is mediated by faith: certainty that the contents of the Scriptures declare trinitarian faith, that the contents of trinitarian faith are imprinted in some manner within the structure of human consciousness, and that such imprinting is impaired in a way that can only be repaired by Christ. To leave out any of these three aspects of the kind of certainty that Augustine wishes to inculcate in his readers is to miss the full dimensions of Augustine's project.

The Trinitarian Image in Humanity

Contrary to the notion that the second half of *De Trinitate* presents a speculative reasoned appropriation of trinitarian faith, we find Augustine at the end of book 7 depending on Scripture for articulating the rationale for the project of locating a trinitarian image in human consciousness. In fact, Augustine's scriptural reflections on this point adumbrate fairly precisely the proper contours and aims of his project. The plural in the divine announcement of human creation, "Let us make the human being to our image and likeness" (*ad imaginem et similitudinem nostram*) (Gen. 1:26), refers to the Trinity of Father, Son, and Holy Spirit. This biblical revelation justifies the assumption that the human being is made in the image of the Trinity. However, Augustine immediately proceeds to clarify that humanity's status as "image" indicates not parity or some kind of reduplication in miniature of the divine being, but rather humanity's dynamic relatedness to God through imitation:

> But the image of God was not made in any sense equal, being created by him, not born of him . . . that is, he is not equated in perfect parity with God, but approaches him in a certain similarity. . . . But as I said, [the human being] is said to be "to the image" (*ad imaginem*) because of the disparity of his likeness to God, and "to our image" to show that [the human being] is the image of the trinity; not equal to the trinity as the Son is equal to the Father but approaching it as has been said by a certain likeness, as one can talk of a certain proximity between things distant from each other, not proximity of place but a sort of imitation (*cuiusdam imitationis*).[48]

Augustine's explanation of what he considers to be the scriptural sense of "image" alerts us again to the fact that the kind of trinitarian knowledge he is looking for is not a simple or punctiliar transaction between a given set of propositions and their objective referent in divine being but rather an all-encompassing way of imitation, purification, and ascent. It will become even clearer by book 13 that such a way can

47. *Trin.* 1.2.4.
48. *Trin.* 7.6.12.

only take place through him who is the Way. For the moment, it is crucial to keep in mind Augustine's selection of scriptural texts for elucidating humanity's being "to the image" of the trinitarian God. He had begun the discussion by referring to Genesis 1:26, but he concludes it by referring to texts that emphasize this more dynamic aspect of humanity's actualization of its likeness to the Trinity: "To this kind of approximation we are exhorted when it says, 'Be refashioned in the newness of your mind' (Rom. 12:2), and elsewhere he says, 'Be therefore imitators of God as most dear sons' (Eph. 5:1), for it is with reference to the new [human being] that it says, 'Who is being renewed for the recognition of God according to the image of him who created him' (Col. 3:10)."[49]

If trinitarian knowledge of God is to be conceived globally as a way of imitation and reformation, its ontological foundations reside in the very structure of human consciousness. A reading of the work as a whole that is not predisposed to cancel out its cataphatic pronouncements by selective recourse to its apophatic caveats would disclose that demonstrating a certain continuity (along with discontinuity) between the structure of human consciousness and the formulations of Nicene theology is integral to Augustine's stated project of "giving a reasonable account" for Nicene faith. As we embark on Augustine's reflections on the trinitarian image in humanity, it is helpful to deal from the outset with the modern complaint that Augustine's locating of this image in the individual human being is solipsistic and a significant moment, via Descartes, in initiating the decline of Western culture as a whole into disembodied individualism.[50] A potent rebuttal to this charge has been to note that Augustine concludes his reflections by clarifying that the fruition of the image comes about not through the mind's mere remembering, understanding, and loving itself but rather through its directing of these activities toward God.[51] A reading of the second half of *De Trinitate* is greatly enhanced if we realize from the outset that Augustine fully intends for there to be a structural dialectic between the mind's remembering, understanding, and loving itself and its intending of God. Understanding trinitarian *similitudo* involves carefully tracing this dialectic in Augustine between the transitive outward orientation of human consciousness toward God and its inner structural dynamism, a dialectic that is fundamentally consistent with Augustine's understanding of the basic structural mutuality of any sign vis-à-vis the object that it signifies. Thus the transitive orientation of the mind to God is the aspect that refers specifically to its nature as a sign oriented to its signified referent; its inner structure indicates that as a sign, it is also a thing in itself. To see the correspondence between these two aspects is to see the human person as image of God. The ultimate goal of this meditation is

49. *Trin.* 7.6.12.

50. On this and other modern misreadings of Augustine, see Barnes, "Augustine in Contemporary Trinitarian Theology."

51. See especially Williams, "*Sapientia* and the Trinity"; cf. Milbank, "Sacred Triads," 91: "Surely we have here the perfecting of a solipsistic interiority? Yet, in truth, the reverse is the case, because, for Augustine, to know oneself *genuinely* means to know oneself as loving what one should love, namely God and one's neighbor as oneself. Hence, not interiority but radical *exteriorization* is implied."

to see the trinitarian (dynamic) structure of human consciousness as transitively attending to the Triune God. Thus Augustine's clarification in book 14 that the mind is not image simply as memory, intellect, and will but as remembering, understanding, and loving God is already embedded in his initial proposal that human consciousness constitutes a trinitarian *similitudo*.

Given the above, it is significant to note that Augustine does not in fact begin his exposition of trinitarian *similitudo* in book 8 directly with an analysis of the inner structure of human consciousness but rather with the mind's innate relatedness to God and with God's radical presence to the mind. That is to say, he is from the outset focused on the mind's intending of God, and his analysis of the mind's own self-relatedness is always subsumed under that focus. He begins book 8 by analyzing the mind's innate outward orientation toward truth, justice, and goodness. He proposes that underlying the universal human desire for truth, as well as the recognition and affirmation of some aspects of reality as just and good, there is an inchoate and, we would now say "transcendental," experience of the presence of God as Truth and as the Good. The innate dynamism of desiring and affirming goodness finds paradigmatic expression in the experience of human love when that love is bound up with the affirmation of the goodness present in another human being. Augustine takes as his example the experience of loving the apostle Paul. At this juncture, he reminds his readers of the scriptural identification of God as love. If God is also Trinity, then the human experience of love must contain some image of the Trinity. Augustine quickly discerns that such a trinity can be found once we realize that the experience of love structurally involves a lover, a beloved, and the love between them. This trinity of love is not simply a self-standing structure that "pictures" the divine Trinity; rather, it manifests the mind's radical relatedness to God, since the love by which we love anything genuinely, according to Augustine, is God himself. (Later, he will clarify that this love is to be particularly associated with the Holy Spirit.) In loving another human being, we are first of all loving to love, and the love by which we love another human being is more present and more inward to us than the human object of this love. This inward presence of a love by which we love others is the presence of God. Thus the trinity of "lover, beloved, and love" manifest in human experience attains a certain participation in God, who is Love.

Modern readers tend to associate the "trinity of love" model with Richard of St. Victor, while those familiar with Augustine's work can lament that Augustine left behind the interpersonal and "social" trinity of love and moved on to a putatively individualistic and more intellectual trinity of mind. However, the matter is decidedly more complex. As to moving from an interpersonal to an "individual" model, Augustine is very far from denying that the performance of this being-in-the-image is manifested on the interpersonal level.[52] As we have seen, that is in fact his starting

---

52. Williams puts it aptly when he says that in Augustine's analysis of the triadic structure of consciousness, "we are given an account of mental life in which the fundamental category is lack of and quest for an other to love" ("Paradoxes of Self-Knowledge," 126).

point, inasmuch as the mediation begins with the example of loving the apostle Paul. But he is also committed to the biblical datum that every person is in himself or herself made "to the image" of the Triune God. It is truer to the flow of Augustine's argument to see his move from the interpersonal performance of the triune image to its roots in the individual as positing a continuity between human relationships and the individual's innate aptness for such relations. Moreover, we must recall that Augustine is involved in a theological inquiry whose goal is to discern a concrete "sight" by which to orient trinitarian faith. Such a sight must meet all the criteria established by the Nicene interpretation of Scripture. The "social-love" model does not meet these criteria. In the case of the love between two persons, we do not have a sight of a consubstantiality that is constitutively inseparable; in the case of self-love, we do not have a proper differentiation of persons, since the lover and beloved are the same person. In neither case do we have a vision of that perfect mutuality which is the touchstone of Augustine's trinitarian vision: "They are each in each and all in each and each in all and all in all and all are one."[53] That mutual inseparability can however be discerned in the mutually intertwined dynamisms of the mind's self-relatedness and its innate relatedness to God.

The objection that Augustine leaves behind love in order to find the trinitarian image in the "intellect" fundamentally misinterprets Augustine's locating of this image in *mens*, which is generally better translated as "consciousness" than "mind" or "intellect."[54] In fact, the foundation of the trinitarian dynamism of human consciousness is the ineradicable interrelatedness of loving and knowing. Love requires knowledge, and the native dynamism of human consciousness is that of a loving knowing and a knowing loving. Consequently, Augustine progresses from the human subject as loving others to a consideration of human consciousness as intrinsically and ineluctably a dynamic of loving-knowing. The fact that he tracks the interrelatedness of love and knowledge in the mind's transitive outward intentionality to an innate interrelatedness of love and knowledge as constitutive of the mind as such should not lead to the unwarranted assumption that he thus leaves behind the mind's outward relatedness; rather, Augustine is simply grounding the former in the latter. Tracking the interrelatedness of love and knowledge to the very constitution of consciousness, we have the trinity of human consciousness discerned as: mind (*mens*) or consciousness or self, its knowledge of itself (*notitia sui*), and its love of itself (*amor sui*). This is the fundamental trinitarian dynamism of human consciousness, as proposed by Augustine in book 9. Further reflections simply refine and elaborate on this dynamism. A more structural, nominative statement of this dynamic is memory, intellect, and will (*memoria, intellectus, voluntas*). The dynamic and, one can say, innately ek-static dimension of this structure is elaborated by speaking of the intellect in terms of the generation or begetting of an inner word by which memory images itself, while the will couples together and rests

53. *Trin.* 6.1.12.
54. As Williams remarks, Augustine is preoccupied with "an analysis of the grammar of the 'subject' (not simply the intellect)" ("Paradoxes of Self-Knowledge," 121).

in the union of the begetting memory with its begotten word. The inner "sight" of this threefold interrelatedness of the dynamism of human consciousness thus appears to meet the Nicene criteria of perfect mutual interrelatedness. But as we have insisted, this structural interrelatedness is always in dialectical interplay with the mind's innate outward relatedness to God. If we have not forgotten the contents of book 8 by the time we get to book 9, we are bound to see that the mind's unified activity of self-knowledge and self-love derives from and is innately oriented to divine truth and divine goodness. Thus, looking ahead to book 14, the full integrity of the image will only be manifest when the mind's self-knowledge is fully integrated into its knowing of God and its self-love is fully enfolded in its love of God. At the same time, this integration of the knowing and loving of self within the loved knowledge of God will include a rightly ordered knowing and loving of the rest of creation in God. Augustine is clear that this integration can only be eschatologically realized. The question then arises, what is the value of this "image" in our present reality, particularly with regard to the project of appropriating trinitarian faith? To answer this question, we must return to the dialectic of certainty into which Augustine wishes to initiate his readers.

Human Certainty and Seeing the Trinity

We have seen that in book 1, Augustine announces that he will try to respond to those who are hankering after indubitable reasons ("reasons which they can have no doubt about") for holding Nicene trinitarian doctrine. Near the end of *De Trinitate*, in book 15, Augustine recapitulates the contents of the work and declares that he has responded to those who "ask for reasons."[55] Despite certain interpretations to the contrary, Augustine is clearly concerned with providing some kind of rational evidence for the credibility of trinitarian doctrine, so a proper interpretation of this work must provide an account of Augustine's efforts and self-proclaimed success in that regard.[56] But we have to be careful to construe the nature of this "rational" appeal in its own terms.

Features of Augustine's Appeal to Reason

In particular, two distinctive features of Augustine's appeal to "reason," already articulated in book 1, must be kept firmly in view. The first is that the reason that

55. *Trin.* 15.20.39.
56. The classic interpretation of *De Trinitate* as not intending to provide any intelligible knowledge of the divine Trinity is Schindler, *Wort und Analogie*, esp. 215–16; a more recent and more nuanced argument that the project of *De Trinitate* is to demonstrate the failure of the Neoplatonic ascent is found in Cavadini, "Structure and Intention." Cavadini's treatment is valuable in highlighting the anti-Platonic dimensions of this work, though I am more inclined to take at face value Augustine's announcements of his qualified success in giving some glimpse of the divine Trinity through the human image. At the same time, my interpretation has a close affinity with Cavadini's in that I argue that Augustine's demonstration of a certain structural failure in the mind's efforts to attain certainty even about itself is crucial to his project of "giving a rationale" for trinitarian faith.

Augustine has in mind is not an autonomous realm separate from the realm of faith but rather an attentiveness to the "signs" and "sights" that faith in divine revelation provides. Once again, Augustine's "reason" must be interpreted within the structural dialectic of faith and sight that pervades the entire *De Trinitate*. Faith calls forth the ascent of understanding by providing discernible sights that lead from themselves to divine realities. In those terms, to provide a rationale (*reddere rationem*) for trinitarian doctrine is not to argue "within the limits of reason alone" but rather to interpret these discernible and intelligible sights of faith properly so as to be led to the contemplation of the realities that are beyond human understanding. Because the realities that are the objects of faith are beyond human understanding, the dialectic of faith and sight/reason is performed in the mode of quest. Thus the motif of the quest, which recurs at various strategic locations throughout the work, is not a merely digressive expression of a pious impulse but is integral to Augustine's theological epistemology and his particular version of the dialectic of faith, sight, and reason. One striking expression of this motif is that the project of knowing God involves a finding that keeps on seeking: we seek in order to find, and we find in order to seek. In this context, Augustine, like Gregory of Nyssa, makes use of Philippians 3:13–14: "Forgetting what lies behind and straining forward to what lies ahead, I press on toward the goal for the prize of the upward call of God in Christ Jesus."[57] Seeking in faith leads to the finding of "sights" that anchor this faith. But a sight of faith is precisely an apprehension that does not arrest the gaze of the beholder but leads her upward to a signified beyond. The sights and reasons of faith are thus always iconic; they are, in Augustine's terms, *signa* or *similitudines*.[58] Therefore, the finding of these sights always leads to the seeking of more sights, toward the ultimate vision of the trinitarian being.

The second distinctive feature of Augustine's project of providing "reasons" for trinitarian faith—again, a feature already announced in book 1—is that these reasons will explain both the intelligibility of trinitarian faith and our incapacity to readily apprehend that intelligibility. Once again, Augustine's dialectical conception of "reason" proves more complex than those interpreters realize who evaluate the program of *De Trinitate* simply in terms of his success or failure in showing that human consciousness somehow pictures the divine Trinity. In fact, however, both the success and the failure involved in seeing trinitarian faith are equally constitutive of the "rationale" of Nicene trinitarian faith, and both are equally referred to the christocentric foundation of that faith. The success of seeing, in some measure, the intelligible content of trinitarian faith provides a warrant for assenting to the "regime of symbols" that culminates in the trinitarian disclosure of God through the incarnation, life, death, and resurrection of Jesus Christ, as that disclosure is interpreted in the Nicene doctrine of co-equal mutuality. But the failures and aporias involved in this seeing are meant to demonstrate that the apparent incoherence and unintelligibility

57. *Trin.* 9.1.1.
58. The implied contrast between the iconic and the idolatrous comes from Marion, *God without Being*, chaps. 1–2. See Anatolios, "Divine Semiotics."

of Nicene faith does not so much pertain to the contents that faith proposes to human understanding, but rather to the innate incoherence and breakdowns of intelligibility that are native to the fallen human condition as such and that can only be redeemed in Christ. We must now retrace Augustine's efforts to lead his reader to an inward "sight" of trinitarian faith that is also revelatory of humanity's need for christological transformation.

Faith, Sight, and the Logic of **De Trinitate**

Augustine's exposition of the trinitarian image in humanity is not a disruption but a continuation and extension of his scriptural reflections on the "regimen of symbols" provided in the first four books. There Augustine analyzed the revealed sights of Christian faith, culminating in the appearance of Christ as the supreme symbol and "sacrament" of divine self-disclosure and in the Spirit's climactic witness to this manifestation of God in Christ. This history of divine self-manifestation, which culminates in the missions of the Son and Spirit "in the fullness of time," is revelatory of the inseparable mutuality of the "Trinity which God is." However, while the constitutive manifestations within the history of divine disclosure, taken altogether and considered in their various interconnections according to a Nicene understanding, issue in a disclosure of the equality and inseparability of the Trinity, there is no single "sight" or manifestation of that inseparable and equal mutuality itself. This is the problem with which book 4 concludes: "Father and Son and Holy Spirit, God the Creator, of one and the same substance, the almighty three, act inseparably. But they cannot be manifested inseparably by creatures which are so unlike them, especially material ones."[59]

This way of stating the problem is emblematic of the way the faith-sight dialectic structures and animates the logic of *De Trinitate* as the logic of quest. The sights of the scriptural history of divine self-disclosure are interpreted coherently, according to Augustine, in the Nicene propositions that assert the inseparable mutuality of the Trinity. But this Nicene "finding" of the inseparable mutuality of the Trinity must lead to further seeking by faith, and this further seeking by faith would be greatly enabled by a creaturely "sight" of inseparable mutuality that could orient and refer faith in its upward ascent to the divine Trinity. Consequently, after books 5–7 clarify and reassert the Nicene interpretation of Scripture as indicating the perfect mutual correlativity of the divine Trinity, book 8 begins the seeking by faith for a sight of perfect mutual correlativity. But Augustine is not about to go looking randomly everywhere for such a sight and, contrary to a tradition of misinterpretation, he is not about to "turn inward" to a solipsistic analysis of the human mind. Rather, in keeping with the faith-sight epistemological dialectic we have already outlined, he is looking for a sight that arises out of the exigencies of faith and enables that faith by providing a kind of "certainty" that anchors faith.

59. *Trin.* 4.20.30.

As we have already pointed out, book 8 begins not directly with an analysis of human consciousness, considered in itself, but rather with the way in which God's presence to human consciousness as truth and goodness grounds and motivates the radical human awareness of and desire for God. Augustine's analysis of the exigencies of this desire bring into clear focus the nexus of dialectics that animate his logic: faith and sight, certainty and quest, love and knowledge. He introduces this set of dialectics as follows:

> But we also have to stand by and cling to this good in love, in order to enjoy the presence of him from whom we are, whose absence would mean that we could not even be. For since "we are still walking by faith and not by sight" (2 Cor. 5:7) we do not yet see God, as the same apostle says, "face to face" (1 Cor. 13:12). Yet unless we love him even now, we shall never see him. But who can love what he does not know? Something can be known and not loved; what I am asking is whether something can be loved which is unknown, because if it cannot then no one loves God before he knows him. And what does knowing God mean except to see (*conspicere*) him and firmly perceive (*percipere*) him with the mind? For he is not a body to be examined with the eyes in your head. But then to behold and perceive God as he can be beheld and perceived is only permitted to the pure in heart—"blessed are the pure in heart because they shall see God" (Matt. 5:8); so before we are capable of doing this, we must first love by faith, or it will be impossible for our hearts to be purified and become fit and worthy to see him. Where after all are those three things to be found which the whole gear of all the inspired books is set up to build in the human spirit; where are faith, hope, and charity to be found if not in the spirit that believes what it cannot yet see and hopes in and loves what it believes? So something can be loved which is unknown, provided it is believed. But naturally the spirit which believes what it does not see must be on its guard against fabricating something that does not exist, and thus hoping in and loving something false.[60]

This passage recapitulates much of the core logic of Augustine's approach in *De Trinitate*. He begins by asserting God's absolute and foundational presence to human existence and consciousness and the corresponding human drive to "enjoy that presence." However, despite the fact of God's presence as the absolute ground of human existence, or rather precisely because of this fact, God is not an object of knowledge within the horizon of objective human knowing. Thus "we walk by faith and not by sight" (2 Cor. 5:7). Yet the walking by faith requires loving ("we must first love by faith"), and this loving works a purification of heart that will ultimately lead to our eschatological seeing of God. But what motivates Augustine's search for a "sight" of trinitarian faith is the consideration that, even now, the loving by faith requires a kind of seeing and knowledge to inform it. Otherwise, the object of faith and love would be quite indeterminate and one could end up believing and loving "what does not exist."

The problematic articulated in this passage harks back to book 1 and thus demonstrates the organic unity of the whole work. There, the reader was told that faith,

---

60. *Trin.* 8.4.6 (altered). I have changed Hill's translation of *percipere Deum* from "to grasp God" to "to perceive God." Cf. CCSL 50A:274.

rather than "reason," was the starting point for Augustine's reflections. However, Christian faith provides divinely ordained revelatory "sights," which provide an intelligible orientation to faith. To bypass these sights is to risk fabricating what does not exist.[61] The assent of faith consists in accepting the revelatory content of these sights, which leads us upward to the divine realties that they signify. This assent constitutes a path of "purification" that animates our ascent from revelatory signs to the divine signified. Book 8 subtly recalls the epistemological problematic presented in book 1 in order to pose the distinctive problem involved in the "seeing" that initiates, informs, and animates trinitarian faith. Faith in general involves a dialectic between the upward ascent, which continually reaches beyond the range of the knowable "sights," and the orienting and structuring of this ascent through intelligible content provided by knowable "sights." Trinitarian faith in particular, however, trades in content that seems inaccessible to knowledge.

Augustine highlights this distinction by comparing trinitarian confession with other aspects of Christian faith, such as the incarnation, virgin birth, or resurrection of Christ. In these other cases, at least the constituent elements of the content proposed to faith are knowable. Thus, faith in the virgin birth assents to a proposition whose constituent elements are objects not of faith but of knowledge. Christians believe, says Augustine, "that the Lord Jesus Christ was born of a virgin who was called Mary."[62] This faith is conditioned on knowledge of "what a virgin is and what being born is and what a proper name is."[63] We do not have to *believe* what these notions mean; we *know* what they mean, as we must if we are to be able to believe in the synthetic proposition that proposes to faith that Jesus was born from a virgin called Mary. Similarly, faith in the resurrection of Christ requires knowledge of the categories of "living man" and "dead man" in order that faith may assent to the proposition that Christ passed from the state of being a dead man to the state of being alive again.

Nicene trinitarian doctrine, however, proposes to faith certain predications of mutual distinction and inseparability that seem utterly inaccessible to knowledge and *consequently unavailable for faith*. Nicene trinitarian doctrine does not simply predicate that God is a "trinity" in the sense of a mere commonplace threeness; it predicates of God a particular kind of threeness for which there are no other examples. What then is the intelligible content of this faith? It should not surprise the attentive reader that, for Augustine, such intelligible content must be provided by a creaturely sight, or object of knowledge, that would constitute a certain "likeness" to the signified object of faith and thus provide an intelligible orientation to the ascending movement of loving faith. What motivates the search for the trinitarian image in humanity is the principle enunciated from the beginning of book 1: faith needs sight.

> What then do we know, either generically or specifically, about the transcendent trinity, as though there were many such trinities and we had experience of some of them, and

61. *Trin.* 1.1.1.
62. *Trin.* 8.4.7.
63. *Trin.* 8.4.7.

thus could believe according to a standard of likeness impressed on us or in terms of specific and generic notions that that trinity is of the same sort, and hence could love the thing we believe and do not yet know from its likeness to what we do know? But this of course is simply not so. . . . Perhaps then what we love is not what any trinity is but the trinity that God is. So what we love in the trinity is what God is. But we have never seen or known another God, because God is one; he alone is God whom we love by believing, even though we have not yet seen him. What we are asking, though, is from what likeness or comparison of things known to us we are able to believe, so that we may love the as yet unknown God.[64]

Reasons of Faith: Image and Distortion

It is clear from this passage in book 8 that Augustine is not about to abandon, half-way through the work, his stated goal of conducting his reflections from "the starting point of faith (*initium fidei*), rather than reason." But he is concerned with providing his reader with "reasons" that amount to an intelligible "sight," which can thus inform the ascent of faith with at least enough intelligible content to keep this faith from being misdirected and malformed. I suggest that Augustine's presentation of these "reasons of faith" is a complex interplay of two intertwined arguments, which together are intended to inculcate a kind of "certainty" that can ground and animate Nicene trinitarian faith. These two lines of argument are not presented sequentially. Their interdependence is rhetorically dramatized by their textual interplay, the overlooking of which renders the whole work maddeningly and ineffectually digressive. These two arguments are: (1) Human consciousness does in fact present a "likeness," albeit not without a measure of dialectical unlikeness, of what Nicene doctrine confesses about the divine Trinity, namely, an inseparably mutual, consubstantial, and irreducibly distinct trinity. Moreover, the nature of this likeness is such as to constitute a kind of certainty regarding trinitarian faith, inasmuch as the phenomenon of certainty is itself ineluctably triadic. The fact of the correspondence between the trinitarian image in humanity and the Nicene interpretation of the scriptural history of divine self-disclosure substantiates Nicene faith. (2) The radical difficulties encountered in the effort to understand what Nicene doctrine says about God correspond to the radical distortions that sin has caused in humanity's imaging of God, and thus even the difficulties attending the understanding of Nicene doctrine substantiate that doctrine. We need to review, albeit briefly, each of these arguments in order to follow Augustine's program of "giving reasons" for Nicene trinitarian faith.

THE TRINITARIAN IMAGE IN HUMANITY

As regards the first line of argument, we have already seen that Augustine analyzes human consciousness as a dynamic outflow of loving-knowing that can be resolved into the triad of memory, intellect, and will. Memory is the dynamic principle from which

---

64. *Trin.* 8.5.8. The last sentence in this quotation runs, "*Sed ex qua rerum notarum similitudine uel comparatione credamus quo etiam nondum notum deum diligamus, hoc quaeritur.*"

emanate the inseparable double processions of the knowing intellect and the loving will. According to Augustine, this threefold dynamic does represent a kind of "inner sight" that can orient trinitarian faith consistently with the Nicene criterion of irreducible threeness conjoined in consubstantial inseparability. Augustine acknowledges that this trinitarian image in humanity also contains significant elements of unlikeness. Most significantly, he concedes that this threefold dynamic in human consciousness in not what we would call "tripersonal." To state the matter from the divine side, the Word is not merely the Father's activity of self-knowing, but the Word himself knows and loves, as do the Father and the Holy Spirit.[65] But it is a misreading of Augustine's entire project to use his concessions of the unlikeness between the trinitarian image in humanity and the divine Trinity as evidence that he is withdrawing his claims that there is also a likeness. The very notion of an "image" or "likeness" denotes a dialectic of likeness and unlikeness, which cannot be reduced to a zero-sum game. The fact that there is unlikeness between the human trinitarian "image" and the reality of the divine Trinity proves not that the former does not contain the likeness of an image but rather that it is precisely an image rather than the reality itself. Augustine's consistent position, throughout the oscillations in the dialectic of likeness-unlikeness, is that the trinitarian image in humanity is "an unequal image, but an image nonetheless."[66]

In the last analysis, however, the most fundamental point of Augustine's project of giving "reasons" for Nicene faith is his attempt to analyze human certainty itself as a trinitarian event. While the second half of *De Trinitate* has been extensively analyzed in terms of the sheer threefoldness of consciousness and its relation to divine Trinity, the underlying theme of how the human triunity of consciousness constitutes the phenomenon of certainty has been virtually ignored. But it is precisely with respect to the latter theme that we can see Augustine's distinctive and subtly executed maneuver of "giving reasons" from the "starting point of faith." In response to those who seek certainty about trinitarian faith, Augustine does not merely presume the phenomenon of human certainty as a given and then use it as a criterion for judging the propositional contents of Nicene trinitarian doctrine. Rather, he presumes the contents of Nicene doctrine as given to faith and uses that as a key to uncovering the ineluctably trinitarian structure of human certainty. This occurs in book 10 of *De Trinitate*, where the quest for indubitable certainty coincides with the locating of the trinitarian image in human consciousness. Here, certainty is construed in terms of the immediate self-presencing of consciousness. There is nothing that the "mind" (*mens*) can be more certain of than what is most immediately present to it, and there is nothing more immediately present to it than itself. This immediate self-presence of consciousness is ineluctably a dynamic act of a conjoined self-knowing and self-loving. The initiative principle of this reflexive dynamism is called "memory." Thus we have memory (*memoria*: the source of the mind's act of self-presencing), intellect (*intellegentia*: self-presencing as self-knowing), and will (*voluntas*: self-presencing

65. *Trin.* 15.7.12.
66. "*Impar imago est humana mens sed tamen imago*" (*Trin.* 10.12.19; cf. *Trin.* 15.23.43).

as self-loving). Certainty consists in the mutual relatedness of these three, which is articulated in a way that resembles the essential criterion of Nicene doctrine, that of a perfectly coincident triunity.

A careful reading of book 10 will reveal this intertwining in Augustine's text between the themes of the mind's self-presence, a phenomenology of indubitable certainty, and the triadic structure of human consciousness. A selection of key sentences from the heart of the argument in book 10 demonstrates this intertwining:

> Let the mind then not go looking for a look at itself as if it were absent, but rather take pains to tell itself apart as present.[67]
>
> But we are concerned now with the nature of mind; so let us put aside all consideration of things we know outwardly through the senses of the body, and concentrate our attention on what we have stated that all minds know for certain about themselves. . . . Nobody surely doubts, however, that he lives and remembers and understands and wills and thinks and knows and judges. At least, even if he doubts, he lives; if he doubts, he remembers why he is doubting; if he doubts, he understands he is doubting; if he doubts, he has a will to be certain; if he doubts, he thinks; if he doubts, he knows he does not know; if he doubts, he judges he ought not to give a hasty assent. You may have your doubt about anything else, but you should have no doubts about these; if they were not certain, you would not be able to doubt anything.[68]
>
> Now let us put aside for the moment the other things which the mind is certain about as regards itself, and just discuss these three, memory (*memoria*), understanding (*intellegentia*), and will (*voluntas*). . . . These three, then, memory, understanding, and will, are not three lives but one life, nor three minds but one mind. So it follows of course that they are not three substances but one substance. . . . For this reason, these three are one in that they are one life, one mind, one being, and whatever else they are called together with reference to self, they are called in the singular, not in the plural. But they are three in that they have reference to each other. And if they were not equal, not only each to the other but also each to them all together, they would not of course contain each other. In fact, though they are not only each contained by each, they are all contained by each as well. After all, I remember that I have memory and understanding and will, and I understand that I understand and will and remember, and I will that I will and remember and understand, and I remember my whole memory and understanding and will all together. . . . Therefore since they are each and all and wholly contained by each, they are each and all equal to each and all, and each and all equal to all of them together, and these three are one, one life, one mind, one being. Are we already, then, in a position to rise with all our powers of concentration to that supreme and most high being of which the human mind is the unequal image but the image nonetheless?[69]

The description of the perfect mutuality of the threefold dynamic pattern of human consciousness closely echoes Augustine's statement of the key principle of inseparable and perfect mutuality in the Nicene doctrine of God: "So they are each in each and all

67. *Trin.* 10.9.12.
68. *Trin.* 10.10.14.
69. *Trin.* 10.11.17–19.

in each, and each in all and all in all, and all are one. Whoever sees this even in part, or 'in a puzzling manner in a mirror' (1 Cor. 13:12) should rejoice in knowing God and should 'honor and thank him as God' (Rom. 1:21)."[70] The similarity between the two passages signals to the attentive reader that Augustine is claiming success in his efforts to "give reasons" for the credibility of trinitarian faith. Thus the first line of argumentation in Augustine's project of "giving reasons" for trinitarian faith is to show that human certainty itself is structured in the image of the Nicene Trinity and that human consciousness manifests a certain threefold mutuality, which gives positive intelligible content to the propositions of Nicene doctrine.

THE DISTORTING EFFECTS OF SIN

But that, of course, is not the whole story. In our reading of book 1, we noted that Augustine immediately follows the announcement of his intention to give positive "reasons" for the credibility of trinitarian faith with the warning that this account will include a demonstration of humanity's sinful incapacity to clearly ascertain these reasons. He hopes that the effect of such a demonstration on those who demand "reasons" for trinitarian faith will be that

> they may actually come to realize that that supreme goodness does exist which only the most purified minds can gaze upon, and also that they are themselves unable to gaze upon it and grasp it for the good reason that the human mind with its weak eyesight cannot concentrate on so overwhelming a light unless it has been nursed back to full vigor on "the justice of faith" (Rom. 4:13).[71]

When we get to book 10, we find the implementation of this dialectical project in Augustine's dizzying analysis of the paradoxical combination of self-knowledge and self-ignorance that conditions human consciousness as existentially a bewildering conundrum of self-presencing and self-estrangement.

For many readers, book 10 presents one of the most bewildering, enigmatic, and inconclusive trajectories in the complex and sprawling argument of *De Trinitate*. But much clarity can be thrown upon this crucial juncture of Augustine's argument if we see it as the dialectical demonstration promised in book 1. In book 10, Augustine intends to demonstrate that Nicene doctrine's paradoxical combination of intelligibility and inaccessibility is actually imaged in the human mind's own paradoxical, indeed conflicted, condition of simultaneous self-grasp and self-abandonment. What is right about Nicene faith is indeed imaged in our human subjectivity; what seems to be wrong with Nicene faith is really wrong with our own "minds": "they will sooner find fault with their own minds than with the truth itself or our arguments." As far as the "reasons they can have no doubt about," we have shown that Augustine endeavors to prove that the mind's very self-presencing and thus its innate experience of certainty has a trinitarian pattern. The mind exists insofar as it images itself in self-knowledge

70. *Trin.* 6.10.12.
71. *Trin.* 1.2.4.

and affirms itself in self-love. Augustine thus draws a link between the "reasons" for Nicene faith and the trinitarian structure of certainty, which delineates the mind's own act of self-presencing.

But the complementary dialectical movement of book 10 insinuates another link, this time between the doubting demand for the "reasons" of Nicene faith and the mind's *innate lack of certainty* even regarding its own act of existence. The real issue, suggests Augustine, is not merely the difficulty of attaining certainty about Nicene faith but rather the mind's radical uncertainty about itself, the constitutional breakdown of the self's own acts of self-presencing. While the mind is demonstrably constituted by the acts of self-knowing and self-willing, it is so alienated from itself that these very acts, which constitute its being, are perceived as *desiderata* and tasks to be accomplished. The mind seeks to know itself as if it did not already know itself, even though it would not be a mind if it did not already know itself! Augustine carefully elaborates and unpacks this maddening paradox. If there is any conclusion to his Zen-like meditation, it is precisely that the paradox must stand as an accurate assessment of the reality of the human condition.

Interiority in Exile

One clarification that Augustine makes is between the mind's knowing of itself (*nosse*) and the mind's thinking about and attending to itself (*cogitare*). The mind, *qua* mind, cannot help but know itself; it ceases to know anything else and to be mind the moment it ceases to know itself. But the mind does not always attend to itself and think about itself. While its self-knowledge underlies all its activities, the mind's constitutive act of self-presencing can become opaque and seemingly absent to the extent that its disordered outward activities overlay and obscure its own underlying movements of self-knowing and self-willing. This distinction between the mind's constant and constitutive self-knowing and its inconsistent, rare, and largely distorted self-awareness does not so much explain or unravel the paradoxical condition of human subjectivity as highlight the gap of self-estrangement that runs through every human consciousness. In book 4, Augustine had characterized the human condition as one of estrangement and alienation.[72] In calling us out of this condition of exile, divine revelation exposes and confirms our situation of estrangement in order to lead us back to the divine source of our being: "But we were exiled from this unchanging joy. . . . So God sent us sights (*visa*) suited to our wandering state, to admonish us that what we seek is not here and that we must turn back from the things around us to where our whole being springs from."[73] In book 10, Augustine seeks to show that our situation of exile is indeed radical to our inmost being; we are exiled even from our very selves. Though our human consciousness, which images divine being, is constituted by a triadic act of self-presencing, that act itself is overlaid by self-forgetfulness. If even certainty about our own act of self-presencing is so far from our grasp, are we in

72. *Trin.* 4.1.2.
73. *Trin.* 4.1.2.

any position to demand certainty about the reality of the divine being? If we are to attain any certainty about the divine, we must first contend with our fundamental and radical uncertainty about the very structure that constitutes our certainty about anything, the structure of our own self-knowledge and self-awareness.

Yet another clarification is necessary. This clarification, though not so explicitly thematized and localized in the text as that between *nosse* and *cogitare*, is clearly presumed throughout Augustine's argument and sometimes explicitly stated: We cannot attain to the "sight" of the trinitarian dynamic of human consciousness as a perfectly mutual, equal, and co-inhering complex act of self-remembering through self-knowing and self-willing simply by perceiving the normal condition of human existence. Rather, this "sight" is an insight, gained through much exertion, into what the mind *ought* to be. Here again, we can draw a connection that is easy to overlook in following Augustine's complex and seemingly randomly digressive argument in the second half of *De Trinitate*. Augustine began his meditation on the "inner trinity" in book 8 with a meditation on how we come to recognize someone else as just, especially in the case of a person who is not just and knows himself to be unjust and yet can recognize another person as just. This analysis led to the conclusion that we recognize justice as a certain presence within us which we can distinguish from ourselves. It is by reference to this presence of justice that I can aspire to be just while knowing that I am not just and admire another person who approximates the justice that I can perceive as a kind of presence that is accessible to me but not simply what I am. A similar dynamic seems to be at play in the case of a human person's access to the reality of her own consciousness. The discrepancy between the constitutive underlying structure of human consciousness and the overlaid layers of self-forgetfulness is such that we cannot peruse the true reality of our own consciousness simply by looking inward. When we do look inward what we see is precisely the discrepancy itself. So it turns out to be just like our perception of justice, which is not attained simply by looking at what we are but most often by way of at least an implicit awareness of the difference between what we are and what we ought to be. In the case of our own consciousness, we discern its true being not simply by noticing its errant operation but in the light of a superior illumination of truth that allows us to bypass the mind's errant operation and see its ineluctable underlying reality: "We gaze upon the inviolable truth from which we define as perfectly as we can, not what kind of thing any particular man's mind is, but what kind of thing by everlasting ideas it ought to be."[74] It is by gazing at the presence of truth in the mind that we can discern that the mind ought to be and must be what it ineluctably is in its fundamental constitution, even if that constitution is overlaid by self-obfuscating distortions.

To the extent that Augustine provides an explanation for the paradoxical combination of self-presencing and self-forgetting that permeates human consciousness, that explanation is moral. This is where Augustine's project of "looking inward" achieves its full existential and social resonances. As it turns out, the quest for the trinitarian

74. *Trin.* 9.6.9.

image in humanity coincides entirely with Augustine's moral schema of the ordering of loves. Charges that Augustine's project is solipsistic can only be sustained if we omit the connections that he himself is at pains to draw between authentic self-knowledge and self-love, and being in right relation with the whole order of reality. The mind's proper self-knowledge is bound up with its correctly placing itself within the hierarchy of being: "Why then is the mind commanded to know itself? I believe it means that it should think about itself and live according to its nature, that is, it should want to be placed according to its nature, under him it should be subject to and over all that it should be in control of; under him it should be ruled by, over all that it ought to rule."[75] If the mind's self-awareness is to correctly image its own existence, so as to safeguard the perfect mutuality whereby it knows itself exactly to the extent that it is, then this self-knowledge must take the exact measure of the mind's creaturely mode of existence.

It is the same with an authentic and true self-love. In both cases, the perfect mutuality and equality between the mind's existence, its self-knowledge, and its self-love is not simply manifest in the human condition. This equality and mutuality, which is integral to the divine image in humanity, is a moral task susceptible to moral failure: "The mind therefore and its love and knowledge are three somethings, and these three are one thing and *when they are complete* they are equal (*cum perfecta sunt aequalia sunt*). If the mind loves itself less than [as] it is—for example, if the mind of a person loves itself only as much as a person's body should be loved, though it is itself something more than body—then it sins and its love is not complete. Again if it loves itself more than [as] it is, for example if it loves itself as much as God is to be loved, though it is itself incomparably less than God, here too it sins by excess and does not have a complete love of itself."[76] The motif of the ordering of loves explains the discrepancy between the mind's ineluctable self-presencing and its habitual self-forgetting. The self-forgetting through which the mind appears to fail to know itself is not due to the real absence of self-knowledge that constitutes the self-presence that is identical with the very being of mind. Rather, this self-forgetting happens when the mind's act of self-presencing is overlaid by an excessive and inordinate attachment to what is external to it. By improperly identifying itself with what it is not, the mind loses sight of its own act of self-presencing. This fate is unavoidable unless the mind attends to God according to its proper creaturely mode of being and thereby knows itself and loves itself in subordinate relation to its knowing of God and loving of God. The human person most properly knows herself and loves herself *through knowing and loving God*. When this happens, the human person also knows and loves other creatures in proper subordinate relation to knowing God. But the mind that does not attach itself to God will become attached to other lesser realities, precisely because the mind is so innately transitive. In that case, the mind will not authentically know God or itself or other creatures, nor will its self-knowledge and self-love be equal and

75. *Trin.* 10.5.7.
76. *Trin.* 9.4.4 (my italics).

identical with its real existence, or even transparent to itself. The trinitarian image imprinted in human consciousness will thereby become obfuscated, and the mind's capacity for certainty will be radically compromised. That is the situation of the human person in exile from the enjoyment of knowing and loving God.

Remembering the Christological Center

The foregoing makes it clear why Augustine insists that the trinitarian image in humanity, whereby the mind remembers itself through knowing and loving itself, is only fulfilled through its remembering, knowing, and loving God. That is true ultimately because the very notion of *imago dei* indicates, for Augustine, a real participation in the life of God. But it is also true because the mind simply cannot properly know itself and love itself without a true estimate of itself, which is only available through recognition of its subordinate and derivative creaturely relation to God.

But how does the mind go about remembering, knowing, and loving itself in God and thus recovering its trinitarian imaging of the divine Trinity? One wrong way for a modern reader to answer this question is to imagine that what is required is something like a method of generic centering prayer in which one attempts to direct the mind's act of recalling-understanding-loving toward a higher being, which can be called "God." What is involved in such an approach—and it is perhaps just such an approach that is presumed in denunciations of Augustine's solipsism—is an unaccountable amnesia with respect to everything that has transpired in *De Trinitate* up to the point where Augustine finally names the trinitarian image of God in humanity. But why should we suddenly forget what Augustine has been telling us from the beginning of book 1 regarding how to go about knowing and loving God? There we were told that the authentic knowing of God cannot happen by humanity's projecting its own material or even spiritual experience onto God. Neither does the apophatic abstraction from human experience guarantee genuine knowledge of God but rather risks being the most erroneous route inasmuch as it is prone to attribute to God what is true neither of God nor even of creatures.[77] The way to true knowledge of God is that provided by God himself, through which he adaptively discloses himself through creaturely "signs" that both accommodate our earthbound sensibilities and purify them by directing them upward to the true reality of God. The supreme such sign and sacrament is Jesus Christ, who perfectly unites in his own person both the human signification of the divine and the divine signified. This supreme and perfect self-signification of God constitutes the mission of the Word, which inaugurates the new covenant in the fullness of time, while the accompanying mission of the Holy Spirit is to enable recognition of and witness to this supreme self-signification of God in Christ.

If we do not suddenly forget all this when we come to Augustine's unveiling of the trinitarian image in humanity as the remembering, understanding, and loving of God, then we must interpret him to mean that all this must happen in no other way

77. *Trin.* 1.1.1.

than through Christ. But in order to entirely secure this point, Augustine follows his analysis of the trinitarian image in humanity in books 8–12 with a renewed insistence on christological mediation in book 13. The structural parallelism between the two christological books, book 4 and book 13, can be gleaned through the framework of signs (*similitudines*). Book 4 presents Jesus Christ as the one through whom all the "signs" of divine revelation achieve their true and climactic signification. Book 13 presents Jesus Christ as the one through whom the sign of the trinitarian image of God in the human *mens* achieves its ultimate signification as participation in the trinitarian life of God. In book 13, the humanity and divinity of Christ are rendered in epistemological terms as respectively the objects of human knowledge and wisdom. Augustine applies this framework to the description of Christ in Colossians 2:3 as the one "in whom are hidden all the treasures of wisdom and knowledge." He explains that "the difference between these two is that wisdom is attributed to divine things and knowledge to human." The totality of knowledge and wisdom, as well as the way from the former to the latter and their ultimate unity, are all enfolded in the person of Christ:

> I acknowledge each of them [i.e., knowledge and wisdom] in Christ and so does every believer with me. And when I read, "The Word became flesh and dwelt among us" (John 1:14), in the Word I understand the true Son of God and in the flesh I acknowledge the true Son of man, and each joined together into one person of God and man by an inexpressible abundance of grace. . . . Among things that have arisen in time the supreme grace is that man has been joined to God to form one person; among eternal things the supreme truth is rightly attributed to the Word of God. That the only-begotten from the Father is the one who is full of grace and truth means that it is one and the same person by whom deeds were carried out in time for us and for whom we are purified by faith in order that we may contemplate him unchangingly in eternity. . . . Our knowledge therefore is Christ and our wisdom is the same Christ. It is he who plants faith in us about temporal things, he who presents us with the truth about eternal things. Through him we go straight toward him, through knowledge toward wisdom, without ever turning aside from one and the same Christ, "in whom are hidden all the treasures of wisdom and knowledge" (Col. 2:3).[78]

The mind's true self-knowledge, then, as well as its knowledge of God, from which true self-knowledge derives, strictly depends on its knowledge of the total manifestation of the human Christ. This knowledge is faith-knowledge inasmuch as it informs and orients our upward gaze from the humanity of Christ to the divinity he shares with the Father and the Spirit. Similarly, the mind's true self-love, as well as its love of God, from which appropriate self-love derives, depend on its love of the same manifestation of the human Christ. Such love is faith-love inasmuch as it is oriented upward toward the divinity of Christ, but it is anchored in the sensible knowledge of the human Christ, "for how can things be loved if they are not known but only

---

78. *Trin.* 13.19.24.

believed? . . . We discovered that no one loves what he is totally ignorant of; but that, when unknown things are said to be loved, they are loved in virtue of things that are known."[79] We can see the utter consistency in Augustine's presentation, throughout *De Trinitate*, of Jesus Christ as the one through whom God is known by a self-disclosure that leads from "sight" to "faith." As we showed in our discussion of book 1, the faith-sight framework is one that delineates the dynamic knowledge of God. But in book 13, Augustine is also concerned with the christological transformation of the will. An awareness of his intention in this regard provides an explanation for his discussion of human happiness in book 13.

This discussion should not be regarded merely as a general statement that we become happy through faith in Christ, but, in keeping with the flow of Augustine's argument, as a treatment specifically of the transformation of the will through Christ. Augustine begins this discussion by designating the universal desire for happiness as the characteristic and defining activity of human willing: "All people have one common will to obtain and retain happiness."[80] Yet this common will is divided through different conceptions of its appropriate object. While happiness is commonly understood as the attainment of whatever is desired, it genuinely exists only when it desires what is authentically good. In that sense, the enactment of a "good will" (*voluntas bona*) is a necessary ingredient of happiness. Consequently, faith, as the desire for God who is the source of all good, is also necessary for happiness: "It is for this reason that the faith by which we believe in God is particularly necessary in this mortal life, so full of delusion and distress and uncertainty. God is the only source to be found of any good things, but especially of those which make a [human being] good and those which will make him happy."[81]

But just as the fulfillment of knowledge is not available in this world, neither is the fulfillment of happiness. This is so because another necessary objective ingredient of happiness is the good of immortality. In book 4, Augustine presented the human manifestation of Christ as a cure for both human pride and despair, and we were told that the latter is healed by the demonstration of God's love in Christ. In book 13, he retrieves the motif of the manifestation of Christ as an antidote to despair in order to present Christ as healer and motivator of the good will and as the proper object for the universal human desire for happiness. While the humanity of Christ provides a demonstrative "sight" of God, which purifies human knowledge and leads it up to God, it also heals and uplifts the will by providing an objective "demonstration" of God's love:

> This faith of ours, however, promises on the strength of divine authority, not of human argument, that the whole man, who consists of course of soul and body, too, is going to be immortal and therefore truly happy. . . . But in case this feebleness that is man, which we see and carry around with us, should despair of attaining such eminence, [the

79. *Trin.* 13.20.26.
80. *Trin.* 13.4.7.
81. *Trin.* 13.7.10.

gospel] went on to say, "And the Word became flesh and dwelt among us" (John 1:14), in order to convince us of what might seem incredible by showing us its opposite. For surely if the Son of God by nature became son of man by mercy for the sake of the sons of men . . . how much easier it is to believe that the sons of men by nature can become sons of God by grace and dwell in God; for it is in him alone and thanks to him alone that they can be happy, by sharing in his immortality; it was to persuade us of this that the Son of God came to share in our mortality. . . . Nothing was more needed for raising our hopes and delivering the minds of mortals, disheartened by the very condition of mortality, from despairing of immortality, than a demonstration of how much value God put on us and how much he loved us. And what could be clearer and more wonderful evidence of this than that the Son of God, unchangeably good, remaining in himself what he was and receiving from us what he was not, electing to enter into partnership with our nature without detriment to his own, should first of all endure our ills without any ill deserts of his own; and then once we had been brought in this way to believe how much God loved us and to hope at last for what we had despaired of, should confer his gifts on us with a quite uncalled for generosity, without any good deserts of ours, indeed with our ill deserts our only preparation?[82]

The Holy Spirit as Love and Gift

While the christological demonstration of divine love objectively informs and orients the "good will" of faith, the working of the Holy Spirit makes interiorly present the love of God objectively demonstrated through the humanity of Christ: "In order that faith might work through love, 'the love of God has been poured into our hearts through the Holy Spirit which has been given to us' (Rom. 5:5)."[83] Augustine follows the exposition of Romans 5 from the association of divine love with the outpouring of the Holy Spirit to the recognition that our access to this love is consequent upon being "justified by [Christ's] blood" while we were yet sinners (Rom. 5:8). This link takes us back to the theme of book 4, that the drama of divine redemption, as a demonstration of God's love in the face of human sinfulness, is an antidote to both despair and pride. It also recalls the presentation of book 4 in that the epistemological motifs of faith-sight (and knowledge-wisdom in book 13) are supplemented by the recognition that the purification required for the quest of the vision of God involves our assimilation to Christ's sacrificial self-offering. The event of Christ's redemptive sacrifice is one in which Father, Son, and Holy Spirit "work all things together and equally and in concord."[84] But within this unified trinitarian agency, the Holy Spirit is to be distinctively associated with the titles of "love" and "gift":

So it is the Holy Spirit of which he has given us that makes us abide in God and him in us. But this is precisely what love does. He then is the gift of God who is love. . . . So the love which is from God and is God is distinctively the Holy Spirit; through him

82. *Trin.* 13.10.13.
83. *Trin.* 13.10.14.
84. *Trin.* 13.11.15.

the charity of God is poured out in our hearts, and through him the whole Trinity dwells in us. This is the reason why it is most apposite that the Holy Spirit, while being God, should also be called the gift of God. And this gift, surely, is distinctively to be understood as being the charity which brings us through to God, without which no other gift of God at all can bring us through to God.[85]

Consistently with the principle outlined in book 4, in which the missions of Son and Spirit are revelatory of their eternal relations, Augustine conceives of the Spirit as both Love and Gift within the divine being, the mutual love of the Father and the Son, which eternally proceeds so as to be the donability of God: *sic procedebat ut esset donabile.*[86] In the economy, the Holy Spirit, as divine Love, is particularly associated with the will, for "what else after all is charity but the will?"[87] The christological economy thus provides the essential "notions of faith" by which the intellect is properly oriented to God and the Holy Spirit uplifts the will to cling to this manifestation with love, and so human memory, intellect, and will are reformed through the economic co-activity of Son and Spirit.[88] Yet even this is not yet the image of God in humanity, because the image of God in humanity is not fulfilled in merely attending to the human economy of Christ but rather in assenting to that economy as referring to the divinity that he shares with the Father and the Spirit. As we saw already in book 1, faith is always the assent to the referential character of the humanity of Christ as signifying his divinity. Therefore, the image of God in humanity finds its fulfillment to the extent that Christ himself leads us from knowing and loving his human manifestation to a real participation in the life of the Father, Son, and Holy Spirit. Along this path, our own self-knowing and self-loving, as well as our knowing and loving other creatures, will be healed and transformed by becoming wholly derivative of our knowing and loving the Triune God. Increasingly, our knowing and loving will become equivalent to our entire existence in a way that approximates the mutual circumincession of the Father, Son, and Holy Spirit. The increase of this trinitarian image within us does not make us "tripersonal" in the way that God is three persons, but it does render our individuality ever more apt to participate, knowingly and lovingly, in the communion of all creation in the divine persons.

᪥   ᪥

The purpose of this chapter was to present a reading of Augustine's classic work on the Trinity from the point of view of the question of what kind of knowledge of the Trinity is possible for human beings. As a way of recollecting the main lines of our interpretation of this difficult and sprawling work, we can end with a brief portrait of the kind of person Augustine wants to form through the spiritual exercise of reading this work and appropriating its contents. Such a person would recognize

85. *Trin.* 15.17.31–15.18.32.
86. *Trin.* 5.15.16.
87. *Trin.* 15.20.38.
88. Cf. *Trin.* 13.20.26.

from the outset that the difference between God and creation is such as to preclude human knowledge of the divine apart from the *initium fidei* of divine self-disclosure. Scripture presents such a program of divine self-disclosure in which God is manifested symbolically through creaturely realities (*similitudines*). This scriptural program names Father, Son, and Holy Spirit as the co-agents of divine self-disclosure and salvific activity. The items of divine self-disclosure prior to the incarnation of the Son cannot be determinately assigned to any of the divine persons distinctly, but their revelatory function is consummated by the manifestation of Jesus Christ, who is thus the supreme sign and sacrament of divine self-disclosure. The Holy Spirit is also manifested through the christological economy precisely through his work of authenticating the manifestation of the Son and enabling human reception of this manifestation. The scriptural program of divine self-disclosure thus consummated through the christological-pneumatological economy reveals Father, Son, and Holy Spirit as existing in perfect co-equality and co-mutuality. Faith searches for a "sight" of such perfect coincidence of distinction and unity in order to avoid misdirecting its orientation away from the God manifested through Scripture as Father, Son, and Spirit. Faith also seeks a remedy for the agitation caused by the lack of certainty that such a "sight" is possible or intelligible. Inspired by the scriptural revelation that the human being is made in the image of God, faith looks for a trinitarian sight in the human person. What it finds there is that the criterion of certainty is itself trinitarian inasmuch as certainty coincides with the self's self-presencing as the dynamic intertwined processions of love and knowledge from a generative source (memory). What it also finds is that problems with certainty afflicting trinitarian faith go all the way down to radical problems with the self's lack of certainty about itself and lack of presence to its own structural act of self-presencing.

The real problem, then, is not how to ratify trinitarian faith by the standards of human certainty but how to heal the deep wounds of a radically uncertain self through the revelation of God through Christ and the Spirit. Nicene faith is thus bolstered both by the realization that there is a sight of perfect trinitarian mutuality that can be glimpsed as constitutive of consciousness and by the acknowledgment that our grasp of this sight is deeply damaged. The latter concession throws us back to the *initium fidei* when we realize that it is trinitarian faith that reveals to us the estranged homeland of our own selves and the degree of our estrangement. This faith also reveals to us the way to the cure in which our self-presencing through the intertwined activity of love and knowledge can be healed by attending to the manifestation of Christ and being assimilated to his purificatory sacrifice ("the blood of the just man"[89]) in the receptive power of the Spirit. Ultimately, the kind of knowledge we can have of the trinitarian God is not so much an enclosing of God within the grasp of a radically damaged human aptitude for certainty but an unrestricted openness to Father, Son, and Spirit, which enfolds our own acts of self-presencing and intentionality toward other creatures. Throughout this chapter, we have used Augustine's framework of

89. *Trin.* 4.2.4; cf. *Trin.* 13.11.15.

signs-things to delineate some of his key insights. A key element of that framework that is decisive for his trinitarian epistemology is that of "referring." Ultimately, what is at stake in trinitarian faith is not having a comprehensive grasp of the *res* of the Triune God but of comprehensively referring oneself to the God who is Father, Son, and Holy Spirit:

> Anyone who has a lively intuition of these three (as divinely established in the nature of his mind) and of how great a thing it is that his mind has that by which even the eternal and unchanging nature can be recalled, beheld, and desired—it is recalled by memory, beheld by intelligence, embraced by love—has thereby found the image of that supreme trinity. To the memory, sight, and love of this supreme trinity, in order to recollect it, see it, and enjoy it, he should refer (*debet referre*) every ounce and particle of his life.[90]

---

90. *Trin.* 15.20.39.

Conclusion

Retrieving the Systematic Scope of Nicene Theology

The purpose of this concluding chapter is to suggest some elements that can contribute toward a creative retrieval of Nicene trinitarian faith. There is not a single and monolithic path for such retrieval, just as fourth-century theologies that accepted the Nicene *homoousios* were not utterly uniform. The burden of this book has been to propose that both the construction of Nicene theology and its reappropriation are systematic endeavors in the sense that they aspire to interpret the entirety of Christian experience in light of the oneness of being of Father, Son, and Holy Spirit. But the exact contours and contents of this project differed from one theologian to another, and rather than trying to homogenize a "Nicene theology," we have chosen to retrieve key insights from three preeminent theologians of that era. This task of retrieval involves both a receptive and an active constructive posture. The receptive element is composed of reconstructing the logic by which questions pertaining to the divinity of Christ and the Spirit in the fourth century led to a trinitarian reinterpretation of Christian faith. Of course, this work of reconstruction, being an interpretive endeavor, cannot itself be purely receptive. I have exercised selectivity and systematization both in my choice of representatives of the Nicene tradition and of aspects of their work. Similarly a constructive retrieval of Nicene theology can take various forms and emphases. The following is an attempt to sketch some themes delineating the systematic scope of Nicene theology that can be valuable in informing a contemporary experience of trinitarian faith. In large part, they refer back to insights gleaned from our analyses of Athanasius, Gregory of Nyssa, and Augustine. At the same time, they demand further elaboration, nuance, and qualification that cannot be adequately provided here. The present task is simply to recommend these themes as worthy of further reflection both in their original setting and in our contemporary context as evocative of the systematic scope of trinitarian doctrine.

Revelation

As Creator, God is both radically other than his creation and positively related to it. The difference between God and world is such that creatures can only know God through his free self-revelation. Any attempt by creatures simply to infer the nature of the divine on the basis of creaturely realities will inevitably amount to a projection of created features onto the divine[1] and will thus amount to a mythology (Athanasius).[2] Divine self-disclosure is available through its inspired witness in the Scriptures, as interpreted by acts of ecclesial communion (synodal councils) and as appropriated and performed in worship and discipleship. The combination of these three elements constitutes what fourth-century theologians referred to as *eusebeia*. That the elasticity of that term combined these elements is evidenced by the range of translated meanings, all of them appropriate in distinct contexts, which are allotted to it: "piety," "orthodoxy," "religion," and so on. An authentic retrieval of Nicene trinitarian theology should endeavor to reappropriate trinitarian *eusebeia* in this global sense: as appropriating determinate ways of reading Scripture through interpretations gleaned from acts of ecclesial communion and ways of celebrating and suffering this divine self-disclosure in worship and discipleship. However, even an integral reception of God's self-revelation does not eradicate divine infinity and incomprehensibility and the incommensurability between the divine and the human. The infinite God cannot be contained by finite human knowing. Yet, human knowing and human existence in its entirety can be so contained and determined by the divine self-disclosure as to be suffused with knowledge and love and union with the divine. Christian eschatological hope looks forward to a consummation of this process in the eternal enjoyment of the sight of the Father, Son, and Holy Spirit. In the meantime, Christian existence consists in the project of referring one's existence toward this sight such that every internal and external act becomes oriented to the love and knowledge of the Triune God.

Scripture

Scripture is not simply God's Word without admixture of human elements, nor is it merely a collection of human words that express experiences of the divine. The inner form of scriptural language is christological and trinitarian.[3] The Scriptures represent the self-communicating accommodation of the divine to human sensibilities. The agency of effecting this translation from the "language" of divine being to human language is especially appropriated to the Holy Spirit, while the contents of this accommodation are objectively manifest in the life, death, and resurrection of Jesus Christ as the climax and recapitulation of the scriptural disclosure of God. In

---

1. Augustine, *Trin.* 1.1.1; see above, 242–44.
2. Cf. Athanasius, *Decr.* 18; see Torrance, "Lazarus Narrative," 245.
3. See above, 168–69 (Gregory of Nyssa).

turn, the manifestation of Christ is to be understood as a revelation of the Father, of whom he is the expressive Word and Image.

Considered as a whole and in all its distinct aspects, Nicene trinitarian faith comprises determinate interpretations of Scripture. At the same time, the retrieval of Nicene ways of reading Scripture cannot be restricted simply to cataloging ways in which the contents of Scripture can be marshaled toward a logical argument for speaking of God as "three persons in one nature." It must be a retrieval precisely of the *reading* and proclamation of Scripture in just these ways rather than using doctrinal formulation to leave behind such reading and proclamation. This means, for example, that we must attend to the trinitarian patterns of naming divine majesty and the narrative of God's salvation in the reading, praying, and proclamation of Scripture. These patterns in and of themselves—not merely the dogmatic conclusions that regulate their logical relations—enable access to the trinitarian God. A retrieval of Nicene theology must therefore include the rhetorical performance of trinitarian doctrine in its original scriptural idiom. How often does one hear Jesus referred to in homilies as Word, Wisdom, Image of the Father? Yet, as we have seen, these scriptural characterizations were crucial to the formulation and appropriation of the dogma that he is *homoousios* with the Father. The way to retrieve that dogma must include resorting to the scriptural *epinoiai* now understood with reference to the controlling interpretation of *homoousios*. Fourth-century trinitarian discourse offers untapped resources for the retrieval of a properly trinitarian scriptural rhetoric in which God is named through the interlocking scriptural patterns of the naming of Father, Son, and Spirit. Moreover, in our own time, a way of reading Scripture that attends to the broad scriptural spectrum of the trinitarian co-naming of the Divine enables us to address legitimate concerns about the masculinization of God through exclusive reliance on Father-Son language.

Tradition and Ecclesial Scriptural Interpretation

That the trinitarian debates provided the impetus for the origins of a theology of church councils and a focused reflection on the relations between Scripture, doctrine, and tradition is not coincidental. If we say that a trinitarian *eusebeia* requires that a determinate reading of Scripture be held as normative, we raise the question of just how a determinate reading of Scripture is to be posited as normative. Athanasius's championing of Nicaea, in his *On the Nicene Council*, offers some enduring guidelines for engaging this question. Athanasius insisted on the "sufficiency" of the Scriptures, although the controversies in which he was embroiled made it abundantly clear that such sufficiency does not preclude misinterpretation. Nevertheless, to assert the sufficiency of Scripture is to claim that Christian teaching (*doctrina*) arises from the Scriptures and cannot essentially represent elements extraneous to Scripture. The formulation and construction of Christian doctrine, therefore, are essentially composed of the labor of demonstrating its basis in Scripture, and thus doctrine is essentially a demonstration precisely of the "sufficiency" of Scripture. The subject who has the authority to declare a particular doctrinal interpretation as an adequate dem-onstration of the sufficiency of Scripture is not any individual but the church in its communal conciliar manifestation.[4] It is certainly true that the debates of the fourth century teach us that the mere occurrence of a council does not guarantee the truth and adequacy of its pronouncements. But the point for the moment is not that the pronouncements of a council are necessarily correct but simply that the sufficiency of scriptural truth requires ecclesial witness. The correct interpretation of Scripture must take the form of "an ecclesiastical sense."[5] Demonstrating the sufficiency of Scripture also involves a constructive retrieval of how the Scriptures have efficaciously guided the church through time and thus of a continuity in the transmission (*traditio*) of scriptural truth.[6] The discernment and formulation of the patterns and inner form of such continuity is a constructive and hermeneutical process, and there may be more or less adequate and sometimes glib and false accounts of such continuity. Never-theless, the task of Christian theology presupposes that the sufficiency of Scripture is in principle demonstrable as effecting a continuity, however complex, of its own reception.[7] The historical dimension of this task includes insuring that accounts of continuity are not overly simplistic or false.

With regard to trinitarian doctrine, all this means that the reception of this doctrine involves appropriating and proclaiming its scriptural basis, professing communion with the conciliar pronouncements by which the ecclesial sense of the scriptural revelation of God as Trinity is articulated, and discerning and constructing patterns of continuity in the church's reception of this revelation.

Worship

A trinitarian *eusebeia* presupposes and prescribes in the first place the unqualified worship of Jesus Christ, inasmuch as his divinity is intrinsic to the perfection of divine being and his humanity does not detract from his divinity but expresses it. A doxological affirmation of the perfection of Jesus Christ also involves affirmations of the perfection of his relations to the Father and the Spirit. The trinitarian content of Christian worship and sacramental life is exemplified in the evocation of the trinitarian name in baptism. Adopting Athanasius's account of the oneness of baptism, we can say that the integrity of this act depends on affirming Father, Son, and Holy Spirit as the one destination to which the act of baptism leads and the unified agency by which

4. We cannot take account here of the question of whether this principle still applies in the Roman Catholic doctrine of papal infallibility and, if so, to what extent. The present discussion is restricted to elements that can be gleaned from a study of the development of trinitarian doctrine in the fourth century.

5. Athanasius, *C. Ar.* 1.44.

6. Cf. Athanasius, *Decr.* 4.

7. For a provocative statement of the continuity of the church's experience of Christ and the limitations of the notion of development from an Eastern Orthodox point of view, see Louth, "Is Development of Doctrine a Valid Category?"

the baptizand is led into divine life. This interpretation of baptism presumes that the content of the sacrament is truly an entrance into the life of the Triune God (deification). Christians are continually invited to renew and deepen their participation in trinitarian life through eucharistic communion, whereby they are incorporated into the self-offering of the Incarnate Son to the Father in the Spirit and in the mutual glorification of the Father and the Son by the Spirit. Participation in the interrelations of Father, Son, and Spirit is simultaneously the goal and the means of Christian sacramental life.

The Primacy of Christ

A Nicene interpretation of Scripture necessarily involves a maximal affirmation of the primacy of Christ. Only such an interpretation can avoid performative self-contradiction with respect to the fact that Christians worship Jesus Christ. Christian faith is essentially faith in the lordship of Christ, and this premise is the first principle of Christian discourse. Christian discourse therefore does not argue to this principle but from it. Or, even better, Christian discourse is an ascending dialectic that argues from the principle of the lordship of Christ toward a deeper and fuller appreciation of the lordship of Christ. This dialectic is manifest in the doctrinal debates of the fourth century, and a contemporary appropriation of that epochal moment of Christian discernment must retrace the logic from the presumption of the primacy of Christ to a fully trinitarian elaboration of this primacy. As we have noted earlier, every participant in these doctrinal debates presumed some version of the primacy of Christ, of what it means to say that Jesus is Lord. Despite the various inflections of difference among individual participants in these debates, it is possible to interpret these debates as fundamentally positing two basic versions of the primacy of Christ. To reconstruct this logic, we must keep in mind that, then as now, the concrete experiential starting point for reflecting on the mystery of Jesus Christ is some vision of the whole person of Jesus Christ and not a conglomeration of abstract categories, such as "humanity," "divinity," and "preexistence." These categories came to be analyzed in view of a global experience of the primacy of Christ and were differently related in view of how that primordial experience was construed.

One construal of this experience conceived the lordship of Christ in terms of his being the perfect creature. As the perfect creature, Jesus Christ is the greatest possible approximation to the God and Creator. This construal of the lordship of Christ is consistent through a trajectory that runs from Arius to Asterius to Eunomius, despite all their unmistakable differences. This version of the lordship of Christ and his perfect creaturehood includes an account of his work of creating all other inferior creatures and of redeeming fallen humanity and returning it to proper relation to God. Precisely as the perfect and uniquely preeminent exemplar of the Creator-creature relationship, from the creaturely side, Jesus Christ maintains and acknowledges the distance between himself and the Creator-Father. His "divinity" consists precisely in his preexistent perfect creaturehood, which is exemplified in his work in creating other creatures, and his "humanity" is assumed for the sake of assimilating our imperfect and sinful creaturehood to his own perfect and sinless creaturehood. In both his "divinity" and "humanity," Jesus is Lord as perfect creature.

On the other hand, the Nicene version of the primacy of Christ cannot be ultimately construed as a simple denial that the primacy of Christ is to be conceived in terms of his perfect creaturehood. Rather, Nicene theology finds its central impetus in the effort to dialectically and simultaneously conceive of the primacy of Christ in terms of *both* his perfect creaturehood *and* his absolute and unqualified divine perfection. The Nicene trinitarian reading of Scripture is based on this central principle of the double primacy of Christ, as encompassing both sides of the God-world relation. Thus we have the assertion that what we would call the hermeneutical key of Scripture and what the ancient theologians called the *skopos* is "a double account of the Savior," declaring both his divine and creaturely preeminence.[8] Christ is Lord as perfect God, as constitutive of the perfection of the divine being, and he is Lord again as the perfect creature, the one whose obedient self-offering to the Father embraces all creation and allows it entrance into the presence of the Father. It is precisely by the union of both kinds of precedence in his own person that Jesus Christ achieves the salvation of humanity. Of course, it need hardly be said that this version is also an absolutely maximal version of the primacy of Christ, encompassing both sides of the Creator-creature distinction.

The Nicene version of the primacy of Christ insists on the absolute perfection of Christ, such that his perfection is in no way secondary to the perfection of God but is in fact constitutive of divine perfection. The identity of Christ and the meaning of divine perfection thus become interdependent and mutually referential. Such a reading of Scripture identifies the "exalted titles" (*epinoiai*) of Christ and finds them to be correlative to the scriptural designation of divine precedence, thereby constructing models of correlativity that signify simultaneously a relation of origin and outflow and a pattern of mutual reference. In the terms of one such model, divine perfection consists in the radiance of the Son as an outflow of the light of the Father by which we are enlightened in the Spirit. The scriptural christological narrative also presents Jesus in terms of his exemplary creaturehood, as the one who was sent by the Father, lived, taught, and died in obedience to the Father's will, and both was anointed by the Spirit and granted his disciples a share in that same Spirit. Then as now, the crucial question was what connection this trinitarian pattern of Christ's earthly life bears to the reality of God. One interpretation was to see patterns of subjection in Jesus's relation to the Father and the Spirit's relation to Christ as reflective of graded levels of ontological precedence. The inherent plausibility of this schema can be expressed simply by saying that it is the most straightforward application of the principle that the economic Trinity is the immanent Trinity. Accordingly, Jesus's obedience and submission to the Father is interpreted as indicative of a lower level of precedence with

---

8. Athanasius, *C. Ar.* 3.29.

respect to the Father, while Christ's sending of the Spirit indicates the Son's higher level of precedence with respect to the Spirit. However, the Nicene account of the identity of the economic and immanent Trinity involves fully integrating both the patterns of co-activity and the patterns of subjection with a maximal interpretation of the absolute primacy of Christ. The absolute primacy of Christ is not qualified by reference to the narrative of Christ's human limitations and suffering but is reasserted through a christological reinterpretation of divine perfection. These human limitations and sufferings are seen to be not reflective of a lower level of transcendence but rather disclosive of divine perfection and transcendence reconceived as loving condescension and self-abasement. This involves the insertion of the categories of *kenōsis*, compassion, and self-humbling into the canon of absolute divine perfections. In this way, the creaturely primacy of Christ manifest in his life of obedience and compassionate suffering comes to be seen as a reflection and not a mitigation of absolute divine primacy. Compassionate self-abasement becomes both a divine attribute and a characterization of the humanity of Christ. A pattern of *kenōsis* binds together the being of God and the life of Jesus Christ and characterizes the double primacy of Christ as both loving Lord and suffering servant. A Nicene trinitarian reading of Scripture thus sees the scriptural account of the absolute primacy of Christ as twofold. It presents both the absolute majesty of Christ as constitutive of the name and being of the divine as well as the human self-humbling for our salvation, while attributing both to a single agent and speaker. Moreover, within this twofoldness, the account of the human self-humbling is to be seen as disclosive of the transcendence of God conceived as love and mercy.

The Person of the Holy Spirit

The Holy Spirit is encountered in the Scriptures as the third inflection of the divine name and characterized correlatively to the characterizations of Jesus Christ and the God he called "Father." The Spirit is the one who makes available and shareable the Word and Son, who perfectly images the Father, thus rendering us "worded" in the Word and sons and daughters in the Son. In sum, the Spirit is the one in whom the relation between the Father and the Son is extended outward.[9] A scripturally mediated experience of the absolute primacy of Christ is simultaneously an experience of the Spirit, who enables the recognition of Jesus as Lord. The Spirit is constitutive of the precedence of Christ as the "Anointed" One, and can thus be characterized as the content of his "kingship" in the economy of salvation and the one who eternally glorifies the Son within the trinitarian "circle of glory." The perfect and reciprocally referencing co-activity of Son and Spirit is manifest in the incarnation, wherein the Son both divinely gives the Spirit and humanly receives it, thus enabling human reception of the Spirit. Correlatively, reception of the Spirit enables us to know and

---

9. See Anatolios, "Divine Disponibilité."

appropriately honor Jesus as Lord and to realize in ourselves the form of Christ. In the economy of salvation, Jesus gives us the Spirit and the Spirit gives us Jesus as Lord and we are thus enfolded into the circle of mutual trinitarian glorification.

Creation

On the basis of the plain sense of Scripture, all significant participants in the fourth-century debates were agreed that Jesus Christ is in some sense Creator of the world. At the same time, as we have seen, there was a newly solidified recognition that absolute divine precedence involves a radical otherness between the ultimate transcendence of God and creation. One strategy for synthesizing the last two statements was to assert that God's absolute precedence is transcendent to any kind of outflow, production, or activity, all of which can be indifferently enfolded in the category of creation. Jesus Christ, inasmuch as he is scripturally designated even in his exalted titles as deriving his being from the Father, enjoys a precedence that is still within the realm of creation and inferior to the Unbegotten and unoriginated God. But inasmuch as he is also scripturally characterized as Creator, then he must be conceived, in his divinity, as created Creator. The Nicene synthesis, however, affirmed that the derivation of the Son from the Father is disclosive and constitutive of absolute divinity and thus cannot be enfolded within the realm of creation. There is an outflow, production, and activity that is constitutive of divine being in the generation of the Son and procession of the Spirit and thus characterizes divine life as an eternal eventfulness. At the same time, the divine activity *ad extra* in bringing about creation from nothing is grounded in the inner fecundity of intra-trinitarian life. Creation is not a necessary outflow of intra-divine generation, but neither is it an arbitrary act that "gains" for God a communion that he does not inherently enjoy. Creation takes place within the mutual delight of Father and Son such that God's delight in creation is enfolded in the mutual delight of Father and Son.[10] As *Deus donabilis*, the Holy Spirit renders the Father-Son relation shareable and thus brings about creation as the site of the extension of the Father-Son relation beyond divine being. Such a trinitarian account of creation speaks to our contemporary ecological crisis, leading us to see that a destructive posture toward creation is blasphemous in its dishonoring of the Father-Son delight and the Spirit's gift-giving of that delight.

In ruling out the notion of a created Creator and the hybrid designation of Jesus Christ as a Servant-Lord, Nicene theology instituted a strict and unqualified demarcation between the eternal perfection of divine being and the contingency of creation from nothing, as well as its global status of servitude. Along with the dismantling of the Greek "chain of being" and the rejection of semi-divine intermediaries, such a demarcation emphasizes the inherent equality of all creatures as servants of God and the qualification of any inter-creaturely lordship. Any form of slavery or any positing

10. Cf. Athanasius, *C. Ar.* 2.82.

of a radical ontological supremacy of one creature over another is thereby proscribed. The relation of humanity to the rest of creation may be cited as a special case inasmuch as humanity is scripturally ordained to "rule over creation." The Christian tradition has typically conceived of humanity as being ontologically superior to other terrestrial creatures, created in God's image and having a special affinity for participation in divine life. But all this can be maintained without mitigating the fundamental insight that any variations of excellence or relations of governing and being governed among creatures can only be understood as modalities of a common servitude. Thus, to return to the ecological theme, the human being is ordained to rule over creation precisely in servitude to the lordship of God and not for her own ends. The same is true for any hierarchical relations among human beings. Contemporary efforts to reflect on the nature of human relationality, in general and in the church, on the basis of the trinitarian mystery, need to incorporate this element of a trinitarian theology of creation into their reflections.

Christian Salvation

The Christian tradition, beginning with the Scriptures, has devised various images and conceptual frameworks for describing the reparation of the human condition through the life, death, and resurrection of Jesus Christ. While employing a wide range of such concepts and images, theologies that affirm the oneness of being of Father, Son, and Holy Spirit typically understand the essential content of Christian salvation in terms of a fairly maximal conception of union with God, which can be designated by the term "deification." Thus the argument that "only God can save us" tends to be equivalent to "only God can join us to God." This soteriological conception can be distinguished from others in which salvation is conceived not so much in terms of union and "joining" but of becoming adept at knowledge and worship of God and obedience to the divine will. These latter accounts do not require that the Son and Spirit, who are scripturally characterized as effecting salvific agency, be themselves fully and perfectly divine. While the notion of "deification" is increasingly appreciated as an important and rich patristic and Eastern Christian *theologoumenon*, there are substantial grounds for raising the question of whether it is simply intrinsic to the scope of trinitarian doctrine as such.

At minimum, a trinitarian account of Christian salvation is solicitous of naming the economic interactivity of Father, Son, and Spirit in its description of the content of Christian salvation. Through Christ's human reception of the Spirit that he divinely gives, humanity is gifted with adoption by grace into the Son's imaging of the Father. Humanity thus becomes "begotten by grace" within the Son's natural generation from the Father and is presented to the Father through the Son's own self-offering. The ultimate content of Christian salvation is to be incorporated into the trinitarian communion, the mutual glorification of Father, Son, and Spirit. Despite a long history of misreadings, Augustine's conception of Christian salvation in *De Trinitate* follows a similar pattern: salvation ultimately consists in a reparation of our remembering, understanding, and willing—which necessarily includes a reparation of our relation to the rest of creation—such that this threefold activity that is constitutive of human consciousness is perfectly correlated to the Father, Son, and Holy Spirit.

We have seen that the trinitarian debates of the fourth century involved different construals of where to locate the soteriological *pro nobis* in relation to the person and work of Jesus Christ. It can be provocatively argued that the theologies of Arius and others who affirmed the creaturehood of the Son were radically soteriological, inasmuch as they located the soteriological mediation of Christ at the very origin of his existence. A dominant strain in modern theology, going back to Melanchthon's famous dictum, "To know Christ is to know his benefits," tends to reduce the primacy of Christ to functional, soteriological categories. It has become a prevalent form of theological piety to reduce the "real meaning" of any theological system to its soteriology. However, it should give us pause that Nicene theology tended to be emphatic about restricting the christological *pro nobis* to Christ's humanity. To properly construe the primacy of Christ is not simply to know his benefits "for us" but to know his glory, for whose sake creation itself exists (cf. Col. 1:16). Retrieving the Nicene account of the primacy of Christ involves extending the range of soteriology into doxology. Of course, ultimately, even the glory of Christ is "for us" inasmuch as its content is a love that is freely shared with creation.

But there is still an important distinction to be made between the glory of the divine nature for the sake of which creation exists and the self-humbling *pro nobis*, which takes place in the human nature so that humanity might rejoice in the glory of the divine nature that Christ shares with the Father and the Spirit.

Humanity in the Image of the Trinity

Athanasius, Gregory of Nyssa, and Augustine all understood human communion to be a certain image of the oneness of the Father and the Son (cf. John 17:21). This was not the subject of extensive discussion but simply taken to be the plain sense of the scriptural text. At the same time, as the trinitarian pattern of salvation indicated above makes evident, humanity is particularly correlated with the position of the Son within the Trinity. The soteriological theme of "adoption" (cf. Gal. 4:6–7) signifies not so much a vague sentiment about humanity's inclusion into the "family of God," but a properly trinitarian logic in which humanity participates in divine life from within the particular position of the incarnate Son. Asserting the consubstantiality of the Son with the Father, in light of the incarnation, has momentous anthropological consequences. It is a revelation of the worthiness of the human state to be joined to divine being, though this worthiness is itself the consequence of divine goodness and mercy. The Christian narrative thus dismantles a binary framework of ontological polarity that sees divine spirit and matter as opposites and replaces it with an ethical framework that sees irreconcilable opposition only between divine goodness and evil. Matter, especially the condition of human bodiliness, which was united to the divine Word, is not in opposition to the divine goodness but a manifestation of that goodness. Moreover, human sexuality is not to be denigrated but honored as bearing a certain image to the divine fecundity. The human spirit, or consciousness, is also mysteriously like the Trinity in the way it is constituted as a dynamic inter-relation of knowledge and love oriented to communion with the rest of creation in the knowledge and love of Father, Son, and Spirit. At the same time, every aspect of humanity's imaging of the Trinity, individually or collectively, is deficient and broken. The latter acknowledgment does not simply negate the likeness but delineates the distance between humanity's likeness to the Trinity and its unlikeness as the space of redemption to be traversed through transformation in Christ. In modern debates about "the psychological analogy" or "the social analogy," the accent tends to be typically misplaced on the question of whether this or that analogy really *works*. Following Augustine, we can take the biblical datum that the human being is made in the image of God and presume that since God is Trinity and the human being is composed of both interiority (consciousness) and relatedness to others (creatures and God), both these aspects will bear a trinitarian image. But it will be a flawed and broken image, the perception of which should return us to Christ as the one who repairs our com-munion with the Triune God.

Divine Being as Trinity

We have learned, most pointedly from Gregory of Nyssa and Augustine, that trinitar-ian faith is not a matter of comprehending the trinitarian being of God as an inert and passive object of human knowing. But neither is it a matter of abstracting the trinitarian form of our relation to God from the reality of God's being, as some mod-ern theology has done. Rather, trinitarian faith stems from the recognition that the trinitarian form of God's relation to us truly reflects God's being and is determined by God's trinitarian being. Trinitarian faith is ultimately the project of allowing our-selves to be determined by God's trinitarian being. To be so determined is to signify or mean the Trinity by our whole being without thereby encompassing the "object" of our signification. The crucial question of trinitarian faith is therefore not: *What* is the meaning of trinitarian doctrine? but, *How* can we mean the Trinity? Yet asking the latter question did and does involve us in speaking of God in the categories of being. A Nicene reading of Scripture advances from the scriptural narrative of trinitarian co-activity to a perception of the divine nature as "co-owned" by Father, Son, and Spirit, though in distinct modes.

The scriptural narrative presents Father, Son, and Holy Spirit as *personas/prosōpa*, each of whom is endowed with consciousness and intentionality. At least to that extent, Father, Son, and Spirit can and should be conceived as "persons" in a sense not absolutely discontinuous from modern notions of personhood. As Gregory of Nyssa proposed that it is the customary usage of language that is mistaken rather than the description of God as three *hypostaseis*, so one of the tasks of a contemporary trinitarian theology is to reveal how contemporary notions of human personhood are distorted in light of the revelation of God as the communion of Father, Son, and Spirit. Moreover, one of the fruits of recollecting the fourth-century debates is to note that a certain synthesis achieved between trinitarian theologies of unity of being and theologies of unity of will in the fourth century has subsequently been overshadowed and largely forgotten. Following Athanasius and, to an even greater extent, Gregory of Nyssa, we should not be afraid to say that the communion of Father, Son, and Spirit is willed by each of them and is thus a genuine interpersonal communion. At the same time, the consubstantial unity of the Trinity can be expressed, with Gregory of Nyssa, by saying that there is no variation in perfection among the three. Father, Son, and Holy Spirit are each equally owners of all the divine perfection such that the divine being is a single perfection. In the last analysis, neither the unity nor the distinctions among the Trinity can be adequately expressed. The task of trinitarian theology is not to claim fully adequate expressions or analyses of divine being but to clarify the rules generated by God's self-revelation that enable us to successfully refer our being and activity, knowingly and lovingly, to Father, Son, and Holy Spirit. Augustine's prayer at the end of his *De Trinitate* is an exemplary statement of trinitarian *eusebeia* so conceived:

> O Lord our God, we believe in you, Father and Son and Holy Spirit. Truth would not have said, "Go and baptize the nations in the name of the Father and of the Son and of the Holy Spirit" (Matt. 28:19), unless you were Trinity. Nor would you have commanded us to be baptized, Lord God, in the name of any who is not Lord God. Nor would it have been said with divine authority, "Hear O Israel, the Lord your God is one God" (Deut. 6:4), unless while being Trinity you were still one Lord God. And if you, God and Father, were yourself also the Son your Word Jesus Christ, were yourself also your gift the Holy Spirit, we would not read in the documents of truth, "God sent his Son" (Gal. 4:4), nor would you, only-begotten one, have said of the Holy Spirit, "whom the Father will send in my name" (John 14:26), and, "whom I will send you from the Father" (John 15:26). Directing my attention toward this rule of faith as best I could, as far as you enabled me to, I have sought you and desired to see intellectually what I have believed.... Do you yourself give me the strength to seek, having caused yourself to be found and having given me the hope of finding you more and more.... Let me remember you, let me understand you, let me love you. Increase these things in me until you refashion me entirely.[11]

---

11. *Trin.* 15.28.51 (ET: Hill, *Trinity*, 436, altered by substituting "Trinity" for "triad" to render *trinitas*).

Bibliography

Ancient Sources

Aetius

Syntagmation. In Epiphanius, *Panarion* 76.11–37. ET: Wickham, L. "The *Syntagmation* of Aetius the Anomean." *Journal of Theological Studies*, n.s., 19, no. 2 (1968): 540–49.

Alexander of Alexandria

"Letter of Alexander to Alexander of Byzantium" (*Hē philarchos*). In Theodoret, *Ecclesiastical History* 1.4.1–61. In Opitz, H., ed. *Urkunden zur Geschichte des Arianischen Streites.* Berlin: de Gruyter, 1934. ET: NPNF² 3:35–41.

Ambrose

On the Holy Spirit. In Faller, O., ed. CSEL 79. Vienna: Hölder Pichler Tempsky, 1964.

Apollinaris of Laodicea

Kata Meros Pistis *and Fragments.* In Lietzmann, H. *Apollinaris von Laodicea und Seine Schule: Texte und Untersuchungen.* Tübingen: Möhr, 1904.

Arius

"Letter of Arius to Alexander of Alexandria." In Athanasius, *De synodis* 16; Epiphanius, *Panarion* 69.7–8. In Opitz, H., ed. *Urkunden zur Geschichte des Arianischen Streites.* Berlin: de Gruyter, 1934. ET: Williams, R. *Arius: Heresy and Tradition*, 270–71. 2nd ed. Grand Rapids: Eerdmans, 2002.

"Letter to Eusebius of Nicomedia." In Epiphanius, *Panarion* 68.6; Theodoret, *Ecclesiastical History* 1.5. In Opitz, H., ed. *Urkunden zur Geschichte des Arianischen Streites.* Berlin: de Gruyter, 1934. ET: NPNF² 3:41.

Thalia. In Athanasius, *De Synodis* 15 and *Orationes Contra Arianos* 1.5–6. ET: Williams, R. *Arius: Heresy and Tradition*, 100–103. 2nd ed. Grand Rapids: Eerdmans, 2002.

Asterius

Fragments. In Vinzent, M., ed. *Asterius von Kappadokien: Die Theologischen Fragmente; Einleitung, kritischer Text, Übersetzung und Kommentar.* Supplements to *Vigiliae Christianae* 20. Leiden: Brill, 1993.

Athanasius of Alexandria

Against the Greeks. In Camelot, P. T., ed. and trans. *Athanase d'Alexandrie: Contre les Païens; Texte grec, introduction et notes.* SC 18. Paris: Éditions du Cerf, 1977. ET: Thomson, R. W. *Athanasius:* Contra Gentes *and* De Incarnatione. OECT. Oxford: Clarendon, 1971.

Festal Letters. In Cureton, W., ed. *The Festal Letters of Athanasius.* London, 1848; and Lefort, T., ed. *Lettres festales et pastorales en copte.* CSCO 150–51 (= *Scriptores Coptici* 19–20). Leuven: Peeters, 1955. ET: NPNF² 4:506–53.

Letter to Adelphius. PG 26:1072–84. ET: NPNF² 4:575–78.

Letter to All Bishops (*Henos sōmatos*). In Athanasius, *De synodis* 35.1–21. Opitz, H., ed. *Urkunden zur Geschichte des Arianischen Streites.* Berlin: de Gruyter, 1934. ET: NPNF² 2:3–5.

Letter to Epictetus. PG 26:1049–69. ET: NPNF² 4:570–74.

Letter to Marcellinus. PG 27:12–45. ET: Gregg, R. C., trans. *The Life of Antony and the Letter to Marcellinus.* New York: Paulist Press, 1980.

Letters to Serapion on the Holy Spirit. PG 26:529–676.

Life of Antony. In Bartelink. G. J. M., ed. and trans. *Athanase d'Alexandrie: Vie d'Antoine; Introduction, texte critique, traduction, notes et index.* SC 400. Paris: Éditions du Cerf, 1994. ET: Gregg, R. C., trans. *The Life of Antony and the Letter to Marcellinus.* New York: Paulist Press, 1980.

On the Council of Nicaea (*De Decretis*). In Opitz, H., ed. *Athanasius Werke*, 2.1:1–45. Berlin: de Gruyter, 1935–1941. ET: Anatolios, K. *Athanasius*, 176–211. New York: Routledge, 2004.

On the Councils of Ariminum and Seleucia (De Synodis). In Opitz, H., ed. *Athanasius Werke*, 2.1:231–78. Berlin: de Gruyter, 1935–1941. ET: NPNF² 4:448–80.

On the Incarnation. In Kannengiesser, C. *Athanase d'Alexandrie: Sur l'incarnation du Verbe; Introduction, texte critique, traduction, notes et index.* SC 199. Paris: Éditions du Cerf, 1973. ET: Thomson, R. W. *Athanasius:* Contra Gentes *and* De Incarnatione. OECT. Oxford: Clarendon Press, 1971.

Orations against the Arians. In Metzler, K., and K. Savvidis. *Athanasius Werke* 1.1. New York and Berlin: de Gruyter, 2000. ET: NPNF² 4:306–432; and Anatolios, K. *Athanasius*, 87–175. New York: Routledge, 2004.

Tome to the Antiochenes. PG 26:796–809. ET: NPNF² 4:483–86.

Augustine of Hippo

On the Trinity. In Mountain, W. J., and F. Glorie. 2 vols. CCSL 50–50A. Turnhout: Brepols, 1968. ET: Hill, E. *The Trinity.* New York: New City Press, 1991.

Basil of Caesarea

Against Eunomius. In Sesboüé, B., with G.-M Durand and L. Doutreleau. *Basil de Césarée: Contre Eunome suive de Eunome Apologie.* SC 299, 305. Paris: Éditions du Cerf, 1982–1983.

Epistles. In Courtonne, Y., ed. *Sainte Basile: Lettres.* 3 vols. Paris: Belles Lettres, 1957, 1961, 1966. ET: NPNF² 8.

On the Holy Spirit. In Pruche, B., ed. *Basil de Césarée: Sur le Saint Esprit.* SC 17. Paris: Éditions du Cerf, 2002. ET: *St. Basil the Great: On the Holy Spirit.* Crestwood, NY: St. Vladimir's Seminary Press, 1980.

Eunomius of Cyzicus

Apology and Confession of Faith. In Vaggione, R. P., ed. and trans. *Eunomius: The Extant Works.* OECT. Oxford: Clarendon Press, 1987.

Eusebius of Caesarea

Demonstration of the Gospel. In Heikel, I., ed. *Die Demonstratio Evangelica.* GCS 6. Leipzig: Hinrichs, 1913. ET: Ferrar, W. J. *The Proof of the Gospel.* 2 vols. London: SPCK, 1920.

Ecclesiastical History. In Lake, K., ed. and trans. 2 vols. LCL. Cambridge, MA: Harvard University Press, 1989.

Ecclesiastical Theology. In Klostermann, E., ed. *Eusebius Werke 14: Gegen Marcell, Über die kirchliche Theologie, Die Fragmente Marcells.* Berlin: Akademie Verlag, 1972.

In Praise of Constantine. In Heikel, I., ed. *Eusebius Werke 1.* GCS 7. Leipzig: Hinrichs, 1902. ET: NPNF² 1.

The Preparation for the Gospel. In Mras, K., ed. *Eusebius Werke 8: Die Praeparatio evangelica.* GCS 43.1–2. Berlin: Akademie Verlag, 1954, 1956. ET: Gifford, E. H., trans. *Preparation for the Gospel.* 2 vols. Eugene, OR: Wipf & Stock, 2002.

Theophany. In Gressmann, H., ed. *Die Theophanie: Eusebius Werke 3.2.* GCS 11.2. Leipzig: Hinrichs, 1904.

Gregory of Nazianzus

Theological Orations 27–31. In Gallay, P., ed., with M. Jourjon. *Grégoire de Nazianze: Discours 27–31 (Discours Théologiques).* SC 250. Paris: Éditions du Cerf, 1978. ET: Wickham, L., and F. W. Norris. *Faith Gives Fullness to Reasoning: The Five Theological Orations of Gregory Nazianzus.* Leiden: Brill, 1991.

Gregory of Nyssa

Against Eunomius. In Jaeger, W., ed. *Contra Eunomium Libri*. GNO 1–2. Leiden: Brill, 1960. ET: NPNF[2] 5:35–314.

Against the Macedonians on the Holy Spirit. In Mueller, F., ed. GNO 3.1. Leiden: Brill, 1958. NPNF[2] 5:315–25.

Catechetical Orations. In Mühlenberg, E. *Discours Catéchétiques*. SC 453. Paris: Éditions du Cerf, 2000. ET: Richardson, C., in Hardy, E. R., ed. *Christology of the Later Fathers*. Philadelphia: Westminster, 1954.

Commentary on the Song of Songs. In Langerbeck, H. GNO 6. Leiden: Brill, 1960. ET: McCambley, C. *Saint Gregory of Nyssa: Commentary on the Song of Songs*. Brookline: Hellenic College Press, 1987.

Life of Moses. In Daniélou, J., ed. *Grégoire de Nysse: La vie de Moïse*. 3rd ed. SC 1. Paris: Éditions du Cerf, 1968. ET: Malherbe, A. J., and E. Ferguson. *Gregory of Nyssa: The Life of Moses*. New York: Paulist Press, 1978.

To Ablabius, On Not Three Gods. In Müller, F., ed. *Opera Dogmatica Minora*. GNO 3.1. Leiden: Brill, 1958. ET: Richardson, C., in Hardy, E. R., ed. *Christology of the Later Fathers*. Philadelphia: Westminster, 1954.

To Eustathius on the Holy Trinity. In Mueller, F., ed. GNO 3.1. Leiden: Brill, 1958. ET: NPNF[2] 5:326–30.

To the Greeks on Common Notions. In Mueller, F., ed. GNO 3.1. Leiden: Brill, 1958. ET: Stramara, D. F. *Greek Orthodox Theological Review* 41, no. 4 (1996): 381–91.

To Peter, On the Difference between Ousia *and* Hypostasis (= Basil, *Ep.* 38).

Hilary of Poitiers

Collectanea Antiariana Parisina (Fragmenta Historica). In Feder, A., ed. CSEL 65. Vienna: Hölder Pichler Tempsky, 1916. ET: Wickham, L. *Hilary of Poitiers: Conflicts of Conscience and Law in the Fourth-Century Church*. Translated Texts for Historians 25. Liverpool: Liverpool University Press, 1997.

On the Synods. PL 10:479–546. ET: NPNF[2] 9.

On the Trinity. In Smulders, P., ed. *De Trinitate*. CCSL 62, 62A. Turnhout: Brepols, 1979, 1980. ET: NPNF[2] 9.

Irenaeus

Against the Heresies. In Rousseau, A., and L. Doutreleau. SC 263–64, 293–94, 210–11 (books 1–3); Rousseau, A., B. Hemmerdinger, L. Doutreleau, and C. Mercier. SC 100 (book 4); Rousseau, A., L. Doutreleau, and C. Mercier. SC 152–53 (book 5). Paris: Éditions du Cerf, 1965, 1969, 1974, 1979, 1982. ET: ANF 1.

Marcellus of Ancyra

Fragments. In Vinzent, M., ed. *Markell von Ankyra: Die Fragmente; Der Briefe an Julius von Rom*. Supplements to *Vigiliae Christianae* 39. Leiden: Brill, 1997.

Methodius of Olympus

On Free Will. In Bonwetsch, G. N. *Methodius: Werke*. GCS 27. Leipzig, 1917.

Symposium. In Musurillo, H., ed. *Méthode d'Olympe: Le Banquet*. SC 95. Paris: Éditions du Cerf, 1963.

Origen

On First Principles. In Görgemanns, H., and H. Karpp. *Origenes: Vier Bücher von den Prinzipien*. 3rd ed. Darmstadt: Wissenschaftliche Buchgesellschaft, 1992. ET: Butterworth, G. W. *On First Principles*. Gloucester, MA: Peter Smith, 1973.

Philostorgius

Ecclesiastical History. In Bidez, J., and F. Winkelmann. *Philostorgius Kirchengeschichte*. GCS 21. Berlin: Akademie Verlag, 1972.

Socrates

Ecclesiastical History. In Hansen, G. C., with M. Sirinian. *Sokrates: Kirchengeschichte*. GCS, N.F. 1. Berlin: Akademie Verlag, 1995. ET: NPNF² 2.

Sozomen

Ecclesiastical History. In Bidez, J., and G. C. Hansen. *Historia ecclesiastica*. GCS 50. Berlin: Akademie Verlag, 1960. ET: NPNF² 2.

Tertullian

Against Praxeas. In Evans, E., ed. *Tertulliani Adversus Praxean Liber: Tertullian's Treatise Against Praxeas*. London: SPCK, 1948.

Secondary and Modern Sources

Abramowski, Luise. "Was hat das Nicaeno-Constantinopolitanum (C) mit dem Konzil von Konstantinopel 381 zu tun?" *Theologie und Philosophie* 67 (1992): 481–513.

Anatolios, Khaled. *Athanasius*. New York: Routledge, 2004.

———. *Athanasius: The Coherence of His Thought*. New York: Routledge, 1998.

———. "Discourse on the Trinity." In *Constantine to 600*. Vol. 2, *The Cambridge History of Christianity*, edited by W. Löhr and F. Norris, 431–59. Cambridge: Cambridge University Press, 2007.

———. "Divine Disponibilité: The Hypostatic Ethos of the Holy Spirit." *Pro Ecclesia* 12 (Summer 2003): 287–308.

———. "Divine Semiotics and the Way to the Triune God in Augustine's *De Trinitate*." In *God in Early Christian Thought: Essays in Memory of Lloyd G. Patterson*, edited by Andrew B. McGowan, Brian Daley, SJ, and Timothy J. Gaden, 163–94. Supplements to *Vigiliae Christianae*. Leiden: Brill, 2009.

———. "Dynamics of Reception in the Fourth Century." In *The Oxford Handbook for the History of the Reception of Christian Theology*. Oxford: Oxford University Press, forthcoming.

———. "The Immediately Triune God: A Patristic Response to Schleiermacher." *Pro Ecclesia* 10 (2001): 159–78.

———. "The Influence of Irenaeus on Athanasius." In *Studia Patristica* 36, edited by M. F. Wiles and E. J. Yarnold, 463–76. Leuven: Peeters, 2001.

———. "Oppositional Pairs and Christological Synthesis: Re-Reading Augustine's *De Trinitate*." *Theological Studies* 68 (2007): 231–53.

———. "Theology and Economy in Origen and Athanasius." In *Origeniana Septima: Origenes in der Auseinandersetzungen des 4. Jahrhunderts*, edited by W. A. Bienert and U. Kühneweg, 165–71. Leuven: Peeters, 1999.

———. "When Was God without Wisdom? Rhetorical Strategy and Trinitarian Hermeneutics in Athanasius of Alexandria." In *Studia Patristica* 41, edited by F. Young, M. Edwards, and P. Parvis, 117–23. Leuven: Peeters, 2006.

Anatolios, Khaled, and R. Clifford. "Christian Salvation: Biblical and Theological Perspectives." *Theological Studies* 66 (2005): 739–69.

Arnold, Duane W. H. *The Early Episcopal Career of Athanasius of Alexandria*. Christianity and Judaism in Antiquity 6. Notre Dame: University of Notre Dame Press, 1991.

Ayres, Lewis. "Athanasius's Initial Defense of the Term *Homoousios*: Re-Reading the *De Decretis*." *Journal of Early Christian Studies* 12 (2004): 337–59.

———. *Nicea and Its Legacy: An Approach to Fourth-Century Trinitarian Theology*. New York: Oxford University Press, 2006.

———. "'Remember That You Are Catholic' (*Serm.* 52.2): Augustine on the Unity of the Triune God." *Journal of Early Christian Studies* 8 (2000): 39–82.

Ayres, Lewis, J. Behr, and K. Anatolios. "*Nicaea and Its Legacy*: A Discussion." *Harvard Theological Review* 100 (2007): 141–75.

Balás, David L. "Gregor von Nyssa." In *Theologischen Realenzyklopaedie* 14, 173–81. New York: de Gruyter, 1985.

———. Metousia Theou: *Man's Participation in God's Perfections according to Saint Gregory of Nyssa*. Rome: Pontificium Institutum S. Anselmi, 1966.

———. "*Plenitudo Veritatis*: The Unity of Human Nature in Gregory of Nyssa." In *Disciplina Nostra: Essays in Memory of Robert F. Evans*, edited by Donald F. Winslow, 115–33. Patristic Monograph Series 6. Cambridge, MA: Philadelphia Patristic Foundation, 1979.

Balthasar, Hans Urs von. *Presence and Thought: Essay on the Religious Philosophy of Gregory of Nyssa*. Translated by Mark Sebanc. San Francisco: Ignatius, 1995.

———. *The Action*. Vol. 4, *Theo-Drama: Theological Dramatic Theory*. Translated by Graham Harrison. San Francisco: Ignatius, 1994.

———. *The Last Act*. Vol. 5, *Theo-Drama: Theological Dramatic Theory*. Translated by Graham Harrison. San Francisco: Ignatius, 1998.

———. *Theology: The New Covenant.* Vol. 7, *The Glory of the Lord: A Theological Aesthetics.* Translated by Erasmo Leiva-Merikakis. San Francisco: Ignatius, 1990.

Barnes, Michel René. "Augustine in Contemporary Trinitarian Theology." *Theological Studies* 56 (1995): 237–50.

———. "*De Regnon* Reconsidered." *Augustinian Studies* 26 (1995): 51–79

———. "*De Trinitate* VI and VII: Augustine and the Limits of Nicene Orthodoxy." *Augustinian Studies* 38, no. 1 (2007): 189–202.

———. "Divine Unity and the Divided Self: Gregory of Nyssa's Trinitarian Theology in Its Psychological Context." In *Re-Thinking Gregory of Nyssa*, edited by Sarah Coakley, 45–66. Oxford: Blackwell, 2003.

———. "The Fourth Century as Trinitarian Canon." In *Christian Origins: Theology, Rhetoric, and Community*, edited by L. Ayres and G. Jones, 47–67. New York: Routledge, 1998.

———. *The Power of God:* Dynamis *in Gregory of Nyssa's Trinitarian Theology.* Washington, DC: Catholic University of America Press, 2001.

———. "The Visible Christ and the Invisible Trinity: Mt 5:8 in Augustine's Trinitarian Theology of 400." *Modern Theology* 19 (2003): 329–55.

Barth, Karl. *Church Dogmatics.* Edited by G. W. Bromiley and T. F. Torrance. Translated by G. W. Bromiley. New York: T&T Clark, 2004.

Behr, John. *The Nicene Faith.* 2 vols. Crestwood, NY: Saint Vladimir's Seminary Press, 2004.

———. *The Mystery of Christ: Life in Death.* Crestwood, NY: Saint Vladimir's Seminary Press, 2006.

———. *The Way to Nicaea.* Crestwood, NY: Saint Vladimir's Seminary Press, 2001.

Bernard, Régis. *L'image de Dieu d'après Saint Athanase.* Paris: Aubier, 1952.

Bienert, Wolfgang. "Zur Logos-Christologie des Athanasius von Alexandrien in *Contra Gentes– De incarnatione*." *Studia Patristica* 21 (1989): 402–19.

Bouchet, J.-R. "Le vocabulaire de l'union et du rapport des natures chez saint Grégoire de Nysse." *Revue Thomiste* 68 (1968): 533–82.

Brakke, David. *Athanasius and the Politics of Asceticism.* Oxford: Clarendon, 1995.

Burrell, David. *Freedom and Creation in Three Traditions.* Notre Dame: University of Notre Dame Press, 1993.

Canévet, Mariette. *Grégoire de Nysse et l'hermeneutique biblique: Études des rapports entre le langage et la conaissance de Dieu.* Paris: Études Augustiniennes, 1983.

Cavadini, John. "The Quest for Truth in Augustine's *De Trinitate*." *Theological Studies* 58, no. 3 (1997): 429–40.

———. "The Structure and Intention of Augustine's *De Trinitate*." *Augustinian Studies* 23 (1992): 103–23.

———. "Trinity and Apologetics." Conference paper presented at "La *De Trinitate* de saint Augustin: Exégèse, logique et noétique." Université Bordeaux, June 17, 2010.

Coakley, Sarah. "Re-Thinking Gregory of Nyssa: Introduction—Gender, Trinitarian Analogies, and the Pedagogy of *The Song*." In *Re-Thinking Gregory of Nyssa*, edited by Sarah Coakley, 1–14. Oxford: Blackwell, 2003.

Congar, Yves. *I Believe in the Holy Spirit.* New York: Crossroad, 1999.

Coolman, Boyd Taylor, and Dale M. Coulter, eds. *Trinity and Creation*. Victorine Texts in Translation 1. Turnhout: Brepols, 2010.

Daley, Brian. "Divine Transcendence and Human Transformation: Gregory of Nyssa's Anti-Apollinarian Christology." In *Re-Thinking Gregory of Nyssa*, edited by Sarah Coakley, 67–76. Oxford: Blackwell, 2003.

———. "A Humble Mediator: The Distinctive Elements in St. Augustine's Christology." *Word and Spirit* 9 (1987): 100–117.

———. "'One Thing and Another': The Persons in God and the Person of Christ in Patristic Theology." *Pro Ecclesia* 15 (2006): 17–46.

———. "Origen's *De Principiis*: A Guide to the 'Principles' of Christian Scriptural Interpretation." In *Nova et Vetera: Patristic Studies in Honor of Thomas Patrick Halton*, edited by John F. Petruccione, 3–21. Washington, DC: Catholic University of America Press, 1998.

Daniélou, Jean. *Platonisme et théologie mystique: Essai sur la doctrine spirituelle de Saint Grégoire de Nysse*. 2nd ed. Paris: Aubier, 1944.

Derrida, Jacques. *Of Grammatology*. Translated by Gayatri Chakravorty Spivak. Baltimore: Johns Hopkins University Press, 1998.

———. *Writing and Difference*. Translated by Alan Bass. Chicago: University of Chicago Press, 1980.

Dossetti, Giuseppe Luigi. *Il simbolo di Nicea e di Costantinopolis*. Rome: Herder, 1967.

Ernest, James D. *The Bible in Athanasius of Alexandria*. The Bible in Ancient Christianity 2. Boston: Brill, 2004.

Fedwick, Paul Jonathan. "A Commentary on Gregory of Nyssa or the 38th Letter of Basil of Caesarea." *Orientalia Christiana Periodica* 44 (1978): 31–51.

Fiorenza, Francis Schüssler. "Schleiermacher's Understanding of God as Triune." In *The Cambridge Companion to Friedrich Schleiermacher*, edited by Jacqueline Mariña, 171–88. New York: Cambridge University Press, 2005.

Fries, Heinrich. *Fundamental Theology*. Translated by Robert J. Daly, SJ. Washington, DC: Catholic University of America Press, 1996.

Gavrilyuk, Paul L. *The Suffering of the Impassible God: The Dialectics of Patristic Thought*. New York: Oxford University Press, 2006.

Gioia, Luigi. *The Theological Epistemology of Augustine's* De Trinitate. New York: Oxford University Press, 2008.

Gregg, Robert C., and Dennis E. Groh. *Early Arianism: A View of Salvation*. Philadelphia: Fortress Press, 1981.

Guarino, Thomas G. *Foundations of Systematic Theology: Theology for the Twenty-First Century*. New York: T&T Clark, 2005.

Gunton, Colin B. *Act and Being: Towards a Theology of the Divine Attributes*. Grand Rapids: Eerdmans, 2002.

———. *The Promise of Trinitarian Theology*. London: T&T Clark, 1991.

Hadot, Pierre. *Philosophy as a Way of Life*. Translated by Michael Chase. Oxford: Blackwell, 1995.

Haight, Roger. *Jesus: Symbol of God*. Maryknoll, NY: Orbis, 1999.

———. "The Point of Trinitarian Theology." *Toronto Journal of Theology* 4 (1988): 191–204.

Halleux, André de. "Hypostase et 'Personne' dans la formation du dogme trinitarian (*ca* 375–381)." *Revue d'histoire ecclésiastique* 79 (1984): 313–69, 625–70.

Hanson, R. P. C. *The Search for the Christian Doctrine of God: The Arian Controversy 318–381.* New York: T&T Clark, 1988.

Hart, David Bentley. *The Beauty of the Infinite: The Aesthetics of Christian Truth.* Grand Rapids: Eerdmans, 2003.

———. "No Shadow of Turning: On Divine Impassibility." *Pro Ecclesia* (Spring 2002): 184–206.

Heine, Ronald E. *Perfection in the Virtuous Life: A Study in the Relationship between Edification and Polemical Theology in Gregory of Nyssa's* De vita Moysis. Cambridge, MA: Philadelphia Patristic Foundation, 1975.

Hendrickx, Ephraem. "La date de composition du *De Trinitate.*" In *Augustine: La Trinité,* 557–66. Bibliothèque Augustinienne 15. Paris: Desclée de Brouwer, 1955.

Holl, K. *Amphilochius von Ikonium in seinem Verhaltnis zu den grossen Kappadoziern.* Tübingen: Mohr, 1902.

Hübner, Reinhard M. *Die Einheit des leibes Christi bei Gregor von Nyssa: untersuchungen zum ursprung der "Physischen" Erlösungslehre.* Leiden: Brill, 1974.

Hunsinger, George. "Election and the Trinity: Twenty-Five Theses on the Theology of Karl Barth." *Modern Theology* 24, no. 2 (2008): 179–98.

Hurtado, Larry W. *Lord Jesus Christ: Devotion to Jesus in Earliest Christianity.* Grand Rapids: Eerdmans, 2003.

Jenson, Robert W. *Systematic Theology.* Vol. 1, *The Triune God.* New York: Oxford University Press, 1997.

———. *The Triune Identity: God according to the Gospel.* Minneapolis: Fortress, 1982.

Kannengiesser, Charles. *Athanase d'Alexandrie, évêque et écrivain: Une lecture des traités Contre les Ariens.* Paris: Beauchesne, 1983.

———. *Athanase d'Alexandrie: Sur l'incarnation du Verbe; Introduction, Texte critique, traduction, notes et index.* Sources Chrétiennes 199. Paris: Éditions du Cerf, 1973.

———. "La date de l'apologie d'Athanase 'Contra les paiens' et 'sur l'incarnation.'" *Recherches de Science Religieuse* 58 (1970): 383–428.

———. *Holy Scripture and Hellenistic Hermeneutics in Alexandrian Christology: The Arian Crisis.* Berkeley: Center for Hermeneutical Studies, 1981.

Kant, Immanuel. *Religion within the Limits of Reason Alone.* Translated by Theodore M. Greene and Hoyt H. Hudson. New York: Harper & Row, 1960.

Kelly, J. N. D. *Early Christian Creeds.* New York: Longman, 1972.

Kinzig, Wolfram. *In Search of Asterius: Studies on the Authorship of the Homilies on the Psalms.* Göttingen: Vandenhoeck & Ruprecht, 1990.

Kittel, G., and G. Friedrich, eds. *Theological Dictionary of the New Testament (TDNT).* Translated by G. W. Bromiley. 10 vols. Grand Rapids: Eerdmans, 1964–1976.

Kopecek, Thomas A. *A History of Neo-Arianism.* Patristic Monograph Series 8. Philadelphia: Patristic Foundation, 1979.

———. "Neo-Arian Religion: The Evidence of the *Apostolic Constitutions.*" In *Arianism: Historical and Theological Reassessments: Papers from the Ninth International Conference on*

Patristic Studies, September 5–10, 1983, Patristic Monograph Series 11, edited by Robert C. Gregg, 153–79. Philadelphia: Patristic Foundation, 1985.

LaBonnardière, Anne-Marie. *Recherches de chronologie augustinienne.* Paris: Études Augustiniennes, 1965.

LaCugna, Catherine. *God for Us: The Trinity and Christian Life.* San Francisco: Harper Collins, 1991.

Laird, Martin. *Gregory of Nyssa and the Grasp of Faith.* New York: Oxford University Press, 2004.

Lienhard, Joseph T. "The 'Arian' Controversy: Some Categories Reconsidered." *Theological Studies* 48 (1987): 415–36.

———. *Contra Marcellum: Marcellus of Ancyra and Fourth-Century Theology.* Washington, DC: Catholic University of America Press, 1999.

———. "Did Athanasius Reject Marcellus?" In *Arianism after Arius: Essays on the Development of the Fourth Century Trinitarian Conflicts,* edited by Michel R. Barnes and Daniel H. Williams, 65–80. Edinburgh: T&T Clark, 1993.

———. "*Ousia* and *Hypostasis*: The Cappadocian Settlement and the Theology of the 'One Hypostasis.'" In *The Trinity: An Interdisciplinary Symposium on the Doctrine of the Trinity,* edited by S. T. Davis, D. Kendall, and G. O'Collins, 99–121. New York: Oxford University Press, 2000.

Lindbeck, George. *The Nature of Doctrine: Religion and Theology in a Postliberal Age.* Philadelphia: Westminster John Knox, 1984.

———. *The Nature of Doctrine: Religion and Theology in a Postliberal Age.* 25th anniv. ed. Louisville: Westminister John Knox, 2009.

Löhr, W. A. "Arius Reconsidered: Part Two." *Zeitschrift für Antikes Christentum* 10 (2006): 121–37.

Lonergan, Bernard. "The Subject." In *A Second Collection,* 69–86. Toronto: University of Toronto Press, 1996.

Lorenz, Rudolf. *Arius judaizans: Untersuchungen zur dogmengeschichtlichen Einordnung des Arius.* Forschungen zur Kirchen- und Dogmengeschichte 31. Göttingen: Vandenhoeck & Ruprecht, 1980.

Louth, Andrew. "Is Development of Doctrine a Valid Category for Orthodox Theology?" In *Orthodoxy and Western Culture: A Collection of Essays Honoring Jaroslav Pelikan on His Eightieth Birthday,* edited by Patrick Henry and Valeria Hotchkiss, 45–63. Crestwood, NY: Saint Vladimir's Seminary Press, 2005.

———. "The Use of the Term *IDIOS* in Alexandrian Theology from Alexander to Cyril." *Studia Patristica* 19 (1989): 198–202.

Lyman, Rebecca. *Christology and Cosmology: Models of Divine Activity in Origen, Eusebius, and Athanasius.* New York: Clarendon, 1993.

———. "Hellenism and Heresy." *Journal of Early Christian Studies* 11 (2003): 209–22.

Marcel, Gabriel. *Reflection and Mystery.* Vol. 1, *The Mystery of Being.* London: Harvill, 1950.

Marion, Jean-Luc. *God without Being: Hors-Texte.* Translated by Thomas A. Carlson. Chicago: University of Chicago Press, 1991.

———. *In Excess: Studies of Saturated Phenomena.* Translated by R. Horner and V. Berraud. New York: Fordham University Press, 2004.

Marshall, Bruce. "The Dereliction of Christ and the Impassibility of God." In *Divine Impassibility and the Mystery of Human Suffering*, edited by James F. Keating and Thomas Joseph White, OP, 246–98. Grand Rapids: Eerdmans, 2009.

———. "The Trinity." In *The Blackwell Companion to Modern Theology*, edited by Gareth Jones, 183–203. Oxford: Blackwell, 2004.

Martin, Annick. *Athanase d'Alexandrie et l'église d'Egypt au IVe siècle (328–373)*. Collection de l'Ecole française de Rome 216. Rome: École française de Rome, 1996.

Maspero, Giulio. *Trinity and Man: Gregory of Nyssa's Ad Ablabium*. Supplements to *Vigiliae Christianae*. Leiden: Brill, 2007.

May, Gerhard. "Die Chronologie des Lebens und der Werk des Gregor von Nyssa." In *Ecriture et culture philosophique dans la pensee de Gregoire de Nysse*, edited by M. Harl, 51–67. Leiden: Brill, 1971.

Meijering, E. P. "The Doctrine of the Will and of the Trinity in the Orations of Gregory of Nazianzus." *Nederlands Theologisch Tijdschrift* 27, no. 3 (1973): 224–34.

———. "*ΗΝ ΠΟΤΕ ΟΤΕ ΟΥΚ ΗΝ Ο ΥΙΟΣ*: A Discussion of Time and Eternity." *Vigiliae Christianae* 28 (1974): 161–68.

Meredith, Anthony. "The Pneumatology of the Cappadocian Fathers." *Irish Theological Quarterly* 48, nos. 3–4 (1981): 196–211.

Meslin, Michel. *Les Ariens d'Occident 335–430*. Patristica Sorbonensia 8. Paris: Éditions du Seuil, 1967.

Milbank, John. "Sacred Triads: Augustine and the Indo-European Soul." In *Augustine and His Critics: Essays in Honour of Gerald Bonner*, edited by Robert Dodaro and George Lawless, 77–102. New York: Routledge, 2000.

———. *The Word Made Strange: Theology, Language, and Culture*. Oxford: Blackwell, 1997.

Moltmann, Jürgen. *The Crucified God*. Translated by R. A. Wilson and John Bowden. 2nd ed. London: SCM Press, 1974.

———. *The Trinity and the Kingdom*. Translated by Margaret Kohl. Minneapolis: Fortress, 1993.

Mortley, Raoul. *From Word to Silence*. 2 vols. Bonn: Hanstein, 1986.

Mühlenburg, Ekkehard. *Die Unendlichkeit Gottes bei Gregor von Nyssa: Gregors Kritik am Gottesbegriff der klassischen Metaphysik*. Forschungen zur Kirchen- und Dogmengeschichte 16. Göttingen: Vandenhoeck & Ruprecht, 1966.

———. *Epochen der Kirchengeschichte*. Uni-Taschenbücher 1046. Heidelberg: Quelle und Meyer, 1980.

———. "Vérité et Bonté de Dieu: Une interprétation de *De Incarnatione*, chapitre VI, en perspective historique." In *Politique et théologie chez Athanase d'Alexandre*, edited by Charles Kannengiesser, 215–30. Théologie historique 27. Paris: Beauchesne, 1974.

Newman, John Henry. *An Essay in Aid of a Grammar of Assent*. Notre Dame: University of Notre Dame Press, 1975.

Norris, Richard. *The Christological Controversy*. Philadelphia: Fortress, 1980.

O'Collins, Gerald. *Fundamental Theology*. Mahwah, NJ: Paulist Press, 1981.

Orbe, Antonio. *La Epinoia: Algunos preliminares históricos de la distinción kat' epinoian*. Rome: Pontificia Universitas Gregoriana, 1955.

Ormerod, Neil. "The Psychological Analogy of the Trinity: At Odds with Modernity." *Pacifica* 14 (2001): 281–94.

Pannenberg, Wolfhart. *Systematic Theology*. Translated by G. W. Bromiley. Grand Rapids: Eerdmans, 1991.

Parvis, Sara. *Marcellus of Ancyra and the Lost Years of the Arian Controversy 325–345*. New York: Oxford University Press, 2006.

Patterson, Lloyd G. *Methodius of Olympus: Divine Sovereignty, Human Freedom, and Life in Christ*. Washington, DC: Catholic University of America Press, 1997.

———. "Methodius, Origen, and the Arian Dispute." *Studia Patristica* 17, no. 2 (1982): 912–23.

Pelikan, Jaroslav. "*Canonica Regula*: The Trinitarian Hermeneutics of Augustine." In *Collectanea Augustiniana: Augustine—Second Founder of the Faith*, edited by Joseph C. Schnaubelt and Frederick Van Fleteren, 329–43. New York: Peter Lang, 1990.

Peterson, Erik. *Der Monotheismus als politische Problem: ein beitrag zur geschichte der politischen theologie im Imperium romanum*. Leipzig: Hegner, 1935.

Polanyi, Michael. *Knowing and Being*. Edited by Marjorie Grene. Chicago: University of Chicago Press, 1969.

———. *Personal Knowledge: Towards a Post-Critical Philosophy*. Chicago: University of Chicago Press, 1958.

Pottier, Bernard. *Dieu et le Christ selon Grégoire de Nysse: étude systématique du "Contre Eunome"; avec traduction inédite des extraits d'Eunome*. Namur: Culture et vérité, 1994.

Rahner, Karl. *The Trinity*. Translated by Joseph Donceel. New York: Crossroad, 2004.

Ricken, Friedo. "Die Logoslehre des Eusebios von Caesarea und der Mittelplatonismus." *Theologie und Philosophie* 42 (1967): 341–58.

———. "Nikaia als Krisis des altchristlichen Platonismus." *Theologie und Philosophie* 44 (1969): 321–41.

———. "Zur Rezeption der platonischen Ontologie bei Eusebios von Kaisareia, et l'Areios, und Athanasios." *Theologie und Philosophie* 53 (1978): 321–52.

Richard of St. Victor. *The Book of the Patriarchs, The Mystical Ark, Book Three of the Trinity*. Edited by Grover A. Zinn. New York: Paulist Press, 1979.

Robertson, Jon. "Divine Mediation in Marcellus of Ancyra: The Concept of the Image of God in the Fragments of His Work *Against Asterius*." In *Studia Patristica* 34, edited by M. F. Wiles and E. J. Yarnold, 217–22. Leuven: Peeters, 2001.

Rush, Ormond. "Reception Hermeneutics and the 'Development' of Doctrine: An Alternative Model." *Pacifica* 6 (1993): 125–40.

———. *The Reception of Doctrine: An Appropriation of Hans Robert Jauss' Reception Aesthetics and Literary Hermeneutics*. Rome: Gregorian University Press, 1997.

Schindler, Alfred. *Wort und Analogie in Augustins Trinitätslehre*. Tübingen: Mohr, 1965.

Schleiermacher, Friedrich. *Der Christliche Glaube: Nach den Grundsätzen der Evangelischen Kirche im Zusammenhang Dargestellt*. Berlin: de Gruyter, 1960.

———. *The Christian Faith*. Translated by H. R. Mackintosh and J. S. Stewart. New York: T&T Clark, 1999.

Schoonenberg, Piet. "Trinity: The Consummated Covenant; Theses on the Doctrine of the Trinitarian God." *Studies in Religion* 5 (1975–1976): 111–16.

Severus ibn al-Mukaffa. *History of the Patriarchs of the Coptic Church of Alexandria*. Vol. 1.4, *Patrologia Orientalis*. Edited by J. Evetts. Paris: Firmin-Didot, 1907.

Simonetti, Manlio. *La crisi ariana nel IV secolo*. Rome: Institutum Patristicum Augustinianum, 1975.

Slusser, Michael. "The Exegetical Roots of Trinitarian Theology." *Theological Studies* 49 (1988): 461–76.

Sokolowski, Robert. *The God of Faith and Reason: Foundations of Christian Theology*. Notre Dame: University of Notre Dame Press, 1982.

Spanneut, Michel. *Le stoïcisme des Pères de l'Église: de Clément de Rome à Clément d'Alexandrie*. Paris: Éditions du Seuil, 1969.

Spoerl, Kelley McCarthy. "Apollarian Christology and the Anti-Marcellan Tradition." *Theological Studies* 48 (1994): 545–68.

———. "Apollinarius and the First Nicene Generation." In *Tradition and the Rule of Faith in the Early Church: Essays in Honor of Joseph T. Lienhard, SJ*, edited by Ronnie J. Rombs and Alexander Y. Hwang, 109–27. Washington, DC: Catholic University of America Press, 2010.

———. "Athanasius and the Anti-Marcellan Controversy." *Zeitscrift für Antikes Christentum* 10 (2007): 34–55.

———. "A Study of the *Kata Meros Pistis* by Apollinaris of Laodicea." PhD diss., University of Toronto, 1991.

Staniloae, Dumitru. *The Experience of God: Orthodox Dogmatic Theology*. Edited and translated by Ioan Ionita and Robert Barringer. Brookline, MA: Holy Cross Orthodox Press, 2005.

Stead, Christopher. "Arius in Modern Research." *Theological Studies* 45 (1994): 24–36.

———. "Athanasius' Earliest Written Work." *Theological Studies* 39 (1988): 76–91.

———. "The Platonism of Arius." *Journal of Theological Studies*, n.s., 15 (1964): 16–31.

———. "Rhetorical Method in Athanasius." *Vigiliae Christianae* 30 (1976): 121–37.

———. "Was Arius a Neoplatonist?" *Studia Patristica* 31 (1997): 39–52.

———. "Why Not Three Gods? The Logic of Gregory of Nyssa's Trinitarian Doctrine." In *Studien zu Gregor von Nyssa und der christlichen Spätantike*, edited by Hubertus R. Drobner and Christoph Klock, 149–63. New York: Brill, 1990.

Stead, G. C. "The Platonism of Arius." *Theological Studies* 15 (1964): 16–31.

Strutwolf, Holger. *Die Trinitätstheologie und Christologie des Euseb von Caesarea*. Göttingen: Vandenhoeck & Ruprecht, 1999.

Teselle, Eugene. *Augustine the Theologian*. New York: Herder & Herder, 1970.

Tetz, Martin. *Athanasiana: Zu Leben und Lehre des Athanasius*. New York: de Gruyter, 1995.

———. "Zur Biographie des Athanasius von Alexandrien." *Zeitschrift für Kirchengeschichte* 90, nos. 2–3 (1979): 304–38.

Torrance, Alan J. "The Lazarus Narrative, Theological History, and Historical Probability." In *The Gospel of John and Christian Theology*, edited by Richard Bauckham and Carl Mosser, 245–62. Grand Rapids: Eerdmans, 2008.

Turcescu, Lucian. "The Concept of Divine Persons in Gregory of Nyssa's *To His Brother Peter, on the Difference between* Ousia *and* Hypostasis." *Greek Orthodox Theological Review* 42 (1997): 63–82.

Vaggione, Richard Paul. *Eunomius of Cyzicus and the Nicene Revolution*. Oxford Early Christian Texts. Oxford: Oxford University Press, 2001.

Vinzent, Markus. *Asterius von Kappadokien: Die theologische Fragmente; Einleitung, kritischer Text, Übersetzung und Kommentar von Markus Vinzent*. New York: Brill, 1993.

Weinandy, Thomas. *Does God Suffer?* Notre Dame: University of Notre Dame Press, 2000.

Widdicombe, Peter. *The Fatherhood of God from Origen to Athanasius*. 2nd ed. New York: Oxford University Press, 2004.

Wiles, Maurice F. *Archetypal Heresy: Arianism through the Centuries*. New York: Oxford University Press, 1996.

———. "Eunomius: Hair-splitting Dialectician or Defender of the Accessibility of Salvation?" In *The Making of Orthodoxy: Essays in Honour of Henry Chadwick*, edited by Rowan Williams, 157–72. Cambridge: Cambridge University Press, 1980.

Williams, Rowan. "Angels Unawares: Heavenly Liturgy and Earthly Theology in Alexandria." *Studia Patristica* 30 (1997): 350–63.

———. *Arius: Heresy and Tradition*. 2nd ed. Grand Rapids: Eerdmans, 2002.

———. "Arius and the Melitian Schism." *Theological Studies* 37 (1986): 35–52.

———. "Baptism and the Arian Controversy." In *Arianism after Arius: Essays on the Development of the Fourth Century Trinitarian Conflicts*, edited by Michel R. Barnes and Daniel H. Williams, 149–81. New York: T&T Clark, 1993.

———. "The Logic of Arianism." *Theological Studies* 34 (1983): 56–81.

———. "The Paradoxes of Self-Knowledge in the *De Trinitate*." In *Augustine: Presbyter Factus Sum, Collectanea Augustiniana*, edited by J. T. Lienhard et al., 121–34. New York and Frankfurt: Peter Lang, 1993.

———. "*Sapientia* and the Trinity: Reflections on the *De Trinitate*." In *Collectanea Augustiniana: Mélanges T. J. van Bavel*, edited by B. Bruning et al., 317–32. Leuven: Peeters, 1990.

Zachuber, Johannes. *Human Nature in Gregory of Nyssa: Philosophical Background and Theological Significance*. Leiden: Brill, 2000.

Zizioulas, John. *Being as Communion: Studies in Personhood and the Church*. Crestwood, NY: Saint Vladimir's Seminary Press, 1985.

Subject Index

Index of Modern Authors

Index of Ancient Sources